Fundamental Concepts for the Software Quality Engineer

ASQ Quality Press
Milwaukee, Wisconsin

NEW AGE

Fundamental Concepts for the Software Quality Engineer

Sue Carroll and Taz Daughtrey, Editors

PUBLISHING FOR ONE WORLD

NEW AGE INTERNATIONAL (P) LIMITED, PUBLISHERS

New Delhi • Bangalore • Chennai • Cochin • Guwahati • Hyderabad
Jalandhar • Kolkata • Lucknow • Mumbai • Ranchi

Visit us at **www.newagepublishers.com**

First Indian Sub-Continent Edition : 2010
by New Age International (P) Ltd., Publishers

This special low-priced edition is for sale in India, Bangladesh, Bhutan, Myanmar (Burma), Sri Lanka, Nepal, Pakistan, Southeast Asia and the Middle East.

Originally Published by *American Society for Quality, USA*

Branches:

- No. 37/10, 8th Cross (Near Hanuman Temple), Azad Nagar, Chamrajpet, **Bangalore**-560 018. Tel.: (080) 2675 6823, Telefax: 2675 6820, E-mail: bangalore@newagepublishers.com
- 26, Damodaran Street, T. Nagar, **Chennai**-600 017. Tel.: (044) 24353401, Telefax: 24351463, E-mail: chennai@newagepublishers.com
- CC-39/1016, Carrier Station Road, Ernakulam South, **Cochin**-682 016, Tel.: (0484) 2377004, Telefax: 4051303. E-mail: cochin@newagepublishers.com
- Hemsen Complex, Mohd. Shah Road, Paltan Bazar, Near Starline Hotel, **Guwahati**-781 008. Tel.: (0361) 2513881. Telefax: 2543669, E-mail: guwahati@newagepublishers.com
- No. 105, 1st Floor, Madhiray Kaveri Tower, 3-2-19, Azam Jahi Road, Nimboliadda, **Hyderabad**-500 027. Tel.: (040) 24652456, Telefax: 24652457, E-mail:hyderabad@newagepublishers.com
- RDB Chambers (Formerly Lotus Cinema)106A, 1st Floor, S.N. Banerjee Road, **Kolkata**-700 014. Tel.: (033) 22273773, Telefax: 22275247, E-mail:kolkata@newagepublishers.com
- 16-A, Jopling Road, **Lucknow**-226 001. Tel.: (0522) 2209578, 4045297, Telefax: 2204098, E-mail: lucknow@newagepublishers.com
- 142C, Victor House, Ground Floor, N.M. Joshi Marg, Lower Parel, **Mumbai**-400 013. Tel.: (022) 24927869. Telefax: 24915415, E-mail: mumbai@newagepublishers.com
- 22, Golden House, Daryaganj, **New Delhi**-110 002. Tel.: (011) 23262370, 23262368, Telefax: 43551305. E-mail: sales@newagepublishers.com

Printed in India at Glorious Printers, Delhi.
C-10-05-4589

ISBN: 978-81-224-3107-0
Original Edition Price: $ 72.00
Indian Edition Price: Rs. 399.00

PUBLISHING FOR ONE WORLD
NEW AGE INTERNATIONAL (P) LIMITED, PUBLISHERS
4835/24, Ansari Road, Daryaganj, New Delhi-110002
Visit us at **www.newagepublishers.com**

Contents

Introduction

What does being a professional have to do with software? We need to continue to add professionalism to the field of software engineering to help mature the practice of developing software. Also, our customers are quickly gaining knowledge and will not tolerate low-quality software. To remain profitable, software producers must have professionals (as opposed to cowboys) guiding the process. To help promote quality software, we advocate that all organizations have software quality professionals on the team.

According to the American Society for Quality (ASQ), "the Certified Software Quality Engineer understands software quality development and implementation, software inspection, testing, verification and validation, and implements software development and maintenance processes and methods."

This encompasses all aspects of quality assurance, including the various methods of assuring quality, adding quality to well known software engineering processes, project management, finding metrics that illustrate aspects of the project, and, of course, verification and validation of the project and good configuration management to keep all the pieces together. These topics all come together to create the Body of Knowledge for software quality engineering professionals. The main topics of the Certified Software Quality Engineer (CSQE) Body of Knowledge are:

I. General Knowledge, Conduct, and Ethics
II. Software Quality Management
III. Software Engineering Processes
IV. Program and Project Management
V. Software Metrics, Measurement, and Analytical Methods
VI. Software Verification and Validation (V&V)
VII. Software Configuration Management

It has been five years since the publication of the last book of reprints from the journal *Software Quality Professional* (*SQP*). *SQP* is a peer-reviewed quarterly publication applying quality principles to the development and use of software and software-based systems. It publishes case studies, experience-based reports, and state-of-the-art reviews in order to provide practitioners with an understanding of those software quality practices that have proven effective in a wide range of industries, applications, and organizational settings. To enhance personal and professional growth, the journal provides a forum for exchanging practical ideas and experiences. *SQP* constantly strives to improve the professionalism of practitioners, the satisfaction of customers, and the well-being of the larger society.

This volume provides all new articles gathered from the last five volumes of *SQP*. It provides insights from authors around the globe, which is vital in today's global economy. Both *SQP* and this reprint volume follow the categories of the CSQE Body of Knowledge (http://www.asq.org/certification/software-quality-engineer/bok.html). All articles are related to one of the seven knowledge areas. Since the last volume of this book was published, the Body of Knowledge has been revised. Audits are no longer a main topic; they have been incorporated into the Software Quality Management category.

We hope you will use this book to broaden your knowledge in several important aspects of software quality. The field keeps growing and expanding to meet the changing needs of technology. Meet the challenge and begin your journey.

Sue Carroll

PART I

General Knowledge, Conduct, and Ethics

What does it take to be a software quality professional? Begin with a good knowledge of quality principles, standards, and ethics, add some skills in leadership and good professional development, and you have the basics. That is what is covered in this section. It is the first area of the CSQE Body of Knowledge because it lays the foundation. Without understanding general quality principles, how can you analyze those principles and make them applicable to software? Standards and ethics allow us to work together, see similarities across different companies, and know that we are all working for the same purpose—to make better software! If you have been in this field for any length of time, you know that good people skills are vital. We don't always get the resources we need, so we must lead a virtual group from all areas of the company to ensure the quality of the final product. It is also necessary to be an advocate for software quality to promote needed changes. And where would we be in this fast-changing, crazy field without continuing education? We must keep up with this evolving discipline and not hold back exciting advances by embracing outdated processes. Our two authors discuss professionalism and how organizational goals and personal beliefs may require examination.

In "Bridging Between Software Management and Software Professionalism," Dave Miller strives to properly balance organizational goals and encouragement of individual professionalism. He claims that techniques for managing professionals can be appropriately applied by considering their characteristic values. Miller shows that quality practitioners can effectively lead software developers to support organizational goals by mastering mediation skills and by demonstrating professional behaviors themselves.

Nicole Radziwill discusses "An Ethical Theory for the Advancement of Professionalism in Software Engineering." Software engineers and their managers are often confronted with difficult situations that require a commitment to personal ethics. Even when a software professional has committed to abiding by the ASQ Code of Ethics, a variety of situations involving peers, clients, and employers can challenge an individual's application of these ethical principles. In this article, the definition of professionalism for software engineers and their managers is examined, and an ethical theory is proposed to help software engineers and software development managers identify the best approach to difficult "right vs. wrong" and "right vs. right" choices. This guiding framework is then evaluated against scenarios that commonly arise in software development to determine the most ethical, and thus the most professional, course of action.

Bridging Between Software Management and Software Professionalism

Dave Miller

The long-term success of an organization depends in part on effective communications between management and developers. Many software engineers consider themselves to be professionals. Techniques for managing professionals can help improve communications between management and software engineers. By understanding how to mediate with professionals and by demonstrating professional behaviors themselves, software quality practitioners can effectively lead developers to support quality initiatives.

Key words: anthropology, communication, discipline, managerial orientation, morale, teamwork, value systems

To Understand or to Discipline Software Engineers?

Various social sciences have been invoked in attempts to explain how managers can better understand software developers. Barry Boehm (1981) orients his book on software engineering economics around the concept of "human economics." Jerry Weinberg (1988) writes about the psychology of software developers. Steve McConnell (1996) offers practical suggestions for customer orientation, motivation, teamwork, and team structures. Tom DeMarco and Timothy Lister (1987) show how management can frustrate developers and vice versa. (These frustrations are also illustrated in Scott Adams' "Dilbert" cartoons.) Recent articles and texts explore the culture and sociology of software developers (Mackey 2000; Wieggers 1996; Weinberg 1992; Glass 2000). An article in *IEEE Computer* even addresses the culture of software programs: programmers come and go and their skill sets change as the program evolves (Rajlich 2001). All of these authors imply that it makes business sense to accommodate software developers' value systems and modes of interaction.

Capability Maturity Model, CMM, and CMMI are registered in the U.S. Patent and Trademark Office by Carnegie Mellon University.

One therefore expects the literature about managing software engineers and about software quality to consider how software engineers think and work. Instead, many books about managing software and software quality recommend discipline, expressing disdain for software developers who fail to see themselves as workers and who resist following standardized processes. For example:

> "Data processing organizations must equate their function to manufacturing a product in order to see the need for a quality control function. Data processing must assume the responsibility of determining an acceptable level of quality, and then establish the mechanism—quality assurance function—to determine that level is maintained. If you, the data processing professional, say, 'My product is hand crafted and it's a one-of-a-kind type product, so it cannot be measured and compared against a standard,' quality assurance has little chance of success in your organization. On the other hand, if you say, 'My skill is finding better ways to perform work, but the end product can be measured and evaluated against a standard,' then the quality assurance function can perform a very viable service for you." (Perry 1991)

The quality industry generally assumes that the best results are to be gained by top-down enforcement of standardization and process control. These are requirements for ISO 9000 and Capability Maturity Model (CMM) certification. Arguments for process discipline center on the assertion that defining and enforcing processes leads to better definition of requirements, improved efficiency and productivity, and overall success of the organization (Schmauch 1994; Dunn 1990; Humphrey 1995; Perry 1991). There is evidence that process discipline can lead to excellent results. For example, Michael Fagan's inspection methods have been shown to result in cheaper, faster, and better results (Fagan 2001).

However, efforts to institute process control sometimes fail. The pattern of failure appears to be the following scenario: upper-level managers vow to "change the software development culture here." Someone is nominated to institute a development process. The process is written without grass-roots involvement or support by the developers. Software developers are then ordered to follow the process. Perhaps a software quality group is set up. Perhaps there will be an initiative to become CMM certified. Sometimes this approach works, and the organization changes for the better. But too often, after a few months it becomes apparent that the process and the initiatives have caused disruption but have not benefited the organization. Projects stop using the process, and the process management initiative fades away. This scenario occurs too often to ignore.

A common denominator of such failures is a breakdown in communication between managers and developers. The success of process improvement initiatives appears to depend largely on how effectively management can influence software developers to support the initiatives, obtaining willing cooperation, fostering job satisfaction, and increasing morale. In other words, building bridges between management and developers helps the organization to improve process discipline. Software quality professionals can help build those bridges by understanding and appealing to the professionalism of the development staff.

Management of Professionals

Software developers are not unique in their attitudes toward process management and quality management. Software developers are famous for working long hours, taking pride in their skills, resenting management, and resisting standardization. But listen to people who manage physicians, lawyers, scientists, and accountants: Those groups have the same behaviors, and can be even more difficult to manage. Moreover, as there are radical differences in ability among software developers, so are there dramatic degrees of abilities among physicians, lawyers, scientists, and accountants. The challenge for managing any of these groups is to control and improve quality while retaining and motivating the best staff members.

Software engineers are increasingly referred to as professionals. Many books about software management suggest that managers should respect developers as professionals and give them more latitude in how they create software.

What techniques are useful for managing professionals? The classic book on the subject is Joseph Raelin's *The Clash of Cultures: Managers and Professionals* (1984). Raelin approaches the question from an anthropological point of view, building on Edward Hall's famous (and very practical) examinations of how different cultures have very different frames of reference (Hall and Hall 1990). Raelin contrasts the beliefs and values of managers and professionals, and then systematically explores techniques to meet both the goals of the organization and the goals of the professional staff. "Professionals" include scientists, physicians, lawyers, accountants, and some engineers: "It is clear that the individual approach must apply in determining the ultimate criterion of membership. Some engineers will act like professionals; others may not." (In my experience, some software engineers identify themselves as professionals, while other software engineers identify themselves as workers and are content to be closely managed. Some who regard themselves as professionals are difficult to manage, while others are very cooperative and supportive of quality efforts.)

Managers Don't Think Like Professionals

Hall and Hall explain how different countries and groups often fail to understand each other's beliefs and thought patterns (1990). Thus, Raelin begins by explaining that value systems of managers are usually very different from the value systems of professionals:

Managers	Professionals
Hierarchy	Participation
Respect for authority	Defiance of authority
Corporate efficiency	Social justice
Team player	Individual initiative
Career	Quality of life

For example, a manager believes strongly in the organization structure (hierarchy), and believes it is right to follow orders (respect for authority). A professional believes that decisions should be the result of intelligent conversation and agreement among peers (participation), and believes it is wrong to follow orders without such conversation and agreement (defiance of authority). The manager will worry about what is best for the organization; the professional will worry about what is best for society. The manager will want to be part of a team; the professional will want to work individually. The manager will offer promotions and "career opportunities" to the professional, who in turn will distain those offers in favor of more enjoyable work and better home life. In short, these different value systems naturally tend to produce mistrust and misunderstanding between these two groups, regardless of whether they speak the same language or work in the same place.

Essentially, management and professionals constitute different cultures (or different subcultures). Neither is "right" or "better." Both are necessary to the organization. Professionals must be guided into activities that help the organization meet its goals. Managers also need to accommodate professionals' value systems and ways of thinking. If not, the better technical staff members will leave or the organization will fail to make effective use of the professionals.

The United States is still experiencing repercussions of the 1960s' social conflict between authorities (governments, armies, corporations) and rebels (civil rights movement, anti-war movement, resistance to "business"). One repercussion is that professionals continue to distrust authority. They take pride in their social conscience, independence, and resistance against authority, as exemplified by the doctors in the movie and TV series "MASH." As another example, the main character in the movie "The Graduate" rebels against society (parents, church, respectability, cocktail parties, and "plastics"). Clearly, people with such sentiments will be difficult to persuade to obey authority and to follow processes.

What Is "a Professional"?

"Professional status" is characterized by six attributes: 1) expertise (education, skills); 2) autonomy ("freedom to select the problems they will study"); 3) commitment to a career in a technical specialty rather than commitment to any organization; 4) self-identification as a professional; 5) ethics (commitment to professional ethics rather than to organizational objectives); and 6) formal and informal standards for measuring competence and self-policing the profession. Raelin uses engineering as an example of a field where some members demonstrate these six attributes of professionalism, while others do not. Some professionals are so focused on manifesting these characteristics that they refuse to conform to organization or corporate goals.

These six attributes provide clues to how to influence and manage professionals. For instance, it is necessary to realize how important education, skills, publications, patents, and expertise are to professionals. The quickest way to alienate a professional is not to show respect for the professional's achievements in these areas. Alternatively, the quickest way to get a professional's willingness to cooperate is to mention the value of the professional's achievements. Similarly, it is more effective to ask for participation than to demand the professional's services. Managers who have to maintain professional staffs should understand that professionals are more interested in enhancing their technical skills and experience than in keeping their jobs with the organization. Referring to development professionals as "workers" or "employees" is bound to have negative consequences; it is better to refer to "engineers" or "professional staff." Finally, the organization can improve morale and teamwork by understanding that professionals wish to be judged in terms of professional achievement rather than evaluated in the same manner as managers, administrative staff, or factory workers.

How to Mediate Between Management and Professionalism

Effective management of professionals is based on careful application of mediation strategies:

- *"Linkage devices" to help professionals identify with the organization's structure and purpose*: Meetings, seminars, bulletin boards, exposure to other parts of the organization, interdisciplinary teams, even beer busts.
- *Opportunities for professional advancement within the company, so the professional does not have to go elsewhere for technical advancement:* Training, career development counseling and courses, negotiation of assignments, abundant information on all job openings, multiple career paths, feedback regarding job opportunities and selections, minimization of politics, open-door policies, ways to "unstick" professionals from dead-ends or unhappy career paths, use of professionals for consulting and troubleshooting, swapping staff members between departments, and recognition of professional achievement.
- *Organizational socialization*: Ways to defuse conflicts between the professional environment and the business activities, good orientation for students and new employees, making it clear how expected contributions fit into the organizational structure and mission, facilitation of social

interaction among professionals to reduce isolation and to help set expectations, performance appraisals based on professional skills and values, and mentorship.

- *Balance control and autonomy*: Restrain managers from trying to over-control the means of professional practice, tell professionals what the company stands for, get professionals to participate in strategic and tactical decisions, get professionals to commit to goals and target dates, leave professionals alone to choose the means to solve the problem, provide a dual ladder where professionals can advance in parallel with managers, use professionals to mediate and facilitate between management and other professionals, allow professionals to transition into management, let professionals control their own work processes, use managers as buffers between professionals and the organization, use peer groups to set criteria, and emphasize results rather than behaviors in evaluation of projects and performance.
- *Provide supervision in a way that is palatable to professionals*: Set goals that lead to self-management, use peer control, build trust and teamwork, make sure reviews are based on performance and not on politics, select supervisors who have superior technical skills, use management by objectives, and develop gatekeepers to keep technical staff in touch with professional developments.
- *Provide incentives that increase professional satisfaction*: Good salary and profit-sharing plans, private offices, reference areas, official titles, publication of papers, private or team secretaries, reporting to higher-level executives, sponsorship of participation in professional organizations and activities, and minimization of supervision.
- *Minimize control of procedures for professionals*: Reduce quantity of control procedures, let professionals develop their own procedures, "flatten" the organization to reduce middle management, keep organizations small with no more than two layers of management, spin off ventures, use a matrix management structure but keep meetings to a minimum, emphasize forms of self-control rather than formalized controls, set ways whereby professionals can earn professional recognition while meeting organizational goals, and break down barriers between professionals and managers.
- *Use strategies to get professionals to help solve real-world needs of the organization*: Job enrichment to challenge professionals to develop horizontal as well as vertical skills, promote entrepreneurship and contact with clients, personalize the administration to treat professionals with dignity and as people rather than as numbers, provide employment stability so that professionals continue to tie their personal goals with organizational goals, avoid reserved parking spaces or executive dining rooms or other

displays of management hierarchy, encourage teamwork, and encourage executives and managers to be approachable and friendly.

- *Promote a sense of ethical consciousness*: Encourage free and open exchange of ideas, set the tone by communicating the goal of ethical behavior and making people aware of consequences of unethical behavior, publicize guidelines and codes of ethics, and make it clear that top management is serious about ethics.

How Have Raelin's Recommendations Fared in Recent Years?

Raelin's book was highly successful. It was well-reviewed, and has been reissued several times, with slight changes to the title and the contents. Other authors appear to have adopted his recommendations. For instance, a recent Massachusetts Institute of Technology (MIT) course for executives appears to be a distillation of Raelin's book (MIT 2002). Watts Humphrey's book, *Managing Technical People* (1997), is also consistent with Raelin's recommendations, though it does not cite Raelin.

In the 1970s when Raelin's book first came out, engineers were still generally perceived as craftsmen or workers, programming COBOL, tending mainframes, and dealing with fanfold green-bar printouts. Since then, the boom in computers, communications, and software in general has given the public a very different image of software engineers. Software engineering has become more important and more immediate to people's lives and jobs. Discussion continues about licensure of software developers, as well as on curricula for training and updating developers. More people than ever know how to program and configure software, and at the same time, today's software developers are expected to have better training and skills. In short, Raelin's guidelines are even more relevant to software development and software quality management than they were when he wrote *The Clash of Cultures*.

The Balancing Act: Improving Processes and Encouraging Professionalism

Software quality activities should encourage professionalism among software engineers. If Raelin is correct, the organization cannot afford the long-term consequences of using heavy-handed management techniques to control professionals. Again, unfortunately, that is exactly what much quality literature insists upon: top-down management directives and process controls.

I am not advising readers to abandon software quality best practices—quite the opposite. Professionals need management for the organization to meet its objectives, and without software quality activities, the organization will not improve, control, or measure the quality of its software. The trick is *balancing* encouragement of professionalism with focus on business and quality objectives. As Humphrey (1997) asserts:

"Many managers see a conflict between the need for strong leadership and the need for more employee participation in decision-making. There is, however, no real conflict. Professionals want to do important work and they want to do it their way. The strong leader reinforces the urgency and importance of the goal, while the participative manager recognizes success and provides the freedom and support his or her people need."

Understand the Software Organization's Culture—and One's Own Culture

To influence a software organization, one should understand how it works. In other words, one should understand his or her culture (or subculture). But first one must understand his or her own culture—how one's expectations are based on beliefs of the quality industry and of management. (See Hall and Hall 1990 for a general background on cultural differences.) Because beliefs and behaviors are deeply rooted, it is difficult for different cultures to negotiate (peacefully and successfully) with each other. The cultures must first try to understand each other, and gradually develop enough shared information and goals to be able to cooperate and compromise.

Here are some difficulties in accommodating professionals' beliefs while also trying to carry out software quality activities:

- There may be practical reasons why software developers behave the way they do. Do software quality practitioners understand these reasons? When trying to institute changes or enforce processes, how much of one's motivation is based on practical business reasons, and how much is based simply on the desire to conform to beliefs of the quality industry?
- Do software quality practitioners understand software developers' professional motivations? How do they differ from one's own motivations? Software professionals do not value money, responsibility, and discipline as much as other organizational subcultures. Software professionals probably want technical growth rather than management responsibility. How can one influence these professionals to help improve software quality and practices? (Raelin's book is an excellent resource. Though it is currently out of print, used copies appear to be widely available.)
- Telling software professionals to follow strictly enforced "cookie-cutter" processes insults them. They do not appreciate being identified as "workers" or being grouped with manufacturing staff or customer service people.
- Rigorous, top-down enforcement of processes violates software cultural beliefs and will probably result in problems with morale, motivation, and staff retention. What techniques can persuade the professional staff to adhere to processes, yet still appeal to their professionalism?

- What sort of development process do software developers really need? There are plenty of cases where improving processes resulted in better products. There are also plenty of cases where attempts to make radical changes or institute elaborate processes resulted in failure—the developers ignoring the processes or management cutting support out from under attempts to enforce the process. An approach that works better is to start with a simple process, then gradually make improvements, while always allowing flexibility and always keeping professionals fully engaged in the improvements.
- Schedule discipline and metrics are easy to define, but they sometimes backfire. Be careful not to use these as whips to beat software developers. Software developers typically face considerable schedule pressure. They also know that requirements will mutate throughout the development cycle, causing schedule changes. Try to balance schedule management by allowing developers to explain where changing requirements have affected schedules. Try to balance metrics by including indications of where developers have done well.
- Software quality professionals are well aware that business realities often clash with "good" development processes. Customer problems and marketing opportunities will frequently cause the organization to turn on a dime, cut corners, and work long hours—often without detailed requirements—to save the day. Understand that software development professionals often find themselves in such compromising positions. The software quality professional should demonstrate understanding, and should help the development professionals explain why such projects may not be well documented or satisfy every activity listed in the development process.
- Process audits and quality assurance checklists can have benefits. But bear in mind that these are being used on professionals who value creativity, believe in their workmanship, and try very hard to meet expectations. It takes great tact to avoid aggravating professionals. They will find it stressful to be cross-examined by "nonprofessionals." The most effective approach is to acknowledge and show respect for their professionalism, and to manifest one's own professionalism.
- Software quality managers and engineers should communicate with developers as if they are all professionals. For instance, it will be more productive to appeal to logic rather than to cite executives or documents. While it is true that some developers lack the education and skills of true professionals, and that some developers have large egos, the best chance for obtaining cooperation and compliance is by appealing to professionalism. Even if some individual developers remain difficult to deal with, the rest of the development staff will respect the professionalism of the software quality staff.

Software Quality Professionals as Leaders

Software quality professionals are portals between management and developers. They are responsible for accomplishing goals for product quality and process quality. They are also responsible for recognizing and addressing opportunities to improve staff morale and communication.

The most obvious way to maintain rapport with development professionals is to be a professional. Professionalism is rooted in an *ethos,* a shared set of beliefs and responsibilities. Professionals place great value in their integrity, their commitment to doing their jobs as well as possible, and their responsibility to seek and speak the truth.

There are no free lunches or silver bullets; orienting an organization's software quality efforts to accommodate the professionalism of its developers will not solve all of the organization's problems. For instance, it will need to consider differences in cultural norms based on where the organization is located, as well as the specific behavior of the specific organization. The organization will, of course, need to understand customer needs and market realities, as well as many other factors that lead to success. But at least it may prevent unnecessary tensions and morale problems, and it may be able to foster better quality practices, if the organization understands and accommodates the professional social values of its developers.

It can be done. There is evidence that successful development and software quality can foster professionalism while also achieving better quality practices and business success.

It is never easy to lead, but that is what software quality professionals should do—help management lead teams to improve practices in such a way that the development professionals participate, understand, and take pride in the improvements.

REFERENCES

Boehm, B. 1981. *Software engineering economics.* Upper Saddle River, N.J.: Prentice-Hall.

DeMarco, T., and T. Lister. 1987. *Peopleware.* New York: Dorset House.

Dunn, R. H. 1990. *Software quality: Concepts and plans.* Englewood Cliffs, N.J.: Prentice-Hall.

Fagan, M. 2001. Hitting the bull's eye—Improving your quality, schedule, cost and performance. In *Proceedings of the 11th International Software Quality Conference,* Pittsburgh. Milwaukee, Wis.: ASQ.

Glass, R. L. 2000. Loyal opposition: The sociology of open source: Of cults and cultures. *IEEE Software* (May/June): 104–105.

Hall, E. T., and M. R. Hall. 1990. *Understanding cultural differences: Germans, French, and Americans.* Yarmouth, Maine: Intercultural Press.

Humphrey, W. S. 1995. *A discipline for software engineering.* Reading, Mass.: Addison-Wesley.

———. 1997. *Managing technical people: innovation, teamwork, and the software process.* Reading, Mass: Addison-Wesley.

McConnell, S. 1996. *Rapid development*. Redmond, Wash.: Microsoft Press.

Mackey, K. 2000. Culture at work: Mars versus venus. *IEEE Software* (May/June): 14–15.

MIT. 2002. *Managing technical professionals and organizations: Improving and sustaining the performance of organizations, project teams and individual contributors*. Cambridge, Mass.: Massachusetts Institute of Technology (MIT).

Perry, W. E. 1991. *Quality assurance for information systems: Methods, tools, and techniques*. New York: John Wiley and Sons.

Raelin, J. A. 1984. *The clash of cultures: Managers and professionals*. Boston: Harvard Business School Press.

Rajlich, V., et al. 2001. Software cultures and evolution. *IEEE Computer* (September): 24:27.

Schmauch, C. H. 1994. *ISO 9000 for software developers*. Milwaukee, Wis.: ASQ Quality Press.

Weinberg, G. M. 1988. *The Psychology of computer programming*, Silver Anniversary Edition. New York: Dorset House.

Weinberg, G. M. 1992. *Quality software management: Volume 1, systems thinking*. New York: Dorset House.

Wieggers, K. E. 1996. *Creating a software engineering culture*. New York: Dorset Hall.

BIOGRAPHY

Dave Miller has managed quality and test organizations for two decades, and has published papers on software quality models, design of surveys, and surveys of engineering groups. He has a master's degree in information technology from Drexel University, a doctorate in English from Duke University, a master's degree in English from the University of Michigan, and a bachelor's degree from Montana State University. He is a member of ASQ and IEEE, and a senior member of ACM. He alternates between several irreconcilable opinions about the role of software quality engineering. He can be reached at dmillers@bellatlantic.net.

An Ethical Theory for the Advancement of Professionalism in Software Engineering

Nicole Radziwill, National Radio Astronomy Observatory

Software engineers and their managers are often confronted with difficult situations, where a commitment to personal ethics is necessary. However, even when a software professional has committed to abiding by the ASQ Code of Ethics, there are a variety of situations that can be encountered with peers, clients, and employers that can challenge an individual's application of these ethical principles. To promote one's commitment to quality, professional behavior and well-considered choices are imperative, even when the most ethical course of action is unclear. In this article, the definition of professionalism is examined for software engineers and their managers, and an ethical theory is proposed to help software engineers and software development managers identify the best course of action for difficult "right vs. wrong" and "right vs. right" choices. This guiding framework is then evaluated against scenarios that commonly arise in software development to determine the most ethical, and thus the most professional, course of action. Software professionals can use this new ethical theory as a tool for upholding their own professionalism when faced with difficult decisions, while ensuring that the following tactical objectives of software quality management are met: to identify, plan, assign, complete, verify, and validate software deliverables according to proper requirements.

Key words: decision making, dilemma, ethics, morality, professional, professionalism, quality, teamwork, values

Introduction

An ethical theory is a suggested theoretical framework for clarifying and assessing the morality of a situation or concept. One example of an established ethical theory is utilitarianism, which defines that a moral choice is the one that maximizes the amount of net benefit to the greatest number of individuals. A corollary is negative utilitarianism, which establishes that a moral act or concept must not only produce the greatest good for the most people, but create the least harm to the greatest number as well.

Ethical theories provide a basis for evaluating ideas, circumstances, and scenarios to determine the most appropriate course of action, or the one that is the most "good" or "right." Often these scenarios pose dilemmas, which reflect underlying tradeoffs to be considered. These dilemmas often involve a need to balance strategic goals with tactical objectives, a key element of software quality management.

J. M. Juran's "big-Q" view of quality aims to improve all organizational processes, not just product quality (Juran and Gryna 1988). This encompasses factors such as communication between individuals, the development of teamwork, and the ability to quickly and effectively resolve conflicts. Delays in conflict resolution can directly impact project schedules, particularly for complex dilemmas, indicating that an effective resolution process is essential to improving other organizational processes.

Professionalism is a required ingredient in an organizational culture wherever the "big-Q" approach is taken, but its definition can be difficult to apply from day to day (see Figure 1). Because organizational culture is dictated by the behaviors that are valued and rewarded by senior management and peers, professionalism can provide checks and balances because professionals must also answer to others like themselves and society in general. Specific guidelines for acting as a professional in a certain field, however, must be derived from specialized knowledge of the field itself.

Even though the definition of professionalism can be nebulous, most skilled workers and managers will agree that it is a desirable characteristic, and they would rather work with professionals than with amateurs. Because professionalism requires ethics, a certain skill level, and the dedication to the pursuit of knowledge in a particular area, contributions from professionals are likely to

pro·fes·sion·al·ism (prə-fĕsh′ə-nə-lĭz′əm) n.

1. Professional status, methods, character, or standards.

pro·fes·sion·al (prə-fĕsh′ə-nəl) adj.

1. Of, relating to, engaged in, or suitable for a profession: lawyers, doctors, and other professional people.
2. Conforming to the standards of a profession: professional behavior.

Source: The American Heritage Dictionary of the English Language, Fourth Edition Copyright © 2000 by Houghton Mifflin Company. Published by Houghton Mifflin Company. All rights reserved.

Figure 1 A dictionary definition of professionalism

result in more successful projects. Without professionalism, variations due to assignable causes related to the work force are more likely.

An ethical theory that upholds and advances the professionalism of software engineers and software development managers can be used as a tool to translate dilemmas into improved quality of processes and products. This article presents an ethical theory based on the foundations of professionalism in software engineering, which can be applied as guidance to a situation to determine the path of greatest "rightness" for software engineers and their managers. Making decisions that are optimally appropriate under diverse circumstances is a critical skill of the professional.

The Profession and Its Responsibilities

Managing software development from a quality perspective requires an understanding of both the quality management and software engineering professions. A quality management professional "understands quality standards and concepts, can implement organizational assessments, can maintain customer satisfaction and focus, manages projects in support of strategic objectives, and motivates human resources to accomplish goals" (Mische 2004).

A software development manager, however, is jointly responsible for upholding the standards of professionalism within that domain. Standards for software engineering are defined by the IEEE Software Engineering Code of Ethics and Professional Practices, which represents the authoritative written code of ethics in the field sponsored by a professional organization. It is intended to be the standard for teaching and practicing software engineering. The information appropriately covers the role of and standards for software development managers as well.

According to this code, the manager is obligated to "promote an ethical approach to the management of software development and maintenance," which includes exhibiting the competencies of promoting quality and reducing risk through software project management, informing software engineers of standards they are expected to abide by, and ensuring realistic quantitative estimates of cost, schedule, personnel, expected results, and product quality. He or she must manage issues of software ownership, confidentiality, and privacy, and is required to uphold the functional responsibilities of the development staff, which includes "detecting, correcting, and reporting errors in software and associated documents," "striving to fully understand the specifications for software on which they work," "ensuring adequate testing, debugging, and review," and "ensuring adequate documentation."

There is a balance of power between the knowledge of these responsibilities and the way in which that knowledge is applied to situational decision making. It is this gap that an ethical theory seeks to fill.

Constituents

An ethical theory has limited utility unless the decision maker's constituents are identified, known, and understood. Constituents are individuals or groups of people to which responsibilities are owed. These responsibilities may be reflected legally, ethically, or through specific expectations or requirements posed by the constituents. In some cases, there may be many constituents, and these constituents may have competing needs. Ethical decision making may require making a value judgment between these needs.

Quality management professionals directing a team of software engineers (and possibly scientists or other engineers as well) have responsibilities to several groups of people: professionals in the field as well as in other fields (for example, subject-matter experts), the software's users and/or customers, the employer who funds the development work, and one's staff. If one works at a federally funded research institution, he or she may also have a responsibility to the funding authority that allocates taxpayers' resources to one's work; to Congress, which authorizes the expenditures; and to the taxpayers who fund the work. The quality management professional's responsibility extends to society in general, especially because he or she is responsible for the actions, behaviors, and outcomes produced by the development team and its members.

Every software development manager has the responsibility to his or her employer to use their software resources (human and material) in a manner that produces the greatest value with respect to its investment, and to ensure that the work performed by individuals is aligned with the goals of the site and organization. Quality management professionals are morally obligated to provide their staff members with clear and reasonable expectations of what they are to accomplish to benefit the organization as a whole, especially when this involves negotiating with other stakeholders or divisions. If one works at a federally funded institution, he or she is responsible to the federal agencies and taxpayers who fund the work to use those funds appropriately and effectively. Ultimately, the collective goal of a development manager and his or her staff is to derive maximum utility from the production of software.

Each of these constituent groups has implicit and explicit expectations of software engineers. Software professionals have responsibilities to all of them. Subject-matter experts (SMEs) expect that they will be consulted for all matters that require scientific, technical, or process guidance, and that the software engineers will use appropriate discretion and judgment regarding which matters to raise to the SMEs and which to creatively implement. If one works in a scientific or engineering software development role, those who use the software may expect that he or she will provide tools that allow them to readily collect and analyze their scientific data. Because their responsibility to their own profession is to challenge established modes of operation in order to discover new scientific results, it is thus the software developer's responsibility to develop software that does not functionally prohibit them from exploring new horizons.

The software professional's responsibilities to his or her constituents directly influence what behaviors and actions will be considered professional.

Professionalism in Software Engineering

In his foreword to the book *The Responsible Software Engineer* by Myers et al., software project management expert Tom DeMarco attempts to define the meaning of professionalism as it pertains to software engineering. He first suggests that in many lines of work, professionalism is merely "compliant uniformity" in which employees are expected to dress and act in certain ways, and not to upset the delicate balance of the status quo. He argues that professionalism should instead be defined by a "4P" model of proficiency, permanency, professing, and promise keeping. A professional, in his opinion, will have: 1) developed mastery of a body of knowledge common to his or her profession, 2) decided upon the profession as a life's calling, and 3) made a statement declaring membership in the professional ranks. Professionalism is reaffirmed each time the individual keeps his or her promises, thus earning respect as a reliable and consistent person, and adding what the author believes to be an ethical dimension to the definition (Myers, Hall, and Pitt 1996).

Software engineering does require a certain level of compliant uniformity. Although progressive high-tech companies may implement radical policies that allow employees to bring their dogs to work or dress in tattered jeans at the office, this is largely dictated by the culture that a company chooses to allow and not the standards deemed acceptable to a profession. Additionally, a professional attitude, which includes respect for others, is necessary to be able to work as a viable and productive team player. It is detrimental for a software engineer to act as if others are not as smart or as important as he or she is. This poisonous belief reflects a lack of respect for the differences between individuals, which are necessary for business to be conducted and for a profession to be embodied.

Because attitude dictates how an individual behaves and responds to situations, true professionalism requires an attitude that will produce the desired effects. What effects are desired in most situations for which professionalism is a requirement? In addition to being able to use one's mastery of a professional body of knowledge, this knowledge must be applied consistently, reliably, and according to a legal and ethical framework. Constituents must trust the individual to consistently execute his or her tasks in a professional manner. By limiting the ethical dimension to promise keeping, DeMarco's model condones behavior that damages or harms people physically or emotionally as long as promises are met. Because the workplace is so dependent upon relationships and the building of trust, an attitude that integrates respect for others with personal humility is required.

Given these considerations, at its most basic level professionalism can be defined as the willingness and ability to continuously earn the trust of one's many constituents over time. This requires exhibiting professional behaviors, including a fundamental level of compliant uniformity, skill-level proficiency and continuous professional development, permanency, professional involvement, displays of consistency and integrity, and a professional attitude that requires respect for others as human beings and as coworkers.

An Ethical Theory for Software Professionals

The purpose of an ethical theory is not to provide an unambiguous prescription for behavior, but to lead the querent through moral reasoning, which is a decision process that will enable him or her to make a choice. An ethical theory does not, as such, require universal applicability. To illustrate, consider the theory of ethical relativism, which establishes that there are no universally acceptable principles. Instead, each group or culture establishes its own principles for deciding the most ethical course of action, which may or may not be situation dependent.

Because there is never only one answer to an ethical problem, many decisions require valuing one principle, or one constituent's needs, over another. So why have an ethical theory at all? A good ethical theory is easily understood and applied, simple enough to be easily remembered, internally consistent, and able to provide guidance in the interpretation and application of ethical principles to situations. An ethical theory will lead different individuals to similar (although not necessarily identical) conclusions, yet does not require those individuals to painstakingly weigh their options against the myriad of principles found in any code of ethics.

The foundational aspects of this study developed the argument that professionalism is focused on the development of trust between an individual and his or her constituents, and between an individual and other members of the profession. Thus, when a software engineer or manager is weighing courses of action to respond to an ethical issue, the ethical theory described in Figure 2, which is based on the foundations of professionalism, can effectively be applied to the software engineering workplace.

This approach integrates concepts from the established ethical theories of consequentialism, utilitarianism, and virtue theory (Velasquez 1998). The first two components of the ethical theory can help one to decide whether an action is the most ethical and thus most appropriate in a given situation; the third component alone will not directly aid in determining whether an action is the most ethical, but will help an individual to choose between otherwise comparable actions.

Note that there are several assumptions implicit in this model. The first is that integrity and humility are the foundational and most desirable virtues, particularly within software engineering teams that want to achieve high levels of quality. The model assumes that the software professional is making a per-

Components of the ethical theory	Implications
The action must yield the optimal increase in the amount of trust between the professional and his or her constituents.	If the scenario involves a software product or software deliverable, the increase in trust must be evaluated over the lifetime of the software, as well as the lifetime of its legacy in the hearts and minds of users. While trust cannot be quantified, the relative increase in trust for different courses of action can be judged. Note that this component of the ethical theory is normative and establishes that trust should be increased as a result of a truly ethical decision; how to accomplish this depends on the situation and the options available to the individual. Note also that constituents may have competing needs, and a value judgment may be necessary to establish their relative merits. The other two components of the ethical theory may be used to do this.
The action must be directed toward the greater good of the employer, and to the advancement or strengthening of the reputation and integrity of the profession as a whole.	Because obligation to the profession itself is valued equivalently to the employee's obligation to the employer, any unethical action encouraged by the employer is thus not considered appropriate according to this ethical theory. Similarly, any action that is illegal is also unethical, since this erodes the integrity of the profession.
The action chosen should best demonstrate the virtue of humility, that is, an individual must place the needs and desires of the employer, and the future of the profession itself, over his or her own intellectual and emotional needs and desires.	This criterion is added to the model to aid in distinguishing between two or more ethically comparable options that meet the first and second criteria. The one that best develops the desirable virtues of the software engineer will be the one that most effectively strengthens his or her professionalism. This may require strength under pressure.

Figure 2 An ethical theory for software professionals. The criteria are strongly interdependent and must be used jointly.

sonal decision, not a decision on behalf of the employer, and may have limited impact on the ethics demonstrated by the employer. It is also assumed that it is necessary to abide by legal statutes and corporate policies to earn trust, so that anything that is illegal is also unethical because breaking the law violates trust. Consequentialism is concerned with the outcome of an action, and this ethical theory determines whether an action is ethical as the result of the outcome. Does the action build trust in an optimal fashion? If so, then it must contribute to the greater good of the employer.

According to utilitarianism, however, an action should contribute to the greater good of society, not just the employer. But employment is a contract between the worker and his or her organization. It is the employer's right to utilize the employee in a manner that the employer deems appropriate for meeting its goals and objectives; it is furthermore the employer's moral obligation to society to ensure that it does not utilize an employee in a way that is harmful to society. The relativistic nature of the ethics of professionalism is assumed in this personal ethical theory, which places the direct responsibility to society on the employer, and limits the employee's professional responsibility to his or her immediate constituents.

This theory effectively captures several behaviors that are recognized as professional. For example, a professional will follow through on commitments. This helps to increase the trust between the professional and the stakeholders associated with a commitment, and also contributes to the greater good of the employer, who can then plan for tasks that require that previous commitments have been met. Being open about problems and issues, even if this means informing a stakeholder that a deadline cannot be met, demonstrates the virtue of humility; the professional recognizes that even if he or she wants to maintain an image of accomplishment, greater good arises when the employer can follow contingency plans. An environment of open communication will, in turn,, promote enhanced trust.

As another example, consider the need to produce documentation, which is particularly critical in software engineering. This task is dreaded by most software developers, who would rather be "more productive" in their own opinions by writing more code. Documenting one's work clearly and succinctly, however, serves the greater good of the employer since it flattens the learning curve for users and other programmers regarding the adoption of new features and functions. A shorter learning curve means less time will be spent trying to understand software, and more time will be spent applying that software to achieve derived benefits. By accepting the chore of documentation, the software engineer demonstrates humility by placing the employer's needs over his or her own desires to work on something more interesting.

Like the consequentialist and utilitarian systems, the proposed ethical theory attempts to provide guiding principles for determining how to act in a given situation. Although developing the virtues of humility and integrity is highly applicable and desirable, reliance on developing an individual's character will not necessarily provide that person with the ethical basis for exhibiting professionalism, since a specific background and education are assumed. Integrity and humility cannot build one's skills and competencies. According to these criteria, no purely self-serving act in software engineering can be ethical. All actions must cultivate profitable interpersonal relationships, founded upon trust, between software engineers and their constituents. For those who might claim that solid, maintainable code is the more desirable outcome, it is time to reflect upon the original definition of professionalism. In order for the software engineer to continually build trust over time, solid and maintainable code is a critical ingredient for developing and sustaining mutually beneficial relationships between engineers and their customers.

As a result, a quality product is an artifact of professionalism. The ethical theory, then, does not supersede or negate the need for quality practices in software engineering. In fact, abiding by the ethical theory presupposes effective software practices and continuous improvement.

Applying the Ethical Theory

An ethical theory with the intent to provide guidance is only useful if it helps one determine a most appropriate course of action in simple ethical problems, as well as "right vs. right" and "right vs. wrong" dilemmas. A dilemma can be described as perceptions brought about because of "interconnected beliefs about a given situation" (Sambrook 2003). In general, individuals who share beliefs will perceive similar dilemmas, whereas individuals with differing beliefs or values may not view a certain situation as a dilemma.

Surrounding every dilemma, various individuals or groups will have differing and sometimes divergent needs, and there will be several potential courses of action. Many times, however, each party's needs are valid and legitimate and it is only the actions that are in conflict. Needs and actions must be examined in every scenario analysis, as well as the circumstances surrounding the dilemma. Such an "environmental analysis" of the dilemma is critical, because depending on the circumstances at the time an issue has escalated to a dilemma, the most appropriate course of action may change.

When evaluating a difficult situation using an ethical theory, one must also consider which party is capable of taking action as a result of the analysis. One assumes that the ethical theory is used only by the party who recognizes that an action must be taken to resolve a work dilemma, and that the other party may have to be convinced that a certain course of action is the most appropriate. With this in mind, three scenarios in software development have been evaluated ethically to determine the most appropriate course of action. The first is a simple "right vs. right" ethical situation, the second is a slightly more complex "right vs. wrong," and the third examines a critical "right vs. wrong" dilemma, where the employee knows that the employer is motivated to act unethically with respect to the customer.

Scenario No. 1: Customer Asks Software Engineer to Cut Corners

An internal customer asks a software engineer to cut corners during the implementation of a new feature, which would make the final product less robust than if the software engineer followed his or her own design. What should the software engineer do?

This is a "right vs. right" case, which illustrates the need to evaluate the context within which the issue is being raised. The software engineer is faced with choosing a course of action that he or she typically believes is right—developing a robust product—versus following the customer's demands, in order to generate customer satisfaction, which is also a beneficial outcome. The tradeoff is between robustness and customer satisfaction. It is important to question whether the internal customer has a genuine need underlying the request. In this case, the key external circumstance affecting the scenario is that the software module is needed to support only one engineer's tests of prototype algorithms. It will not be delivered in any production software, thus its impact on users is limited to the impact on the internal customer only. The compelling need is that the internal customer must be able to explore the algorithms to satisfy his or her own deliverable two months away to keep another major, high-priority project on schedule.

What action would yield the optimal increase in the amount of trust between the software engineer and the customer requesting the work? Clearly, the internal customer will lose trust in the software engineer if the engineer does not follow the customer's directives. It is the responsibility of the software engineer, however, to inform the customer about the consequences of choosing such a design, and ensure that the customer is willing to bear the risks associated with his or her requests. The action that would yield the optimal trust is to disclose the shortcomings of the customer's requested design in writing, forge a mutual agreement on the plan of action to be taken, and ultimately seek customer satisfaction since the software itself is not the essence of the problem to be solved.

What action would yield the optimal increase in the amount of trust between the software engineer and the external customer represented by the internal customer? In this scenario, there is no external customer being represented. The internal customer requests that software be developed purely for his or her own use during engineering tests, and it is unlikely that the software module will be used under any other circumstances. Furthermore, once it has served its purpose, it is unlikely to be used again. Because there is no external customer, "cutting corners" may be pragmatic rather than inappropriate under these circumstances.

What action would result in the greatest good for the employer, and the advancement of the profession? It is in the greatest good of the employer to have the results the internal customer needs according to the schedule of the major, high-priority project. If the software engineer spends time making the module as robust as it can possibly be, there will be time lost that the internal customer could have spent investigating the algorithms. Because the software engineer is morally obligated to disclose risks he or she is aware of, and obligated to his or her profession to do the same, the best course of action would be to let the customer bear the burden of risk, but only since the impact of the risk is localized to the internal customer only.

What action would exemplify the virtue of humility? In this case, the software engineer should balance his or her own sense of duty as it pertains to this single coding exercise against the needs of the employer. It is the software engineer's responsibility to disclose risks, but it is also his or her responsibility to enable the employer's achievement of higher-level goals through its projects. The software engineer should humbly put the situation in perspective, disclose the risks in writing to the internal customer, get a sign-off acknowledging that the internal customer assumes the risk, and deliver what is needed to accomplish the overarching goals.

Scenario No. 2: Feature Creep During Development Time

A team of software engineers is busily working toward their ship date, when a customer comes and asks if a certain "very important requirement" can just "be slipped in." The lead developer identifies that the addition carries moderate risk systemwide, but would be a very straightforward addition to the code. What should the lead developer do?

This is a "right vs. wrong" case, except the action that is most appropriate will differ depending upon the external circumstances. The internal customer may think that implementing the extra requirement is right because it will best serve the external customer, and not addressing the need that the requirement represents would be wrong. The software engineer may also believe that the addition is right, because it is not difficult and will not negatively impact the remainder of the development schedule. Both parties may believe that the addition would be wrong if the risk outweighed the benefits, and so these issues must also be considered. Any decision made by either the software engineer or the internal customer, however, would not take into account external factors of interest to the development manager or other senior managers, and these unknown external factors will be critical to resolving this dilemma.

What action would yield the optimal increase in the amount of trust between the software engineer, his or her manager, and the internal customer requesting the work? The internal customer may perceive a legitimate need to squeak in the requested enhancement. Particularly in rapidly changing business environments, it is important that the value of potential last-minute additions not be overlooked. If the software engineer acknowledges the need of the internal customer for the requirement to be acknowledged, this will generate more trust than if the request was immediately rejected. If the software development manager is asked to be involved, this will generate trust because the manager will recognize the employee's acknowledgment of organizational goals. The best course of action would involve all parties.

What action would yield the optimal increase in the amount of trust between the software engineer and the external customer represented by the internal customer? To evaluate this question, one must determine whether the value added to the customer as a result of the newly requested addition is large enough to merit management intervention. If the software shipped without the newly requested feature, would the external customer be able to accomplish the required tasks with the software? Would the external customer be at a disadvantage without the addition? How much would it cost, in terms of schedule and monetary outlay, to adjust the plan at this stage? Is the adjustment economically worthwhile for the company? To answer the last question, other senior managers must be involved, so the best course of action is one that decentralizes the decision making.

What action would result in the greatest good for the employer, and the advancement of the profession? If one item can be slipped in, then the internal customer may think that many more can be slipped in as well. Unfortunately, this may encourage the internal customer to make more requests, eventually resulting in a schedule slip or even lowered morale in the software development group (the result of added pressure caused by too much work in the late stages of a project). Any action that promotes responsible requirements management will contribute to the advancement of the profession, and responsible requirements management will help keep the project on track and keep customers satisfied. In order to manage this late entry requirement, the software engineer should use the management structure in his or her organization.

What action would exemplify the virtue of humility? The lead developer should escalate this case to the software development manager, understanding that he or she is better positioned to work with other managers to determine whether an adjustment should be made to the scope or schedule. This requires a demonstration of the virtue of humility since the engineer must show respect to the managers, the organization, and, ultimately, the customer by using organizational structures and processes properly to resolve the issue.

Scenario No. 3: The Employer Pressures the Software Engineer or Manager to Behave Unethically

A computer company is working on an experimental fighter. Based on her experiences during the development process, a quality control software engineer suspects that the flight control software is not sufficiently tested, although it has (finally) passed its contracted test suites; she believes that the test suites simply did not cover all safety-critical elements, some of which were not evident at the time that the requirements and test plans were developed. She is being pressured by her employers to sign off on the software. Her employers say they will go out of business if they do not deliver the software on time, and "strongly suggest" that she approve the tests as executed. Should she sign off? (Adapted from Gotterbarn 2005)

This is a "right vs. wrong" dilemma, since the software engineer's conscience motivates her not to compromise the safety of a yet-to-be-released control system. This situation is made more complex because flight control software, if inadequate, can pose threats to human life through unpredictable or unreliable behavior.

What action would yield the optimal increase in the amount of trust between the software quality engineer and her organization, as represented by senior management? What action would yield the optimal increase in the amount of trust between her and her major group of constituents, the future users of the flight control software? Senior managers deal in schedules, budgets, constraints, tradeoffs, and metrics to characterize progress. Usually, all of these are evaluated over time. In this situation, the employers perceive that the future of their company depends on delivering this software on time, and on-time delivery requires the software quality engineer to sign off immediately. To increase trust between herself and her employers right now, she might be inclined to sign off; problems may not be detected for months or years, and in the meantime, her employers might entrust her with higher-profile projects. Trust, however, is cumulative. If the flight control software is released, and accidents or deaths attributable to software occur, the employers' trust in her will wane. Furthermore, costs of litigation or loss of reputation should accidents occur could cause the company to go out of business anyway. The optimal amount of trust will be generated when the software quality engineer considers the welfare of the company today, as well as in the future. This must be balanced with the users' need for safe control software; their trust is earned by consistent, reliable performance of the released code. That these constituents have not yet had the opportunity to develop trust in the engineer is immaterial.

What action would result in the greatest good for the employer, and the advancement of the profession? In this case, the greatest good for the employer must be considered not only now, but over the life of the flight control software. Because there is considerable risk associated with signing off, both to the future of her company and to the safety of users, she is morally obligated to express her objections. If there were no risks to the employer due to future litigation or loss of reputation, the greatest good for the employer might come by signing off without comprehensive safety testing. But would this advance the profession? The answer is no, because the software quality engineer's professional judgment includes fulfilling professional responsibilities to the end user and representing the integrity of the profession to society. Certainly a "professional" would not endanger users of a software package, in the perception of the general public.

What action would exemplify the virtue of humility? Presumably, the software engineer wants to be part of a successful project team, and it is likely that if she presses the issue of incomplete tests, her managers may perceive that she contributed to the problem. Were she arrogant or prideful, she might choose to ignore inadequacies in the testing process, rather than admitting that the quality assurance team (which she is a part of) did not adequately capture the tests needed to ensure safety. The action that develops the most humility will be one that admits prior errors or omissions, and provides a plan of action to rectify them before the well being of constituents is unnecessarily compromised.

In this example, the software quality engineer should admit to the errors of omission made by the quality assurance team, yet hold firm to her position that the software should not be released and should refuse to sign off. Perhaps the company could also make concessions to the client, providing a discount on development costs or not charging for the extra tests, explaining the company's commitment to safety and its respect for its engineers as morally responsible professionals.

The company, however, may not respond in such an ethical way, and refusing to sign off may cost the employee her job. Furthermore, the employer may choose to go ahead with the software release, regardless of her recommendation. Although the example is from engineering and not software, consider the case of Roger Boisjoly, who objected to the launch of the space shuttle *Challenger* on January 28, 1986, based on his experiences with the fatally flawed O-ring. He argues that intimidation of his employer Morton Thiokol by its customer led to the "management decision" that resulted in loss of life and damage to the reputation of the space program for years. Boisjoly's personal ethical approach led him to write memos to officials at various levels of his organization both prior to and after the disaster, which ultimately led to a demotion. His commitment to the safety of his constituents (the passengers on the doomed launch), however, was recognized when he received the Prize for Scientific Freedom and Responsibility, awarded by the American Association for the Advancement of Science (Boisjoly 1987). Both scenario no. 3 and the Boisjoly case illustrate the personal nature of an ethical theory; although an individual may apply an ethical decision process to determine which action to take, an employer's actions may not be similarly guided.

Conclusions

The software development workplace is dependent upon relationships and the building of trust, so an attitude that combines respect for others with personal humility is essential. Professionalism can thus be defined as the willingness and ability to continuously earn the trust of one's many constituents over time, even when this requires valuing the various constituents' needs differently. For the software engineer to continually build trust over time, quality in the processes he or she follows and attention to the many dimensions of product quality is critical, so a quality product can be considered an artifact of professionalism.

Based on the aforementioned development of the concept of professionalism in software engineering, this study presents a testable proposition (in the form of an ethical theory) to help a software engineer or manager navigate through a complex landscape of ethical considerations using simple heuristics. Each dilemma is highly specific and must be considered as a unique case when the ethical theory is applied. The theory establishes that given an ethical issue to resolve, the most appropriate choice:

- Develops optimal trust between the professional and his or her constituents
- Results in effecting the greatest good for the employer while advancing the profession itself
- Demonstrates the virtue of humility in the software professional

The theory can be applied to a simple ethical problem or a complex dilemma, as illustrated by three scenarios ranging in complexity and level of ethical conflict. Under all circumstances, the needs of the software professional must be balanced against the needs of the constituents, understanding that both may represent legitimate needs of the employer. The circumstances surrounding an ethical choice must also be fully recognized, since these often impact the decision process. Keep in mind that not all ethical choices are dilemmas, and despite good personal ethical choices, employers may still choose to act unethically. Applying this ethical theory to situations encountered in the workplace can enable the software engineer or manager to exemplify professionalism, thereby ensuring that their behavior engenders quality in communications, processes, and, ultimately, products.

REFERENCES

Boisjoly, R. 1987. Ethical decisions, Morton Thiokol and the space shuttle Challenger disaster. *ASME paper #87 WA/TS-4, presented at ASME Winter Meeting, Boston*. See URL: http://onlineethics.org/essays/shuttle/index.html.

Gotterbarn, D. 2005. Ethical considerations in software engineering. See URL: http://www-cs.etsu.edu/gotterbarn/artge2.htm. Case adapted from McFarland in *IEEE Computer*, May 1990.

Juran, J. M., and F. M. Gryna. 1988. Juran's quality control handbook, fourth edition. New York: McGraw Hill.

Mische, M. A. 2004. Defining systems integration. In *Enterprise Systems Integration*, ed. J. Wyzalek. Boca Raton, Fla.: Auerbach.

Myers, C., T. Hall, and D. Pitt, eds. 1996. *The responsible software engineer*. New York: Springer-Verlag.

Sambrook, J. 2003. Dealing with dilemmas in software engineering. *Common Sense Systems Internal Paper #3FE5F965-513E-0863B*. See URL: http://www.common-sense.com/Articles/DWD_SE.

Velasquez, M. G. 1998. *Business ethics: Concepts and cases, fourth edition*. Upper Saddle River, N.J.: Prentice-Hall.

BIOGRAPHY

Nicole Radziwill is the division head for software development at the National Radio Astronomy Observatory (NRAO) in Green Bank, W.Va. She has 10 years' experience in strategy development, business and technology consulting, and managing software development teams for scientific R&D, telecommunications, and e-business applications. Radziwill has an undergraduate degree in meteorology from Penn State, an MBA from Regis University, and is pursuing a doctorate in technology management with a quality systems specialization at Indiana State. Her research interests include management metrics, quality improvement (particularly for scientific applications), and optimization of decision support processes. She can be reached by e-mail at nradziwi@nrao.edu.

PART II

Software Quality Management

Digging down from the foundation information in the first section, we move on to software quality management, where general quality principles are applied to software. Knowing about ISO-compliant quality management systems may not prepare you for understanding software quality concepts. Many concepts have been adapted to software—or are original to the development of quality software. They include setting quality goals, planning how to meet those goals, outsourcing when applicable, determining what documentation will support the process, reviewing the documentation generated during the process, finding defects through various methods, controlling change and determining the cost of quality, ensuring the availability of quality data, robust change control, process improvement, and finally audits—why, how, when, and how to report results. As you can see, this is a huge area. We have selected four articles to guide you in your efforts to understand more about software quality management. These four articles describe using checklists, keeping an eye on the so-called soft factors, modeling the cost of quality, and process improvement.

In "The Value of a Good Checklist" Dan Houston relates how Six Sigma's five process improvement phases of define, measure, analyze, improve, and control were applied to two processes: the repair of defects and the review of system test specifications. Well documented savings resulted from reducing "bad fixes" by 90 percent and from identifying several high-priority defects through more effective testing.

"Soft Factors Affecting Software Quality," by Fred Heemstra and Rob Kusters, addresses the influence of behavioral and organizational factors on the quality of business software. Quality "drivers" such as motivation, commitment, experience, working conditions, and organizational culture are considered. The article may be seen as a plea to learn from other disciplines and to pay more attention to what are regarded as the "soft" factors in the "hard" software world.

Daniel Galin offers his views "Toward an Inclusive Model for the Costs of Software Quality." He expands on the traditional cost-of-quality model by considering separately those costs associated with software development activities and those associated with managerial activities. His goal is to identify an optimal level of managerial appraisal and quality-control costs. Evaluation and reporting of improvements are identified as necessary for an organization to implement this more inclusive model.

To finish our overview of software quality management, we look at "Sustaining Best Practices: How Real-World Software Organizations Improve Quality Processes," by Diana Mekelburg. The most publicized methods that organizations are advised to use for improving their software quality processes are two opposites: continuous improvement models and quick-fix best practices. A two-year study of quality process improvements in 10 organizations, however, determined that all 10 organizations followed similar stages of improvement that grouped complementary practices at each stage. Organizations' progressions through these stages were based on evolutionary changes in their motivations and philosophies rather than on continuous quantitative analysis or the evidence of the effectiveness of best practices. The sustainability of new best practices depended more on the stage in which they were introduced than on the proven benefit of the practices themselves.

The Value of a Good Checklist

Dan Houston, Honeywell, Inc.

Checklists are widely used in software development for a variety of purposes, such as measuring phase completion and readiness to proceed with work, guiding reviews of work, and ensuring adherence to procedures. The quality of a checklist, and thus its usefulness, often depends on how it was produced.

This article describes two Six Sigma projects, both of which produced a checklist and resulted in savings through avoidance of costly rework. One project looked at the defect fixing process as it is performed across two sites to discover why a high percentage of defect fixes were unsuccessful.

The other project looked at how system test specifications are reviewed, and developed a checklist for the reviews.

Keywords: defect processing, DMAIC, FMEA, process improvement, reviews

Six Sigma

Six Sigma is a quality improvement program that looks at processes with a view to analyzing process steps, determining what process elements most need improvement, developing alternatives for improvement, and then selecting and implementing one. It relies on a variety of qualitative and quantitative tools, emphasizing the use of data and statistical analysis within a method called DMAIC, an acronym for the names of its five phases (define, measure, analyze, improve, and control) (see Figure 1). Six Sigma projects are typically selected for their potential to derive savings from process improvements, whether the process is in production, administration, engineering, or services.

A Six Sigma project typically begins with a high-level definition of a process using a diagram to specify the process boundaries, inputs, outputs, customers, and requirements. In the measure phase, a process metric is selected and used to baseline the current performance of the process. In the analysis phase, the process is analyzed, usually with a process map and a failure modes and effects analysis (FMEA), but may include other types of analysis. The process map shows each process step with its inputs and outputs and provides the basis for either an FMEA or a quantitative, usually statistical, analysis. Areas for improvement are pinpointed and alternatives are generated and evaluated.

Phase	Steps
Define	Identify an opportunity and define a project to address it.
Measure	Analyze the current process and specify the desired outcome.
Analyze	Identify root causes and proposed solutions.
Improve	Prioritize solutions; select, plan, validate, and implement a solution.
Control	Develop a plan for measuring progress and maintaining gains.

Figure 1 DMAIC method for process improvement

Once an improvement option is selected and implemented, the project enters the control phase. In this phase, a plan is established for monitoring and controlling the process to ensure that gains are maintained.

Breyfogle (2003) and Pyzdek (2000) both provide comprehensive treatments of Six Sigma and DMAIC.

Improving Integrity of Defect Fixes

A very experienced software metrician once said that one of the best metrics for indicating a software development organization's health is the fix integrity rate, or its opposite, the bad-fix rate. Fix integrity is essentially the percentage of fixes that correct the problems logged and do not have undesirable side effects. Fix integrity rates can vary widely: Some published figures suggest a range of 45 percent (Freedman and Weinberg 1990) to 96 percent (Baan 1996).

A U.S. Honeywell team, dedicated to maintaining a process control system, relied heavily on an offshore team for customer-funded enhancements. However, the complexity and age of the control system presented challenges to the offshore team. The U.S. team's deep knowledge of the system allowed them to judge the quality of the offshore team's fixes. At about the time that Six Sigma was being introduced in Honeywell Industry Solutions, the U.S. team noticed a large number of bad fixes and decided to address the problem in a Green Belt project. Green Belt projects are chartered to improve a business process, are executed by a team of people who have attended a DMAIC course, and are expected to produce a measurable savings. Figure 2 lists the major activities of each phase of the defect fix integrity Green Belt project.

The project was initiated and led by the U.S. team, with the cooperation of the offshore team. The Green Belt candidates were on the U.S. team and were responsible for drafting the work products and analyzing the data. Work products were reviewed in teleconferences. When the team worked on the FMEA, they took advantage of the offshore manager's visit to involve him in this exercise.

Define	Measure	Analyze	Improve	Control
Problem statement	As-is process map	Failure modes and effects analysis	Defect fixing process	Control plan
List of knowns/unknowns	Collect baseline defect fix data		Checklist	Results
SIPOC (Supplier-Input-Process-Output-Customer diagram)	Refined savings estimate		To-be process map	
Macro process map			Checklist implementation	
Savings estimate				

Figure 2 Activities by phase of the defect fix integrity quality improvement project

Define Phase

In the define phase, the team formulated the problem statement, in this case, a fairly simple one. Team members listed what they did and did not know about the problem, an exercise that demonstrated the potential scope of the project. Using a supplier-input-process-output-customer (SIPOC) diagram the team defined the beginning and end of the process being improved, in addition to the process inputs and outputs, customers and suppliers, and requirements on the inputs and outputs. At this point, an important scoping decision was made: The project would not study the whole development process; rather, it would study only the process of fixing defects. Furthermore, results would not consider all defects, only those that were considered bad fixes (either did not fix the reported problem or created undesirable side effects). By limiting the measurement of results to bad fixes, the project's data gathering and analysis task was simplified.

A high-level map of the process (see Figure 3) started with defect discovery and ended with released product. This process map identifies inputs and outputs for each step (inputs below each step, outputs above).

In the define phase, the project team also estimated savings from improving the defect fixing process by calculating the cost of bad fixes in the previous release and then normalizing this cost using the developer effort in each release. A target was set for reducing bad fixes by 50 percent, thereby saving 150 hours of rework and associated effort (management, retesting, configuration management, and release). These savings did not attempt to include less tangible costs, such as those due to customer dissatisfaction, warranty service, and late releases.

Measure Phase

In the measure phase, the process map was refined. Each process step was detailed and the inputs were categorized. Both the U.S. and offshore teams made an initial assessment of critical inputs.

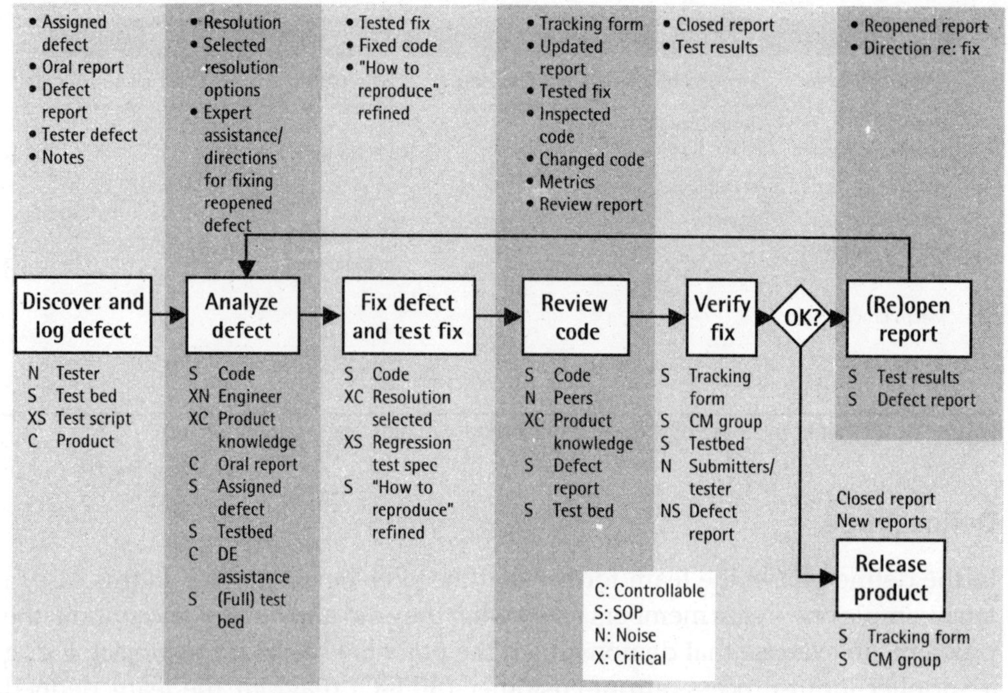

Figure 3 Process map of defect fixing process

Also, in this phase, the bad-fix data for the previous release were collected and analyzed. The target improvement ratio was increased from 50 percent to 90 percent, and the savings estimate was refined. Because of the refixing costs, substantial savings (between $15,000 and $23,000) could be realized from reducing the bad-fix rate.

Analysis Phase

An FMEA was performed on the process map. The failure modes for each process step were listed and causes and effects of the failure modes were evaluated. The results of the FMEA were used to identify the critical inputs of the process, as well as actual and potential problems, in the process.

In an FMEA, it is important to understand the causes of the failure modes. Actions based on intermediate, rather than root, causes may not effectively control the risks of failure. In the course of this FMEA, one cause was cited repeatedly, indicating that the root causes had not been identified. To overcome this limitation, bad fixes in the previous release were analyzed and their root causes identified (see Figure 4). Branches on the fishbone diagram were given weights based on occurrence of the causes.

The highest priority risks identified in the FMEA provided the basis for producing actions to take on the defect fixing process. These actions included additional training for inspection moderators, additional training for offshore

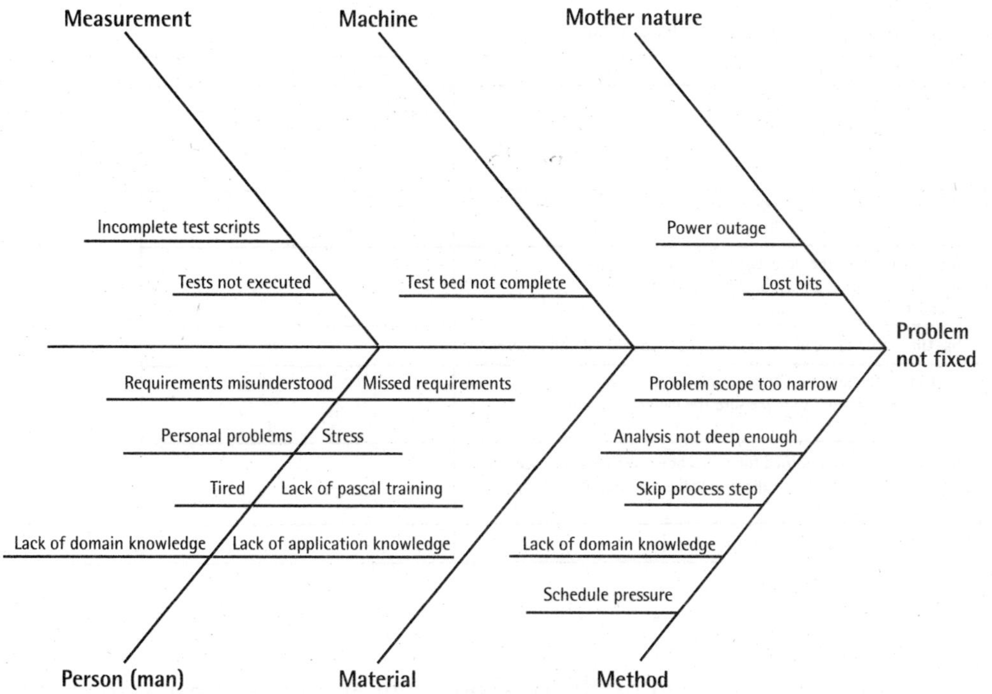

Figure 4 Cause-and-effect diagram for incorrect defect fixes

developers on the legacy control system, definition of a new defect fixing process, sending an offshore developer to the United States during the period of defect fixing, a checklist for the defect fixing process, modifying the inspection process to accommodate discussion between sites, and delaying a release to accommodate longer reviews. Most of these actions were expensive and would have required more time than was available. The process improvement(s) had to be made within a month, prior to the start of system testing and the subsequent reporting of defects.

Improve Phase

The Green Belt team elected to improve the defect fixing process by producing a checklist and requiring the development team to use it as a means of ensuring proper execution of each defect fixing step. The cost of this action was low and the checklist could be produced and in use within a relatively short period of time. The United States and offshore teams used the process map and the FMEA to produce the checklist. They walked through the process map and, while referring to the FMEA for the significant failure modes and to the root-cause analysis for the underlying causes, they asked what was required for a correct output at each step. They constructed the checklist from these requirements. A portion of the checklist is shown in Figure 5.

Defect Correction Process Guide/Checklist

Defect # >>	Date >>	
Engineer's name >>		
Step description	Each answer should be "Yes" before proceeding to the next step.	Reviewer team lead
1. Has the quality database been updated to indicate the "analyze" status for this PAR?		
2. Are all aspects of the defect understood (symptoms, how to reproduce, and so on)? If not, contact the submitter for clarification.		
3. Has the "root" cause of the problem been identified and entered?		
4. Have all potential modified functions been researched to see where they are called from to make sure the calling functions aren't negatively impacted?		
5. Have all potential modified functions been researched to see what other functions they are calling to make sure the called functions aren't negatively impacted?		
6. Have all possible solutions been analyzed?		

Figure 5 Sample of the defect fixing checklist

The checklist was tried by the offshore team and revised using their feedback. A "To-Be Process Map" was created by editing the original process map to show each completed checklist item as a step output.

Control Phase

In this phase, a control plan was written to ensure that the process improvement and its consequent benefits would continue. The control plan provides: 1) controls on the process for detecting when the defect fixing process outputs are not as specified, and 2) five responses to process failures.

As a result of working on the control plan, the teams realized the need for a control to ensure correct use of the checklist. For this reason, the Reviewer column was added to the checklist form and the Team Lead is required to review the completion of each checklist item with the developer who fixes the defect.

The control phase lasted throughout the release cycle in which the checklist was installed and no bad fixes were found in that release cycle. At the end of the project the benefit of checklist usage, based on rework and additional releases avoided in one version, was estimated at $30,000.

Reviewing Test Specifications

As Fagan-style inspections were being applied to all work products in the Honeywell IAC's Development Engineering organization, system testers realized the need for guidance in reviewing test specifications. Although the inspection process was structured, reviewers found little structure and guidance for the content of inspected test specifications. Lacking such support, testers feared that test specifications might be incomplete, allowing testing to be incomplete and defects to pass through the system test phase. Consequently, this project focused on the test specification process, with emphasis on the quality of test specification content. At the outset of the project, no savings were anticipated, but as the project progressed, the project team saw an opportunity to measure savings from use of the checklist. Figure 6 lists the major activities in each phase of this project and the remainder of this section explains these activities.

Define Phase

The scope of the project was defined as the test specification process in an SIPOC diagram (see Figure 7). The important part of this document was the list of requirements on both the process inputs and outputs.

Define	Measure	Analyze	Improve	Control
Problem statement SIPOC	As-is process map	Failure modes and effects analysis	To-be process map Checklist drafted and reliability measured	Control plan Results

Figure 6 Activities by phase of the test specification project

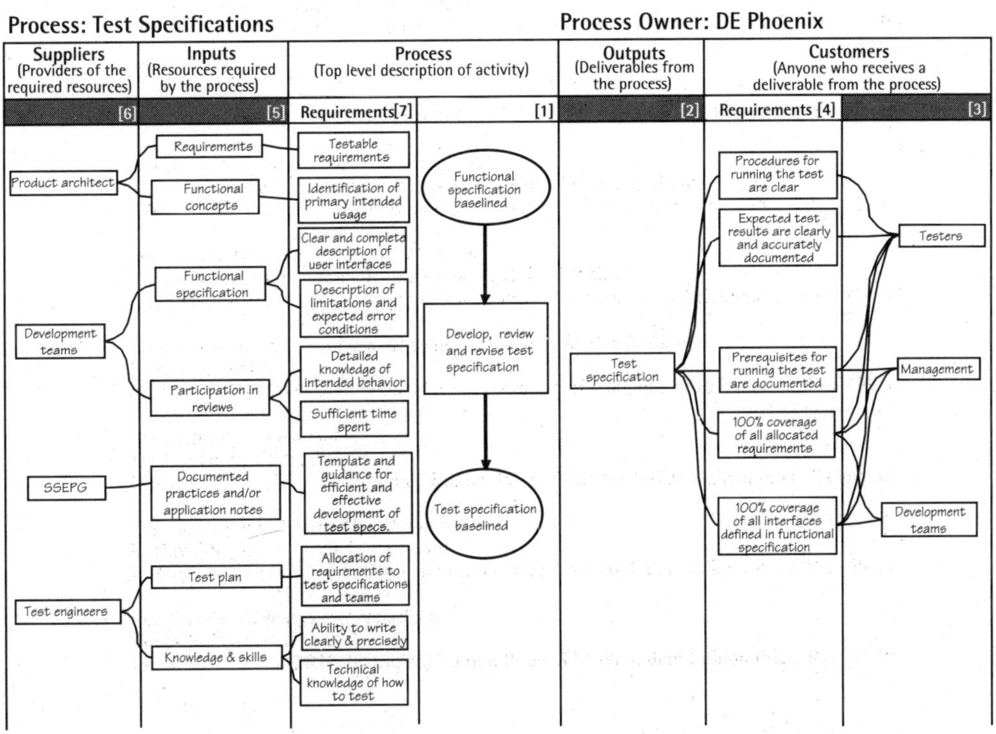

Figure 7 SIPOC for test specification project

Measure Phase

An "As-is process map" was used to identify the test specification process (see Figure 8). When this map was compared to the SIPOC, the process was meeting all the customer requirements.

Analysis Phase

The FMEA performed on the process map identified 39 failure modes and recommended actions for 28 of them. The majority of the risks to the process could be addressed in the steps of writing and reviewing test specifications if prior experience were used to ensure the completeness of a specification. Therefore, most of the recommended actions listed items that could be put in a checklist, but other actions included use of different types of experts in reviewing specific parts of a test specification.

The FMEA led to identifying five desirable attributes for test specification authors:

- Analytical skills (identifying completeness of coverage with minimal redundancy)
- Communications skills (clarity of instructions)
- Customer usage knowledge
- Technical systems knowledge (the architecture and interaction of components)
- Testing experience

Furthermore, the most critical attributes were found to be analytical skills and technical systems knowledge.

Improve Phase

The project team used the recommended actions to develop a test specification checklist and specified the type of expertise required for each checklist item. At the same time, they revised the test specification process such that: 1) specifications could be written incrementally and a draft specification could be inspected prior to baselining, and 2) test specifications can be revised and reviewed after execution.

The first version of the checklist was tested using the Kappa technique, a statistical technique for measuring the reliability of a subjective rating system (Futrell 1995). A number of judges, or raters, are asked to rate a set of objects using the rating system. The variation in the ratings is analyzed in a contingency table, and the observed ratings are adjusted for chance, to produce a score that indicates the reliability of the rating system. The highest Kappa score is 1.0, and .7 or higher usually indicates a reliable rating system.

In this case, four people were provided with a test specification and the 20-item checklist (rating system), and asked to independently indicate whether the specification conformed to each item in the checklist. The high degree of

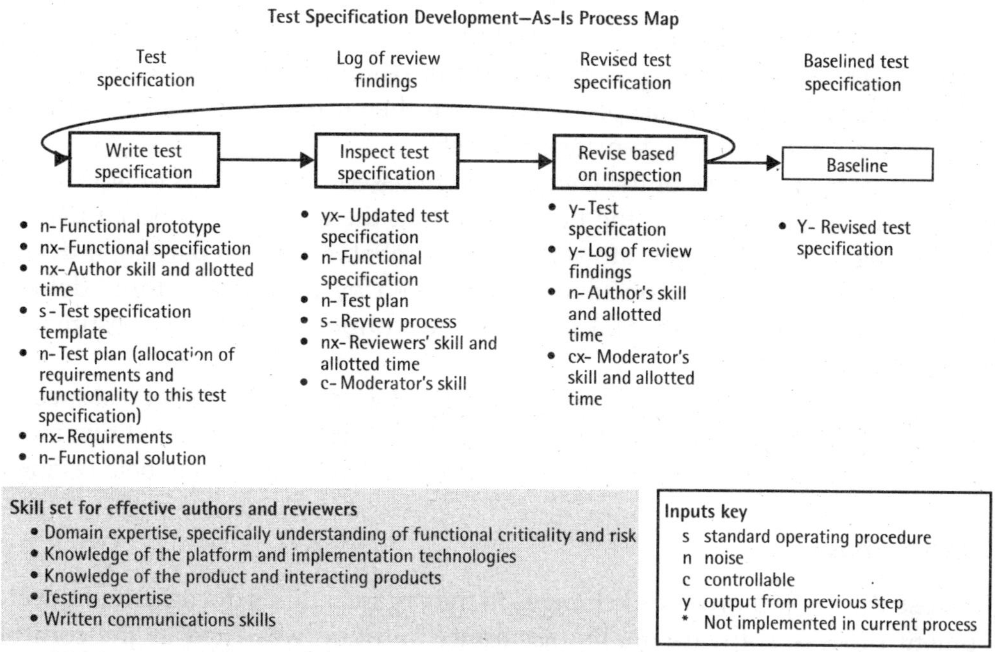

Figure 8 As-is process map for test specification

variation in their responses produced a score of .3. This low score showed that the checklist needed improvement if it was to serve as a reliable guide for judging the quality of test specifications.

Using the results of the Kappa exercise, the team determined which checklist items had produced disagreement and studied ways to improve those items. The revised checklist was retested on the same test specification with four new raters, producing a score of .8 and indicating reliability suitable for general usage. Parts of the checklist are shown in Figure 9.

General

Reviewer	Checklist item
Architect	1.1. Does the scope clearly specify the boundaries of the testing covered by this document?
Test expert	1.3. Does this spec tell the tester where to find all the files necessary to run each test?

Overall coverage

Reviewer	Checklist item
any	2.1 Are all requirements allocated by the test plan to this test team covered by this set of test cases?
(technical) Domain expert	2.4 Are there test cases with loads to stress the functionality to at least the level of the maximum realistic customer usage?

Individual test cases

Reviewer	Checklist item
Test expert	3.1 Are the required files/databases and their location identified?

Figure 9 Sample of the test specification checklist

The revised checklist was then used to inspect a test specification that had already been used for testing. Deficiencies were found in the specification and it was revised. The revised test specification was then used to run some additional tests, which found three high-priority defects.

Savings from the use of the checklist were based on estimates of additional costs to fix defects found in the field, including the costs of additional regression testing releases (taking into account the probability that a particular defect might trigger a release). The savings, produced by finding the three defects through the single use of the checklist and the additional testing, was estimated at $10,100.

The checklist was further validated by using it to reinspect another test specification. Additional testing with this second test specification discovered two more defects at the same time they were being discovered by customers in beta testing.

Control Phase

Because this project produced changes to the organization's documented development process, software quality assurance auditing was cited as the control on continued use of the test specification process, including the checklist for reviewing test specifications.

Summary and Conclusions

Two different Green Belt teams used process mapping and FMEA to distill their experience into checklists for improving development work. In addition, the second project demonstrated that the reliability of checklists can be measured and ensured through application of the Kappa statistical technique. Both projects produced savings by avoiding rework costs.

In the defect fix integrity project, a checklist was chosen as the low-cost solution to the fix integrity problem. The FMEA was used to identify critical points in the process that were later addressed in the checklist. The checklist usage by developers during the fixing process became a tool for preventing problems.

One of the challenges of this project was the distributed development. Though the project was based in the United States, it required that offshore team members use the new process and the new checklist. This challenge was met through teleconferences to review the process maps. The team also took advantage of the offshore manager's visit to involve him in the FMEA.

In the test specification project, a checklist became a tool for indirectly detecting defects and preventing their leakage. An FMEA was used to distill the experiences of testers by identifying the risks in test coverage. The reliability of subjective content in the resulting checklist was measured so that its effectiveness could be improved. Measurement and rework produced a checklist that resulted in savings by eliminating defects that would otherwise have shipped.

Checklists are widely used in software development because they are relatively low-cost quality assurance tools. However, a checklist is valuable only to the extent that it incorporates expert knowledge of a process, including lessons accrued from experience, and makes it readily available for application. Because good checklists are based on process knowledge, a particular checklist is not necessarily valuable outside the organization and process for which it was created. Consequently, the process of producing a checklist can be a value-generating one.

REFERENCES

Baan. 1996. Esprit Project 21799. See URL: http://www.cordis.lu/esprit/src/21799.htm.

Breyfogle, Forrest W., III. 2003. *Implementing six sigma: Smarter solutions using statistical methods,* second edition. New York: John Wiley & Sons.

Freedman, D. P., and G. M. Weinberg. 1990. *Handbook of walkthroughs, inspections and technical reviews,* third edition. New York: Dorset House.

Futrell, D. 1995. When quality is a matter of taste, use reliability indexes. *Quality Progress* 28, no. 5 (May): 81–86.

Pyzdek, T. 2000. *The six sigma handbook.* New York: McGraw-Hill.

BIOGRAPHY

Dan Houston is a Six Sigma Black Belt for Honeywell Automation and Control Solutions in Phoenix, Arizona. This article is based on two of the process improvement projects he has mentored. Most of his work during the last two years has been devoted to software Design for Six Sigma (DFSS): developing and delivering training, and leading a team of Black Belts in mentoring and certifying more than 500 software engineers.

He has more than 15 years' experience in software training and support, and in developing applications software, primarily for process control engineering. Prior to joining Honeywell's Six Sigma organization, he spent five years leading globally distributed development teams.

Houston earned a doctorate in industrial engineering from Arizona State University. His research and subsequent work have focused on applications of industrial engineering to software engineering. He is a member of ASQ, IEEE-CS, and ACM. He can be reached by e-mail at dxhouston@ieee.org.

The Six Sigma Toolkit

Evolved from years of process improvement in manufacturing and engineering, the Six Sigma toolkit is expansive. Following are short descriptions of two frequently used methods that are readily applicable in software development improvement projects.

Process Mapping

Process mapping is a representation of major activities/tasks, subprocesses, process boundaries, key process inputs, and outputs. In addition to its use as a detailed process descriptor, it is often used in the refinement of a Six Sigma project's scope and scale. A process map may be an input to cause-and-effects matrices, failure modes and effects analysis, design of experiments planning, and the control plan that is assembled to sustain performance. And, a process map may evolve to a value map, in which process steps are evaluated for their "value added" contribution to the overall outcome. Unnecessary steps are eliminated to improve cycle time and reduce risk of error.

The basic steps of process mapping are as follows:

- For the overall process, list inputs and outputs. Figure A lists types of inputs and outputs to consider.
- Identify all steps in the process: value-added and nonvalue-added.
- Show key outputs at each step (process and product).
- List key inputs and classify process inputs. Figure B shows a process map with a partial listing.
  —Controllable inputs: key inputs that can be changed to see the effect on key outputs, sometimes called "control knobs."

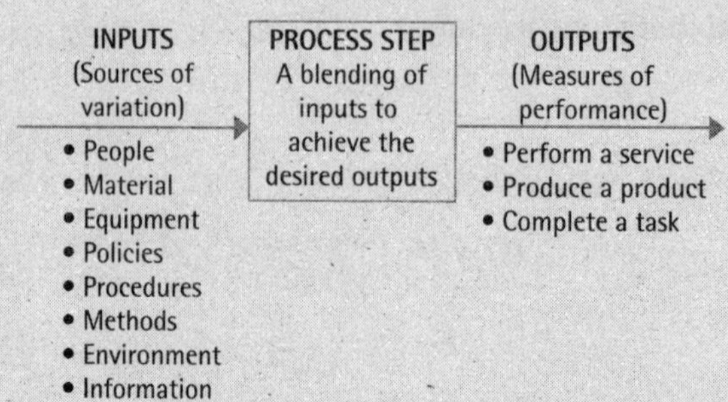

Figure A Black box process with types of inputs and outputs

—Critical inputs: key inputs that have been statistically shown to have a major impact on the variability of the key outputs.

—Noise inputs: Input variables that impact the key outputs but are difficult or impossible to control.

—Standard operating procedures: A standard procedure for running the process.

- Add the operating specifications and process targets for the controllable and critical inputs.

When developing process maps, it is important to go to the actual place where the process is performed, talk to the actual people involved in the process, and chart the actual process. Few processes work the way that we think they do!

FMEA (Failure Modes & Effects Analysis)

FMEA is a systematic method for:

- Identifying, analyzing, prioritizing, and documenting potential failure modes
- Determining their effects on system, product, and process performance
- Determining possible causes of failure
- Establishing actions to reduce risk

Unlike statistical process control charts, which flag existing problems and call for response, FMEA is a risk mitigation and reliability improvement method that is intended to prevent problems from occurring. Ultimately,

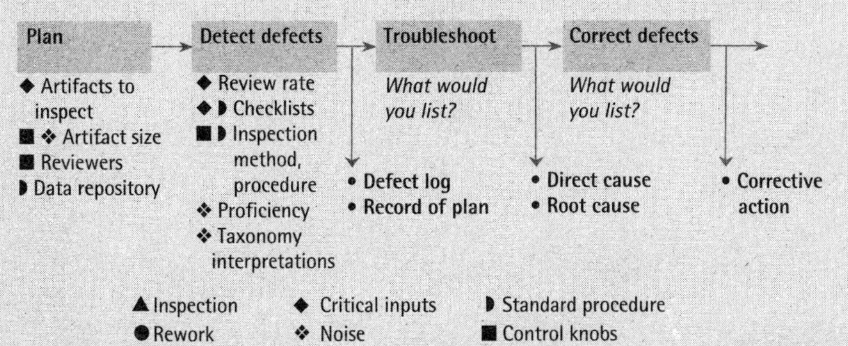

Figure B Partial process map of an inspection process

this will decrease rework, reduce cycle time, reduce cost, and so on. It is most effectively conducted with a cross-functional team.

Its basic steps are as follows:

- For each process function, list what could go wrong, the potential failures
- Describe the effects of each failure and rate in terms of its severity on a 1–5 scale
- Identify root causes of failure and rate for their probability of occurrence on a 1–5 scale
- Identify means of detecting the failures and rate for their ability to detect on a 1–5 scale
- Calculate risk by multiplying the ratings: severity × occurrence × detection
- Prioritize using the risk factor
- Identify (and implement!) ways to reduce risk by decreasing occurrence, reducing severity or increasing detection

These and many other tools are described in Six Sigma reference handbooks and on Internet sites such as http://www.isixsigma.com. In the next issue, the final "official" issue for this series, several such references will be listed.

Six Sigma Toolkit sidebar provided by Jeannine M Siviy, Software Engineering Institute, e-mail jmsiviy@sei.cmu.edu.

Soft Factors Affecting Software Quality

Fred J. Heemstra, Open University, The Netherlands, and Rob J. Kusters, Open University, The Netherlands and Eindhoven University of Technology

In recent discussions about improving software quality, much emphasis is placed on technically oriented activities regarding the development process. Developments such as ISO 9000:2000, CMM-I, validation and verification techniques, metrics, and so on, are examples of this orientation. Unfortunately, less attention is paid to quality drivers such as motivation, commitment, labor conditions, organizational culture, experience, skills, and knowledge. In the authors' opinion, this is a missed opportunity. Looking at other disciplines, it is obvious how important these "soft" factors are for achieving high product quality (Crosby 1979; Baatz 1991; Prahalad and Hamel 1990).

In this article, the authors look beyond technically oriented factors and give an overview of the impact of soft factors on product quality. The main goal of the article is to open the mind to, and obtain a higher understanding of, soft factors in the "hard" software world. The main question is, "Which human and organizational factors determine the quality of (business) software." This is not a simple question to answer, because the number of quality drivers is large, the impact of a specific quality driver depends on the characteristics of the local development situation, and there is no consensus as to which factors should be looked at. The authors present a framework that can be used as a tool for ordering software quality drivers. They explain the framework and focus on the description of the so-called resources and context dependent quality drivers.

Key words: human factors, quality drivers, software quality improvement

Introduction

To improve software quality, insight is required into the factors that influence software quality and the way these factors can be manipulated. Only then can quality improvement be realized using well-directed actions. In principle, many factors can be identified. However, the relevance of these factors to a specific situation, the effects these factors can have on software quality, and the way these factors can be influenced to further a positive result is often not clear.

PSP and TSP are service marks of Carnegie Mellon University.

In this article, the authors develop a framework for identifying software quality drivers and discuss a number of the less technical, "softer" drivers and their impact on software quality.

The Quality Framework

To develop a framework of software quality drivers, the authors began by identifying the main categories of quality drivers in a top-down approach. Figure 1 depicts the basic process of software development, where input is translated into a finished software product through a process of requirements engineering and software engineering.

When looking at the categories of software quality drivers that influence this process one can see that the engineering activities are supported by a large and continuously expanding set of standards and techniques that can be grouped as *software engineering technologies*. It is evident that the correct use (*correct* meaning proper use as well as meaning a proper match between the selected aid and the development setting) of these technologies will strongly influence the quality of the resulting software.

Software engineering technologies, however, do not form the only category of software quality drivers. Another category can be identified under the common denomination *resources*. Potential users, user management, and various types of domain experts provide the input into the engineering process. Also, people, collaborating in teams, often carry out the engineering effort. A third resource factor can be found in the constraints that result from the availability of resources, such as development time or funds. Together these resources have a strong influence on the way the quality of the resulting software is defined and realized.

A final category of software quality factors can be identified when one realizes that software development does not take place in a vacuum. The *context* in which the development effort takes place will undoubtedly influence the quality of the result. In this context one can first identify the software organization as a group of factors influencing software quality. Beyond this, the environment in which the organization operates will also exert its influence, such as in the form of legislature. Figure 2 depicts the results of this discussion in which the three categories of software quality factors are split into seven subcategories.

Given the top-down approach and the high level of abstraction, it is fairly certain that the selected categories *context* (environment, organization), *resources* (people, team, constraints), and *technologies* (standards, techniques) are both

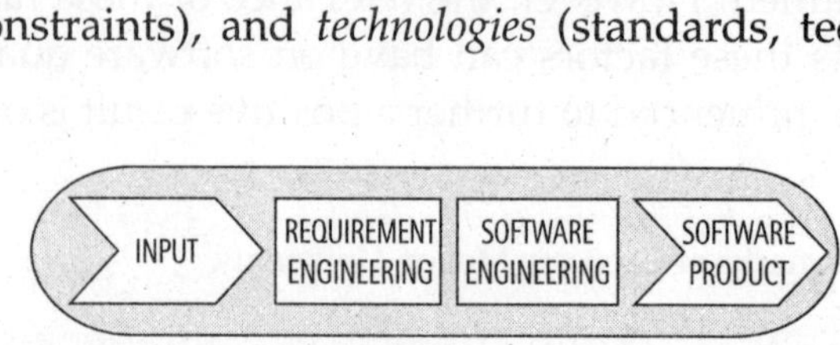

Figure 1 Overview of the software development process

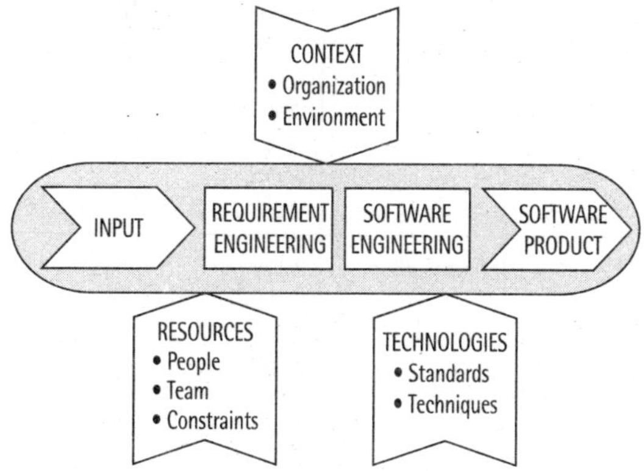

Figure 2 The main groups of software quality factors

logically consistent as well as complete. Going one-step further, the matter is less straightforward. In Figure 3, the authors present a number of relevant quality drivers.

At this level the authors claim no completeness, as it is hard to give such a selection a scientific basis. Most research on the influence of (resource and context) dependent factors on software quality is qualitative. The lack of hard numbers is due to the low maturity of the software engineering discipline (Shaw 1990), the abundance of factors (quality drivers) (Glass 1998), the difficulties of making these factors operational and measurable (McConnell 2000), and the underestimation of the influence these kinds of factors have (Sharp, Robinson, and Woodman 2000). Furthermore, not all drivers will be relevant or applicable to each situation. Relevancy and applicability are locally and situational dependent. Based on an extensive study of available literature, however, one would claim this to be a representative sample of the type of software quality driver that should be looked into.

Important examples of *environmental quality drivers* are the impact of the user, customer, law, competitor, and business sector. Users will impact software quality by the way they are willing and capable of providing useful and stable requirements. Customers (clients/principals) have a strong influence in the way they understand the repercussions of the trade-offs that are required during a development project. Legislation can influence software requirements, such as through privacy regulation. The level of quality that is considered acceptable can be influenced by the level of quality competitors do or do not offer. Also, the business sector can play a role, for example, by setting fair trading standards.

Examples of *organizational* quality drivers are organizational policy, culture, and structure. An important aspect of culture deserves special mention. The degree to which a multiperspective view on quality has found its way into the organization is also an important driver, as shown by staff (including top management) involvement, focus on training, organizationwide approach, and so on. The authors will refer to this driver as "quality culture." Total quality

Category	Subcategory	Software Quality Driver
Context	*Environment*	User Customer Legislator Branch Competitor
	Organization	Policy Culture and structure Reuse Quality culture
Resources	*People*	Motivation & commitment Behavior Professionalism
	Team	Team composition Team maturity
	Constraints	Time Money
Technologies	*Standards*	CMM-I ISO 9000:2000
	Techniques	Methodology Models Tools

Figure 3 A framework of software quality drivers

management (TQM) is an example of an approach for improving this quality culture. Similarly, the idea of software reuse is mentioned here. It can be seen as a part of the software engineering technologies, but since reuse requires a proper embedding in both organizational culture and organizational structure, it is mentioned here as a specific quality driver.

People can be regarded as the most important "means of production." One cannot overestimate the influence of the people driver on software quality. Important people-related quality factors have to do with knowledge and skills as furthered by professionalism, motivation, and commitment as well as behavior of software engineers. Certainly in safety critical software development one would prefer the work being carried out by certified professionals. Given the abstract character of software development, motivation and commitment will have a large impact on the resulting quality. In general, stressing the importance of quality will only succeed if developers adapt their behavior, too.

Most software engineers work as a *team*. Examples of team-dependent quality drivers are team composition (for example, division of team roles) and team maturity. A well-structured and smoothly functioning team will usually deliver better quality products.

With regard to the subcategory *constraints*, this article will only look at money and time. It is well known that budget restrictions and shortening the development time have a primarily negative effect on software quality. Proper identification of a suitable level of quality to aspire to needs to consider these constraints.

Examples of *standards* that influence software quality are ISO 9000:2000 and CMM-I, which play an important role in organizing and improving processes. There is not just an increasing emphasis on standardizing development processes, but also a growing interest in standards for the purpose of software acquisition, control, and maintenance processes.

Moreover, properly developing, implementing, and employing development techniques is a prerequisite for realizing high-quality software. Methodologies play an important part in gathering and using best practices. They also impact the visibility of the development process allowing a more explicit management of quality-related aspects. Software engineering makes extensive use of various types of models. They allow explicit discussion and reliable communication of intermediate results. Finally, tools provide an important positive impulse toward software quality (see, for example, Kusters and Wijers 1993).

In the remainder of this article the authors will focus on the so-called soft software quality drivers since they believe this area needs additional attention. Software engineering technologies are therefore outside the further scope of this article. Environmental quality drivers are also left out because the article is oriented to the internal software development organization. This article will concentrate on organizational and resources dependent factors. A comprehensive discussion of all the factors mentioned in the framework can be found in Heemstra, Kusters, and Trienekens (2001).

Organizational Quality Drivers

In literature, the influence of the software development organization on software quality is often ignored. This is remarkable because people do their work within an organization. An organization is organized and structured, it has a level of formalization and decentralization, and work task responsibilities are allocated. These factors influence the quality of the software development process, and as a result, that of the final product—the software.

Following is a brief discussion of the four organizational quality drivers: 1) policy, 2) structure and culture, 3) reuse, and 4) quality culture.

Quality Policy and Software Quality

The integration of quality as a part of the organization policy and of the quality targets in the organization's strategic goals evolves, according to Wentink (1999), along several levels. At each higher, more mature level, an organization pays more attention to a growing number of aspects such as products, processes, means, human capital, management, strategy and policy, customers, and, of course, quality. Wentink explains the progress of "investing in quality" and "realizing quality policy" by the transition from one level to the next.

At the first level, any kind of quality policy is not available. Quality efforts happen on an ad hoc basis, quality policy is not formally defined, and responsibilities with regard to quality are vague. At the mature level, on the other hand, quality policy has been applied to all aspects and has been fully integrated in the work processes.

Only a few organizations have reached the mature level. Quality policy as an integrated part of the strategic policy is still in its infancy for most companies.

Structure and Culture and Software Quality

According to Boer's model (Boer 2000) relations between organizational characteristics and the quality of a software development process can be defined. The organizational characteristics are a set of structurally oriented characteristics (for example, level of centralization, standardization, formalization, specialization) and culturally oriented characteristics (for example, level of cohesion, anticipation, discipline, motivation, expertise). Both sets of characteristics can be used to analyze an organization. For example, with regard to the characteristic "level of anticipation," an organization can be characterized as proactive, and with regard to the characteristic "level of centralization," as decentralized.

The most interesting conclusion of Boer's model is the possibility of defining relations between organizational characteristics and software development characteristics. By doing so, changes in culture and structure can be considered in order to realize quality improvements. An exact definition of the relations, however, cannot be offered yet. The research is ongoing. However, it can be concluded that a software development organization will encounter trouble if there is a mismatch between organizational characteristics and software development characteristics.

Reuse and Software Quality

One goal of a software development organization is to create a development environment in which the development process will be simplified, in which complexity will be handled by dividing it into smaller and less complex parts, and in which errors and faults will be prevented. A possible and important way to reach these goals is applying reuse, which, in turn, requires adaptations of both organizational culture and structure as well as policy (Cusumano 1989; van Genuchten 1992).

Swanson extensively describes the introduction, application, and results of reuse (Swanson et al. 1991). The results are promising: the number of errors per 1000 lines of source code is somewhere between 0.01 and 0.25 with reuse, compared with 4.4 without reuse.

Experiences with reuse at Hewlett-Packard (HP) showed a 51 percent reduction in the number of errors (Lim 1994). However, HP claims that an organization must have reached capability maturity model (CMM) level three in order to realize such figures. NEC (Braun 1994) improved software quality by a factor of 2.8 thanks to reuse.

Morisio, Ianino, and Okumoto (2000) investigated the effects of reuse on "time to market," productivity, costs control, flexibility in product assortment, reliability, and rework within four organizations. It proved to have caused significant improvements.

These and other investigations show that reuse helps to significantly improve software quality (Prieto-Diaz 1993). Lim (1994), for example, mentions studies that show reliability improvements by a factor of 10 just by applying reuse concepts. Analyzing studies on reuse one can conclude that among important success factors are the attention for organizational characteristics such as organizational culture, for issues such as responsibilities, centralization-decentralization, the level of formalization, and so on. Practical experiences show how difficult it is to introduce reuse successfully if such an organizational perspective is missing (Hall and Jin 1997).

Quality Culture and Software Quality

Quality culture can be described as the importance an individual, a department, and an organization attach to quality. Quality culture at the individual level will be explained later in this article. To underline the importance of quality culture at an organizational level, quality awards are distributed at a national, international, and sometimes at a branch level. In the Netherlands, the Dutch Quality Award is the most prestigious quality award; in Europe, the European Foundation for Quality Management Award is the most well-known award; and the United States has the Malcolm Baldrige National Quality Award.

These awards are focused on the introduction of an overall quality system, of which TQM is by far the most important. It is interesting to question the influence of TQM on software quality. From the perspective of software quality, TQM should be an important approach because three of the main TQM principles—customer orientation, continuous improvement, and teamwork—are central aspects in developing software. This is supported by an extensive study among 247 software development organizations in which the effects of applying TQM on software quality have been investigated (Parzinger and Nath 2000). The results showed that:

- The TQM factor "using the employees' capabilities" was by far the most important in realizing high customer satisfaction.
- The TQM factors "evaluating customer needs and requirements" and "training of special skills" are the most important to realize a higher CMM-I level or ISO 9000:2000 compliance.

Human Factors

The effects of human factors on software quality are increasingly regarded as the most important factors (DeMarco and Lister 1987). All investments in process improvement, methodologies and techniques, tools, and so on are of lesser value, when the employee applying them does not have the skills, capabilities, and/or professionalism for their proper use, or is not willing to use them. Lack of professionalism, neglecting education and training, a large turnover of labor staff, a high level of absenteeism, and the inability to recruit the right people are examples of factors that hamper the realization of well-meant improvements. An organization must not only invest in so-called businesslike factors, but also in the "psychological welfare" of its staff. In addition to the inability of employees to employ the potential benefits of improvement initiatives, it is possible for employees to be unwilling to accept such initiatives. Improvements often cause changes in the way people do their job, sometimes even cause reorganizations. People must be prepared and supported in order to handle these changes. Changes in the method of working often go hand in hand with necessary behavioral changes. A software department wanting to change its informal, reactive, ad hoc organization into an ISO certified organization with procedures for measuring, documentation, and evaluation, demands from its staff considerable behavioral changes. The cultures of both types of organizations differ tremendously.

The next three items will be explained briefly:

1. Motivation and commitment
2. Behavior and changes in behavior
3. Professionalism

Motivation and Commitment and Software Quality

Based on the well-known research of Herzberg (1959), Fitz-enz (1978) answers questions such as "What motivates a software developer?" and "What makes him or her enthusiastic?" According to Fitz-enz, a software developer is motivated by factors such as job content, the product produced, and the recognition. Some motivators differ strongly depending on the individual's position. Programmers, for example, ranked responsibility ninth on a list of motivational factors, while project managers rank this as fourth and line managers put this factor first. Although the Fitz-enz study was done more than 30 years ago, the results are still valid today. This can be seen in Whitaker's (1997) updated overview of the most dominant motivator, which, surprisingly, shows many similarities. Moreover, it is remarkable that most motivators have an egocentric tendency, which means that "what's in it for me" prevails over "what's in it for my organization."

In light of insight on motivators and demotivators, management is able to coordinate and manipulate factors more precisely motivating employees to maximize software quality. Fitz-enz's results contradict a job satisfaction investigation among information technology (IT) professionals described by Sijtstra (2000). They are reported to be less happy with their job compared with employees in general services organizations and other similar sectors in industry. A similar study in Great Britain also looks bleak. Almost 75 percent of British IT employees with an annual salary greater than $100,000 are looking for another job; 63 percent of them are registered in nine or more job-hunting bureaus (IT Research House 2000). Only 9 percent are not registered in any bureau at all. The

British IT employees, surprisingly, regard money as a very important satisfier, over factors such as "an exciting job" and "a challenge." Factors such as "status," "security," and "corporate benefit" are hardly of importance.

Behavior and Behavioral Changes and Software Quality

Berkman (1999) distinguishes behavior that characterizes an organization at a low maturity level and behavior that characterizes an organization at a high maturity level. The differences are considerable (see Figure 4).

Behavior at a low level implicates no coordination between departments and always running out of time. The consequences are loss of efficiency and poor product quality. A behavioral change cannot be simply bought; it is a complex artifact. That is why behavioral changes from a low to a high maturity level are hard to realize. From that perspective, it is necessary to pay attention to the following (Berkman 1999):

- Everyone must work in the same direction (realizing the same well-known goals).
- Staff members must have specific skills. The organization must invest in obtaining these skills.
- Without incentives, people will not change their behavior.
- Time, money, information, people, and facilities are vital for behavioral changes.

Professionalism and Software Quality

In their study, Ford and Gibbs (1996) show that professionals follow a professional development path regardless of their specific discipline. Mature professions should include the following elements:

- Initial professional education
- Accreditation

Maturity level: low	Maturity level: high
• Actions based on perception	• Actions based on data/facts
• Reactive behavior (fire fighting)	• Proactive behavior
• Focus on problems	• Focus on solutions
• Ample use of performance indicators	• Use of performance indicators is stimulated
• Responsibility: top management	• Responsibility: lower organization levels
• Ample communication	• Much communication and coordination

Figure 4 Organizational behavior at different maturity levels

- Skills development
- Certification
- Licensing
- Professional development
- Professional societies
- Code of ethics

In the area of software development the Association for Computer Machinery (ACM) and the IEEE Computer Society cooperated with joint task forces in the areas of:

- Software Engineering Body of Knowledge and Recommended Practices (SWEBOK)
- A code of ethics and professional practices
- A software engineering curriculum

The SWEBOK project offers a structure for answering questions regarding professional education and skills development (Bourque et al. 1999). In the Netherlands, the so-called L_PASO model (Dietz 1999) focuses on the same topics. A proposal for a code of ethics and professional behavior was developed (ACM 2001), and considerable effort is being directed at a software engineering curriculum. Despite these initiatives the process of certification and licensing is yet in its infancy (Ford 1994; Werth 1998). McConnel and Tripp (1999) conclude that the professionalism of the software engineering field is in its early stage.

Looking for concrete examples of professional educational programs in which software developers learn to apply the basics of process improvement on an individual level, Humphrey's Personal Software Process (PSP) is the best the authors could find (Humphrey 1996). PSP applications show that developers improve their estimates (Ferguson et al. 1997), productivity, and quality (making better software in less time and according to plan) (Kamatar and Hayes 2000; Zhong, Madhavji, and Emam 2000).

Team Factors

Software development is improving its record in composing the "best" teams for making the "best" software. Many quality problems in software development are due to poor team performance. In interviews with software developers, the question "What hampers good team performances?" was answered (Krasner 1999):

- "Issues brought to the table by us are not taken seriously."
- "We are evaluated based on criteria that are unrelated to the project goals."

- "The influence of the individual's (team member's) agenda dominates the team's agenda/goals."
- "We are unable to offer our opinion regarding the pros and cons of the project goals and working methods."
- "The project goals are not clear."
- "Vagueness with regard to authority and responsibilities"
- "Ever-changing team compositions"
- "Endless discussions about the scope of the project"
- "Communication problems within the team and between team and environment"

Project managers were asked the same question. They too came up with a long list of problems:

- "Team members suffer lack of professionalism"
- "Not enough people to execute the project properly (understaffing)"
- "Team members confront us with estimates of their work without any explanation or foundation."
- "Team members come up with deadlines even before the work has been defined and specified properly (over-optimism)."
- "Changes are badly managed."
- "Lack of on-the-job training"

These kinds of problems can cause enormous damage. Poorly performing teams result in time and cost overruns, and more specifically, in products that do not obtain the required level of quality. This section will focus on team composition and team maturity.

Team Composition and Software Quality

Team quality depends on the way people are allowed, willing, able, and obliged to fill in the team roles with their knowledge, capabilities, and experiences. A team must evolve from a set of individuals into a solid entity, one that performs at a high level of quality, and whose members support one another, viewing conflicts and diversity as positive success factors rather than as a threat to the project. Organizations able to offer the right conditions for effective software team performance differ from organizations failing to do so in the conscious evolution of teams according to a team maturity process. The phases in such a maturity process are:

- *Team composition.* In this phase, team composition goals are defined, roles are formulated, and authority and responsibilities are determined.
- *Making a solid team.* In this phase, the team must realize a unified vision regarding the goals that should be fulfilled.

- *Execution.* The focus is on realizing the goal.
- *Discontinuance.* Relevant questions to be answered are, "When has the time come to end the project," and "How should the discontinuance take place."

Team Maturity and Software Quality

From Humphrey's perspective, a software development organization is only able to maximize its performance when the best possible team members for the best possible team composition are available (Humphrey 1998). In order to materialize this vision the Team Software Process (TSP) has been developed following the basics of PSP and CMM.

Recent experiences with TSP are promising. A TSP team at the Embry-Riddle Aeronautical University, for example, solved more than 99 percent of all development errors before the system tests were executed. Another TSP team at Hill Air Force Base was able to reduce its test time by a factor of eight and at the same time increase its productivity by a factor of two. One of the most important consequences of applying TSP is the support team management receives in order to tackle the complex project environment. A good example is handling unrealistic time pressure from outside the project. TSP advises how to make well-founded plans that invalidate unrealistic demands and pressure. Furthermore, TSP emphasizes the role of the manager as a coach. TSP teaches management at what moment in time which means must be available for a team, how the interface to a higher management level must be realized, how the team must be coached, and how a continuous pressure on quality must be organized.

Constraints

Quality costs time and money. Specifying quality, for that reason, implies continuously balancing between demands and the costs to fulfill these demands. This recognition for the impact of constraints and the need for balancing between them is supported by Boehm (Boehm 2000), who presents a case in which development costs were $30 million rather than $100 million if average response time were set to four seconds instead of one second, a difference of $70 million. Therefore, quality *is* money, and money is a condition for quality.

To answer the question of how to perform this balancing activity, two schools of thought can be distinguished in the quality world. The first school implies that quality is a matter of finding the right balance between quality and other organizational goals, such as realizing a shorter development time. According to this school, there must be an optimal quality level somewhere. Beyond the optimum, more investments in error detection and prevention lead to higher software quality, indeed, but the prevention costs do not counter-balance the costs caused by extra errors; each extra level of quality improvement requires a higher expenditure. The main question is of course, "Where is the cost optimum?" and "When are more investments, from an economical perspective, of less use?" Studies show (see, for example, Abdel-Hamid 1988) that the optimal expenditure level for quality-related activities is more or less 15 percent of the total development costs.

A second and relatively new school is called "good enough software." Currently, this approach is receiving a lot of attention and the reviews are mixed; mistakenly, the "good enough software" approach often is compared with mediocrity. In order to realize software quality, considerations such as on-time delivery, flexible and fast anticipation of customers' needs, and selling cheap software at the marketplace, also play an important role besides economic considerations (Jones 1993). Fast, cheap, and flexible delivery implies a deliberate devaluation of quality and a deliberate choice for not solving errors, even though their existence in the software is known. Solving implies, after all, loss of time and additional costs, resulting in higher cost prices (Bach 1997).

The difference between the good enough software approach and the first school is in the acceptance that errors are still present in the software, and a deliberate cessation of quality actions before the optimum has been reached.

Some information regarding the relationship between quality requirements and constraints can be found in software cost estimation models, although these models often do not agree as to the exact nature of this relationship. Chulani (1999) describes an explicit approach that makes use of this relationship.

Conclusions

In the article, the authors have tried to give an overview of factors that have an important impact on software quality. The overview is fragmentary because the authors have only focused on factors that are related to so-called organizational and human factors dependent affairs. Furthermore, they have only paid attention to what they believe are the most important factors. The overview is also quite depressing; there are so many quality drivers with an enormous diversity in characterization and impact and there is so little existing knowledge of its relation with software quality. How can software management be expected to guarantee high-quality software under such uncertain and complex circumstances? There is some hypocrisy in this question. After all, the software world has only itself to blame. For years, software development emphasized specifying functionality; quality was always treated as the ugly duckling.

Software quality determination requires considerable user involvement and intense consultation between software engineer and software user, even more than during software functionality determination. Involvement and consultation was not exactly the thing either party was waiting for; the user wanted the software as soon as possible, while the software engineer wanted to jump to the next profitable order as fast as possible. Software has been developed in this unrealistic and overstrained atmosphere for many years. It does not come as a surprise that little effort has been spent to find out "which buttons must be pressed" to realize better software. Apparently, no one benefited from solving this problem.

It is the consumer market rather than the software engineering discipline that finally has grown up. Confronted with poor quality software that is too expensive and not delivered on time, customers have started demanding error-free software products. They are coming up with insurance claims for the damage software errors cause to the organization, demanding software contracts that stipulate that the software meets the specified requirements with penalties for noncompliance, asking "maintenance for free" product, and so on. The marketplace has forced the software producer to invest in improving its software products and software processes.

The software industry responds by developments such as CMM-I, Bootstrap, SPICE, and so on. These kinds of software process improvement initiatives have their golden age. Recent initiatives, such as TSP and PSP, have a warm welcome in the software industry. Much time and money is spent on refining testing techniques such as walkthroughs, reviews, inspections, pair programming, and so on.

Does it help? Referring to Hatton, an authority in the software world, all the efforts are more or less useless. Hatton (1998) argues that at this moment an average of six errors per thousand lines of code is regarded as a standard for good software from a commercial point of view. Comparing this figure with the state of the art 10 years ago (Musa, Ianino, and Okumoto 1987), one can conclude that the number of errors per thousand lines of code hardly has been improved, despite developments such as software improvement, object orientation, automated tools for error detection, improved test tools and compilers, and more sophisticated languages such as Java and Ada.

The authors have to take into account, however, that the consumer world asks for applications that can be applied to problems with growing complexity. Applications have to offer an increasing functionality and quality. Comparatively speaking, software quality has been improved. However, no one will admit that an optimal situation has been reached. Looking at the current developments it is striking that comparatively much emphasis is on technically oriented techniques and methodologies for improving the software product and the software process, and less attention is paid to the quality drivers mentioned in this article. This is a pity and a missed opportunity. One must look at other disciplines to realize how important factors such as motivation, involvement, labor conditions, atmosphere, knowledge, and skills are for the quality of the end result. This article must be regarded as a plea to learn from other disciplines and to pay more attention to the soft factors in the hard software world.

REFERENCES

Abdel-Hamid, T. 1988. The economics of software quality assurance: A simulation-based case study. *MIS Quarterly* (September).

ACM. 2001. *ACM code of ethics and professional conduct*. New York: The Association for Computing Machinery (May). See URL http://www.acm.org/constitution/code.html.

Baatz, B. 1991. The chancing face of the organization. *Electronic Business* (18 March): 60–64.

Bach, J. 1997. Good enough quality: Beyond the buzzword. *IEEE Computer* (August).

Berkman, W. 1999. Performance improvement by changes in behavior. *Information* (December).

Boehm, B. W. 2000. Verifying software and systems engineering. *IEEE Computer* (March).

Boer, H. 2000. Quality of software development in organizations: The influence of structure and culture. *Information* (January/February).

Bourque, P., R. Dupuis, A. Abran, J. W. Moore, and L. Tripp. 1999. The guide to the software engineering body of knowledge. *IEEE Software* (November/December).

Braun, C. L. 1994. Reuse. In *Encyclopedia of software engineering*. New York: John Wiley and Sons.

Chulani, S. 1999. COQUALMO (COnstructive QUALity MOdel): A software defect density prediction model. In *Project control for software quality*, eds. R. J. Kusters, A. Cowderoy, F. J. Heemstra, and E. van Veenendaal. Maastricht, The Netherlands: Shaker Publishing.

Crosby, P. 1979. *Quality is free: The art of making quality certain*. New York: McGraw-Hill.

Cusumano, M. A. 1989. The application software factory: A historical interpretation. *IEEE Software* (March): 23–30.

DeMarco, T., and T. Lister. 1987. *Peopleware, productive projects and teams*. New York: Dorset House Publishing.

Dietz, J. 1999. *The passage to professionalism, a framework*. TU Delft.

Ferguson, P., W. S. Humphrey, S. Khajenoori, S. Macke, and A. Matvya. 1997. Introducing the Personal Software Process: Three industry case studies. *IEEE Computer* 30, no. 5 (May): 24–31.

Fitz-enz, J. 1978. Who is the DP professional? *Datamation* (September).

Ford, G. 1994. Software licensing and certification. SEI Report (CMU/SEI-94-TR-01, ESC-TR-94-01). Pittsburgh: Software Engineering Institute, Carnegie Mellon University.

Ford, G., and N. E. Gibbs. 1996. A mature profession of software engineering. SEI Report (CMU/SEI-96-TR-004). Pittsburgh: Software Engineering Institute, Carnegie Mellon University.

Glass, R. L. 1998. Defining quality intuitively. *IEEE Software* (May/June).

Hall, P. A. V., and L. Jin. 1997. The reengineering and reuse of software. In *Software engineering*, eds. M. Dorfman and R. Thayer. Palo Alto, Calif.: IEEE Computer Society.

Hatton, L. 1998. Does OO sync with how we think. *IEEE Software* (May/June).

Heemstra, F. J., R. J. Kusters, and J. Trienekens. 2001. *Software quality: Towards better software*. Den Haag, The Netherlands: Ten Hagen & Stam.

Herzberg, F. 1959. *The motivation to work*. New York: John Wiley & Sons.

Humphrey, W. S. 1996. Using a defined and measured Personal Software Process. *IEEE Software* 13, no. 3 (May): 77–88.

Humphrey, W. S. 1998. Pathways to process maturity: The Personal Software Process and Team Software Process. *CrossTalk* (February-April).

IT Research House. 2000. British top-IT staff not loyal. *Automatiseringsgids* (21 July).

Jones, T. C. 1993. Software quality: Analysis and guidelines for success. Cambridge, Mass.: International Thomson Press.

Kamatar, J., and W. Hayes. 2000. An experience report on the Personal Software Process. *IEEE Software* (November-December).

Krasner, H. 1999. Teamwork considerations for superior software development. In *Constructing Superior Software*, ed. P. C. Clements. Indianapolis: MacMillan Technical Publishing.

Kusters, R. J., and G. M. Wijers. 1993. On the practical use of CASE tools: Results of a survey. In *Proceedings of the sixth international workshop on computer aided software engineering*, eds. H-Y Lee, T. F. Reid, and S. Jarzabek Singapore. Los Alamitos, Calif.: IEEE Computer Society Press.

Lim, W. C. 1994. Effects of reuse on quality, productivity, and economics. *IEEE Software* 11: 23–30.

McConnell, S., and L. Tripp. 1999. Professional software engineering: Fact or fiction? *IEEE Software* (November/December).

McConnell, S. 2000. Quantifying soft factors. *IEEE Software* (November/December).

Morisio, M., C. Tully, and M. Ezran. 2000. Diversity in reuse processes. *IEEE Software* (July/August).

Musa, J. D., A. Ianino, and K. Okumoto. 1987. *Software reliability: Measurement, prediction, application*. New York: McGraw-Hill.

Parzinger, M. J., and R. A. Nath. 2000. Study of the relationships between total quality management implementation factors and software quality. *Total Quality Management* 11, no. 2: 353–371.

Prahalad, C. K., and G. Hamel. 1990. The core competence of the corporation. *Harvard Business Review* (May/June): 79–91.

Prieto-Diaz, R. 1993. Implementation of multiple classification for code reuse. *Information* no. 6.

Sharp, H., H. Robinson, and M. Woodman. 2000. Software engineering: Community and culture. *IEEE Software* (January/February).

Shaw, M. 1990. Prospects for an engineering discipline of software. *IEEE Software* 7, no. 6. (November): 15–24.

Sijtstra. 2000. IT employees are seldom happy in their job. *Automatiseringsgids* (21 July).

Swanson, K., D. McComb, J. Smith, and D. McCubbrey. 1991. The application software factory: Applying total quality techniques to systems development. *MIS Quarterly* (December).

Van Genuchten, M. J. I. M. 1992. *Towards a software factory*. Dordrecht: Kluwer Academic Publisher.

Wentink, A. A. L. G. 1999. Learning from quality management. *Bestuurskunde* 8, no. 6.

Werth, L. 1998. Certification and licensing for software professionals and organizations, software engineering education. In *Proceedings of the 11th Conference on Software Engineering Education and Training*. Palo Alto, Calif.: IEEE Computer Society.

Whitaker, K. 1997. Motivating and keeping software developers. *Computer* (January).

Zhong, X., N. H. Madhavji, and K. E. Emam. Critical factors affecting Personal Software Process. *IEEE Software* (November/December).

BIOGRAPHIES

Fred J. Heemstra is a professor of industrial engineering and computer science at the Dutch Open University in Heelen, where he is responsible for the master's program "ICT Management." He received his master's degree in industrial engineering in 1976 and his doctorate in software cost estimation and control from Eindhoven University of

Technology in 1989. His research interests include software management issues such as project management, cost-benefit analysis, risk management, and software quality.

Rob J. Kusters is a professor of ICT and business processes at Dutch Open University in Heerlen where he is responsible for the master's program "Business process and ICT." He is also an associate professor of IT enabled business process redesign at Eindhoven University of Technology, where he is responsible for a section of the program in management engineering. Kusters is also an associate member of the research school BETA, which focuses on operations management issues. He received his master's degree in econometrics from Tilburg University in 1982 and his doctorate in operations management from Eindhoven University of Technology in 1988. His research interests include enterprise modeling, software quality, and software management. He can be reached by e-mail at r.j.kusters@tm.tue.nl.

Toward an Inclusive Model for the Costs of Software Quality

Daniel Galin, Ruppin Academic Center, Israel

This article shows that the classical cost of quality (CoQ) model, which is applicable to the manufacturing industry, fails to serve the software industry by not differentiating between costs of software quality (CoSQ) generated by the software development team and those created by the managerial level. By not presenting CoQ separately, it is difficult to identify and analyze these costs of quality.

Improved presentation of the components of CoSQ in the inclusive model, targeted at the software industry, presents separately management's share in the costs of failure of control in addition to management's share in the costs of appraisal and control. This model demonstrates that by defining the optimal level of managerial appraisal and quality control costs, one can reduce the total management-based costs of software quality to a minimum.

The article concludes with a discussion of the difficulties involved in the collection of cost of quality data, particularly data on managerial activities, and outlines the framework of activities for implementation of the inclusive CoSQ model.

Key words: analytical models, cost of quality models, software product quality costs

Introduction

It is generally accepted that cost of quality (CoQ) data are important tools for managers eager to control expenditures on quality, namely costs of prevention and costs of appraisal, while taking into account the costs of failure. The results obtained with the classic CoQ model (see Figure 1) are used as managerial tools when analyzing the extent and sources of the failure of quality costs in the current period. They likewise serve as a basis for making decisions regarding the size of the budget for quality assurance activities (of prevention and appraisal) in the manufacturing departments and quality assurance units in subsequent periods. These decisions are intended to effectively minimize total CoQ. Dobbins (1999) and Knox (1993) discuss the implementation of the classic CoQ model at the software development project level.

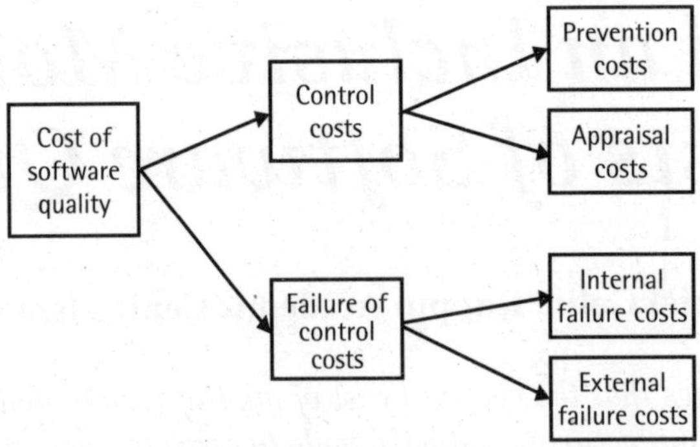

Figure 1 The classic cost of quality (CoQ) model

Despite its proven contribution to manufacturing, this article raises the following question about the classic CoQ model's suitability to software development projects: Is the classic CoQ model, which was developed for the manufacturing industry about 50 years ago, also applicable, as is, to software development projects? In particular, does it present an appropriate classification of quality assurance costs that will effectively support making decisions regarding budgeting the quality assurance activities by the relevant bodies, those that substantially affect costs of failure?

In response to this question, the article suggests an alternative, more inclusive model, targeted at the software industry.

The Need for an Inclusive CoQ Model Targeted at Software Development Projects

The classic CoQ model, which was developed for the manufacturing industry (Feigenbaum 1991; Juran 1988), classifies costs of quality into four subclasses, where the responsibility for these costs lies almost entirely on the manufacturing departments and on the quality assurance (QA) unit.

There are significant quantitative and organizational differences between the software and manufacturing industries regarding CoQ issues. These differences emphasize the need for a specific CoQ model targeted at the software industry.

Quantitative Difference in the Level of CoQ

Typical costs of software quality (CoSQ), measured as a percentage of total development costs, have thus been found to be significantly higher than those applicable to the manufacturing industry. While CoQ usually consumes from 5 percent to 25 percent of company sales, CoSQ ranges between 10 percent and 70 percent of the total software development costs (Krasner 1998). Additional results pointing at the high level of CoSQ were published for software development projects in the United Kingdom and the United States. A Price Waterhouse study, carried out with 19 software suppliers in the United Kingdom during the 1980s, concluded that 40 percent to 55 percent of total development costs are due to quality costs. Several papers refer to the correlation between the level of the software quality assurance system and the expected level of CoSQ. Dion (1993) and Haley (1996) present CoSQ results for Raytheon Electronic Systems (RES) for a period of three years during its development of a software quality assurance system; a total of 15 projects were tracked. They found that at CMM level 1, the CoSQ for the RES projects ranged between 55 percent and 67 percent of total development costs. Three years later, when RES had reached CMM level 3, CoSQ had dropped to 40 percent of total development costs (again based on the 15 projects tracked).

Fundamental Differences in the Organization's Units that Generate CoQ

In the manufacturing industry quality assurance (QA) deals mainly with repetitive production of established products; however, software quality assurance (SQA) deals mainly with development of new software products. Accordingly, while in the manufacturing industry the production level departments and the QA unit are responsible for almost all CoQ substance, in the software industry, in addition to the production level (development teams) and SQA units, management is responsible for significant portions of the CoSQ. Management's CoSQ may be classified into three categories: 1) managerial appraisal and control costs; 2) managerial internal failure costs; and 3) managerial external costs. The costs of managerial failures, internal and external, may be defined as those caused by managerial action or inaction in performing managerial appraisal and control tasks.

To clarify the organizational differences between the two industries, Figure 2 presents a comparison of the organizational units responsible for each class and subclass of CoQ in the classic model.

		Units of the organization responsible for CoQ	
Classes of CoQ	Subclasses of CoQ	Manufacturing project	Software development project
Costs of control	Prevention costs	1. Quality assurance unit 2. Manufacturing unit team	1. Software quality assurance unit 2. Software development project team
	Appraisal costs	1. Quality assurance unit 2. Manufacturing unit team	1. Software quality assurance unit 2. Management 3. Software development project team
Costs of failure of control	Internal failure costs	Manufacturing unit team	1. Management 2. Software development project team
	External failure costs	Manufacturing unit team	1. Management 2. Software development project team

Figure 2 The classic CoQ model: Comparison of organizational units responsible for CoQ in the manufacturing software industries

High evaluation of management's share in the costs of software quality, specifically in software failure costs, is demanded by Glass (1998) and by Flowers (1996), with the title of the latter's book, *Software Failure: Management's Failure,* reflecting management's share in these costs.

This aspect of management's substantial share of CoSQ is likewise reflected in: a) management's share of software development risks, and b) its actions and inactions resulting in catastrophic cases of software failure, the latter being a tangible threat for any software project of considerable scale. These two matters thus further support the need for a targeted yet inclusive CoQ model for the software industry.

Management's Share of Software Development Risks

According to Boehm (1991), the first two software development risks in the "top 10 software risk items" refer to managerial actions or failure of actions, namely: a) personnel shortfalls, and b) unrealistic schedules and budgets. Management's failure to recruit sufficient and adequate staff may result from deficient project progress control or unrealistic project team planning at earlier stages of implementation. Unrealistic schedules and budgets are usually products of overly optimistic estimates driven by management anxiety when compiling a competitive proposal. Similar results were found in an international study on software project risks carried out in the United States, Finland, and Hong Kong (Schmidt et al. 2001; Keil et al. 1998). Many of the risk factors identified in this study relate to project management, staffing, funding, and corporate environment.

Management Share in Cases of Catastrophic Results of Software Failure

The software industry suffers frequently from "standard" cases of external failure costs, which range from 10 percent to 30 percent of total software development costs. These are spent on software corrections performed at the customer's site, compensation for customer inconvenience, and so forth. In addition, the software industry faces "catastrophes," cases where the level of software failure damage is valued at 10 or more times the total software development costs.

Well-known examples of such catastrophic failures of software development projects are the automated baggage handling system of Denver's International Airport and the updated vehicles and drivers handling system for the California Department of Motor Vehicles (DMV). Flowers (1996) and Glass (1998) describe and analyze these and other instances of catastrophic failures. Further illustrations and analyses of such extreme cases can be found in Montealegra and Keil (2000). Common to all these failing projects are their severe budget overruns and very late completion dates. While such failures are very rare in the manufacturing industry, they are real, ongoing threats to every large-scale software development project.

Another type of catastrophe is the case of abandoned software projects. A 1995 study reveals that the software development budget of 53 percent of the projects reviewed were completed at an average of 189 percent over budget (Ewusi-

Mensah 1997). This tendency for costs to soar is also reflected in the statistics of unfinished and completed projects that were abandoned (were never brought into service)—31 percent of all projects according to Ewusi-Mensah (1997).

A Proposed Targeted, Inclusive CoQ Model for Software Development Projects

As shown previously, the classic CoQ model (see Figure 1) does not represent the circumstances surrounding software development projects effectively. By not presenting CoQ generated by management separately, it is difficult to identify and analyze these costs of quality. Improved presentation of the components of CoSQ in the inclusive model, targeted at the software industry, presents separately management's share in the costs of failure of control in addition to management's share in the costs of control. This model demonstrates that by defining the *optimal level* of managerial appraisal and quality control costs, one can reduce the total management-based costs of software quality to a minimum.

A seven-subclass model for CoSQ has been developed on the basis of the aforementioned observations. The control costs and failure of control costs of software quality that relate to managerial activities have been separated and presented in an additional three subclasses of CoQ, to create an inclusive model for CoSQ (see Figure 3).

Typical quality cost items for each of the seven subclasses of the proposed CoSQ model, are presented in Figure 4.

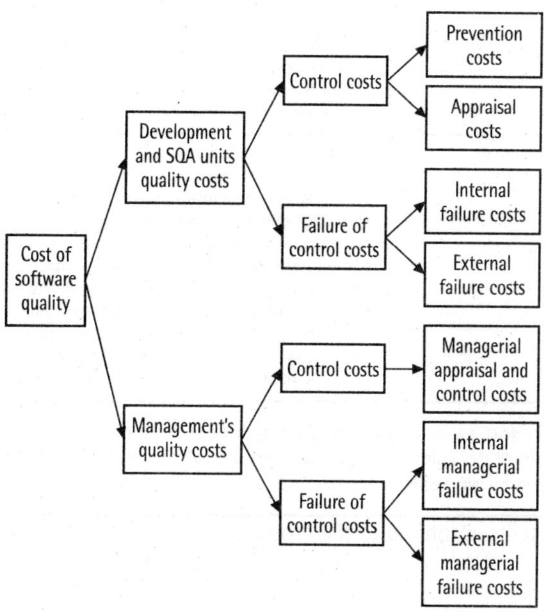

Figure 3 The proposed inclusive CoSQ model—targeted at software development projects

Body in the organization responsible for quality costs	Class of costs of software quality	Typical quality cost items for each subclass
Software development and SQA teams	Control costs	Prevention costs: • Investments in development of and updating of procedures and work instructions • Investments in development and regular operation costs of software configuration management system • Investments in development and regular operation of software quality metrics • Instruction of new employees in those SQA subjects and procedures required by their positions • Certification of employees for positions that require special certification • Internal and external quality audits
		Appraisal costs: • Performance of various reviews • Performance of unit, integration, and software system tests • Participation in acceptance tests • Quality assurance of subcontractors and other external participants
Software development teams	Failure of control costs	Internal failure costs: • Redesign or corrections subsequent to design review and test findings • Reprogramming or correcting programs in response to test findings • Repeated design review and retesting (regression tests)
		External failure costs: • Resolution of customer complaints during the warranty period • Correction of software defects detected during regular operation • Damages paid to customers in case of a severe software failure • Reimbursement of customer's purchase costs, in case of total dissatisfaction • Insurance premium against customer damage claims in case of severe software failure • Hidden external failure costs, that is, reduction of sales as a result of damaged reputation, increased investments in sales promotion under-pricing of tender bidding to counter the effects of past software external failures
Management	Control costs	Managerial appraisal and control costs • Costs of conduct of contract reviews • Costs for preparation of project and quality plans and their periodic updating • Costs for performance of regular progress control
	Failure of control costs	Internal managerial failure costs: • Unplanned development costs resulting from underestimation of resources for submitted proposals • *Domino effect:* Damages to other projects planned to be performed by team members involved in delayed projects due to extra costs for recruitment of replacement team members*
	Failure of control costs	External managerial failure costs: • Damages paid to customers as compensation for late project completion resulting from an unrealistic schedule presented in proposal • Damages paid to customers as compensation for late project completion resulting from failure to recruit sufficient and appropriate team members • *Domino effect:* Damages for delayed completion paid to clients of other projects planned to be performed by team members involved in delayed projects* • Hidden external failure costs, that is, reduction of sales as a result of damaged reputation, increased investments in sales promotion under-pricing of tender bidding to counter the effects of significant past delayed completion of projects due to managerial failures in appraisal and/or progress control tasks

Note: * These damages should be considered managerial failure costs belonging to the original project, whose scheduling problems interfered with the progress of other projects. Should they materialize, one can expect the domino effect to obstruct the progress of several other projects and induce considerable hidden external failure costs.

Figure 4 Typical cost items according to the proposed CoSQ model (examples)

To Sum Up

The proposed targeted inclusive model for CoSQ clarifies the importance of management's share in total software quality costs side by side with the other participants in originating CoSQ—the software development teams and the SQA units. The proposed CoSQ model sheds light on activities that management performs, that is, contract review and project progress control, and promotes decisions of budgeting these activities at a level that will prevent or at least drastically decrease the unfavorable costs of managerial internal and external failures. These decisions are intended to bring the total managerial quality costs to an optimum.

Discussion

The route for implementing this model, more specifically for collecting the data required to determine quantitatively the extent of each of the subclasses of the CoSQ, is the subject of this discussion. While collecting the required data for CoSQ subclasses, for which the development team and the SQA unit are responsible, presents substantial difficulties, gathering the data about management's share in control and failure of control costs appears to present greater difficulties.

Data collection on CoSQ components originating from development teams and SQA units is generally accompanied by inaccuracies and incompleteness resulting from:

- Incomplete reporting of quality costs.
- Biased and/or negligent reporting of quality costs, particularly the tendency to "reduce" reported internal and external failure costs.
- Biased recording of external failure costs due to indirect if not "camouflaged" compensation for failures (for example, by supply of free services) recorded as other costs.
- Difficulties in identifying and quantifying hidden external failure costs, in cases of clearly identified development team's external failures. Hidden external failure costs may be realized by loss of sales, increased difficulties in winning tenders, and so on. These, by definition, are difficult to identify and quantify.

Problems are encountered also when collecting data on managerial CoSQ matters. These include:

- Difficulty in determining appraisal and control costs. Contract review and progress control activities are often performed in a "part-time mode" and/or subdivided into several disconnected activities of short duration. The reporting of time invested in these activities is usually inaccurate and often neglected.

- Difficulty in obtaining time reports for many of the participants in performing appraisal and control activities, resulting from their being senior staff members who, in most cases, are not required to report use of their time resources.
- Difficulty in identifying and quantifying hidden external quality costs in cases of clear identification of management's external failure costs.

In addition to the aforementioned difficulties in collecting CoSQ data, there are also problems encountered in determining responsibilities for identified CoSQ matters. Problems of this nature include:

- Difficulties in placing responsibility for schedule failures. These costs of failure may be assigned to:
  a. *The customer*, for instance, in cases that the customer failed to fulfill his or her share of the contract. Examples of such situations are failure to install the required hardware and communication systems, or failure to complete on time the staff's instruction program (in such cases no quality costs are assigned to the contractor, as the customer is required to compensate the contractor).
  b. *The development team*, in cases where the developer fails to complete the development process on time, typically because of excessive failures in the testing stage (considered as the development team's internal failure cost), or because of a high rate of failures identified by the customer's acceptance tests and running in phase (considered as development team's external failures).
  c. *The management*, in cases of failure to recruit sufficient professional team members (considered as a managerial failure cost).
- Discussions on the contribution of each body to schedule failures are frequently lengthy and inconclusive.
- Difficulties in placing responsibility for project budget overruns whether: a) caused by underestimation of costs at the project proposal stage (management's internal failure costs), or b) caused by lack of project team's professional and/or organizational capacity (development team's internal failure team).
- Difficulties involved in determining the body responsible for the need for compensation payments to customers (in cases that are not "camouflaged") usually occurs a while after the project is completed and much too late for efficient application of the lessons learned. At that late date, it is very difficult to determine objectively whether the failure was management's or the development team's responsibility.

One may conclude that while the proposed CoSQ model provides a more comprehensive picture of software project quality costs, its implementation requires substantial efforts from the SQA unit. These include:

- Adaptation of the time resources usage reporting system to include the classifications required for the CoSQ analysis, namely, time spent on appraisal tasks, quality instruction tasks (preventive costs), reprogramming according to test results (internal failure costs), or project progress control (managerial appraisal and control costs), and so on.
- Initiation of general reporting procedures regarding the use of time resources. It might require the application of special reporting procedures for seniors.
- Adaptation of the bookkeeping classification to include the specific items that refer to CoSQ issues, that is, quality instruction expenses (preventive costs), payments made to compensate clients for failure damages (external failure costs), payments made to a quality expert for his or her review of a software product (appraisal costs), and so on. The SQA should define the needed rules for classification of software quality costs.
- Initiation of ongoing contacts between the bookkeeping department and the SQA unit to discuss cases of unclear classification of CoQ.
- Initiation of a procedure for evaluating the extent of external failure costs and determining the responsible unit. Upon completion of each project the procedure that takes care of professional estimates of external failure costs as well as hidden external failure should be applied.
- Development of a software system that will store all CoSQ records, perform follow up of the reporting of the data regarding CoSQ in the organization's units, and process all required reports and queries.
- Application of follow-up procedures to control the correct and full implementation of all components of the data collection system.

The efforts required to complete these tasks should not be underestimated, but the rewards of effective control of CoSQ is of utmost importance for the management of SQA activities.

It is expected that the adoption and implementation of the proposed inclusive CoSQ model will contribute to improved decision making regarding the budgeting of SQA resources.

REFERENCES

Boehm, B. W. 1991. Software risk management: Principles and practices. *IEEE Software* 8, no. 1: 32–41.

Dion, R. 1993. Process improvements and the corporate balance sheet. *IEEE Software* 10, no. 4 (July): 33–41.

Dobbins, H. D. 1999. The cost of software quality. In *Handbook of Software Quality Assurance*, third edition, eds. G. G. Schulmeyer and J. I. McManus. Upper Saddle River, N.J.: Prentice Hall PTR.

Ewusi-Mensah. 1997. Critical issues in abandoned information systems development systems. *Communications of the ACM* 40, no. 9 (September): 74–80.

Feigenbaum, A. V. 1991. *Total quality control*, third edition. New York: McGraw-Hill.

Flowers, S. 1996. *Software failure: Management failure*. West Sussex, U.K.: John Wiley & Sons.

Glass, R. L. 1998. *Software runaways*. Upper Saddle River, N.J.: Prentice Hall PTR.

Haley, T. J. 1996. Software process improvements at Raytheon. *IEEE Software* 13, no. 6 (November): 33–41.

Juran J. M. 1988. *Quality control handbook*, fourth edition. New York: McGraw-Hill.

Keil, M, K. Cule, K. Lyytinen, and R. C. Schmidt. 1998. A framework for identifying software project risks. *Communications of the ACM* 41, no. 11 (November): 76–83.

Knox, S. T. 1993. Modeling the cost of software quality. *Digital Technical Journal* 5, no. 4: 9–16.

Krasner, H. 1998. Using the cost of quality approach for software. *Crosstalk*, no. 11.

Montealegra, R., and M. Keil. 2000. De-escalating information technology projects: Lessons from the Denver International Airport. *MIS Quarterly* 24, no. 3: 417–447.

Schmidt R., K. Lyytinen, M. Keil, and P. Cule. 2001. Identifying software project risk: An international Delphi study. *Journal of Management Information Systems* 17, no. 4: 5–36.

BIOGRAPHY

Daniel Galin is head of the information systems studies at the Ruppin Academic Center. He is also an Adjunct Senior Teaching Fellow at the Technion, Faculty of Computer Sciences. His professional experience includes numerous consulting projects in the areas of software quality assurance, analysis and design of information systems, and industrial engineering.

Galin has a bachelor's degree in industrial and management engineering, and a master's degree and doctorate in operations research from the Faculty of Industrial and Management Engineering of the Technion, Israel Institute of Technology, Haifa, Israel.

Galin's publications include many papers that have appeared in professional journals and in conference proceedings. He is also the author of several books in software quality assurance and in analysis and design of information systems. He can be reached by e-mail at dglin@bezeqint.net.

Sustaining Best Practices: How Real-World Software Organizations Improve Quality Processes

Diana Mekelburg, All-Hands PM

The most publicized methods that organizations are advised to apply for improving their software quality processes are two opposites: continuous improvement models and quick-fix best practices. However, a two-year study of quality process improvements in 10 organizations determined that all 10 of the organizations followed similar stages of improvement that grouped complementary practices at each stage. Organizations' progressions through these stages were based on evolutionary changes in their motivations and philosophies, rather than on continuous quantitative analysis or on the evidence of best practices effectiveness. The sustainability of new best practices depended more on the stage in which they were introduced than on the proven benefit of the practices themselves.

Key words: best practices, motivation, process improvement, stages

Introduction

"The users were very involved in early prototype reviews and testing when we first built the system, but since we switched to maintenance, we've had trouble getting them to do even minimal acceptance testing."

"The e-business group claims that their independent test team is the key to their high-quality systems, but no other development groups have followed their lead and established their own test teams."

"We tried using formal test cases, but the system requirements never were adequately documented or kept up to date, so most of the test cases were wrong or incomplete."

These are just a few of the comments the author has heard from clients, colleagues, and students who have tried to implement quality-related best practices in their organizations. They complained that industry practices like peer reviews and process quality assurance did not last long in their organizations and were never extended beyond one or two groups. The bottom line is that many best practices they attempted didn't "take." That is, they weren't sustainable as standard practices. All of the organizations, however, had progressed in their quality practices beyond ad hoc testing. Several were conducting user acceptance tests, customer reviews of requirements, and technical reviews of designs.

In the last two years, the author has conducted quality process analyses comparing the practices of 10 software development organizations with others in their industry. These companies ranged in size from 200 employees to more than 10,000 employees. Nine were in the financial industry and one was in pharmaceuticals; all were aspiring to zero-defect goals.

Initially, the author's analysis relied on a checklist of practices that industry leaders had found to be the most effective. Each practice was evaluated independently, assuming that each could exist without the others. However, patterns of sustainable practices gradually emerged. Quality improvements appeared to follow an inherent sequence of stages.

The author originally assumed that sustainable improvements in these organizations would follow one of the predominant continuous improvement models, such as the Software Engineering Institute's Capability Maturity Model Integration (CMMI), the Software CMM, and the Testing Maturity Model (SEI 1995; 2001; Burnstein 2003). However, none had used a process improvement approach based on careful measurement, analysis, and implementation, nor were their improvements limited to testing. The quality-related practices that they were able to sustain appeared to rely on the support of other practices, beyond project management and requirements processes, and were not independently identified, evaluated, and implemented. In other words, the progression of quality-related practices seemed to occur in pre-defined groups, rather than as independently selected and implemented practices. Organizations improved by leaps in process, rather than continuously.

The organizations studied reported that even the well-planned attempts to institute practices in isolation were unsuccessful. Even extensive training in best practices didn't guarantee success. Jumping ahead of the typical improvement sequence didn't seem to work.

For example, half of the organizations studied attempted formal peer reviews and failed to sustain them as an organizational practice. Two of these organizations, however, made extra effort in introducing formal peer reviews. Both documented their review processes, allocated project time, and trained participants. Yet, a year later, few, if any, formal peer reviews were being held in either organization. Similarly, in three organizations, test automation tools were conscientiously selected and purchased, specialists were trained, and the products were installed. After brief use, however, the tools were abandoned in all three organizations, most often because of the effort of creating and maintaining automated test scripts in competition with changing requirements and project schedule compressions. In none of these attempted improvements were the practices seen as unbeneficial; they were just not sustainable in the organizations' environment at the time.

Improvement Patterns

During this study, the author found that software development organizations tend to absorb whole groups of related processes as a logical collection, rather than as single, independent processes. (This finding especially contradicts the CMMI continuous model, which allows organizations to achieve a high capability level in any one of 21 process areas independently.) In every case, the practices that comprised these processes were sustainable when complemented by other interrelated processes and practices. These groups of processes occurred in a rational order, in a sequence of stages. The general progression was toward more control and optimization. Organizations did not make great leaps from weak quality processes to optimal processes. They first passed through a series of improved, but not optimal, process groups. In contrast, the Testing Maturity Model (Burnstein 2003) describes levels that are in some cases similar to the stages that the author found; however, the scope of that model was too narrow to fully explain complementary improvements, focusing instead on testing practices.

The two factors that most influenced the new practices' sustainability are the practitioners' abilities and motivations. Acquiring the right abilities required training and/or hiring. In some cases, new tools, such as templates or software packages, were required. Though many clients scrimped on training, hiring, and tools, the lack of ability was not the main factor. Instead, the lack of proper motivation was the more pervasive and influential factor. While individuals whom the author interviewed were personally motivated to improve their quality processes, their organizations often lacked any coherent motivation to change the practices already in place. The individuals who shaped the organizational motivations included business partners as well as software management and staff.

Making the leap to new practices required both negative and positive motivation. In organizational development circles, strong negative motivation is referred to as "the burning platform." Its complement—positive motivation—is "the clear path to success" or, in more stressful situations, "the clear path to safety." The organizations studied were not able to sustain changes to established practices unless they had both a reason to change and a reasonable way to change. Reasonableness was determined by individual and organizational philosophies. Related to quality, philosophies defined each group's responsibility for ensuring quality, what is "good enough" quality for each product, and so on. Invariably, when there was a difference in motivation in an organization, there was also typically a difference in philosophy.

At each stage of improvement, the author found that a common set of motivations caused a common set of practices to be instituted. Organizations were not generally successful in mixing and matching practices from the cornucopia of best practices in use throughout the software development community. Instead, they tended to adopt those that most directly addressed their perceived needs, or "burning platform," at the time. And, they tended to follow a common sequence of improvement stages.

Empirical Model for Improved Quality (EMIQ)

The EMIQ Stages

Each of the organizations studied operated at one of these four stages of quality improvement, as described briefly here:

1. Ad hoc quality—Reliance on unstructured, unplanned testing for quality control. All the organizations studied had operated at the ad hoc quality stage at some time in the past.
2. Release control—Test phases late in the project life cycle just before release. After post-release defects had risen beyond their customers' tolerance levels, each organization studied had advanced at least to the release control stage.
3. Quality discipline—Quality processes planned and measured; quality assets managed. The three organizations studied were operating at the third stage, quality discipline, for more than six months at the time of the study. They advanced to this stage because they were dissatisfied with the extra delays and costs that isolated testing had caused.
4. Quality optimization—Risk-based quality management throughout the life cycle. Only one organization, an e-business, had advanced through the first three stages (at Internet speed) and was instituting practices at the quality optimization stage. Their need for quality, cost-effectiveness, and speed forced them to cut out excess work by preventing defects and risk-based testing.

At least one person in each of the lower-stage organizations told the author that he or she was convinced of the value of the optimizing practices that characterize the quality optimization stage. Attempts to establish these practices at the organizational level, however, had either failed or had not been attempted. Extreme programming techniques (Beck 2004) related to quality control were in use at six organizations, but only in small, specialized development groups. Attempts to expand the use of these techniques had not succeeded.

Stage Conditions

The study found that organizations' motivations to improve their quality-related processes differed at each stage. The appropriate philosophy was needed to sustain the stage's quality practices. The results of each stage justified remaining at that stage or inspired the motivation to advance to the next stage. Table 1 summarizes the conditions and results for each stage.

In summary, most organizations' initial philosophy is to respond quickly to requests and complaints in the ad hoc quality stage. This stage emphasizes development without explicit quality methods. When unacceptable defect levels are evident, the response is to dedicate more resources to quality control. However, the resulting testing and rework delay delivery and sap development reserves. Getting control of quality management activities is seen as the remedy, which lays the foundation for making more dramatic improvements in the way that quality is assured. Testing and rework impacts, however, are still seen as being too high. Ultimately, the organization implements a better balance of defect prevention and control to reduce rework costs and increase productivity.

Motivation

Sustainable quality management methods depend on the organization's experiences in dealing with defects, rather than on the purported "goodness" of the methods. Despite organizations' keen interest in best practices, few highly touted practices become ingrained standard methods in most organizations. The methods that are adopted are those that help to relieve the organization's current, most intolerable conditions.

Organizations must perceive these conditions as significant enough to motivate them to act. Other significant conditions may exist, but unless the organization perceives them as requiring action, they have little motivational force. In many cases, the most pressing problems obscure the lesser ones. Each EMIQ stage identifies those problems that are most motivating at that stage.

	Stage			
Condition	1. Ad hoc quality	2. Release control	3. Quality discipline	4. Quality optimization
Beginning motivation	n/a	Unacceptable released defect levels (SLA noncompliance)	Desire to reduce testing and rework costs	Desire to reduce rework costs and increase productivity
Sustaining philosophy	Features and speed over quality; reaction-driven	Features maximized; isolated testing = quality control	Features and speed focus; quality efforts coordinated and reduced	Balanced features, speed and quality; shared quality roles
End results	Low development costs; released quality unpredictable	Lower defect levels; higher testing costs; increasing technical defects	Efficient testing; no noticeable rework savings	Reduced testing and rework costs

Table 1 EMIQ stage conditions

As exceptions, one or two groups within the organization may use quality management methods that are more advanced than those used by the rest of the organization. Or, they may use more regressive methods. These groups can sustain these methods through persistence and force of personality. Specifically, the group must repeatedly defend its anomalous behavior in two ways:

1. By insisting that their business and/or technical environment requires their unique methods
2. By following a persistent champion who reinforces the group's commitment to their unique methods

The group ultimately gives up its unique methods either when the environment changes, often through outside intervention, or when the champion's commitment or influence diminishes. Alternately, the organization may eventually advance or regress to a stage that includes the group's methods.

Philosophy

Motivation provides the impetus to change quality methods. It does not, however, identify the changes to be made; philosophy does this.

Philosophy is more than a set of methods. It is a coherent belief in the organization's role and abilities. Here are some examples. When a software development organization sees its role as order taker rather than as full partner with its customers, quality methods are implied or vaguely defined. When developers are seen as unable to define and run efficient or effective tests, quality management efficiency is limited to late phase testing by nondeveloper groups. These groups are either testing specialists or user representatives. When rework is perceived as impossible for the development team to measure, expanding defect prevention is unjustified.

Results

No improvement is perfect. All have both positive and negative results. Expecting a set of best practices to provide a silver bullet that solves all quality problems leads to disappointment. Successful improvements require that the organization:

1. Monitor positive results to see if the change has in fact been an improvement
2. Plan for handling the inevitable negative results, which may increase over time

A method that seems to have only positive results initially may turn out to be a disappointment because of the Hawthorne effect; that is, performance may improve temporarily while it receives increased attention. For example, organizations that establish a new test team see a decrease in in-development defects because developers work with the new testers to build a foundation of test cases. During this initial phase, the developers are more aware of the potential defects in their systems and pay more attention to the quality of their code. Once the test team is up and running, however, the developers' attention returns to code production, and the initial benefit of the test team diminishes.

Stages' Characteristics

The characteristics of EMIQ stages identify the activities, organizations, tools, and processes used at each stage. These characteristics result when the right philosophies merge with the right motivations, as explained previously. The characteristics are:

- **Defect monitoring**—tracking and analyzing defects at various phases of development
- **Release control**—gatekeeper methods to prevent defects from moving from one phase of development to another
- **Development life cycle**—explicit timing of quality-related activities, in parallel or integrated
- **Personnel assignments**—groups responsible for quality-related activities
- **Planning and monitoring**—extent and basis for planning and monitoring quality-related activities
- **"Testware"**—condition and storage of components used to guide and support testing, such as test cases
- **Testing tools**—software tools used to automate, manage, and otherwise support quality-related activities
- **Scope of testing**—types of active and passive testing performed
- **Requirements**—quality of requirements and correlation with other work products
- **Documented procedures**—extent of process documentation supporting quality-related activities

Table 2 summarizes the quality improvement stages' characteristics the practices performed. The extent of the defect monitoring and methods used form the foundation for each stage. Without information about defects both after the product's release and during development, efforts to improve quality are hit and miss. The progression of the other characteristics follows the organization's awareness, measurement, and analysis of defects and their causes.

	Stage			
Characteristic	1. Ad hoc quality	2. Release control	3. Quality discipline	4. Quality optimization
Defect monitoring	Partial production defect tracking	Production defects and status tracked; test phase defects and resolution logged	Test-phase and production defects classified and analyzed	Causal analysis of defect histories; risk-based prevention and detection
Release control	Unplanned; dependent on individual developer	Release approval; staged platforms	Expanded release control automation; test phase entry qualification	Intermediate builds; release risk assessments
Development life cycle	Quick-fix cycles	Separate testing phase(s) late in life cycle	Parallel test planning and definition started early and maintained throughout	Integrated test planning and definition
Personnel assignments	Some developer and user testing	Formal test group (users and/or quality control); decreasing developer testing	Testing specialists/coordinators support testing	Developers responsible for quality w/user, quality assurance, and expert assistance
Planning and monitor-ing	Minimal formal planning; little or no test tracking	Project plans; testing timelines scheduled and tracked at a high level	Detail testing phase work plans and tracking; collaborative planning	Test plans based on product/project risks and history
"Testware"	Few or no documented test cases	Test cases; inconsistent depth and coverage; separate storage by project	More efficient test items storage; standard formats; detail test logging	Test repository organized by components/suites, supporting reuse and eval
Testing tools	"Shelfware" automated test tools	Word processing and spreadsheet use; limited version control tool use	Extensive test mgt. and version control tool use; limited performance and automated test tool use	Extensive CM tool and performance and automated test tool use
Scope of testing	Unstructured developer testing; ad hoc user reviews/tests	Structured system inte-gration test; ineffective user acceptance test; unstructured developer ("unit") testing	Verification and validation assigned appropriately; pre-integration component testing	Risk-based inspections and reviews; all testing structured
Requirements	Missing, vague, volatile	Initial requirements documented and partially mapped to tests and releases; major scope changes approved	Bidirectional tracing through work products; requirements changes controlled and tracked; deferred items tracked	Improved requirements definition and mgt. processes based on testware changes and defects history
Documented procedures	Determined by individ-ual and situation	Standard approval-based release and change management forms and process	Testing policies and guidelines; project test mgt. plans	Review guidelines and criteria; project quality assurance plans

Table 2 EMIQ stages' characteristics

As shown in Table 2, the general trend, from stage 1 through stage 4, ranges from free-form, quality-related practices to structured, strategic practices. Initially, the focus of quality improvements is on establishing barriers between groups and phases. In later stages, these barriers are replaced with integrated controls based on collected quality data. Monitoring, both strategic and quantitative, ensures that the best product is delivered within scope, cost, and time constraints.

EMIQ Stage Descriptions

Each stage of the EMIQ addresses certain conditions and has a specific set of characteristics and results.

Ad Hoc Quality Stage

The terms that succinctly describe the ad hoc quality stage are: 1) responsive, and 2) personal.

The motivation at this stage is to get product out the door. Productivity is tempered by quality activities in an ad hoc manner, relying on development team members' personal assessment of their own fallibility. Developers rewarded for closing customer requests as quickly as possible are typically intense code generators, quickly bored by the repetition and reflection needed for quality assurance and control. In fact, the discovery of a production defect creates another opportunity for the developer to respond to the customers' requests for a fix.

Because of the personal and covert nature of quality activities at this stage, defect tracking or quality measurement are scarce or missing entirely. Any decision to improve quality activities risks failure because of a lack of objective information. Most improvement attempts intend:

- To make testing less painful for development teams
- To respond to users' requests to see new products before they are deployed

Ultimately, this stage becomes too uncomfortable for its participants. Defect levels are perceived as being too high, especially after one or more major production defects cause noticeable damage. This usually follows a leading-edge product release, high developer turnover, or a development staff cutback.

Release Control Stage

The terms that succinctly describe the release control stage are: 1) restricted, and 2) isolated.

The motivation for this stage is to stop bad products from going out the door. Management enacts rules that govern when products are releasable. Final product approval by user representatives is required to enforce the rules, at least superficially. To support their approvals, the condition of products is first evaluated, invariably by one or more testing phases.

To avoid disrupting the continued drive for development productivity, individuals outside the development team perform formal testing. These may be users or testers. Prevention during development is not a high priority, because the value of its benefits is assumed to be too unpredictable and its costs too high. No real data exist to contradict this assumption.

Initial requirements are often documented at the request of the testers and are sometimes subject to approval procedures. However, requirements change management is sporadic, leading to tests that are based on obsolete or incomplete requirements. Figure 1 illustrates the logical relations of the dependent processes in this phase.

Notice that user representatives' approvals and quality checks are shown as required, but they may be performed in superficial or inconsistent ways. In contrast, documenting requirements is not required and not always done, although test planning and management benefit from well-defined product requirements. Documenting requirements suggests that the requirements would need to be approved and that their changes are managed. But, at this stage, these follow-up processes are often superficially performed, if performed at all.

This stage does allow for defect tracking and some minimal measurement, such as overall test phase duration and effort. The scope and use of these data, however, is restricted to ensure that defects are fixed and that resources are assigned. Cost and quality analysis is not performed.

This stage has the initial effect of reducing the defects that are found after release. However, the costs and delays due to testing are high. Staffing a separate testing group is expensive. User representatives, who have real jobs outside of testing, become increasingly reluctant to dedicate time to test planning and execution. Eventually, these costs are seen as unjustifiable. Testing and fixing defects late in the development life cycle delays product release and ties up valuable resources that could be working on the next release. Eventually, these delays are seen as unjustifiable.

A few organizations regress from the release control stage by eliminating the testing phase(s) and shifting testing responsibility back to the development team members, who have little or no reason to spend their coding time on quality assurance or control. In fact, during the release control stage, developers tend to increasingly rely on the testing groups to find the defects in their code. Quality checks during development typically have deteriorated, and the organization returns to the ad hoc stage.

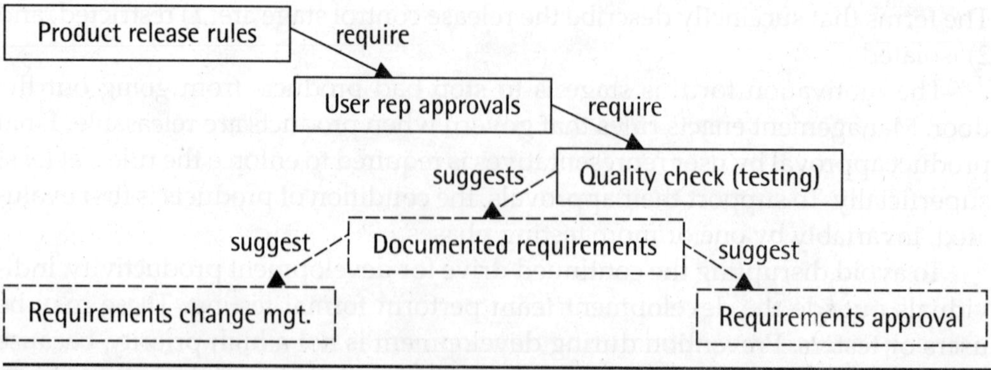

Figure 1 Release control process relationships

Quality Discipline Stage

The terms that succinctly describe the quality discipline stage are: 1) planned, and 2) monitored.

The motivation for this phase is to make the testing phase work more effectively. This includes using testing resources more efficiently and reducing rework. However, the steps that most organizations take to accomplish this at this stage do not noticeably reduce rework.

The approach is to streamline quality efforts and reduce duplication of effort by coordinated planning. At this stage, organizations blend their test planning and definitions with their overall project work. Many morph their traditional waterfall life cycle into a v-shaped life cycle, which links verification and validation with comparable analysis and design phases throughout the project. Most organizations, however, defer structured test execution until late in the life cycle. Few perform in-development testing, except for static tests, such as requirements and design reviews.

Roles and responsibilities for defining and performing tests are assigned to the most appropriate personnel, rather than over-burdening either technical or user testers. Time spent in testing-related activities is tracked in more detail and reviewed to determine testing efficiency. Terminology is also clarified. "Defects" are no longer called "issues" unless their importance or insolubility elevates them to issue status. "Unit" testing is not used to describe the full breadth of "developer" or "in-process" testing.

Test cycles and scope focus on high-yield conditions, rather than full coverage. All testing assets are viewed as valuable resources for reuse and automation. Test results reports are used to plan subsequent testing. Configuration management and requirements management are expanded to provide testing execution with a solid foundation. Requirements are traced through at least design and test to ensure full test definition.

Ultimately, the costs and durations of testing are reduced. Rework levels stay relatively unchanged, however, because of the lack of in-process quality control and assurance.

Quality Optimization Stage

The terms that succinctly describe the quality optimization stage are: 1) preventive, and 2) predictable. Despite organizations' efforts in previous stages, the time spent in the testing phases—by both developers and testers—is not adequately reduced. Productivity at the end of the projects still takes a hit. Organizations are motivated to move to this stage when they run out of ways to cut testing efforts without some assurance that defects won't reach the testing phases in the first place.

In this phase, organizations are forced, by the lack of other alternatives, to incorporate defect prevention and detection into the earlier project phases. The biggest change is the formalization of developer testing. Some of the methods that organizations adopt are risk-based code inspections, pre-coding test definition, test-driven coding, weekly builds and smoke tests throughout coding, and others. While the types of preventive methods may differ, the common feature of this stage across organizations is the assignment of responsibility for product quality to development teams. Analysts and customer representatives are included in this responsibility, with more structured, quantified quality reviews and analysis of requirements.

The habit of collecting measurements for quality efforts and using measures as the basis for improvements continues from the previous stage to this one. While the number of measures doesn't necessarily increase, the types and precision of the measurements usually do. Common uses for the measurements collected in this stage include the analysis of the defect causes as well as process effectiveness and product or component quality.

Conclusion

The EMIQ can be used by software development organizations to assist with:

- Characterization of the organization's current quality-related processes
- Explanation for some of the organization's past failures to adopt and sustain best practices
- Identification of practices that are more likely to be sustainable in the organization
- Identification of the motivations and philosophies that are likely to enable organizations to adopt and sustain new quality-related practices.

Taken together, these EMIQ features describe the most likely next steps for organizations to improve their quality-related practices.

Further Research

EMIQ is a representation of how the 10 organizations studied improved their quality-related practices. The small sample size, especially at the top two stages, is not adequate to confirm the details of these stages. Additionally, the top stage, quality optimization, may be the initial step into a continuous improvement model, but none of the organizations in this study had stabilized at this top stage long enough to confirm or refute this possibility.

Summary

The EMIQ model represents the sequence of quality improvements that the organizations experienced. As each stage was reached, some problems diminished while others increase or became more noticeable. New solutions were sought.

This study found that testing best practices alone does not drive sustainable improvements. Instead, durable changes require complementary changes in release control, development life cycle, personnel assignments, planning and monitoring, and other characteristics. The four stages defined in the EMIQ model are intended to help explain where an organization is likely to seek solutions for its current quality shortcomings. It is a predictive, not prescriptive model.

REFERENCES

Beck, K. 2004. *Extreme programming explained: Embrace change, 2nd edition.* New York: Addison-Wesley Professional.

Burnstein, I. 2003. *Practical software testing.* New York: Springer.

SEI (Software Engineering Institute).1995. *The capability maturity model: Guidelines for improving the software process.* New York: Addison-Wesley Professional.

SEI. 2001. *Capability maturity model integration (CMMISM), version 1.1.* Pittsburgh: Software Engineering Institute (SEI), Carnegie Mellon University.

BIOGRAPHY

Diana Mekelburg has been a consultant, instructor, coach, and assessor for the last eight years, specializing in the SEI CMM and CMMI, testing, requirements, and project and program management. Prior to this, her obsession with risk management and effective communications helped her succeed as a program, product, and project manager for software development in various industries and systems environments. She has been a popular speaker at PMI and SPIN chapters throughout the United States and at national PMI and international PM conventions. She has authored several PM-related articles in a variety of industry publications, including *CrossTalk*. Mekelburg can be reached by e-mail at dianamek@earthlink.net.

Appendix

Cliffs and Fences—A Fable

The following fable illustrates the relationship between motivations and quality practices.

People came from all over to see the beautiful view from a cliff on the edge of the town of Edgefield. The view was especially beautiful at night. Unfortunately, sightseers fell off the cliff.

1. Ad hoc stage: The town stationed the ambulance and its crews full-time at the bottom of the cliff. The same number of sightseers fell, although fewer died. Meanwhile, the town folk had to wait longer for ambulance service.
2. Release control stage: The citizens complained about the poor ambulance service, and tourists still avoided the town, because the cliff had a reputation for being unsafe. The council contracted with an ambulance service to station a second ambulance and crew at the cliff and hired round-the-clock guards to keep people away from the cliff's edge. Fewer sightseers ventured near the edge, and only two fell off the cliff. However, the round-the-clock guards and overtime pay for ambulance crews were not justified by the number of people being saved.
3. Quality discipline stage: Guards told the council that their biggest problems were with young men who drank at night in the park. The council assigned two guards to the "graveyard" shift and fired the rest. They also cut the ambulance contract to graveyard shift only. Again, two sightseers fell off the cliff in the first month after these changes, but the cost-per-death ratio was better. Then the council noticed that tourism was still falling. More young men than ever before came to the park at night to drink and wander near the cliff's edge, believing that the guards would keep them from falling. Guard turnover was high.
4. Quality optimization stage: The council agreed that prevention would have to be started earlier. Large signs about cliff safety were installed all over the parking lot and sightseeing area. A sightseeing platform with an excellent view was built far back from the edge and a fence discouraged people from approaching the cliff's edge. Eventually, the ambulance was no longer needed at the bottom of the cliff. Tourism reached record numbers, yet only one tourist fell off the cliff during the first year of this stage. The council was re-elected to another term and turned their attention to rising sewage problems.

PART III

Software Engineering Processes

The end product is quality software; the path to get there is the application of quality software engineering processes. But what makes a good software engineering process? First, you need to have a repeatable process. If you have ever worked at a company that did not have a software engineering process, then you know how difficult it is to ensure the quality of the end product. The CSQE Body of Knowledge acknowledges that there are many paths to a good process and discusses the individual steps that make up that path. These include having a specified life cycle and a solid architecture as the base of all software engineering work. The rest of the steps are as expected—requirements, design, coding, maintenance—but the details behind them include change management, traceability, requirements engineering, design methods, reuse, formal methods, and tools. In this section, our authors discuss requirements, design, and the collaboration needed to work in an agile programming environment.

Linda Westfall discusses "Software Requirements Engineering: What, Why, Who, When, and How." If software requirements are not right, companies are very unlikely to end up with the software they need. This article discusses the various levels and types of requirements that need to be defined (what), the benefits of having the right software requirements (why), the stakeholders of the software requirements and getting them involved in the process (who), requirements activities throughout the software development life cycle (when), and techniques for eliciting, analyzing, specifying, and validating software requirements (how).

How many times have we heard that it is the early work that really pays off in software engineering? In "Rule-Based Design Reviews" Tom Gilb provides some insights on specifications and design reviews. He notes that by using relevant rules, it should be possible to ensure prior to a review that all the relevant information for the review is present in the design specifications and that all the minimum review criteria are met. This will ensure that management time is not wasted and it will aid in decision making. The article recommends that the specification quality control method be used to do this additional quality control and outlines the impact of evolutionary project management on the design review process.

We hear from Scott Ambler on "Quality in an Agile World." Quality is an inherent aspect of true agile software development. The majority of agilists take a test-driven approach to development: They write a unit test before they write the domain code to fulfill that unit test, with the end result being that they have a regression unit test suite at all times. They also consider acceptance tests as first-class requirements artifacts, promoting not only regular stakeholder validation of their work but also their active inclusion in the modeling effort itself. This article explores the challenge for quality professionals—that agilists work in a highly collaborative and evolutionary (iterative and incremental) manner, often requiring traditional quality professionals to adapt their usual approach.

Software Requirements Engineering: What, Why, Who, When, and How

Linda Westfall, The Westfall Team

If software requirements are not right, companies will not end up with the software they need. This article discusses the various levels and types of requirements that need to be defined (what), the benefits of having the right software requirements (why), the stakeholders of the software requirements and getting them involved in the process (who), requirements activities throughout the software development life cycle (when), and techniques for eliciting, analyzing, specifying, and validating software requirements (how).

Key words: requirements analysis, requirements elicitation, requirements engineering, requirements management, requirements specification, stakeholder

Introduction

If software requirements are not right, companies will not end up with the software they need. This article will discuss:

- What: The various levels and types of requirements that need to be defined
- Why: The benefits of having the right software requirements
- Who: The stakeholders of the software requirements and getting them involved in the process
- When: Requirements activities throughout the software development life cycle
- How: Techniques for eliciting, analyzing, specifying, and validating software requirements

What

Requirements must be determined and agreed to by the customers, users, and suppliers of a software product before the software can be built. The requirements define the "what" of a software product:

- *What the software must do* to add value for its stakeholders. These functional requirements define the capabilities of the software product.
- *What the software must be* to add value for its stakeholders. These nonfunctional requirements define the characteristics, properties, or qualities that the software product must possess. They define how well the product performs its functions.
- *What limitations there are on the choices* that developers have when implementing the software. The external interface definitions and other constraints define these limitations.

Most software practitioners just talk about "the requirements." However, by recognizing that there are different levels and types of requirements, as illustrated in Figure 1 and adapted from Karl Wiegers (2004), practitioners gain a better understanding of what information they need to elicit, analyze, specify, and validate when they define their software requirements.

Business requirements define the business problems to be solved or the business opportunities to be addressed by the software product. In general, the business requirements define why the software product is being developed. Business requirements are typically stated in terms of the objectives of the customer or organization requesting the development of the software.

User requirements look at the functionality of the software product from the user's perspective. They define what the software has to do in order for the

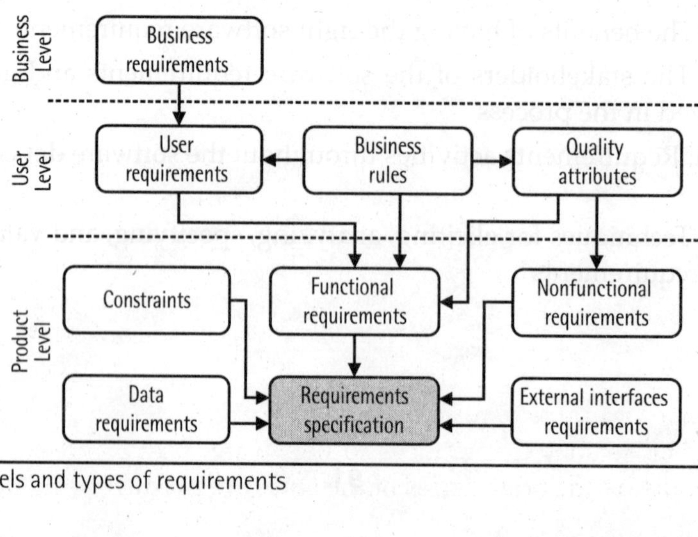

Figure 1 Levels and types of requirements

users to accomplish their objectives. Multiple user-level requirements may be needed in order to fulfill a single business requirement. For example, the business requirement to allow the customer to pay for gas at the pump might translate into multiple user requirements, including requirements for the user to:

- Swipe credit or debit card
- Enter a security PIN number
- Request a receipt at the pump

The product's functional requirements that define the software functionality must be built into the product to enable users to accomplish their tasks, thereby satisfying the business requirements. Multiple functional level requirements may be needed to fulfill a user requirement. For example, the requirements that the users can swipe their credit card might translate into multiple functional requirements including requirements for the software to:

- Prompt the customer to put his or her card into the reader
- Detect that the card has been swiped
- Determine if the card was incorrectly read and prompt the customer to swipe the card again
- Parse the information from the magnetic strip on the card

As opposed to the business requirements, business rules are the specific policies, standards, practices, regulations, and guidelines that define how the users do business (and are therefore considered user-level requirements). The software product must adhere to these rules in order to function appropriately within the user's domain.

User-level quality attributes are nonfunctional characteristics that define the software product's quality. Sometimes called the "ilities," quality attributes include reliability, availability, security, safety, maintainability, portability, usability, and other properties. A quality attribute may translate into product-level functional requirements for the software that specify what functionality must exist to meet the nonfunctional attribute. For example, an ease of learning requirement might translate into the functional requirement of having the system display pop-up help when the user positions the cursor over an icon.

A quality attribute may also translate into product-level nonfunctional requirements that specify the characteristics the software must possess in order to meet that attribute. For example, an ease-of-use requirement might translate into nonfunctional requirements for response time to user commands or report requests.

The external interface requirements define the requirements for the information flow across shared interfaces to hardware, users, and other software applications outside the boundaries of the software product being developed.

The constraints define any restrictions imposed on the choices that the supplier can make when designing and developing the software. For example, there may be a requirement that the completed software use no more than 50 percent of available system memory or disk space in order to ensure the ability for future enhancement.

The data requirements define the specific data items or data structures that must be included as part of the software product. For example, a payroll system would have requirements for current and year-to-date payroll data.

The software may be part of a much larger system that includes other components. In this case, the business and user-level requirements feed into the product requirements at the system level. The system architecture then allocates requirements from the set of system requirements downward into the software, hardware, and manual operations components.

Why

The following quote from Fredrick Brooks illustrates why requirements are so important: "The hardest part of building a software system is deciding precisely what to build. No other part of the conceptual work is as difficult as establishing the detailed technical requirements, including all of the interfaces to people, to machines, and to other software systems. No other part of the work so cripples the resulting system if done wrong. No other part is more difficult to rectify later" (Brooks 1995). Eliciting, analyzing, and writing good requirements are the most difficult parts of software engineering. However, to quote Karl Wiegers (2004), "If you don't get the requirements right, it doesn't matter how well you do anything else." One can end up doing a perfect job of building the wrong product.

There are many issues that can have a negative impact on software development projects and products if practitioners don't do a good job of defining their software requirements. These issues include:

- Incomplete requirements
- Lack of user involvement
- Requirements churn
- Wasted resources
- Gold plating
- Inaccurate estimates

If the requirements are incomplete, software practitioners end up building a software product that does not meet all of the customer and user's needs. As illustrated in Figure 2, Noriaki Kano developed a model of the relationship between customer satisfaction and quality requirements (Pyzdek 2000). The expected quality line represents those quality requirements that the customer explicitly states. For example, they will state their preferences for the make, model, options, and gas mileage when shopping for a car. The customer will be dissatisfied (and go buy a car somewhere else) if their explicit requirements are not met. The customer's satisfaction increases as more of their explicit requirements are met. When enough of their explicit requirements are met, the customer shifts from being dissatisfied with the product to being a satisfied customer. There is a basic level of quality requirements that a customer expects the product to have. These are requirements that are assumed by the customer and are typically not explicitly stated. For example, they expect a car to have four tires, a working engine, and a steering wheel. This level of requirements does not satisfy the customer. Note that the entire basic line is in the dissatisfaction region. Absence of this level of quality requirements will increase a customer's dissatisfaction. Exciting quality is the innovative requirements level and represents unexpected items. These are items that customers do not even know they want, but they love them when they see them. For example, remember when cup holders in cars were first introduced? Note that the entire excited quality line is in the satisfied region. It should be remembered, however, that today's innovations are tomorrow's expectations. The expected quality requirements are the ones practitioners can elicit fairly easily if they talk to the product's stakeholders. However, it is easy to miss both the basic and exciting quality requirements if they do not do a thorough job of detailed requirements elicitation and analysis. In addition, if practitioners miss a stakeholder group or if they do not get the users involved in the requirements process, they can end up with gaps even in their expected requirements.

Requirements churn refers to changes in the requirements after they are initially agreed to and baselined. Some of this change is a part of refining developers' understanding as they develop the software. Changes also occur because of changes in the environment or the user's needs over time that occur as a

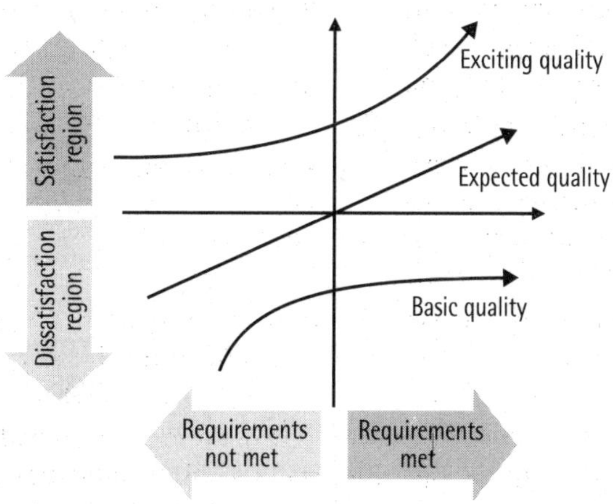

Figure 2 Kano model for quality requirements

natural part of a project of any significant duration. If requirements are poorly defined, however, requirements churn occurs because of missing requirements that should have been included in the original specification or because of poorly written or ambiguous requirements. These are the types of requirements churn that good requirement engineering practices will help avoid.

Requirements errors account for 70 percent to 85 percent of the rework costs on a software project (Wiegers 2003). If one finds a requirements defect during the requirements phase and it costs one unit to fix (for example, three engineering hours, $500), the cost of fixing that same defect will typically increase as it is found later and later in the life cycle. In fact, studies show that it can cost more than 100 times more to fix a requirements defect if it is not found until after the software is released to the field.

Another waste of resources occurs when gold plating is added to the software. Gold plating can take place when a developer adds functionality to the software that was not in the requirements specification but that they believe "the user will just love" without putting that functionality through the requirements engineering process. Users may or may not want the new functionality. If they don't, the cost of developing it is a waste. Cycling these "good ideas" through the requirements engineering process helps ensure that they truly are something that's needed in the product so that gold plating does not occur. A second kind of gold plating comes from the users. For example, if practitioners ask the users "what they want" rather than "what they need to be able to do with the system," they may end up with a wish list of nice to haves or things that they might want sometime in the future but do not really need right now. This is a good reason to prioritize the requirements and focus resources on the most important requirements first. Gold plating can result in wasting resources on implementing functionality that is not of real value or that's never actually used. It also creates the risk that defects in that part of the functionality will cause reliability problems for the rest of the software.

The requirements define the scope of the products that are being developed. Without a clear picture of that scope, estimates of the project schedule, cost, and quality will be less accurate.

Who

Stakeholders are individuals who affect or are affected by the software product and therefore have some level of influence over the requirements for that software product. The requirements engineering process provides the best opportunity to consider all of the various stakeholders' interests in context with one another. There are three main categories of stakeholders: the acquirers of the software product, the suppliers of the software product, and other stakeholders.

The *acquirer* type stakeholders can be divided into two major groups. First there are the customers who request, purchase, and/or pay for the software product in order to meet their business objectives. The second group is the users, also called end-users, who actually use the product directly or use the product indirectly by receiving reports, outputs, or other information generated by the product.

The *suppliers of the software product* include individuals and teams that are part of the organization that develops the software product or are part of the organizations that distribute the software product or are involved in other product delivery methods (for example, outsourcing). The requirements analyst, also called the business analyst or system analyst, is responsible for eliciting the requirements from the customers, users, and other stakeholders, analyzing the requirements, writing the requirements specification, and communicating the requirements to development and other stakeholders. The designers are responsible for translating the requirements into the software's architectural and detailed designs that specify how the software will be implemented. The developers are responsible for implementing the designs by creating the software products. If the software is part of a larger system, hardware designers and developers may also be interested in the software requirements. The testers use the requirements as a basis for creating test cases that they use to execute the software under specific, known conditions to detect defects and provide confidence that the software performs as specified. The documentation writers are responsible for using the requirements as inputs into the creation of the user documentation including user/operations manuals, help files, installation instructions, and training materials as necessary. The project managers are responsible for planning, monitoring, and controlling the project and guiding the software development team to the successful delivery of the software. Technical support, also called operations or the help desk, is responsible for interfacing with the user community to support the software once it has been deployed to the field. Product change management, which may take the form of a change control board (CCB), is responsible for reviewing proposed changes to the requirements, analyzing their impacts, approving/disapproving changes, and ensuring that approved changes are implemented and validated.

There may also be *other stakeholders* interested in the requirements. Examples of other requirements stakeholders include:

- Legal or contract management
- Manufacturing or product release management
- Sales and marketing
- Upper management
- Government or regulator agencies
- Society at large

Identifying and considering the needs of all of the different stakeholders can help prevent software product requirements from being overlooked. For example, if a company is creating a payroll system and it does not consider charities as one of its stakeholders, it might not include the requirements for the software to:

- Allow the payees to specify from one to three charitable deductions
- Withhold charitable deductions from payees' checks each pay period
- Report current and year-to-date charitable deductions on payees' pay slips
- Print a check to each charity for the accumulated amount deducted from payees

The requirements analyst will never know as much about a stakeholder's work as that stakeholder. By identifying and involving key stakeholders, the analyst gains access to their experience base and domain knowledge. The analyst's job is then to analyze, expand on, synthesize, resolve conflicts in, and combine the inputs from all the stakeholders into an organized set of requirements at the appropriate level of abstraction for the target audience.

Identifying the stakeholders and getting them involved in the requirements engineering process brings different perspectives to the table that can aid in a more comprehensive set of requirements early in the software development life cycle. As Wiegers puts it, getting stakeholders involved eliminates the need for two of the most ineffective requirements elicitation techniques: clairvoyance and telepathy (Wiegers 2003).

Remember, people hate change and a new software product means changing the way the stakeholders will perform part or all of their jobs. Obtaining stakeholder input and participation gets them involved in the solution to their needs. Involved stakeholders are more likely to buy in to the completed software product, which can create champions for the software product in the stakeholder community. This can be beneficial in transitioning the software product into the operational environment.

The first step in identifying the stakeholders is to make sure that one considers all of the potential stakeholders. The following checklist can help in identifying potential stakeholders:

- What types of people will use the software product?
- What business activities are supported by the software product and who performs, is involved in, or manages those activities?
- Whose job will be impacted by the introduction of the new software product?
- Who will receive the reports, outputs, or other information from the software product?
- Who will pay for the software product?

- Who will select the software product or its supplier?
- If the software product fails, who could be impacted?
- Who will be involved in developing, supporting, and maintaining the software product?
- Who knows about the hardware, other software, or databases that interface with this software product?
- Who established the laws, regulations, or standards governing the business activities supported by the software product?
- Who should be kept from using the software product or from using certain functions/data in the software?
- Whom does this software product solve problems for?
- Whom does this software product create problems for?
- Who does not want the software product to be successful?

It is almost impossible for the development of a software product to take into consideration the needs of all of the potential stakeholders. The needs of stakeholders may also contradict each other. For example, the need to keep unfriendly hackers from breaking into the payroll software conflicts with the accountant's need for quick and easy access to the software.

The second step in identifying the stakeholders is for the practitioners to decide how they are going to deal with these conflicts. They accomplish this by determining which stakeholders have higher priorities based on their contribution to the success of the software product. This allows practitioners to make appropriate trade-offs when conflicts occur. Gause and Weinberg (1989) discuss what they call the user-inclusion strategy, which the author has expanded to the stakeholder-inclusion strategy. In this strategy, software practitioners can look at the list of potential stakeholders and determine if:

- They want to be friendly to this stakeholder and consider how to accommodate their needs in the software product (for example, make access to the software quick and easy for the accountant).
- They can afford to simply ignore their needs because they are not key to the success of the software product (for example, decide that the specific needs of a little-known charity are not important enough to consider when defining the requirements).
- They want to be unfriendly and consider how to counteract their needs in the software product (for example, prevent hackers from breaking into the software).

The third step is to decide who will represent each stakeholder group that one has designated as friendly or unfriendly. There are three main choices:

- *Representative.* Select a stakeholder champion to represent the group of stakeholders. For example, if there are multiple testers who will be testing the product, the lead tester might be selected to represent this stakeholder group. The lead tester would then participate in the requirements engineering activities and be responsible for gathering inputs from other testers and managing communication with them.
- *Sample.* For large stakeholder groups or for groups where direct access is limited for some reason, sampling may be appropriate. In this case, it would be necessary to devise a sampling plan for obtaining inputs from a representative set of stakeholders in that particular group. For example, if the company had several thousand employees, it may decide to take a sample set of employees to interview about their needs for the new accounting system.
- *Exhaustive.* If the stakeholder group is small or if it is critical enough to the success of the system, it may be necessary to obtain the input from every member of that stakeholder group. For example, if the software product has only one customer or a small set of customers it might be important to obtain input from each of the customers.

Software practitioners must determine when the stakeholder group needs to participate in the requirements engineering activities. Are they going to participate throughout the entire process or only at specific times? For example, practitioners may want the stakeholder champion for the accountants to be a member of the requirements team and to participate throughout the requirements engineering process. They may not need the human resource stakeholder representative to participate on the requirements team, but may need them on a continuous, on-call basis in case there are questions. However, practitioners may only need to sample the employees during the requirements elicitation activities.

Software practitioners must also determine how they are going to have each stakeholder group participate. Are they going to send them questionnaires; do one-on-one interviews; have them participate in a focus group or in a facilitated requirements elicitation workshop; or show them prototypes, mock-ups, or simulations, and gather their inputs?

The final decision is to establish the priorities of the stakeholder team members based on their relative importance to the success of the software product. These established priorities help one determine whose voice to listen to when conflicts arise between the needs of various stakeholders or stakeholder groups.

When

Requirements development encompasses all the activities involved in identifying, capturing, and agreeing upon the requirements. This includes the definition and integration of the business requirements, the user requirements, and software product-level requirements. The majority of the requirements development activities occur during the early concept and requirements phases of the life cycle. Continued elaboration of the requirements, however, can progress into the later phase of the software development life cycle.

Requirements management encompasses all of the activities involved in requesting changes to the base-lined requirements, performing impact analysis for the requested changes, approving or disapproving those changes, and implementing the approved changes. Requirements management also includes the activities used for ensuring that all work products and project plans are kept consistent and tracking the status of the requirements as one progresses through the software development process. Requirements management is an ongoing activity throughout the software development life cycle.

The implemented software product is validated against its requirements during the testing phases of the life cycle to identify and correct defects and to provide confidence that the product meets those requirements.

Requirements engineering is an iterative process. Practitioners must first develop the business requirements and baseline them. The business requirements are input into the development of the user-level requirements. Based on that effort, practitioners may discover gaps in their business requirements that result in their further refinement. They can then use the information they gain from refining the business requirements for further update of the user-level requirements. The business and user-level requirements feed into the definition of the product-level requirements. This may lead to further refinement of the business and user-level requirements. The product requirements are then input into the software design and development process, which may uncover implicit requirements or the need for further refinement of the business, user, and product-level requirements.

How

Software requirements engineering is a disciplined, process-oriented approach to the definition, documentation, and maintenance of software requirements throughout the software development life cycle. As illustrated in Figure 3, software requirements engineering is made up of two major processes: requirements development and requirements management. Requirements development encompasses all of the activities involved in eliciting, analyzing, specifying, and validating the requirements.

The requirements elicitation step includes all of the activities involved in identifying the requirements' stakeholders, selecting representatives from each stakeholder class, and determining the needs of each class of stakeholders. The elicitation process is the information-gathering step in the requirements development process. Many different techniques may be used to elicit requirements, including stakeholder interviews, focus groups, facilitated requirements

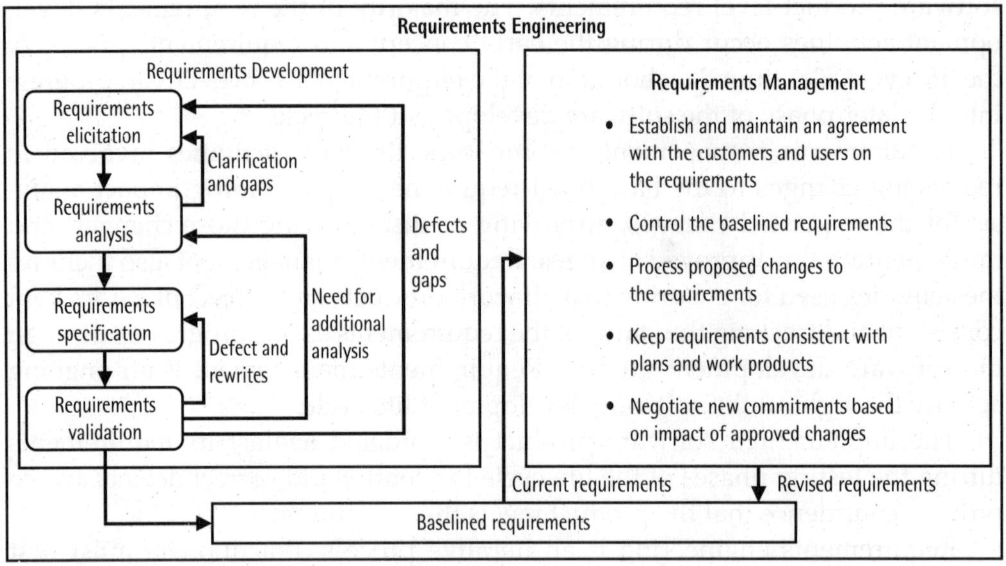

Figure 3 Requirements engineering process (based on Wiegers 2003)

workshops, observations of current work processes, questionnaires and surveys, analysis of competitors' products, and benchmarking of industry practices. Requirements elicitation may also involve documentation studies of:

- Industry standards, laws, and/or regulations
- Product literature (one's own or the competition's)
- Process documentation and work instructions
- Change requests, problem, or help-desk reports
- Lessons learned from prior projects or products
- Reports and other deliverables from the existing systems

During the requirements analysis step the stakeholders' needs, assumptions, and other information identified during requirements elicitation are melded together and refined into further levels of detail. This step includes representing the requirements in various forms including prototypes and models, performing trade-off analysis, establishing priorities, analyzing feasibility, and looking for gaps that identify missing requirements. The information gained in the analysis step may necessitate iteration with the elicitation step as clarification is needed, conflicts between requirements are explored, or missing requirements are identified.

The requirements are formally documented during the specification step so they can be communicated to the product stakeholders. The requirements specification can take one of many forms. For example, on small projects the requirements information may be documented in a single Software Requirements Specification (SRS) document. On larger projects, the requirements may be specified in multiple documents. For example:

- Business requirements may be documented in a business requirements document (BRD), marketing requirements document (MRD), or project vision and scope document.
- User requirements may be documented in a set of use cases in a tool or in a user requirements specification (URS) document.
- If the software is part of a larger system, the product-level requirements may be documented in a system requirements specification and a system architecture specification may document the allocations of those requirements to the software, hardware, and manual operations components of that system.
- The software functional and nonfunctional requirements and the constraints may be documented in an SRS.
- External interfaces may be included in the SRS or in separate external interface requirements documents.

One good practice for requirements specification is to have predefined requirements specification templates. These templates allow the requirements analyst to focus on content instead of format and can help ensure that key items are not overlooked as the requirements are being documented. For example, if assumptions are not documented, they may lead to future misunderstandings or other problems. Another good practice is to use a requirements tool (or database). A requirements tool can be a major asset in both requirements management and project management.

The last step in the requirements development process is to validate the requirements to ensure that they are well written, complete, and will satisfy the customer needs. Validation may lead one to iterate the other steps in the requirements development process because of identified defects, gaps, additional information or analysis needs, needed clarification, or other issues.

One of the primary tools for requirements validation is to conduct formal peer reviews of the requirements specification documents before they are baselined. Empirical evidence from many different companies shows that peer reviewing the requirements documentation has the highest return on investment of any defect detection activity. The peer review process should look at the requirements specification as a whole to ensure that it is:

- *Complete.* The requirements document includes all of the necessary requirements information. For example, the SRS includes all the functions and nonfunctional requirements, constraints, external interface requirements, and data requirements that must be satisfied.

- *Consistent*. Internal conflicts do not exist between requirements in the document that result in the requirements contradicting each other. The requirements also do not conflict with higher-level requirements including business, user, or system-level requirements. Terminology should also be used consistently within the document:
  —A word has the same meaning every time it is used.
  —Two different words are not used to mean the same thing.
- *Modifiable*. The requirements document is organized and written in a manner that will facilitate making future change:
  —Nonredundant: Each requirement is stated in only one place.
  —Changeable: Each requirement can be changed without excessive impact on other requirements.

The peer review process should also look at each individual requirement to ensure that it is:

- *Unambiguous*. Each requirement statement should have only one interpretation, and each requirement should be specified in a coherent, easy-to-understand manner. For example, the author searches for words that end in "ly" (for example, quickly, user-friendly, automatically) because adverbs by nature are almost always ambiguous.
- *Concise*. Each requirement should be stated in short, specific, action-oriented language.
- *Finite*. The requirement should not be stated in an open-ended manner. For example, words like "all," "every," and "throughout" should be avoided in requirements statements.
- *Measurable*. Specific, measurable limits or values should be stated for each requirement as appropriate.
- *Feasible*. The requirement can be implemented using available technologies, techniques, tools, resources, and personnel within the specified cost and schedule constraints.
- *Testable*. There exists a reasonably cost-effective way to determine that the software satisfies the requirement.
- *Traceable*. Each requirement should be traceable back to its source (for example, user-level requirements, system-level requirements, standard, enhancement request). It should also be specified in a manner that allows traceability forward into the design, implementation, and tests.

Another major tool for validating the requirements is to start writing the test cases for functional (black box) testing of the software. Since functional testing only requires knowledge of the requirements and not of the internals of the software product, practitioners can start writing test cases against their requirements as soon as they start writing them. The major advantage to writing the functional test cases early in the life cycle is that it will uncover defects in the requirements. Writing test cases early may result in some rework if the requirements change, but the cost of that rework will be more than offset by the savings resulting from finding and fixing more requirements defects earlier.

Requirements development is an iterative process. One should not expect to go through the steps in a one-shot, linear fashion. For example, the requirements analysts may talk to a user, then analyze what the user had to say. They may go back to that user for clarification and then document what they understand as that part of the requirements. They may then go on to talk to another user, or hold a joint requirements workshop with several user representatives. Their analysis may then include building a prototype that they show to a focus group. Based on that information the analyst documents additional requirements and holds a requirements walk-through to validate that set of requirements. The analyst then moves on to eliciting the requirements for the next feature and so on.

After one or more iterations through the software requirements development process, part or all of the requirements are deemed "good enough" to baseline and become the basis for software design and development. A good saying to remember at this point is, "When is better the enemy of good enough?" The requirements will never be perfect—one can always do more refinement and gather more input. Requirements baselining is a business decision that should be based on risk assessment.

Requirements management starts with getting stakeholder buy-in to the baselined requirements. Requirements management encompasses the activities involved in requesting changes to the baselined requirements, performing impact analysis for the requested changes, approving or disapproving those changes, and implementing the approved changes. Requirements management also includes the activities used for ensuring that work products and project plans are kept consistent and tracking the status of the requirements as one progresses through the software development process.

Conclusion

Practitioners must understand the different types and levels of requirements to do a good job of requirements engineering. It requires an understanding of the benefits of having good requirements so that adequate resources and time are dedicated to the requirements engineering process throughout the software development life cycle. Doing requirements engineering correctly requires an interdisciplinary approach that considers the needs of multiple stakeholder groups. It also requires expertise in the various skills of requirements engineering including requirements elicitation, requirements analysis, requirements specification, requirements validation, and requirements management.

REFERENCES

Brooks, F. 1995. *Mythical man-month: Essays on software engineering, 20th anniversary edition.* Reading, Mass.: Addison-Wesley.

Gause, D., and G. Weinberg. 1989. *Exploring requirements, quality before design.* New York: Dorset House Publishing.

Pyzdek, T. 2000. *Quality engineering handbook.* New York: Marcel Dekker.

Wiegers, K. E. 2003. *Software requirements,* **2nd edition.** Redmond, Wash.: Microsoft Press.

Wiegers, K. E. 2004. *In search of excellent requirements.* Process Impact Web site. See URL: http://www.processimpact.com.

BIOGRAPHY

Linda Westfall is the president of The Westfall Team, which provides software metrics and software quality engineering training and consulting services. Prior to starting her own business, Westfall was the senior manager of the Quality Metrics and Analysis at DSC Communications where her team designed and implemented a corporatewide metrics program. Westfall has more than 25 years of experience in real-time software engineering, quality, and metrics. She has worked as a software engineer, systems analyst, software process engineer, and manager of production software.

Very active professionally, Westfall is the past chair of the American Society for Quality (ASQ) Software Division. She has also served as the Software Division's program chair and certification chair and on the ASQ National Certification Board. Westfall is a past chair of the Association for Software Engineering Excellence (ASEE). She is a professional engineer in software engineering from the state of Texas and is an ASQ Certified Software Quality Engineer (CSQE) and Certified Quality Auditor (CQA). Westfall can be contacted by e-mail at lwestfall@westfallteam.com or visit her Web site at www.westfallteam.com.

Rule-Based Design Reviews

Tom Gilb

Design reviews would benefit from the support of formal rules. By the use of relevant rules, it should be possible to ensure, prior to a review, that all relevant information for the review is present in the design specifications, and that all the minimum review criteria are met. This will ensure management time is not wasted and aid better decision making. This article recommends that the specification quality control (SQC) method be used to do this additional quality control. In addition, this article outlines the impact of evolutionary project management (Evo) on the design review process.

Key words: evolutionary project management, peer review, quality control of specifications, review, review standards

Introduction

It is known that most projects are a partial or total failure, and few are totally successful (Morris 1994; Taylor 2001; Johnson 2001). A key reason for this lack of success is the failure of design reviews. In other words, designs must have been approved that were in some way inappropriate.

Based on reading the literature and participating in numerous requirement and design inspections in many different industries internationally, I fear that most design reviews are carried out:

- On poorly written design specifications (in the sense that the design specifications lack sufficient detail for them to be safely evaluated)
- Using highly polluted requirement specifications (requirements being the basis for evaluating any design).

I find it unacceptable that design reviewers are given *no quantified knowledge* of the quality of the design specification, or of the estimated ability of the design(s) to impact on the requirements (that is, the system performance and costs). A common underlying problem is that specification of design is carried out on the basis of inadequate design standards. I suggest the following remedies:

- A high, defined standard of requirements should be met before entry to the design process itself is permitted.
- Design specification should initially pass quality control against design specification rules to ensure the designs are clearly and fully described.
- Designs should be specified in enough detail to accurately estimate their dominant performance and cost characteristics.
- A set of designs should be seen to credibly and numerically contribute to meeting the requirements (the set of performance targets within the resource budgets).
- The design review process should work in the context of evolutionary cycles of design (for example, in 50 steps), and not operate on a large monolithic total initial design set.

In other words, this article recommends that design specifications undergo specification quality control (SQC) to establish their conformance to the *standards for design specification*, and on successful exit from that, undergo a second SQC to determine their conformance to the *standards for design review* (see Figure 1). Only on successful exit from this second SQC should the actual review, by a body of senior people, take place. One should not waste their time on substandard design proposals.

This recommendation for a second SQC represents an extension of the current practices. It suggests that the use of SQC be expanded to specifically assist the various classes of review. The idea is that SQC can assist reviews by checking that all the information required by the decision makers, that is available, has been gathered and processed as necessary, and that the minimum criteria required to take design specifications forward to review has been met.

Note that this article does not explain how the impacts of designs on the requirements are estimated or how tradeoffs are made. (Impact estimation is a process for achieving this; see Gilb 1998.)

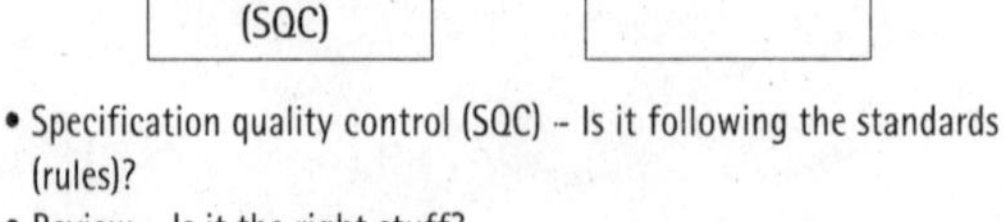

- Specification quality control (SQC) – Is it following the standards (rules)?
- Review – Is it the right stuff?

Figure 1 The two necessary distinct processes

Terminology

Specification Quality Control (SQC)

SQC is also known by the name "inspection." Given that inspection has another meaning to engineers within manufacturing, I prefer to use the term SQC and avoid the collision of using a term with two different meanings. For example, Boeing refused to use the term inspection and used process error prevention (PEP) instead. SQC is also sometimes termed "peer review." I do not use this term because I want to make a clear distinction between "quality control" and "review."

SQC is a rigorous quality control discipline concerned with defect detection, defect measurement, defect removal, process improvement, and entry/exit controls. It is based on evaluating specification conformance to specification rules.

Traditionally, SQC does not pretend to judge the specifications in terms of their relevance or profitability in the real world. It is primarily concerned with making sure that the specifications are clear, complete, and consistent by checking a specification and any of its source and kin documents against "specification rules." It judges whether the specification is suitable to be used in subsequent engineering or management processes. However, by using a different type of rules, "specification review rules," it is possible to extend the SQC process to checking the readiness of specifications for review. This could be for a business review, a progress review, or a technical review. See Figure 2 for an outline of the extended SQC process.

Review

A review is any process of human examination of ideas with a defined purpose and defined standards of inquiry.

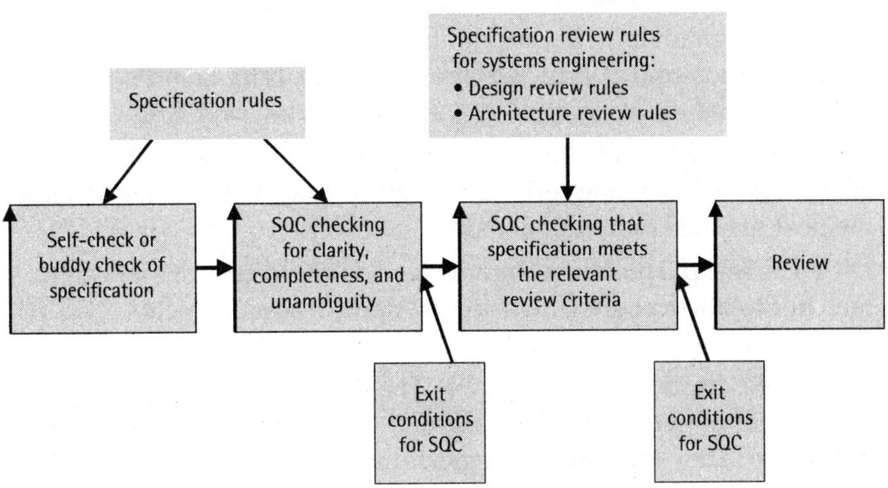

Figure 2 SQC and review processes. Review should follow successful exit from SQC

Design Specification

A design specification is the written specification of a design idea. A set of design specifications attempts to solve a design problem. Identification and documentation of the individual design ideas, and their potential contribution toward meeting the requirements, helps selection of the "best" design ideas for implementation.

The design specifications should contain information about the *expected* attributes of the designs for meeting requirements. This 'expected attributes information' of a design specification might be expressed in the form of an impact estimation table, or it can be as simple as an assertion of impacts on requirements, referenced by their tags (see example in Figure 3).

This article is presented in terms of a set of design review principles.

- DR1: If the specifications are unclear, one is not ready to review whether the design is the "right thing" to do.
- DR2: Individuals cannot review designs if they are unclear whether each specific design is mandatory (a design constraint, which is a requirement) or optional (one of many possible design solutions).
- DR3: Design impacts must be calculated and submitted to a review; they cannot systematically be developed *during* the review.
- DR4: It is part of the purpose of a design review to identify any defective information in the design impact estimates.
- DR5: Certain objective review criteria must be met prior to actually carrying out a review; otherwise, the review may be wasted.
- DR6: The review process should not wait until a large amount of specification is completed; sampling reviews should be held early, and frequently, to spot systemic problems early.
- DR7: A design review process should be carried out on a realistic amount of information and conducted at an effective rate. Don't so overwhelm reviewers that they become incapable of spotting problems.
- DR8: To benefit from feedback, the design review process should be done evolutionarily, as a long series of design reviews, each review deciding on the next planned evolutionary step.
- DR9: The real purpose of design reviews is not to approve a design as correct, but to uncover specific risks and specification defects.

These principles are not scientific laws. They are observations and opinions based on decades of personal experience and empirical data collected and published by clients. They are simply suggestions as to useful ways to think about reviews.

Engineer motivation:
Gist: Motivate and use of free time off
Type: Design idea
Impacts (Objectives): (engineering productivity, engineering costs)
Impacts (Costs): (staff costs, available engineering hours)
Definition: Offer all engineers up to 20 percent of their normal working hours per year as discretionary time off to invest in health, family, and knowledge (studies, write papers, go to conferences)
Source: Productivity Committee Report 1.4.3
Implementor: Human Resources Director

Figure 3 Example of a design specification showing some impacts (though no specific numeric estimates) for the design on the requirements

SQC Principles

Principle DR1: If the specifications are unclear, one is not ready to review whether the design is the "right thing" to do.

Have you ever actually counted the quantity of unclear and ambiguous expressions per page in a real specification? I get my clients to do this using SQC almost every week. The result is consistent and always provides an element of shock.

I define a specification defect as any violation of a set of specification rules. As a simple introduction to SQC, I ask a team of two to five people to select a random page of their "typical" specification and then spend about 15 minutes checking it individually, applying these two rules:

- Rule 1: The specification must be unambiguous to all in the intended readership.
- Rule 2: The specification must be clear enough to test for correct implementation.

For the first rule, it is not a matter of whether the people looking for defects understand the specification; they must role-play the weakest link in the set of people who might have to correctly understand it (for example, "Imagine you had just started here right out of school," or that "You were an Indian subcontractor in Bangalore"). They need to check that there is only one possible plausible interpretation.

I also ask the participants to judge whether the rule violations they find (the "specification defects") are major (or minor). Defects are major if it is judged *possible* (as opposed to *impossible*) that the faulty specification *could* cause something wrong to happen during systems engineering or in the operational system (for example, product faults, test case faults, procurement errors, estimation errors, software bugs, and delays).

Note that if the rules are strongly formulated, then it is less critical whom one selects to be a checker. Ideally, one can use less experienced people to carry out the SQC checking, and then bring in the more experienced people to conduct the actual review. This is because the experience of what to look for is built into the rules and corresponding checklists (of how to interpret the rules). The actual number of checkers is not critical from the point of view of measurement of conformance to standards. It does make a measurable difference, but this can be considered in adjusting the estimates of major defects per page.

Most people (for example, the writer of the specification and his or her peers) consistently manage to find between five and 15 defects in a single sample page of a specification within the 15 minutes.

From experience, I know that for a small team of two to five checkers, doubling the number of majors found by the checker who finds the most majors tends to reveal the total number found by the entire team. I also know that the initial effectiveness in such a situation for finding majors is in the range of 25 percent to 35 percent. (This is partly due to the time allowed, and partly due to the source information available.) For the sake of simplicity, say it is 33 percent.

So if 15 majors were found, I would estimate that there were $15 \times 2 \times 3 = 90$ defects on the single sample page. This means there are about 90 potential misunderstandings of a specification per page. This is "normal" technical specification "pollution," but it is not a good or necessary basis on which to decide if the design itself is a good one. Any one of those major defects alone is capable of corrupting one's understanding of a whole design, and capable of making one's judgments, in a design review, worthless.

The bad news is that this level of majors per page will continue to persist unless management changes the game. The good news is that it is possible to bring down the average level of majors per page by two orders of magnitude within weeks of doing the right things.

One can bring down the majors per page density by stating the specification rules (such as "clear" and "unambiguous"), and then training individual engineers to follow these simple rules. One does that by teaching the rules, and then making sure that rule violations are measured. Work is considered unacceptable when a defined level of pollution (such as one major per page) is exceeded. Under such conditions, an individual will learn at a rate of about 50 percent defect injection reduction per cycle of specify/check/correct (see Figure 4). We proved this initially in 1988 at Douglas Aircraft for hundreds of engineers work-

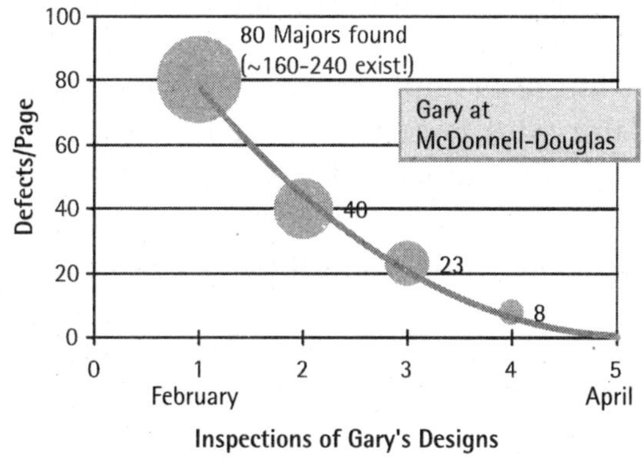

Figure 4 The individual engineer is generally capable of reducing the defect injection density by 50 percent per cycle of personal learning and feedback

ing on airplane drawings. We repeated it the year after at Boeing, and later we experienced this same improvement rate at Ericsson. It doesn't matter where or with which technology this is done, it works. Others, such as Raytheon Defense Electronics, have reported the same experience working within military software projects (Haley et al. 1995).

What does all this mean for design reviews? In summary, all specifications need to be quality controlled to make sure they are not polluted before one can seriously undertake a design review.

I suggest the need for at least three entry conditions into a design review:

- All requirement specifications have successfully exited on a numeric basis from SQC.
- All design specifications have successfully exited on a numeric basis from SQC using design specification rules.
- All design specifications have successfully exited on a numeric basis from SQC using design specification review rules.

I recommend setting the numeric level at "less than 1.0 estimated remaining major defect/page." Anything less is wasting the review team's time and project time. What quality levels does the current review process demand in its entry process?

Principle DR2: Individuals cannot review designs if they are unclear whether each specific design is mandatory (a design constraint, which is a requirement) or optional (one of many possible design solutions).

What most people title "Requirements" often includes some design specification, which is not actually part of the requirements. Only *design constraints* should be specified as part of the requirement specification: any design that is optional has no place there; it should be only in the design specification. (Requirements are the end states needed by stakeholders, irrespective of implementation detail. Design is a decision about the means of implementing those requirements in practice.)

Of course, mandatory designs (the required design constraints) must also have detailed design specifications. Individuals need to ensure they have the design specification for any mandatory design (clearly marked as mandatory), and that it is considered alongside the optional design.

Principle DR3: Design impacts must be calculated and submitted to a review; they cannot systematically be developed *during* the review.

There is no time in a design review to begin a process of collecting facts and making estimates about the multiple impacts on performance and costs of each design. The proper time to do that is before the review, not during it.

If the estimates are not made, this fact should be caught in the SQC preceding the review. Note that such SQC merely observes that such estimates are not made, or not made properly (for example, they lack any evidence).

Principle DR4: It is part of the purpose of a design review to identify any defective information in the design impact estimates.

See Figure 5 for an example of an impact estimation table containing some design impact estimates. (See Gilb 1998 for further details on the impact estimation process.)

The design reviewers are allowed to question the accuracy of the impact estimates, and the evidence and credibility claimed. The design reviewers are experts in their fields and should consider if they agree with the presented data.

Step Target Requirement	Step 1 Plan % (of target)	Actual %	Deviation %	Step 2 to Step 20 Plan %	Plan % cumulated to here	Step 21 [CA, NV, WA] plan %	Plan % cumulated to here	Step 22 [all others] plan %	Plan % cumulated to here
Performance 1	5	3	-2	40	43	40	83	-20	63
Performance 2	10	12	+2	50	62	30	92	60	152
Performance 3	20	13	-7	20	33	20	53	30	83
Cost A	1	3	+2	25	28	10	38	20	58
Cost B	4	6	+2	38	44	0	44	5	49

Figure 5 This is a conceptual example. Three goals (performance targets) and two resource targets are having real (% of impact needed to reach the target) impacts on the performance and cost attributes, and are tracked as steps are delivered. The same table is also being used to specify the impact estimates for the future planned steps. So at each step, the project can learn from the reality of the design impacts included on a step, and the deviation from design impact estimates.

SQC carried out prior to a design review is mainly concerned with finding out that the required impact estimation process for designs was apparently performed.

Principle DR5: Certain objective review criteria must be met prior to actually carrying out a review; otherwise, the review may be wasted.

In addition to making sure the design engineer has adhered to the design specification rules (see Figure 6), there needs to be a check against design specification review rules in preparation for a design review. Only if the design meets the design review rules should a review proceed.

Examples of Specification Rules for Design

AR1: Cost detail: The architecture must be specified in enough detail to permit at least correct order of magnitude impact estimation for costing.

AR2: Cost estimates: Estimates must be made and included as to the order of magnitude of all critical costs of the architecture (particularly for those resources that are budgeted requirements).

AR3: Performance detail: The architecture specification must include enough detail to allow order of magnitude correct estimation of the specification's impact on all specified performance goal levels (that is, all the qualities, resource savings, and work capacity requirements).

AR4: Performance estimates: Estimates will be included for the impacts on all the critical performance requirements, at correct order of magnitude.

AR5: Background detail for estimate: Each impact estimate must be supported by:

- The factual experiential evidence for the estimate
- The source of these facts
- The uncertainty boundaries/error margins (±%)
- A credibility rating (on a 0.0 to 1.0 scale)

These data ideally will be presented using an impact estimation table.

AR6: Additional data: The architectural specification must include additional specification as detailed in the current architecture specification template. This will include stakeholders, detailed design reference (if any), QC level, review approval level, risks, issues, and dependencies.

Figure 6 Some examples of design specification rules. These would be used in an SQC of a design specification. Rule AR6 would likely be expanded into several distinct rules. Only if the defect level was sufficiently low (say, less than one remaining major defect per page) would the specification be submitted for further SQC to see if the specification was ready for review.

Principle DR6: The review process should not wait until a large amount of specification is completed; sampling reviews should be held early and frequently to spot systemic problems early.

Once on a German Air Traffic Control project carried out in Sweden, I saw the signatures of seven managers approving the detailed logic of the air traffic management: 40,000 pages of logic design (the next stage was the programming). Later that day, using the sampling process described earlier, they found 19 major defects in a random representative sample of three of the 40,000 pages of logic design. This was, of course, about one-third of what was actually present in the pages. Their divisional director took 30 minutes to personally check the 19 majors while the eight of us waited in his office, and agreed that they were serious. At about 20 majors per page present, that meant there were about (20 × 40,000) 800,000 majors *approved* for coding by the management review committee. I asked signature no. 3 on the list why he signed off on what we now recognized was a very polluted document. His reply will not surprise the experienced reader: "Because the other two signed it before me." This is why I am skeptical about review committee approvals!

We had many interesting discussions on the basis of this finding. Mainly, if they had bothered to do some simple samples early, for example, after 100 pages had been written, they might have been able to prevent most of this work from being totally wasted. In other words, if reviews had been carried out earlier, and if they had demanded numeric quality controls were in place, then it is unlikely that the defect injection would have been allowed to continue at such a level.

So there is a lesson to be learned here about early sampling of partial work. Don't wait for the entire specification before doing some basic quality control on it—a point I will return to toward the end of this article.

Principle DR7: A design review process should be carried out on a realistic amount of information and conducted at an effective rate. Don't so overwhelm reviewers that they become incapable of spotting problems.

If an attempt is made to review too much design at once, then the analysis is unlikely to be done sufficiently, and the truth is likely to be obscured. If 40 or more (try 40,000 pages, as in the previous example) of design specifications are delivered at once to a design review, then the review group will not have time to study, discuss, or criticize anything in detail. The reality of risks and problems will be lost and, as a result, the review team will not learn about its misjudgments. The project or product will probably fail and the team will not be clear about the cause of failure.

I suggest only feeding a small volume of ideas into a design review committee so that:

- The committee has a chance to do its work properly.
- One can better ensure that any preparatory work has been done properly.

I would suggest one page of design per committee hour as a rough guide.

Deciding what is a realistic sample is the responsibility of the SQC team leader. Of course, he or she should ask questions of the author and the design team to ensure they have a representative sample. One key point to grasp is that if a small sample shows a high defect density, then it is not worth continuing—there clearly is a problem that the document author has to address. Of course, if the sample is "clean" that doesn't imply the entire specification is fine. It does demonstrate, however, that the author knows and conforms to the design specification rules.

Principle DR8: To benefit from feedback, the design review process should be done evolutionarily, as a long series of design reviews, each review deciding on the next planned evolutionary step.

Ideally, most projects should be carried out using evolutionary project management (Evo). The critical distinction between Evo methods and their generic cousins iterative and incremental is that evolutionary processes (which are both iterative and incremental, too) gather facts about impacts, analyze those facts, and change behavior, if necessary, in order to succeed in the higher-level objectives.

Evo means testing the stakeholder effects of a design idea in the field. I suggest maybe 50 ideas, one a week for a year of development effort. The design review committee becomes a learning process; that is, the review team will benefit from the Evo cycle experience feedback concerning the implementation of each previous design, and the team will learn quickly and realistically, by real experience, how to evaluate designs.

Principle DR9: The real purpose of design reviews is not to approve a design as correct, but to uncover specific risks and specification defects.

Design reviews are about risk analysis, and one must build a much better foundation in order to reliably carry out that function. This is where Evo methods are helpful. If individuals do not implement their designs evolutionarily, they might never learn that a particular one of them was their downfall. Even if they do learn which one it was, it is probably too late to do anything about it on that particular project.

If individuals are using Evo, a review could even deliberately decide to implement a high-risk step to find out the results. It is the benefits obtained that count; total avoidance of risk is not the aim!

The key benefit of more frequent reviews is that risk is made more manageable. This might mean that lower-level management can be empowered to make the review decisions. Alternatively, it could mean the design review itself might become obsolete, since reality is going to give designers more reliable advice than any committee of experts.

Implementing SQC

The Costs of SQC

So what are the costs of implementing SQC? In an organization already using SQC, the additional costs would be in deriving the specification review rules and carrying out the additional SQCs.

An organization unfamiliar with SQC could refer to Chapter 2 of the book *Software Inspection* (Gilb and Graham 1993). The main message is that the measurable benefits of using SQC outweigh the direct costs; for example, Haley et al. (1995) report benefits outweighing costs by 8 to 1. The direct costs are the training of the SQC team leaders, which takes about a week, and the operational costs of running the SQCs, which is about one hour of review per page (300 words) of text per reviewer.

For effective reviews, four to five reviewers should carry out the checking. For efficient reviews, two or three reviewers should be used. SQC should always be cost effective; otherwise, it should not be used.

Checking Rate

One critical factor for successful SQC is that the correct checking rate must be adhered to. If SQC is carried out at too fast a checking rate then some defects that should be found will not be found, which will give a spurious quality level. Too slow is equally bad, as that will make the SQC less cost effective.

Rate of Quality Improvement

SQC can reduce defect density by one to two orders of magnitude (from 100-plus to 10 to less than one per page) in six to 30 months for an organization, but it operates at the level of motivated individuals. New employees have to go through the process from their initial level of technical writing capability in relation to the defined rules that apply.

Level of Quality Improvement

A typical and simple example of the reduction of defect densities, which was cited in (Haley et al. 1995), was a factor of about three. Many other studies confirm such substantial reductions, for example, Hewlett-Packard (Grady and Van Slack 1994) and Ericsson (MacFarland 1998).

Management Support

One key factor required for successful SQC is strong support for SQC from management. Quantified exit criteria must be set and adhered to, such as a maximum of one remaining defect per page.

Limitations of the Defined Rules

The main limitation of the method is that it is limited by the defined rules. The ability to detect issues is dependent on the quality of the rules. One way of ensuring the coverage of the rules is to separate the different types of rules into different rule sets. That way it is clearer to everyone the extent of the checking in each different dimension; for example, one rule set can focus on design costs, another on the relevance of the design specifications to the requirements, and another on architectural considerations.

Deadline Pressure

People often are worried about introducing additional tasks into their systems development process, but SQC can actually help reduce schedule pressures by reducing rework! Using SQC at early stages in the development cycle means that some defects are removed earlier. This is beneficial because the later in the development cycle that a defect is detected, the more it costs to correct. Even better, by identifying the causes of repetitive defect insertion, one can put in place corrective actions (by process improvement), and actually eliminate certain defects. The documented reduction in rework is about 40 percent (Gilb and Graham 1993; Haley et al. 1995).

Agile or Simplified SQC

By using such techniques as sampling, SQC can be implemented in an agile systems development environment. I have developed a cut-down, simplified version of SQC, which has been successfully used at one of the largest financial institutions in the world. The initial results after six months were a reduction from on average 88 major defects per page to about 11 defects per page. The expectation is to reduce by another order of magnitude within the next one to two years.

The main ideas behind "agile" SQC are:

- A shift of focus from cleaning up all the defects on a page to defect density measurement by sampling
- A shift from defect correction to motivating specification writers to follow the defined rules
- Use of the measurement and exit process to motivate specification writers to change behavior

This cut-down version also has benefits for smaller organizations. The agile SQC version of the method is designed to work with two people and one single sample page, with an elapse time of approximately 30 minutes.

- The agile SQC version is presented in Figure 7. Note, there are several limitations to this simplified process:

—It does not directly deal with process improvement.

—It is only a small sample so the accuracy is not as good as a full or larger sample.

—The team will not have time or experience to get up to speed on the rules and the concept of major defect.

—A small team of two people does not have the known effectiveness of three or four people.

Agile or Simplified SQC Process

Tag: Simplified SQC.	Version: October 7, 2004.	Owner: Tom@Gilb.com.	Status: Draft.

Entry conditions

- A group of two or more suitable people* to carry out Simplified SQC is assembled in a meeting.
- These people have sufficient time to complete a Simplified SQC. Total elapse time: 30 to 60 minutes.
- There is a trained SQC team leader at the meeting to manage the process.

Procedure

P1: Identify checkers: Two people, maybe more, should be identified to carry out the checking.

P2: Select rules: The group identifies about three rules to use for checking the specification. (Some favorites are clarity ("clear enough to test"), unambiguousness ("to the intended readership"), and completeness ("compared to sources").

P3: Choose sample(s): The group then selects sample(s) of about one page in length (300 non-commentary words). Choosing a page at random can add credibility, as long as it is representative of the content subject to quality control. The group should decide whether all the checkers should use the same sample or whether different samples are more appropriate.

P4: Instruct checkers: The SQC team leader briefly instructs the checkers about the rules, the checking rate, and how to document any issues and determine if they are major defects (majors).

P5: Check sample: The checkers use between 10 and 30 minutes to check their sample against the selected rules. Checkers should "mark up" their copy of the document as they check (underlining issues, and classifying them as major or not). At the end of checking, checkers should count the number of possible majors they have found in their page.

P6: Report results: The checkers each report to the group their number of possible majors. The SQC team leader leads a discussion to determine how many of the possible majors are likely to be majors. Checkers determine their number of majors and report it.

P7: Analyze results: The SQC team leader extrapolates from the findings the number of majors in a single page (about six times** the most majors found by a single person, or alternatively three times the unique majors found by a two-to-four person team). This gives the major defect density. If using more than one sample, average the densities found by the group in different pages. The SQC team leader then multiplies this average major defects per page density by the total number of pages to get the total number of major defects in the specification.

P8: Decide action: If the number of majors per page found is large (10 majors or more), then there is little point in the group doing anything, except determining how they are going to get someone to write the specification properly. There is no economic point in looking at the other pages to find all the defects, or correcting the majors already found. There are too many majors not found.

P9: Suggest cause: Choose any major defect and think for a minute why it happened. Then give a short sentence, or better still a few words, to capture the verdict.

Exit Conditions

- Exit if less than five majors per page extrapolated total density, or if an action plan to "rewrite" has been agreed.

Notes:

* A suitable person is anyone who can correctly interpret the rules and the concept of "major."

** Concerning the factor of multiplying by 6 : We have found by experience (Gilb and Graham 1993) that the total unique defects found by a team is approximately twice that of the number found by the person who finds the most defects in the team. We also find that inexperienced teams using Simplified SQC seem to have about one-third effectiveness in identifying the major defects that are actually there. So 2 x 3 = 6 is the factor we use (Or 3x the number of unique majors found by the team).

Figure 7 The "agile" or simplified SQC process.

—One will not have the basis for making corrections to the entire specification.

—The checking will not have been carried out against all the possible source documents. (Usually, in the simplified SQC process, no source documents are used and memory is relied on. While this means that the checking is not nearly as accurate, it does considerably speed up the process.)

However, if the sample turns up a defects density estimation of 50 to 150 major defects per page (which is normal), this is more than sufficient to convince the people participating and their managers that they have a serious problem.

The immediate long-term solution to the problem of high defect density is neither to remove the defects from the document, nor to change the corporate process. The most effective practical solution is to make sure each individual specification writer takes the defect density criteria (and its "no exit" consequence) seriously. They will then learn to follow the rules and, as a result, will reduce their personal defect injection rate. On average, a personal defect injection rate should fall by about 50 percent after each experience of using the SQC process. Widespread use of SQC will result in large numbers of engineers learning to follow the rules.

Conclusions

Any design specifications input into a design review must be of known high clarity and completeness: they should have successfully exited from SQC using both design specification rules, and then later using design specification review rules.

Design reviews should be held throughout the life of a system. They should be held at early stages on samples of the design work to ensure initial problems and misunderstandings are detected as soon as possible. Reviews should also be held at appropriately frequent intervals to avoid giving reviewers too much to review at one time.

For an evolutionary project, reviews should be held to decide/agree on each "next" evolutionary step. By utilizing feedback, reviewers will learn more about their mistakes and successes, and any actions required to correct/improve project progress can be taken.

A design review should not be an informal management meeting to collect unfocused opinions under pressure.

REFERENCES

Gilb, T., and D. Graham. 1993. *Software inspection*. Reading, Mass.: Addison-Wesley.

Gilb, Tom. 1998. Impact estimation tables: Understanding complex technology quantitatively. *Crosstalk*. (December). See http://www.stsc.hill.af.mil/crosstalk/1998/12/index.html/.

Grady, R. B., and T. Van Slack. 1994. Key lessons in achieving widespread inspection use. *IEEE Software* (July): 46–58. This paper also appears in (Wheeler, Brykczynski, and Meeson 1996). This paper is available for a fee at http://csdl.computer.org/comp/mags/so/1994/04/s4046abs.htm.

Haley, T., B. Ireland, ed., Wojtaszek, D. Nash, and R. Dion. 1995. *Raytheon Electronic Systems experience in Software Process Improvement*, Raytheon. This paper is available online at http://www.sei.cmu.edu/publications/documents/95.reports/95.tr.017.html/.

Johnson, J., K. D. Boucher, K. Connors, and J. Robinson. 2001. Collaborating on project success. *Software Magazine* (February).

MacFarland, R. 1998. Improvement program spreading effective use of reviews and inspections (R&I) throughout the switching organization of a multinational telecommunications company. Presented at Eurostar 98 Software Testing Analysis and Review Conference.

Morris, P. W. G. 1994. *The management of projects*. London: Thomas Telford.

Taylor, A. 2001. IT projects sink or swim. *BCS Review*. See URL: http://www.bcs.org.uk/review/2001/articles/itservices/projects.htm/.

BIOGRAPHY

Tom Gilb was born in Pasadena, Calif. He emigrated to London in 1956 and to Norway in 1958. He took his first job with IBM in 1958, and became a freelance consultant in 1960. He coined the term "software metrics," and is credited as the main inspiration for SEI CMM Level 4.

His interests include corporate strategy, requirements engineering, inspection, and evolutionary methods. He has worked with numerous multinational clients, including BAE Systems, Sun Microsystems, CitiGroup, Philips Medical Systems, Nokia, Ericsson, HP, Intel, Microsoft, British Airports Authority, Symbian, and Canon.

He is the author of nine books. More recent books include *Principles of Software Engineering Management* (1988) and *Software Inspection* (coauthored with Dorothy Graham in 1993). His latest book, *Competitive Engineering,* was published in July 2005. Many of his current papers are available on his Web site, www.Gilb.com. Gilb can be reached at: Tom@Gilb.com.

Quality in an Agile World

Scott Ambler, Ambysoft, Inc.

Quality is an inherent aspect of true agile software development. The majority of agilists take a test-driven approach to development where they write a unit test before they write the domain code to fulfill that unit test, with the end result being that they have a regression unit test suite at all times. They also consider acceptance tests as first-class requirements artifact, not only promoting regular stakeholder validation of their work but also their active inclusion in the modeling effort itself. Agilists refactor their source code and database schema to keep their work at the highest possible quality at all times. The challenge for quality professionals is that agilists work in a highly collaborative and evolutionary (iterative and incremental) manner, often requiring traditional quality professionals to change their approach.

Key words: agile model driven development, agile software development, collaborative development, evolutionary, incremental development, iterative development, refactoring, software processes, test-driven development

Introduction

Modern software processes are evolutionary, iterative, and incremental in nature. This includes processes such as Rational Unified Process (RUP) (Kruchten 2004), Extreme Programming (XP) (Beck 2000), Enterprise Unified Process (EUP) (Ambler, Nalbone, and Vizdos 2005), and rapid application development (RAD), to name a few. Furthermore, many modern processes are agile, which for the sake of simplicity I will characterize as both evolutionary and highly collaborative in nature. The fundamental nature of software development is changing, and quality professionals must change with it. In this article I introduce readers to common agile software development techniques and argue that they lead to software that proves in practice to be of much higher quality than what traditional software teams usually deliver. It is common to say that agilists are "quality infected," and that the greater emphasis on quality implies a changed and perhaps even smaller role for quality professionals on agile software development projects.

Why are developers adopting evolutionary, and more often, agile software processes? Over the years developers have discovered that traditional software development processes, in particular the "well-defined" prescriptive processes, work poorly in practice (Larman 2004). First, the Chaos report, published by the Standish Group (http://www.standishgroup.com), still shows a significant failure rate within the industry, indicating that prescriptive processes simply aren't fulfilling their promise. Second, it appears that most developers do not want to adopt prescriptive processes and will find ways to undermine efforts to adopt them, either consciously or subconsciously. Third, the "big design up front" (BDUF) approaches to software development, where significant modeling and documentation occurs before a single line of code is written, are incredibly risky in practice because they don't easily support change or feedback. For example, one might build what was defined in the specifications, but if the specifications don't reflect what people actually require then there is serious trouble. This risk is often ignored, if it is recognized at all, by the people promoting these approaches. Fourth, most prescriptive processes promote activities that are only slightly related to the actual development of software. In short, the bureaucrats have taken over in many traditional information technology (IT) organizations. Something has to give.

The Agile Movement

To address the challenges inherent to traditional development a group of 17 methodologists formed the Agile Software Development Alliance (http://www.agilealliance.org), often referred to simply as the Agile Alliance, in February 2001. Although all members of this group came from different backgrounds they were able to come to an agreement on issues that methodologists typically do not agree upon. They concluded that to succeed at software development one must focus on people-oriented issues and follow development techniques that readily support change.

The "agile movement" started when they published their manifesto of four values and 12 principles (see sidebar, "The Values and Principles of the Agile Alliance"). A software process is considered agile when it conforms to these values and principles. Agile software processes include XP, Scrum, dynamic system development method (DSDM), the Crystal family, feature-driven development (FDD), agile modeling (AM), and the agile data (AD) method. Although XP is clearly the most popular agile process, there are a variety to choose from.

Just as there are common development techniques and concepts, such as code inspections and data modeling, within the traditional world, there are also common development techniques within the agile world. Interestingly, many of these techniques are focused on the creation and delivery of high-quality software. These agile techniques and concepts include:

- Refactoring
- Test-driven development (TDD)
- Tests replace traditional artifacts
- Agile model driven development (AMDD)

Some Definitions

This article uses the terms collaborative, incremental, and iterative development, and it is important to understand how each term is used:

1. **Collaborative development.** When a team takes a collaborative approach they actively strive to find ways to work together effectively; teams should even try to ensure that project stakeholders such as business customers are active team members. They should strive to adopt the "hottest" communication technique applicable to their situation: prefer face-to-face conversation around a whiteboard to a telephone call, prefer a telephone call to sending an e-mail, and prefer an e-mail to sending someone a detailed document. The better the communication and collaboration within a software development team, the greater its chance of success (Cockburn 2002).
2. **Incremental development.** With an incremental approach a team organizes its system into a series of releases instead of one big one.
3. **Iterative development.** Working iteratively, a team does a little bit of an activity such as modeling, testing, coding, or deployment at a time, and then does another little bit, then another, and so on. This is different than a serial approach where they identify all of the requirements they are going to implement, create a detailed design, implement to that design, test and, finally, deploy the system.

Refactoring

Refactoring (Fowler 1999) is a disciplined way to make small changes to source code to improve its design, making it easier to work with. A critical aspect of a refactoring is that it retains the behavioral semantics of the code—developers neither add nor remove anything when they refactor, they merely improve its quality. An example refactoring would be to rename the getPersons() operation to getPeople(). To implement this refactoring they must change the operation definition and then change every invocation of this operation throughout the application code. A refactoring isn't complete until the code runs again as before.

Similarly, a database refactoring (Ambler 2003a) is a simple change to a database schema that improves its design while retaining both its behavioral and informational semantics. Developers could refactor either structural aspects of the database schema, such as table and view definitions, or functional aspects, such as stored procedures and triggers. When they refactor their database schema, not only must they rework the schema itself but also the external systems, such as business applications or data extracts, which are coupled to their schema. Database refactorings are clearly more difficult to implement than code refactorings; therefore, developers need to be careful.

Many agile developers, and in particular extreme programmers (XPers), consider refactoring to be a primary development practice. It is just as common to refactor a bit of code as it is to introduce an "if" statement or a loop. Agile developers will refactor their code mercilessly because they understand that they are most productive when they are working on high-quality source code; therefore, they will refactor their code whenever needed. When agilists have a new feature to add to their code, the first question they ask is, "Is this code the best design possible that enables me to add this feature?" If the answer is "yes," then they add the feature. If the answer is "no," they first refactor their code to make it the best design possible and then add the feature. On the surface this sounds like a lot of work, but in practice if they start with high-quality source code, and then refactor it to keep it so, this approach works incredibly well.

Test Driven Development (TDD)

TDD (Beck 2003; Astels 2003), also known as test-first programming or test-first development, is an evolutionary (iterative and incremental) approach to programming where agile software developers must first write a test that fails before they write new functional code. The steps of TDD, as shown in Figure 1, are:

1. Quickly add a test, basically just enough code so that the tests now fail.
2. Run the tests, often the complete test suite, although for sake of speed they may run only a subset to ensure that the new test does in fact fail.
3. Update the functional code so it passes the new test.
4. Run the tests again.
5. If the tests fail return to step 3.
6. Once the tests pass the next step is to start over (agilists may also want to refactor any duplication out of their design as needed).

There are several advantages of TDD for agile software development. First, TDD forces developers to think about what new functional code should do before they write it—in other words, to do detailed design just in time (JIT) before writing the code. Second, it ensures that agile developers have testing code available to validate their work, ensuring that they test as often and early as possible. Third, it gives them the courage to refactor their code to keep it the highest quality possible, because they know there is a test suite in place that will detect if they have "broken" anything as the result of refactoring.

Tests Replace Traditional Artifacts

When agile developers become "test infected" they start to realize that tests are truly first-class artifacts that need to be developed and maintained throughout

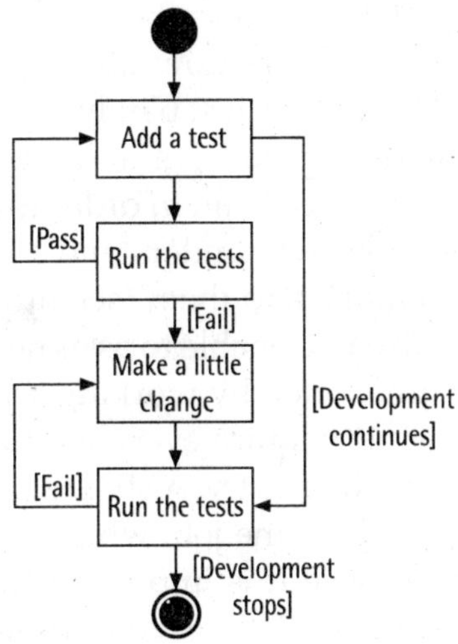

Figure 1 Test-driven development

a project. They also realize that tests, when created properly, are more than just tests. For example, agilists consider acceptance tests to be first-class requirement artifacts—if an acceptance test defines a criteria that the system must exhibit, then clearly it is a requirement. Another common philosophy is that unit tests are detailed design artifacts. With a TDD-based approach agilists write their unit test before writing their source code; in other words, they think through what the source code must do before they write it. The implication is that a unit test, when written before the domain code, effectively becomes a design specification for that portion of code.

These philosophies can dramatically reduce the amount of work agilists need to do. The AM methodology version 2 (http://www.agilemodeling.com) includes a practice called Single Source Information, which advises them to record information once, ideally in the best place possible. Often, the best place to record technical information is in their tests and source code, not in voluminous documentation that rarely gets updated. Furthermore, because the agile developers are creating far less documentation, their traceability needs are thereby reduced, once again reducing their overall work effort.

Agile Model Driven Development (AMDD)

Some people may have heard that agile software developers don't model, but frankly nothing can be further from the truth. They still model, they just don't write as much documentation because they know it is not a good investment of their time. Because they work closely with their project stakeholders, they discover that they don't need a lot of documentation telling them what they are doing; instead, they simply look for themselves. Because they don't need to write as much documentation they can instead focus their efforts on building high-quality working software.

The agile approach to modeling is described in the AMDD method (Ambler 2003b; Ambler 2004). AMDD describes how developers and stakeholders can work together to create models that are just barely good enough. It assumes that each individual has some modeling skills, or at least some domain knowledge that he or she will apply together in a team in order to get the job done. It is reasonable to assume that developers will understand a handful of modeling techniques, but not all of those available to them (see http://www.agilemodeling.com/artifacts for a list). It is also reasonable to assume that people are willing to learn new techniques over time, often by working with someone who already has those skills. AMDD does not require everyone to be a modeling expert, it just requires him or her to be willing to try. AMDD also allows people to use the most appropriate modeling tool for the job, which is often a simple tool such as a whiteboards or paper, because it is important to find ways to communicate effectively, not document comprehensively. There is nothing wrong with sophisticated CASE tools in the hands of people who know how to use them, but AMDD does not depend on such tools.

The life cycle for AMDD is shown in Figure 2. Each box represents a development activity. The initial upfront modeling activity occurs during the first week or so of a project. The goal of this activity is to identify the initial requirements and a potential architecture for the system. The end result might be a stack of index cards or a spreadsheet of point-form text representing the initial requirements and some sketches representing the architecture. It is not necessary to have comprehensive documentation to start development; developers

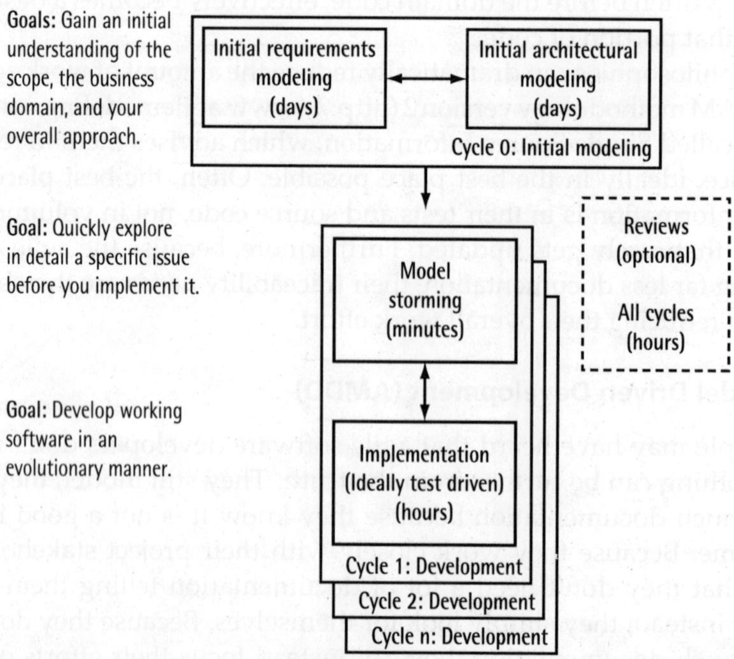

Figure 2 Agile model driven development life cycle

just need a good idea as to the scope of the system and how they think they are going to implement it. The details come later in model storming sessions, where they model JIT and just enough to address the issue at hand. Perhaps developers will get together with a stakeholder to analyze the requirement they are currently working on, create a sketch together at a whiteboard for a few minutes, and then go back to coding. Or perhaps they will sketch out an approach to implement a requirement, once again spending several minutes doing so. Or perhaps they will use a modeling tool to model in detail and then generate the code for that requirement. Model storming sessions should not take more than 15 to 20 minutes.

The Values and Principles of the Agile Alliance

The Agile Alliance developed a manifesto defining four values for encouraging better ways of developing software. These values indicate preferences, not alternatives, encouraging a focus on certain areas but not eliminating others. While developers should value the concepts on the right-hand side (for example, processes and tools), they should value the things on the left-hand side (for example, individuals and iteractions) even more. The four values are:

1. **Individuals and interactions** *over* **processes and tools.** The most important factors to consider are the people and how they work together, because if developers don't get that right the best tools and processes won't be of any use.
2. **Working software** *over* **comprehensive documentation.** The primary goal of software development is to create software, not documents; otherwise, it would be called documentation development. Documentation has its place, and written properly it is a valuable guide for understanding how and why a system is built and how to work with the system.
3. **Customer collaboration** *over* **contract negotiation.** Only one's stakeholders can state what they want. They likely do not have the skills to exactly specify the system, they likely won't get it right at first, and they will likely change their minds. Working together with customers is hard, but that's the reality of the job. Having a contract with customers is important, but a contract is not a substitute for communication.
4. **Responding to change** *over* **following a plan.** Change is a reality of software development, a reality that the software process must reflect. People change their priorities for a variety of reasons, their

understanding of the problem domain changes as they see the developer's work, the business environment changes, as does technology. Although one needs a project plan, it must be malleable and it can be very simple (unlike many Gantt charts seen in the past).

Because the agile values are not sufficient to form a foundational philosophy for software development, the Agile Alliance also identified 12 principles to which an agile software process must conform:

1. Our highest priority is to satisfy the customer through early and continuous delivery of valuable software.
2. Welcome changing requirements, even late in development. Agile processes harness change for the customer's competitive advantage.
3. Deliver working software frequently, from a couple of weeks to a couple of months, with a preference to the shorter time scale.
4. Business people and developers must work together daily throughout the project.
5. Build projects around motivated individuals. Give them the environment and support they need, and trust them to get the job done.
6. The most efficient and effective method of conveying information to and within a development team is face-to-face conversation.
7. Working software is the primary measure of progress.
8. Agile processes promote sustainable development. The sponsors, developers, and users should be able to maintain a constant pace indefinitely.
9. Continuous attention to technical excellence and good design enhances agility.
10. Simplicity, the art of maximizing the amount of work not done, is essential.
11. The best architectures, requirements, and designs emerge from self-organizing teams.
12. At regular intervals, the team reflects on how to become more effective and then tunes and adjusts its behavior accordingly.

An interesting aspect of Figure 2 is that it indicates that model reviews are optional (Ambler 2003c). Is this heresy? No, it is just common sense. With an AMDD approach developers follow practices such as model with others, collective ownership, and apply modeling standards, which say one should never model alone, that everyone should have access to every project artifact, and that one should follow a common set of modeling and documentation conventions, respectively. These two practices, combined with the highly collaborative environment common to agile projects and the desire to work with the right people at the right time effectively, result in "mini-reviews" occurring whenever one is working. With AMDD developers are never in a position where one person works on an artifact, nor where a subset of people work on "their" artifacts. Better yet, everyone works to the same set of conventions (with collective ownership it can't be any other way). In practice, because developers are doing in-progress reviews as they are working they quickly find that reviewing things after the fact offers little value.

It is important to point out that AMDD works on both large and small projects. If needed, one can take an agile approach to architecture (Ambler 2002) to ensure that all of the subteams involved in a larger effort work to the same vision.

Implications for Quality Professionals

There are several interesting implications of agile software development for quality professionals:

1. **Greater quality implies less need for quality assurance activities.** Higher-quality code implies less need for quality assurance activities, such as reviews and inspections, elsewhere in the life cycle. Agilists are quality infected; they have accepted what the quality assurance community has been saying for decades, and they are actively developing high-quality system artifacts as a result. The implication is that they will find that they can start diverting quality assurance resources away from agile projects and focus more on traditional projects where the risk of low-quality work is much higher.
2. **Get used to "incomplete" artifacts.** Models, documents, and source code evolve over time. The only time when agilists can honestly say that something is done is when they are ready to release it into production. For example, they won't have a finalized requirements document from which to develop test cases until the very end of the project. The implication is that if they are going to be involved with agile software projects then they need to get used to working with in-progress artifacts.

3. **Become a generalizing specialist.** A critical concept is that agilists need to move away from being narrowly focused specialists to become more of what I like to call generalizing specialists (Ambler 2003d). A generalizing specialist is someone with one or more technical specialties who actively seeks to gain new skills in his or her existing specialties as well as in other areas. A person needs one or more specialties so he or she can add value to the team, but one needs a general understanding of the software process and of the business domain so he or she can interact effectively with others on the team. With evolutionary approaches to development there is no longer room to invest several hours, let alone days or weeks, on a given activity. One does a little bit of requirements elicitation, then some analysis and design, then some implementation. Specialists who want to focus on one narrow task, such as facilitating a review, will not be very effective in this environment.

Conclusion

These ideas are not new, but their popularity is. Agile software development is real, it works, and it's here to stay. Agilists are arguably taking to heart what quality professionals have been saying for decades, and because of that the role of quality professionals now needs to evolve to reflect this new reality. The IT industry is undergoing yet another paradigm shift. Are you willing to shift with it?

REFERENCES

Ambler, S. W. 2002. Agile modeling: Effective practices for extreme programming and the unified process. New York: John Wiley and Sons.

Ambler, S. W. 2003a. Agile database techniques: Effective strategies for the agile software developer. New York: John Wiley and Sons.

Ambler, S. W. 2003b. Agile model driven development. See URL: http://www.agilemodeling.com/essays/amdd.htm.

Ambler, S. W. 2003c. Model reviews: Best practice or process smell? See URL: http://www.agilemodeling.com/essays/modelReviews.htm.

Ambler, S. W. 2003d. Generalizing specialists: Improving your IT career skills. See URL: http://www.agilemodeling.com/essays/generalizingSpecialists.htm.

Ambler, S. W. 2004. The object primer, 3rd edition: Agile model driven development with UML 2. New York: Cambridge University Press.

Ambler, S. W., J. Nalbone, and M. J. Vizdos. 2005. The enterprise unified process: Extending the rational unified process. Upper Saddle River, N.J.: Prentice Hall PTR.

Astels, D. 2003. Test driven development: A practical guide. Upper Saddle River, N.J.: Prentice Hall.

Beck, K. 2000. Extreme programming explained—Embrace change. Reading, Mass.: Addison-Wesley Longman, Inc.

Beck, K. 2003. Test-driven development: By example. Boston: Addison-Wesley.

Cockburn, A. 2002. Agile software development. Reading, Mass: Addison-Wesley Longman, Inc.

Fowler, M. 1999. Refactoring: Improving the design of existing code. Menlo Park, Calif.: Addison-Wesley Longman, Inc.

Kruchten, P. 2004. The rational unified process, 3rd edition. Reading, Mass.: Addison-Wesley Longman, Inc.

Larman, C. 2004. Agile and iterative development: A manager's guide. Boston: Addison-Wesley.

Palmer, S. R., and J. M. Felsing. 2002. A practical guide to feature-driven development. Upper Saddle River, N.J.: Prentice Hall PTR.

BIOGRAPHY

Scott W. Ambler is the Practice Leader Agile Development within IBM's Methods group. He is founder and thought leader of the Agile Modeling (http://www.agilemodeling.com), Agile Data (http://www.agiledata.org), and Enterprise Unified Process (http://www.enterpriseunifiedprocess.com) methodologies. He helps organizations adopt and tailor these processes to meet their exact needs as well as provides training and mentoring in these techniques.

Ambler is the coauthor of several books, including *Agile Modeling* (John Wiley & Sons), *The Elements of UML 2.0 Style* (Cambridge University Press), and the forthcoming *Database Refactoring* (Prentice Hall PTR). Ambler is a contributing editor with *Software Development* magazine (http://www.sdmagazine.com) and his personal page is http://www.ambysoft.com/scottAmbler.html. He can be reached by e-mail at swa@ambysoft.com.

PART IV

Program and Project Management

Software is typically developed in a constrained environment. We speak of the "iron triangle" in which schedule, budget, and deliverables are in tension and undergoing trade-offs. Is it really necessary to settle for two out of three among these constraints? Sadly, there is a specialized discipline for dealing with "runaway projects." Even more sadly, the conventional measure of a project reaching "runaway" status is that it is one year late and at double the original budget. But how does a project get to be one year late? One day at a time. The plan-do-check-act cycle should certainly be applied throughout any development project. Risk management can be an overarching approach to all these concerns. "Today's risks are tomorrow's problems." What is the likelihood of an unfavorable situation occurring? If it does occur, what are the consequences? Identifying risks and then intervening at the most significant leverage points is the goal of good project management practice.

We begin this section with "Creating Accurate Estimates and Realistic Schedules" by Steven Rakitin. How does one address the persistent difficulty of estimating tasks, building schedules, and then meeting those schedules? The author provides insight into why estimates and schedules are usually wrong and then describes a technique that has proved useful in providing more accurate estimates and realistic schedules. He proposes the use of sticky notes to visualize scheduling forward. Much depends on successful team communication. By following an approach that differentiates "must haves" from "wants," Rakitin shows how organizations can more properly conduct development projects. He concludes that management plays a key role in helping to create a culture of accountability, thus improving productivity, morale, customer satisfaction, and the bottom line.

The next article picks up the problem of over-commitment and under-delivery. Neil Potter and Mary Sakry are concerned about the attitude of "We Must Overcommit—We Must Win Business." If one is focused on trying to gain a new customer, "Sure, we can do that," can appear to be the most appropriate reaction when the customer asks for anything. However, this response so often leads to over-commitment, project chaos, financial loss, and unhappy customers—the exact opposite of what is desired. The authors see two distinct camps of project management. Camp One believes that "it is not realistic to make realistic commitments." Camp Two believes that "it is not realistic to make unrealistic commitments." The article describes how to overcome the common intuitive thinking of Camp One with the counterintuitive solutions found in Camp Two.

How does one best manage the testing that must be completed for a project? "A Test Manager's Guide to Risks Analysis and Management," by Rex Black, probes that question. Testing any real-world system is potentially an infinite task. Of this infinite set of possible tests, test managers need to focus on the most significant risks to system quality. These are the potential failures that are likely to occur in real-world use or would cost a lot if they did occur. This article includes a comparison of five risk-analysis techniques: informal, standards-based, cost of exposure, failure modes and effects, and hazard analysis. Through case studies and a general-purpose process, the author shows how risk analysis provides a foundation for smart test design and development, as well as a continuing basis throughout a project to reassess and manage the risks to system quality.

Creating Accurate Estimates and Realistic Schedules

Steven R. Rakitin, Software Quality Consulting, Inc.

The ability of an organization to accurately estimate tasks, build realistic schedules, and then meet those schedules is critical. Yet few organizations have demonstrated the ability to do this consistently. As a result, many software development and appraisal groups have little or no credibility when it comes to estimating and scheduling. Organizations may be deficient because of a lack of training, inability to manage commitments made to customers, poorly defined requirements, or lack of management support. Some organizations believe project management tools can improve their estimating and scheduling abilities. Unfortunately, tools cannot solve this problem—identifying and implementing best practices can. This article describes a technique based on team communication that has proved to be a useful method for estimating and scheduling the work required to develop and evaluate software products.

Key words: estimating, project management, scheduling, team communication, Wideband Delphi Method, Yellow Sticky Note Method

Introduction

The ability of an organization to produce accurate estimates, build realistic schedules, and then meet those schedules is critical. What happens when a software project is behind schedule? Often, features are dropped at the last minute, activities such as inspections are eliminated, and testing time is reduced. The result is a product that is delivered late, with fewer features than were promised, and often with far too many defects. When this happens, everyone loses:

- The company's *customers* lose because they may receive the software later than promised, without key features, and with more defects than were expected.
- The company's *employees* lose since no one wants to be associated with projects that are deemed failures.
- The *company* loses as its reputation suffers from not meeting customer commitments.

The objective of this article is twofold: 1) to provide insight into why estimates and schedules are usually wrong, and 2) to describe a technique that has been proven to provide more accurate estimates and realistic schedules.

Why Are Estimates Often Wrong?

From participating in and observing dozens of projects at dozens of organizations, the author has found several common factors that result in inaccurate estimates and unrealistic schedules. These include:

- *Companies play ridiculous negotiating games.* Project managers typically find themselves in a position where they must "negotiate" the project schedule with management. Frequently, this negotiation occurs at the beginning of a project, before all the requirements have been defined and all the variables identified, and it usually continues throughout the project, as key milestones are missed. These negotiating games, many of which have been identified by Thomsett (1996), are eloquently explained by Yourdon (1997). A few examples of these games are shown in Figure 1.
- *Companies over-commit and under-deliver.* Many organizations fail to manage commitments made to customers and frequently over-commit. When

Doubling and Adding Some	In this game, the project manager comes up with an estimate for the schedule and then doubles it. For good measure, a few extra weeks or months are then added in.
Reverse Doubling	Most managers are aware of the "doubling and adding some" game. They take the initial estimates from project managers and immediately cut them in half.
Spanish Inquisition	In this game, the project manager walks into a meeting unaware that he/she will be asked to provide management with an on-the-spot, instant estimate. Usually, the schedule has already been determined and the unwitting project manager is coerced into accepting it.
Low Bid	When outsourcing software, competitors often are encouraged to match or beat the competitor's schedule in order to win the contract. Of course, the competitor's schedule is not realistic, so the project manager must agree to match someone else's folly in order to get the contract.
"Guess the number I'm thinking of..."	Management has decided what an "acceptable" figure is for the schedule but doesn't reveal it. The project manager meets with management and attempts to guess what it is by starting with a realistic estimate and whittling it down until it reaches management's "acceptable" figure.

Figure 1 Yourdon's Negotiating Games [1]

an organization over-commits, it cannot deliver what was promised when it was promised. Over-committing is caused by many factors, including competitive pressures; failure to consult with the development, quality assurance, and technical writing groups; overeager sales people; and a lack of understanding of the implications of commitments. When the project manager realizes that the organization has over-committed, he or she is often forced to take drastic measures in an attempt to meet these unrealistic commitments and schedules. Features are cut, design reviews and inspections are cancelled, and testing is curtailed.

- *Projects start with a predetermined release date and without well-defined requirements.* All too often, a project begins with a predetermined release date that has been communicated to customers. The release date is often set before the requirements are clearly defined. It is not possible to commit to a realistic delivery date before the requirements are defined. This would be similar to building a house before the architectural drawings were done. Without these drawings, how can builders give you a realistic completion date? They cannot. Yet, people frequently ask software engineers, appraisal personnel, and technical writers to build, evaluate, and document a software product *without* well-defined requirements.
- *Tasks are estimated based on time available rather than time required.* When a project team commits to a delivery date before the requirements are defined, the project manager is forced to *schedule backward*—that is, create the schedule by starting from the release date and working backward to today. When this happens, tasks are estimated based on *how much time is available* rather than *how much time the task actually requires*. Estimating tasks based on time available rather than time required means that from the beginning of the project, the estimates are incorrect and the schedule is unrealistic.
- *Task interdependencies are not identified.* Software development projects frequently require several groups within the organization to work together. At a minimum, these groups include software engineers, quality assurance, and technical writers. Often, other groups may be involved as well. However, interdependencies between tasks are frequently ignored when scheduling backward. Why? Because the release date has already been set, and the interdependent groups have not been involved in producing the schedules.

A Typical Scheduled-Backward Project

Consider what happens on a typical scheduled-backward project—a project that starts with a predetermined release date, usually resulting from one of the negotiating games listed in Figure 1, and lacks well-defined requirements.

Sooner or later, a critical task will be very late or, worse, will be unable to be completed. Then the ripple effect begins. The test plans, documentation, and coding take longer than expected because the tasks were never fully understood from the outset, dependencies between tasks were never identified, contingency plans for staffing were never implemented, and so forth.

When it becomes obvious that the project team will not meet the schedule, the project manager often abandons whatever development process the team was following in hopes this will somehow speed things up. The focus is shifted to paring down features and cranking up coding. Verification activities such as design reviews and inspections are now viewed as unnecessary and are eliminated. The time planned for validation testing is drastically cut, since testing is typically one of the last activities on the schedule. No design reviews, no inspections, less testing, and more hurrying often results in releasing an unfit product.

The product eventually gets released, usually weeks or months after the scheduled date. The project team is demoralized since it worked extremely hard to get the product released and knows that customers will not be satisfied because the product is missing key features and has far too many defects. The most amazing thing about this whole scenario is that no matter how many times this happens, management is still:

- Appalled at the high support costs
- Upset that so many defects were missed
- Quick to blame the team for doing shoddy work

Clearly, focusing *only* on time-to-market or *only* on quality or *only* on features to the *exclusion of the other two* is not desirable. Having a quality product delivered months late, and as a result, not sell can be just as bad as releasing a poor quality product on time. What is needed is a proper balance of quality, features, and schedule (Rakitin 2001).

Yellow Sticky Note Method

The yellow sticky note method facilitates communication within the project team, and as a result, helps people develop more accurate, realistic estimates of tasks they will perform. It also includes identification of dependencies between tasks. By starting with more accurate estimates and including task dependencies, it is a more straightforward process to create a project schedule that is accurate and realistic.

This method is based on the following simple principles:

- Start with well-defined requirements.
- People who will be doing the work create estimates for the tasks they will do and then help build the schedule.
- Project team members critique each other's estimates.
- People are held accountable for meeting their commitments.

- The organization under-commits. Customers are promised less than what can realistically be delivered.
- Everyone is trained in the yellow sticky note method.
- Management has "bought into" the process and supports its use.

With these simple principles in mind, consider how to create accurate estimates and build realistic schedules.

Start with a Complete Requirements Specification

To create accurate estimates and build a realistic schedule, the project team must have a relatively complete description of what it is being asked to build, that is, a software requirements specification (SRS) (IEEE 1998). Having a relatively complete SRS is essential regardless of what method is used to create estimates and build schedules.

The author has taught this to thousands of people. In doing so, it never fails that when he mentions that a relatively complete SRS is required, people laugh. People often say, "We never start projects with an SRS. We're lucky if the SRS ever gets written!"

So the first step in learning how to create accurate estimates and schedules is to start with an SRS. At this point, it would be helpful to plan a requirements review or inspection. This way, problems with the requirements can be worked out early and problems avoided. Developers, quality assurance, and technical writers should be invited to participate and should each bring his or her unique perspective. That is:

- Developers should ask, is each requirement implementable?
- Quality assurance should ask, is each requirement verifiable?
- Technical writers should ask, is each requirement explainable in simple terms?

Once the requirements are reviewed, they then can be grouped.

Group Requirements into Must-Haves and Wants

Once the SRS is written and reviewed, the requirements must then be grouped into *must-haves* and *wants*.

- *Must-haves:* the product is not worth introducing if it lacks these features
- *Wants:* features that customers want but could be put into a future release if necessary

Frequently, marketing people are involved in making these decisions since they are supposed to be in close contact with customers and should be aware of customers' needs.

Suppose that marketing goes through the SRS and determines that all the requirements are in the must-have group. This is not an acceptable answer, since team communication depends on some requirements being more important than others. If this happens, then use the no-tie ranking method to force a ranking of requirements. Each requirement is ranked according to importance to the customer from 1 to N, where N is the number of unique requirements. The team then determines that requirements numbered 1 through M (where M < N) are must haves and all the rest are wants.

Commit to Deliver Only the Must-Haves Not the Wants

The problem that many organizations have is they over-commit—they promise customers more than can be delivered in the promised time frame. When using the yellow sticky note method, management commits to deliver *only the must-haves not the wants*. Customers are not told about the wants. By committing to deliver only the must-haves, management is setting the customer's expectation lower so that it is more likely to be met. Setting the bar too high and consistently failing to meet it causes customers to become dissatisfied.

In developing the schedule, the project team plans to deliver a product that contains all the requirements—must-haves *and* wants. To account for those unexpected things that happen on every project and for overly optimistic estimates, the project manager works with the project team to try to get back on schedule. If that is not possible, then, as a last resort, the project manager can choose to drop one of the wants. This way, in the worst case the team delivers exactly what was promised (that is, just the must-haves), and in the best case the team delivers more than was promised (that is, must-haves and some or all of the wants). By following this approach, organizations can *under*-commit and *over*-deliver.

Yellow Sticky Note Rules

There are a few simple rules that must be followed when preparing task estimates and building schedules. These are:

- *The people doing the work identify and estimate their tasks based on the SRS.*
- *Each task should be small.* A larger number of shorter tasks is preferable to a smaller number of longer tasks. Decomposing overly long tasks into smaller subtasks provides better visibility and flexibility in building and managing the schedule. Each task should take five working days or less to complete.
- *When building the schedule, use the 80 percent rule.* In a given week, most people do not have 40 hours to apply to project tasks. At most, people have 80 percent of that or 32 hours. This is because people spend time

in meetings, attend training classes, talk on the phone, surf the Web, and participate in other nonproject-related activities. Some people may actually have less than 80 percent to apply to a project because they may be working on two or three projects at the same time.

- *Include vacation, holidays, and tradeshows on the schedule.*

Identifying Tasks and Creating the Initial Estimates

Once the project team has been trained, team members review the SRS. This review is conducted either individually (on smaller projects) or as a group within group members' own disciplines (on larger projects).

The purpose of this review is to identify every task that is required to develop, evaluate, and document the product and determine who will be responsible for that task. Note that tasks are identified for all requirements, both the must-haves and wants.

After the tasks are identified, the person responsible for that task estimates how long (in days) it would take him or her to complete the task *assuming he or she could work on that task uninterrupted*. The 80 percent rule is not used to determine how long a task takes but rather, when the task will complete, as discussed next.

If the task is something that the organization has never done, use the Wideband Delphi Method (Rakitin 2001) to develop a reasonable estimate. Once the task duration is estimated, each person then identifies the dependencies for starting this task. That is, what other task must be completed before this task can start.

All of this information is written onto a Post-It note—commonly referred to as a yellow sticky note—as illustrated in Figure 2. Different groups on the project team should use different color sticky notes so they can be visually

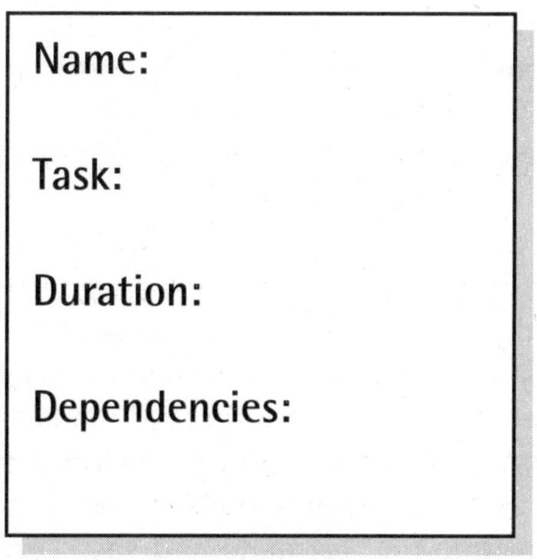

Figure 2 "Sticky note" information requirements

distinguished. Others have reported using similar mechanisms, such as index cards and push pins (Phillips 2001). The important concepts are that individuals responsible for doing the work estimate the task and that the schedule is built going forward.

Each person goes through the process of completing an appropriately colored sticky note with the information shown in Figure 2 for each task he or she has been assigned. The understanding with respect to the task estimates is that *each person is making a personal commitment to complete that task in that amount of time.* Because of this personal commitment, there is immediate buy-in to the schedule from each member of the project team. Each person understands that he or she will be held accountable for meeting his or her commitments.

It is a good idea to identify on each sticky note whether this task is related to a must-have or a want. (An "M" or "W" in the corner works well.) When everyone is finished with this part of the process, the project manager schedules a schedule-building session.

Building the Schedule Going Forward

The first schedule-building session includes the entire project team and should occur at an off-site location. The project manager should coordinate this activity. The room used for this activity should have a long wall upon which some plain chart paper can be affixed. Week marks (not dates) are indicated along the top of the chart paper.

The project team brings all of its colored sticky notes to the session. The process of building the schedule going forward is based on each task having at least one dependent task. When the project team is ready, team members approach the chart paper with their sticky notes and place them on the chart in the location where the task should complete. Here is where the 80 percent rule is applied. Say one has identified a task that should take five days (40 hours) to complete if not interrupted. By applying the 80 percent rule, a five-day task requires six working days to complete. So the sticky note is placed on the sixth day after it can begin. Refer to Figure 3 for an example of what a schedule might look like.

Now this is where it gets interesting and exciting. Recall that the whole project team is in the room. Each person is now standing in front of this wall with a handful of colored sticky notes. As the sticky notes start to go up, discussions start happening. Quality assurance people talk to developers, developers talk to technical writers, everyone talks to the project manager. In addition, peers review each other's estimates. For example, a developer might put up a sticky note for a task with an estimate of three days. Another, perhaps more experienced developer will critique that estimate and say, "You know, I did a task similar to that on the last project and it took me eight days not three." Thus, with peers critiquing each other's estimates, the *estimates get better*.

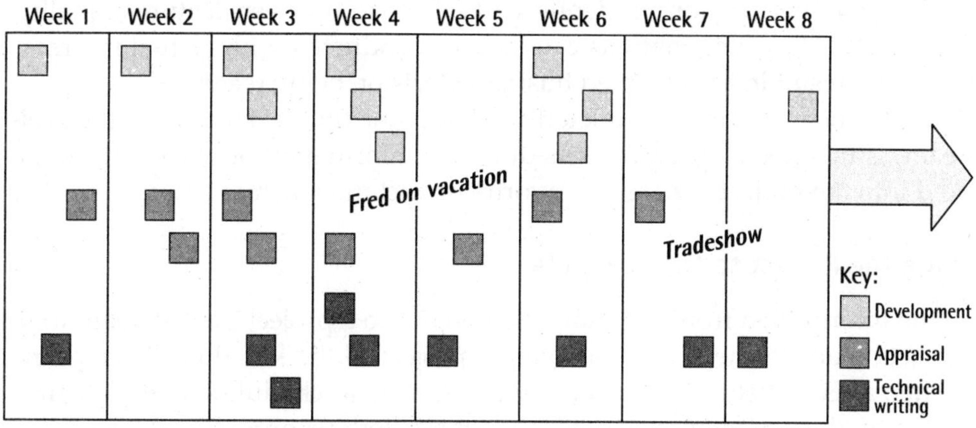

Figure 3 Building the schedule going forward

Further, by working together to build the schedule, the project team will often identify several tasks that no one had thought of previously. This aspect of the process serves to ensure that nothing is overlooked and that an accurate and realistic schedule is created.

When placing tasks on the chart, the team tries to place all of the tasks related to must-haves first and the tasks related to wants last. The reason for this will be apparent in the next discussion.

Finally, the team looks at the schedule it is building. The fact that the team owns the schedule is a powerful motivator. Because team members are talking with each other, sticky notes are put up and pulled off many times until the team as a whole is satisfied that they have developed the best possible schedule.

Negotiate Based on Factual Information

Once the project team completes the task of building the schedule going forward, it will be able to tell management with certainty when it can deliver the product. Frequently, management will not be pleased with this date and a negotiation session is usually required. Management will want to know how the delivery date can be pulled in. By looking at the chart with all of the colored sticky notes, the answers to this question should be obvious. Management can:

- Change the requirements (and the commitment to customers)
- Add resources

Two points need to be highlighted about this scenario. First, it is the people who will be doing the work telling management when they can deliver and, second, the negotiation can be conducted with factual information that everyone can see. For example, the chart will clearly highlight any resource bottlenecks (as evidenced by the lack of certain colored sticky notes in an area of the chart). The chart also has the estimates for each task.

During the negotiation, tradeoffs will be made between features, quality, and schedule. These negotiations can now be conducted with factual information that can result in an informed business decision being reached.

Once the negotiation is completed and everyone (management and the project team) is in agreement on the schedule, the information on the chart can be entered into the project manager's favorite project management tool.

Manage the Project to the Schedule

Once the information from the chart is entered into a project management tool, the project manager needs to manage the project to the schedule. This means that when a task is behind schedule, the result is not a schedule slip. By scheduling forward, the project manager now has the following options:

- Work with the individual to understand if he or she can recoup lost time by working weekends or extra hours or by rearranging other tasks.
- Work with management to identify additional resources.
- As a last resort, the project manager can decide to drop off a want (but not a must-have) to help keep the project on schedule.

Here then, is the reason why it is so important at the outset that the project team is able to categorize requirements as either must-haves or wants. The project manager must remain on top of the situation on a daily basis, meeting with team members and tracking progress for each task on the schedule. As the project progresses, the project manager works with the team to ensure the must-haves are delivered according to the agreed-upon schedule.

Summary

The track record of the software industry with respect to meeting schedules is abysmal. To change the performance of an organization, management must recognize that:

- Continuing to use the same mechanism for estimating and scheduling will result in continued inability to meet schedules.
- The organization needs to find an estimating and scheduling process that works.
- People who will be doing the work are best able to estimate how long the work will take.
- The organization needs training in good estimating and scheduling practices.
- People doing the work need the ability to set the schedule and then need to be held accountable for meeting it.

- The way to improve estimating skills is to learn from past estimates.
- People who create accurate estimates and schedules and then meet them should be rewarded.

By adhering to this process, dozens of project teams have been able to develop better, more accurate estimates and build accurate, more realistic schedules. Using this method, the project manager has more ability to help the project team meet its commitments to the organization and to customers.

Management plays a key role in helping to create a culture based on developing accurate, realistic schedules and then meeting them. By encouraging the organization to use proven methods such as team communication, management will improve efficiency, productivity, morale, customer satisfaction, and the bottom line.

REFERENCES

IEEE. 1998. ANSI/IEEE Standard 830-1998, IEEE Recommended Practice for Software Requirements Specifications. New York: IEEE.

Phillips, D. 2001. Cards-on-the-Wall Session. *Software Development* (July): 53–56.

Rakitin, S. 2001. *Software verification and validation for practitioners and managers*. Norwood, Mass.: Artech House.

Thomsett, R. 1996. Double dummy split and other estimating games. *American Programmer* (June).

Yourdon, E. 1997. *Death march: The complete software developer's guide to surviving 'mission impossible' projects*. Englewood Cliffs, N. J.: Prentice-Hall.

BIOGRAPHY

Steven R. Rakitin is president of Software Consulting Inc. where he helps companies establish a more predictable software development process. He has more than 25 years of experience as a software engineer and software quality manager in a broad range of industries. He has written several papers on the subject of software quality and published a book titled, *Software Verification and Validation for Practitioners and Managers.* Rakitin has a bachelor's degree from Northeastern University and a master's degree from Rensselaer Polytechnic Institute. He has earned certifications from ASQ as a software quality engineer and quality auditor. He is a member of the IEEE Computer Society, the ASQ Software Division, and is on the editorial review board for *Software Quality Professional*. He presents tutorials and workshops at conferences nationally. He can be reached at info@swqual.com.

We Must Overcommit— We Must Win Business

Neil Potter and Mary Sakry, The Process Group

Project planning and establishing achievable commitments continue to challenge software projects. Approximately 60 percent of software professionals that the authors meet complain about being overcommitted, under-resourced, and unable to negotiate deadlines, scope, and resources. The remaining 40 percent have little difficulty establishing achievable commitments with their management team and customer. During the authors' observations since 1989, they see two distinct camps. Camp One believes that, "It is not realistic to make realistic commitments." Camp Two believes that "It is not realistic to make unrealistic commitments."

At face value, intuition within Camp One appears to be the most appropriate reaction when dealing with managers, customers, and commitments. Quick intuitive promises to please the customer and manager have an immediate appeal. However, intuition can lead to overcommitment, project chaos, financial loss, and unhappy customers, the exact opposite of what is desired.

Counter-intuition within Camp One (for example, thinking before promising and promising with sound data) initially appears to be an inappropriate reaction to "please the customer" since it can slow one's response and provide a level of transparency that might be negatively critiqued. In hindsight, however, the counter-intuitive response is the one that builds credibility and satisfied customers.

This article describes the common intuitive thinking of Camp One and the counter-intuitive solutions found in Camp Two.

Key words: commitment, customer satisfaction, data, management, negotiating, planning, schedules

Introduction

Project planning and establishing achievable commitments continue to challenge software projects. Approximately 60 percent of software professionals that the authors meet complain about being overcommitted, under-resourced, and unable to negotiate deadlines, scope, and resources. The remaining 40 percent have little difficulty establishing achievable commitments with their management team and customer. During the authors' observations since 1989, they see two distinct camps. Camp One believes that, "It is not realistic to make realistic commitments," and makes quick intuitive promises. Camp Two believes that, "It is not realistic to make *unrealistic* commitments," and makes promises based on data. This article describes the common intuitive thinking of Camp One and the counter-intuitive solutions found in Camp Two.

Intuitive and Counter-Intuitive Thinking—An Analogy

The following are short profiles of two wine sellers.

Jim: Jim is a wine salesman in the Crafty Corner Restaurant, a fancy establishment in a large city. Jim enjoys selling wine and uses the following sales process:

1. Mention to each customer that the finest wines in the restaurant are the two most expensive wines on the wine list.
2. Always tell each customer that the wines in the middle of the wine list had a bad year last year and should not be considered.
3. Explain that the least expensive wines are really not worthy of the patron's time, but are included to make the list complete.

Jane: Jane is a wine salesperson at the Panache Restaurant, a fancy establishment in a large city. Jane's sales process is:

1. Mention to each customer that the first two wines on the list (the most expensive) are excellent, but the third and fourth listed taste equally as good and are considerably less expensive than the first two.
2. Tell each customer that the wines in the middle of the list are very good, except for number 12, which actually had a bad year last year (the truth).
3. Explain that the least expensive wines at the bottom of the list are grocery-store quality, except for the one at the very bottom that tastes "cheap."
4. Offer the customer a sample of any of the wines before purchase.
5. Give each customer the one-page review by *Wine Critique* magazine.

Most people prefer to do business with Jane rather than Jim. Why? Because Jane is focused on the customer's agenda rather than her own agenda, and when she puts herself in their shoes, she knows that customers want to be provided with credible information, educated about possibilities, and undersold rather than oversold.

Initial intuition might lead one to think that sales are maximized by Jim's approach (that is, sell more expensive wines). Counter-intuition would lead to Jane's approach, since that is the way individuals want to be treated. This treatment, in turn, creates repeat business.

Background to Overcommitment

Overcommitment is certainly not new and not unique to software development. The following summaries help explain why people overcommit.

Summary 1

"Under extreme pressure, software managers often make a guess rather than a plan. When the guess is drastically low, as it usually is, chaos ensues. Intuitive commitments occasionally are accurate, but generally only when the project scale and function are similar to the guesser's experience.

When the going gets rough, there is a strong temptation to believe in magic. Some "savior" may appear, or a new technology may be the answer. Since this hope is often an excuse for not planning, it merely postpones the problems.

The scale of software projects follows an escalating cycle:

- Programs generally take far more code than expected.
- As the programs become larger, new technical and management issues come up.
- Since these are unlike previous experience, they are a surprise.
- As the scale increases, the surprises continue, but at a dramatically increased cost.

Even after a higher maturity level is reached by an organization, new management, increased competition, or new technical challenges put pressure on the process. With the maturity of our field and the general lack of training for our people, this often means that organizations under pressure revert to the Initial [overcommitment] process."

—Watts Humphrey, *Managing the Software Process* (1989)

Summary 2

"The root causes of overly optimistic schedules are deep and manifold.

- There is an external, immovable deadline such as the date of a computer trade show, change in tax laws, or Christmas shopping season.
- Managers and customers refuse to accept a range of estimates and make plans based on a single-point "best case" estimate.
- Managers and developers deliberately underestimate the project because they want a challenge or like working under pressure.
- The project is deliberately underestimated by management or sales in order to submit a winning bid.
- Developers underestimate an interesting project in order to get funding to work on it.

- The project manager believes that developers will work harder if the schedule is ambitious and therefore creates the schedule accordingly.
- Top management, marketing, or an external customer wants a particular deadline, and the project manager can't talk them out of it.
- The project begins with a realistic schedule, but new features are piled on to the project, and before long the project is running under an overly optimistic schedule.
- The project is simply estimated poorly."

—Steve McConnell, *Rapid Development* (1996)

Camp One and Camp Two

Camp One believes that the only way to react to a request for an unrealistic deadline, and succeed as a development organization, is to overcommit to the customer. Among the phrases used to explain their position are:

- "We agree to crazy schedules because we are customer focused."
- "We must promise more than we can do so that we can win sales."
- "It's not realistic to make realistic commitments."
- "We tell management personnel what they want to hear."
- "The business climate makes us overcommit."

Customer satisfaction is cited as the primary motive for these actions.

Camp One's behavior is the result of having one or more of the following underlying beliefs (intuitive thoughts):

- **Belief 1:** Managers believe that their job is to commit the organization to "please the customer."
- **Belief 2:** Project managers and engineers think they must take scope and deadline requests from management almost verbatim and run as fast as they can to "please the manager."
- **Belief 3:** Project managers and engineers don't believe that they need to sell their proposal. "Take this option or give us more resources" is considered sufficient.

Belief 1: Managers Believe Their Job is to Commit the Organization to "Please the Customer."

Pleasing the customer by committing the organization to whatever the customer requests is a risky approach to running a business. The credibility of each commitment becomes suspicious when too many quick promises are made to the customer. If the commitments are unachievable, credibility plummets.

When an individual receives a request, he or she should not assume that the person making the request needs a response immediately. The person might need it by the end of the day, or by the end of the month. Asking how much time one has to work on a proposal and determining how solid his or her commitment can be, given the time available to work on it, is a good strategy. For example, if the request is simple and it is possible to commit to a solution, one should commit. If there is some research needed, the individual can explain that he or she can have a tentative commitment by the end of the day and a firm commitment in three days.

For very complex or large requests, one should explain the steps needed to develop a proposal and establish dates when estimates, ranges, and a final commitment can be provided. If there are many deliverables in the commitment, he or she can commit to the pieces of the project that are known and that can be estimated, and establish subsequent deadlines when the remaining pieces can be defined and promised.

If the company has sales personnel (or an equivalent business analyst or manager who interfaces with the customer), it is helpful to send engineering representatives on sales calls with them, particularly if there is a history of sales personnel making unachievable commitments on behalf of engineering. Joint visits enable customer requirements to be communicated in parallel to both parties, minimizing communication and commitment problems later.

It is easy to resist the suggestion of sales and engineering working jointly on a client visit. The authors hear complaints such as, "There is no time for both company representatives to visit the customer," and "The customer might become confused from two opinions." However, the opposite of these comments is also true. If the addition of the engineering representative adds four more hours of company time to a sales call, then only one mistake of four hours has to be saved anywhere downstream for the additional time to be valuable.

Once the sales process works correctly, where customer requirements are clarified and sound commitments are made, engineering representatives can be reserved for high-risk requests that require the expertise of sales and engineering together.

Managing Commitments

One should use a commitment process to manage expectations between parties and clarify the steps an initial request goes through to become a final commitment. Without such a process, projects and organizations can easily overcommit and mismanage expectations, resulting in chronic crises. An example process is shown in Figure 1.

The process for managing commitments should not be lengthy or complex. The example described can be used as a basis for one's project or group. Typically, one page or less is sufficient to explain how a group will derive sound commitments.

Step 1:	The project team determines high-level product needs (or scope of work) from customer and marketing input.
	Note: For a small request, a short document may be adequate to capture the customer's needs. For a large request, initial needs are collected and a plan is established to refine the requirements, either in one phase or through several iterations.
Step 2:	The project team develops an initial estimate and project plan to determine what is feasible.
	Note: For a large project, state that two estimates will be provided, one on date x, and one on date y. The first will be a range based on the current understanding of the requirements; the second will be based on a final collection of requirements. For iterative projects, state that each iteration consists of a requirements, estimation, and commitment phase.
Step 3:	The project team meets with management, marketing, customers, and related groups to determine: a) whether the product (or change request) is feasible, b) there is agreement to the resource, cost, and schedule estimates, and c) the risk is acceptable.
	Note: This might be a brief meeting, e-mail, or phone call. The focus is to visibly agree to the work, estimates, and risks.
Step 4:	A commitment is made or further negotiation is held.

Figure 1 Example commitment process

"To be effective, the commitment process must reach the top of the organization (Humphrey 1989). This requires that:

- All commitments for future software delivery are personally made by the organization's senior executive.
- These commitments are made only after successful completion of a formal review and concurrence process.
- An enforcement mechanism ensures that these reviews and concurrences are properly conducted.

The senior executive's personal involvement is what motivates the entire commitment process. The people know they must justify their recommendations in a visible process and that poor work will likely be exposed."

Belief 2: Project Managers and Engineers Think They Must Take Scope and Deadline Requests from Management Almost Verbatim and Run as Fast as They Can to "Please the Manager."

The reaction of the project manager and team to jump when the manager says "jump" is probably the weakest link in the organization's ability to handle commitments. The quick reaction of the team to agree to any and all commitments handed to them, regardless of feasibility and risk, is usually the team's first large error. The underlying intuitive thought is, "I can keep my job if I play along and agree to whatever I am asked to do; I can always seek forgiveness later." Changing the way a team reacts to commitment requests might be the toughest behavior to change since it is supported by ego and deep-rooted beliefs that quick and pleasing reactions make people look the most capable.

What is missing is the realization that the person requesting a commitment wants a sound commitment, not just any commitment. When project managers and team members internalize this, their reaction to complex requests changes from "Yes, sure we can do that," to "The team will develop a first-pass estimate range, list of assumptions, risks, and schedule options. When is the latest time by which you need a sound commitment?"

Providing Complete Data

Making sound commitments requires a project team or organization to accompany any estimate with assumption, risk, and resource availability data.

- *Assumptions:* Assumptions are statements regarding any part of the project that help define the commitment. Example assumptions are: "All the code must be developed from scratch," "A new operating system version is required to implement the desired functionality," and "Component B will arrive January 16." Assumptions can refer to resource availability, dependencies, items that are not in scope, and expected quality levels. If any assumption is false, the commitment itself might be in jeopardy.
- *Risks:* Risk assessment enumerates potential technical, schedule, or resource problems that might be encountered by the project. When identifying risks, one should also consider the assumptions that accompany the commitment. Assumptions are statements that need to be true to enable the commitment, but in reality, might become false. An example risk management plan is shown in Figure 2 (Sakry 2001).
- *Resource availability:* The deadline one can achieve will be based on specific availability of resources. When discussing a commitment with a customer or manager, individuals might have an idea of the resources required. If they do, they should verify that they are available to meet this commitment, given their current workload. If they do not have a clear idea of the estimate or resource availability, they need to state that, and develop action items to investigate further.

One should tailor his or her planning response based on the complexity and magnitude of the request; a trivial request can have a quick response, and a complicated request can have a comprehensive response. It is important to respond consistently with a statement that meets the requesters' need, not one

Risk items (potential future problems derived from a brainstorm session)	Likelihood of risk item occurring (1-10)	Impact to project if risk item does occur (1-10)	Priority (likelihood x impact)	Actions to reduce likelihood of risk occurring	Actions to reduce impact if risk does occur	Who should work on actions	When should actions be complete	Status of actions
New operating system might not be stable.	10	10	100	Test OS 2 more weeks.	Identify 2nd OS. Test with second OS.	Joe	3/3/XX	✔
Communication problems over system issues and dependencies.	8	9	72	Develop system interface document.	Add replan milestone to realign the team's schedule.	Cathy	5/6/XX	✔
We may not have the UI requirements right.	9	6	54	Build prototype of UI screens, #2 and #3.	Limit initial product distribution.	Lois	6/6/XX	
Requirements may change late in the cycle.	7	7	49	Get signoff on top 10 requirements. Establish change review board.	Ship core five features and limit initial product distribution to validate approach.	Cecil	6/7/XX	
Database S/W may be late.	4	8	32	Check with supplier.	Make application compatible with a substitute DB.	Joe	7/7/XX	
Key people may leave.	2	10	20	Make sure Jim is happy with current workload and travel schedule.	Earmark Fred as a backup and cross train.	Pete	7/8/XX	

Figure 2 Example risk management plan

that immediately results in a no-win situation. Intuitively, one might think the manager needs a response immediately. But in most cases he or she does not; that is just an assumption. What the manager really wants is a credible supplier who can respond with considered and enlightening feedback.

Individuals might believe that they cannot choose any response other than the one *they* have historically chosen. They should realize, however, that their customer and manager would change their reaction based on the way individuals respond to the commitment request.

When asked for a commitment one should:

- Enumerate credible options to the request and develop alternatives that the requester has not considered.
- Provide planning data that can be examined for options regarding approach and errors in assumptions.
- Communicate project risks and suggested mitigation actions.
- Explain his or her conclusions regarding deadline and cost options using data.

The example in the appendix following this article illustrates one team's reaction to a commitment request.

Belief 3: Project Managers and Engineers Don't Believe They Need to Sell Their Proposal. "Take This Option or Give Us More Resources," is Considered Sufficient.

Customers and managers want sound data on what is possible so they can succeed in their goals. The project team uncovers project details and communicates insight that neither the customers nor managers have. This information is then packaged and communicated in a way that leads the customer to the right solution for all parties. Even if the customer or manager was initially demanding, abrupt, or blue-sky in his or her request, it is still in *everyone's* best interest to package and sell achievable options.

When communicating project options, one should:

- *Know by how much he or she is over- or under-committed:* Compare the total number of effort-days required to complete the project (that is, the effort estimate) with the number of effort-days one has available to spend (that is, number of workdays between today and the deadline × number of people assigned to the project × the availability of each resource (for example, 50 percent or 80 percent)). If the estimate is 20 percent more than the resources available, one might be able to recover by working one weekend day each week, or 1.6 additional hours each day. If one's work estimate is 20 percent to 30 percent more, then one can potentially recover and meet the deadline by working additional hours again, hiring more labor, or increasing the availability of each resource. If the estimate is more than 30 percent larger, then one should consider the following options.
- *Understand what the deadline is based upon:* Understand what is driving the current deadline. Is it a stake in the ground that a manager established to keep people focused? Is it based on a client's need to go live with a system or to avoid the delay of the next release? Unless one knows the details behind the expected deadline, he or she can only guess what can be changed, negotiated, or dropped to achieve it (Fisher and Ury 1981).
- *Propose an incremental delivery:* Once it is known what is important to the customer and manager, and how the system will be used, suggest smaller increments that can be delivered earlier. Identify with the customers the most important features that help them perform their work tasks. Split the requirements into at least three buckets that reflect the requirements' priority (for example, bucket one contains features that must be included in this release; bucket two contains features that must be included but can

wait for a later release; bucket three contains features that would be nice to have if they can be included).

- *Check assumptions with others:* Detailing the project- and task-level assumptions provides more potential options to make one's deadline achievable. Include technical, schedule, resource availability, and quality assumptions. For example, one might assume that version 16 of module X must be used, when in fact, version 15 is simpler and adequate. He or she might assume that it is necessary to wait until the company's sister division completes the hardware in order to test, but in fact, the customer is on vacation during August, and the company could use his hardware at no cost. It is helpful for individuals to write their assumptions down and share them with others to see what options appear.
- *Examine the critical path of the schedule:* The deadline that one will achieve is at the end of the longest calendar path through the schedule (the critical path). Some tasks can be performed more quickly to bring the deadline in, and other tasks that appear to be important can be accelerated with no positive impact on the deadline. Calculate the critical path using a scheduling tool and determine if reducing delays or adding more resources to the critical-path tasks will finish the project more quickly.
- *Clarify resource availability:* All schedules assume the availability of specific resources (for example, Jane must be available 80 percent for tasks 1 through 20, and 30 percent for tasks 21 through 30). An interruption in Jane's availability adds risk to the schedule completion date. Clarify what availability is needed to attain the desired deadline. Take action to reduce chronic interruptions if team members cannot spend the required time on their tasks. If one resource is performing three or more project tasks in parallel, assume that a nonproductive tax must be paid when switching between tasks (it takes a finite time to put one task down and pick up the next). In this situation, schedule the person to complete one task before starting the next, or reduce the number of parallel tasks performed at any one time, thereby reducing the tax. Look specifically at the critical path for examples where resources are being shared. If a resource is performing two parallel tasks, and one of them is on the critical path, the whole schedule is being delayed. Consider having the resource complete the critical path task first, and then work on the other task.
- *Define the customer's quality expectations:* Is the customer expecting a proof-of-concept prototype, a completely error-free system, a product with known defect density (for example, no more than two defects per thousand lines of code), specific reliability (for example, mean-time between failure is no more than five days), or a mature product with all import and export features. Each quality definition corresponds to a different set of project tasks, effort, and duration.

- *Simplify the solution:* Look at the project and identify areas that have been overcomplicated or overengineered. Evaluate each item from the end-user's perspective; that is, if this complication didn't exist, would the user ever know or care? Consider simplifying algorithms, database structures, complicated graphics, wizards, operating system versions, and features that are unnecessary for project success. What can be simplified to achieve the deadline?
- *Investigate process changes that could relieve deadline pressure:* Process changes can make the project complete earlier. However, each process change brings with it a change in risk that must be assessed. For example, a team waiting for an approval at the end of one project phase could start the next phase early and assume the risk of rework if unforeseen changes are introduced during the approval process. A team could also perform inspections (peer reviews) on 50 percent of the code base while assuming the risk of defects being undetected in the remaining 50 percent. Testing could be reduced to final acceptance testing while replacing selected unit testing with inspections.
- *Determine sections of the project that should be purchased or built:* Look at the project for areas that can be delegated to others to save time, money, or risk. Can the team use standard libraries that are pre-tested? Are there sections of the project that can be adequately completed by a third party at similar cost? Are there components that have been delegated that should be brought back in-house because of the available expertise within the company?

When communicating project data to managers and customers, individuals should state how the data were derived (for example, Wideband Delphi process, historical data, intuition, fit to please) and their confidence in the estimate (for example, high, medium, low). One's confidence level indicates how likely this number is to change and whether further planning is necessary.

Obtaining and communicating planning data is not only key to setting stakeholder expectations, it changes how managers and customers react to the data. Communicating "Take this estimate or else!" elicits a limited set of reactions that are usually unpleasant. Communicating the planning data described previously elicits a constructive reaction that results in a project team with a negotiated scope, schedule, and risk. (Project teams do not need permission to perform this level of planning and communication. It is a choice available to all.)

Moving from Camp One to Camp Two

Camp One can continue for years before its behavior and results change, either because customers become used to schedule and quality problems, or because the team comes through at the end of the project with heroic efforts. Usually, neither the organization nor the customers are happy.

The current economic climate is commonly used to support Camp One's position. If the economy is booming, it is declared that there is no time for practices such as planning and risk management. Intuition says, "We are successful without those practices," or "We are too busy making money, we don't have time for *process*." If the economy is in a slump, it is declared that one must underbid and overpromise to "get in the door with the customer," or "tell the customers what they want to hear."

When the economy is booming, activities such as planning and risk management enable a company to maintain a rapid rate of production and prevent problems that could cause major setbacks (such as releasing poor quality products and overcommitting the organization to the breaking point). When the economy is sagging, success is dependent on distinguishing an organization's performance from its competitor's. Success is not achieved by overpromising (and therefore underdelivering) to the customer. Regardless of the economy, customers always want dependable suppliers that deliver quality work. Planning matches one's commitments and capability with the customer expectations. Risk management keeps the company out of trouble by actively identifying and mitigating downstream problems that could occur.

It is very difficult to convince Camp One that its own intuitive thinking is the cause of its problems. Suggestions that the customer's needs should be better understood, or that estimates should be created and risks assessed before commitments are made, are seen as luxurious or theoretical approaches. Camp One is sure that "this is the way we must work," and perceives that Camp Two has an easy life in an easy industry.

The route from Camp One to Camp Two is to match the problems that Camp One cares about with the solutions used in Camp Two and practice them until they become intuitive (Potter and Sakry 2002). This transition can occur proactively or reactively. The proactive approach requires some faith, thought, and the desire to learn by trying. This can be accelerated by a few projects leading the way, using Camp Two practices, and promoting the benefits to the remainder of the organization.

The common alternative is to delay change until the organization sinks under the weight of over-commitment and there are no longer any alternatives other than to plan and make sound commitments that customers can trust.

Watts Humphrey (1989) summarizes the change in the following quote:

> "When people are directed by top management to run a mile in two minutes, what should they do? Experienced hardware engineers have learned to first test the directive. If it is truly firm, the best ones develop a comprehensive comparison of this job with their prior experience to show management why this schedule is unrealistic. They also dig in their heels and insist that management either change the schedule to

one that makes sense or relieve them of responsibility for meeting the dates. When the better engineers all do this, the managers have little choice, unless they want to do the design themselves. Unfortunately, all too many programmers start looking for their running shoes."

Conclusion

At face value, quick promises to please the customer and manager have immediate appeal. The intuitive Camp One response, "Sure, we can do that," can appear to be the most appropriate reaction to "get in the door." However, intuition can lead to over-commitment, project chaos, financial loss, and unhappy customers, the exact opposite of what is desired.

Counter-intuition (for example, thinking before promising and then promising with sound data, assumptions, and risks) can appear to be an inappropriate reaction to "please the customer" since it can slow one's response and provide a level of transparency that might be negatively critiqued. In hindsight, however, the counter-intuitive response is the one that builds credibility and satisfied customers.

REFERENCES

Fisher, R., and W. Ury. 1981. *Getting to yes*. New York: Penguin Books.

Humphrey, W. 1989. Managing software organizations. In *Managing the Software Process*. Reading, Mass.: Addison-Wesley.

McConnell, S. 1996. *Rapid development: Taming wild software schedules*. Redmond, Wash.: Microsoft Press.

Potter, N., and M. Sakry. 2002. *Making Process Improvement Work—A Concise Action Guide for Software Managers and Practitioners*. Reading, Mass.: Addison-Wesley.

Sakry, M. 2001. Keep your project on track. *Software Development Magazine* (April).

Wiegers, K. 2003. *Software Requirements*, second edition. Redmond, Wash.: Microsoft Press.

Wiegers, K. 2000. Stop promising miracles. *Software Development* (February).

BIOGRAPHIES

Neil Potter is cofounder of The Process Group, a software engineering process improvement consultancy. He has 20 years of experience in software and process engineering. For six years Potter was a software engineer at Texas Instruments (TI). For two years he managed a TI Software Engineering Process Group spanning the United States, England, and India. Potter is a Software Engineering Institute (SEI) authorized assessor for CBA-IPI and SCAMPI appraisals, Intro to CMMI instructor, and Six Sigma Green Belt. He has a bachelor's degree in computer science from the University of Essex (UK) and is the coauthor of *Making Process Improvement Work—A Concise Action Guide for Software Managers and Practitioners* (Addison-Wesley). Potter can be reached by e-mail at help@processgroup.com.

Mary Sakry is cofounder of The Process Group, a software engineering process improvement consultancy. She has 29 years of experience in software and process engineering.

For 15 years she was a manager and software engineer within Texas Instruments (TI). In 1989 she led TI's worldwide process assessment effort and was a member of a Software Engineering Process Group. Sakry is an SEI authorized assessor for CBA-IPI and SCAMPI appraisals and Intro to CMMI instructor. She has an MBA and bachelor's degree in computer science. She is the coauthor of *Making Process Improvement Work—A Concise Action Guide for Software Managers and Practitioners* (Addison-Wesley).

Appendix

One Team's Reaction to a Commitment Request—An Example

The group in this example is a large IT division of a multinational product manufacturer. The IT group provides computer services for company sales forecasts, sales transactions, and marketing events. The development team supporting a very old legacy mainframe system was tasked with moving the sales applications to a commercial database product. The team identified 60 business processes currently supported by the legacy system, and each one was required in the new system. The team was committed to move all 60 processes within an impossible timeframe with little or no involvement from the team members. This was the fourth time that the team had been challenged to complete this work, with three previous failures.

Before this last attempt, the team members attended two of the authors' workshops, one on requirements development and one on project planning. In the requirements workshop, they took their ambiguous paragraph-styled requirements and rewrote them as clear single sentences. They expanded the highest risk requirements into detailed use cases and set requirement priorities using the example format shown in Figure 3 (Wiegers 2003). These priorities were shared with their management for feedback. This resulted in the elimination of half of the requirements from the first release of the project.

In the planning workshop, the team estimated the project effort using the Wideband Delphi technique (Wiegers 2000). In the Delphi process, the team creates an initial project task list, followed by individual preparation to derive esti-

Requirement	Benefit (B) if present (1-9)	Penalty (P) if absent (1-9)	Total value (V=B+P)	Value % (V%)	Relative cost (C) to implement (1-9)	Cost % (C%)	Relative risk (R) to implement (1-9)	Risk % (R%)	Priority (V% / C%+R%)
Reqt 4	5	4	9	22%	1	5%	1	6%	1.83
Reqt 1	6	8	14	35%	3	15%	2	12%	1.25
Reqt 3	4	3	7	18%	5	25%	3	19%	0.41
Reqt 2	4	2	6	15%	7	35%	3	19%	0.28
Reqt 5	3	1	4	10%	4	20%	7	44%	0.16
Total	22	18	40	100%	20	100%	16	100%	-

Figure 3 Example format for setting requirements priorities

mates and underlying assumptions. The team members then come together to share their data. Individual estimates are kept anonymous, while task descriptions and assumptions are publicly shared and refined. The process results in a clear task list, assumptions, and estimate range for the work. The output is then reviewed with management.

Here is the story from the team for the requirements and planning phases.

"The analytical nature of the requirements development and prioritization process provided a thorough evaluation of all options. As we reviewed the analysis with key decision makers, we educated them about the potential solutions for each requirement and the benefits, penalties, costs, and risks of each solution option. They participated with us in the evaluation process, providing valuable insight into the analysis and ensuring buy-in with the results. When the process was complete, the analysis clearly showed the best strategies going forward.

Since the key decision makers all participated in the analysis process, they agreed with its outcome, and they were willing to abandon prior strategic decisions, even ones they had personally made. Their involvement in the analysis provided a win-win method for all involved to leave behind failed strategy decisions without losing face. Involving management was a counter-intuitive approach for the team.

With this critical win in our pocket, we then improved our planning skills to give us a fresh start with our new strategy. From the outset of the planning session, we were challenged to think differently. We had managed projects for years using a very disciplined process. We were experienced in project planning and work estimation, and we were quite good at it. The fact that we rarely completed projects on time was obviously due to management, work culture, and other things out of our control!

During the Wideband Delphi process, the team agreed to a high-level work breakdown structure (WBS) followed by each individual estimating the tasks without discussion with the other team members. This already was different. Normally, we would sit around a table as a team and work through the WBS, estimating as we went, until we had a full project schedule. Everyone on the team would be there, everyone would participate, and we would have the right information, correct? However, this time, when we first came back to the table with our individual Delphi estimates, we were all over the map. Way off. Not even close.

What happened next was even more puzzling—we discussed our assumptions and task definitions, but we couldn't talk about specific estimates or formulas. What we didn't realize at the time was that we were level setting. In our previous group session, a few people typically dominated the discussion. As time rolled on, those not heavily involved became bored. Now, our individual preparation in the Delphi process enabled critical and unique assumptions to be surfaced. When we came together we combined them to establish a comprehensive and clearer answer.

The hardest discussion (but most critical) of the planning phase was the review of our planning data with senior management after the team session. The output from the high-level plan did not match their expectations. However, we now understood what it would take for a successful implementation. Management pressured the team to reduce their estimates, to conform to their expectations for delivery, but the team did not budge. Having followed the process, we had detailed assumptions behind each estimate, which we were willing to review, but not willing to arbitrarily change to meet a date. The team's decision to obtain good data provided the level of detail that senior management needed to change their expectations to meet our estimates.

Throughout the project, we continued to use the planning and requirements techniques. We utilized the requirements prioritization process again to determine how we would satisfy each detailed requirement. We revisited the planning process to develop our WBS for the detailed implementation plan. Unlike the previous four attempts, this time the team implemented the agreed-to functionality, on time and under budget!"

A Test Manager's Guide to Risks Analysis and Management

Rex Black, RBCS, Inc.

Testing any real-world system is potentially an infinite task. Of this infinite set of possible tests, test managers need to focus on the most significant risks to system quality. These are the potential failures that are likely to occur in real-world use or would cost a lot if they did occur. This article describes practical ways to analyze the risks to system quality, providing guidance along the way to achieving effective and efficient testing.

Key words: analysis, quality, risk, testing

Introduction

For any real-world system, there are an infinite number of tests that one can conceivably run. How does one choose the best possible subset? A smart approach would be to pick those tests that address the most important risks.

Testing reduces risks to system quality. It helps identify areas of the system that work properly (that is, the tests pass). It also helps identify opportunities to make the system better (that is, the tests fail, detecting defects). So smart test managers should ask, "How do we test the most critical areas and find the most critical defects?"

This article will explain how to apply the powerful techniques of risk analysis and risk management. The author provides five techniques for analyzing quality risks. Using these techniques, one can make informed, objective decisions about where to focus testing resources. By reassessing risk at major milestones during the project, one can continually optimize the effectiveness and efficiency of testing throughout the system development life cycle. The author illustrates the ideas using three case studies.

Why Risk Matters—and What It Has to Do with Testing

Any significant project involves risk. Risk increases with complexity, the number of participants, effort, budget, and duration. Capers Jones (1995) cites probabilities of software project failure ranging from 2 percent to 85 percent. He identifies inadequate testing as one of the four leading causes of failure, along with poor estimation, planning, and project tracking.

Many managers are familiar with project risk management. For example, they manage risks such as loss of key personnel and late deliverables from vendors. Classical risk management says to mitigate these risks using both proactive means (such as cross-training of staff) and reactive means (such as redundant component sourcing). One can mitigate risks to system quality through proactive means like reviews and through reactive means like testing.

The author prefers J. M. Juran's definition of quality: fitness for use. Quality is the presence of that which satisfies users, customers, and other stakeholders, and the absence of that which dissatisfies them. A quality system is fit for the users' purposes, provides the needed features, and contains few, if any, important bugs (Juran 1988).

A risk is a *potential* undesirable outcome. So, a risk to the quality of the system is any potential problem that could cause the system to fail to meet reasonable expectations of quality (Black 2003).

When one starts testing a system, he or she evaluates the quality of the system in terms of particular functions, characteristics, and behaviors. While the presence of some defects is expected, knowing exactly which activities will find them is the challenge.

As testing continues, some of the defects are discovered. These known defects are no longer risks; they are now *actual* undesirable outcomes. It is possible to fix these defects and improve the quality of the system. The overall risk is reduced.

When running the tests, one also discovers where the defects are not. The tests that pass show that the system works as expected under the tested conditions. Again, the overall risk is reduced.

The more thoroughly one tests the system, the more of the remaining defects he or she finds. The more defects one finds, the more defects one can fix. The more thoroughly one tests the system, the more known-good, tested conditions one identifies. So, the more one tests, the lower the risk to the quality of the system. But the risk will never be reduced to zero, because there's always one more test one could run.

Which Quality Risks Should We Worry About?

Since it is not possible to test everything, it is necessary to pick a subset of the overall set of tests to be run. Quality risks analysis can help one focus the test effort.

While the phrase *quality risk analysis* may sound forbidding, mystifying, and complex, the underlying ideas—and the techniques—need not be. Simply put, quality risk analysis is a process for identifying, analyzing, and prioritizing categories of potential quality problems (that is, defects) in one's systems.

Because quality risks are potential problems—with probabilities between zero and 100 percent—one factor that influences the relative importance of a risk is the likelihood of the undesirable outcome. In other words, is it likely that these kinds of defects exist in the system and is it likely that users will encounter these kinds of defects if they exist?

Another factor that influences the relative importance of a risk is the impact of that undesirable outcome on the users, customers, or other stakeholders. In other words, if these kinds of defects exist in the system and users encounter them, how will the symptoms of the defects affect the users? The impact of defects can range from trivial to catastrophic on some systems, even deadly.

For example, suppose one is developing an online banking application. This application allows users to log into their bank accounts over the Internet. They can then pay bills, transfer funds between accounts, and download statements.

For such an application, security is clearly a major quality characteristic. In the area of security, risks to system quality include the possibility that criminal hackers gain unauthorized access to other customers' accounts or that hackers intercept account information in transit between the data center and customers' PCs.

As the steady stream of Internet hacking exploits point out, the likelihood of such problems are all too high. When they do occur, such problems have serious impacts on customers, businesses, and other stakeholders. Clearly, to have confidence in such a system, one would want to develop and test in such a way as to reduce these risks.

Quality Risk Analysis Techniques

There are a variety of risk analysis techniques available these days. Each has its strengths and weakness, depending on the needs and practices of the project team. So, selecting the right technique is essential.

All of these techniques involve identifying and prioritizing the risks to the quality of the system under test. Typically, the risks are grouped or organized by major risk categories, such as functionality, performance, security, and so forth. A cross-functional team of project stakeholders usually identifies the risks. Rather than rely only on the stakeholders' opinions and recollections, the analysis should also draw upon historical defect and field failure data from past projects, requirements and design specifications, sales figures, market research, and anecdotal information from customers, competitors, or clients.

Once the risks are identified, each risk is assigned a level—a measure of its degree of importance. In a later section, the author discusses the factors that affect the level of risk and how one can combine these factors to come up with an aggregate measure of risk, as well as how to use the aggregate measure of risk to decide on the level of effort to expend on testing. Following are five techniques for analyzing risk (see also Figure 1):

Technique	Informal (Black 2002)	ISO 9126 (ISO 2000)	Cost of exposure (Black 2003)	Failure mode/ effect analysis (Stamatis 1995)	Hazard analysis (Craig and Jaskiel 2002)
In a nutshell	Rely on history, experience and checklists	Follow industry-standard quality characteristics	Estimate costs of testing versus not testing	Identify the potential bugs and the effects on stakeholders	Analyze causes of hazards (sources of risk)
Strengths	Easy, lightweight, flexible	Predefined, thorough, common	Balanced, pecuniary, traditional	Precise, meticulous, general	Exact, cautious, systematic
Weaknesses	Participant-dependent, gappy, imprecise	Potentially over-broad, over-regimented	Data-intensive, exclusively monetary	Lengthy, document-heavy, hard-to-learn	Easily overwhelmed by complexity
Consider on projects	Low-risk or agile	Standards-compliant	Financial or actuarial	High-risk or conservative	Medical or embedded
Avoid on projects	Safety-critical or regulated	Very unusual or structure-intolerant	Safety- or mission-critical	Chaotic, fast-changing, or prototyping	Unpredictable or complex

Figure 1 A comparison of risk analysis techniques

1. *Informal quality risk analysis* techniques do not entail much beyond what is described in this section so far. Such techniques provide an easy way to get started in quality risk analysis. One is likely to miss some important areas of risk, especially during early risk analyses, but even informal techniques make it possible to achieve a better degree of test focus and coverage than one can achieve without any risk analysis at all.
2. *For ISO 9126 quality risks analysis* techniques, one should use the quality characteristics and subcharacteristics described in the ISO 9126 system quality standard as the categories for the risk analysis. The six main characteristics of quality are:
   - Functionality
   - Reliability
   - Usability
   - Efficiency
   - Maintainability
   - Portability

   In each category are two or more subcharacteristics. ISO 9126 provides a more structured approach and reduces the likelihood of missing some major risk elements. It also tends to add a bit in terms of time and paperwork.
3. *Cost of exposure quality risk analysis* techniques focus on the following question: What are the expected losses associated with various risks, and how much should one spend to reduce those risks? An expected loss is the product of the probability of the loss multiplied by the cost of the loss. Such techniques allow the project management team to make a hard-nosed, economic decision about testing. For this technique to

work well, however, the risk analysis team must be able to accurately estimate the probabilities and costs of various losses.

4. *Failure mode and effect analysis* goes beyond discussing risks. Using this technique, the risk analysis team tries to identify the different ways the system could fail and all the possible effects those failures would have on customers, clients, the business, society, and so forth. This technique is quite detailed. It can produce finely calibrated testing, but it also can produce a ton of paperwork and lots of invested time.
5. *Hazard analysis* techniques are like failure mode and effect analysis, but done backward. One starts first with the effects—the hazards—and tries to work backward to causes. Along the way, the likelihood of those causes should become clear. In some cases, though, there are many causes of different kinds of bad behavior, so this technique tends to work best with systems that do only a few things.

Case Studies: Quality Risks Analyses

To provide an idea of the documentation and information produced by some of these techniques, look at two case studies, Figure 2 and Figure 3. These figures show excerpts from the two documents the author and his associates developed for these projects.

Figure 2 shows a portion of the document produced during an informal quality risk analysis for an Internet appliance. Such devices allow users to send and receive e-mails, browse the Web, purchase items at e-commerce Web sites, and so on.

Figure 3 shows a portion of the document produced during a formal quality risk analysis, following the failure mode and effect analysis technique. The author analyzed the risks for a utility that ensures file security on PCs by forcing the complete erasure of all digital information related to a file upon deletion.

Quality Risks Analysis Process

Whichever technique one chooses, he or she can follow a similar process for quality risk analysis.

1. Identify the quality risk analysis team.
2. Select a technique.
3. Identify the quality risks. Prioritize the risks. Select appropriate risk mitigation actions. (One may include not only testing at various stages, but also reviews of requirements, design, and code, programming techniques such as array bounds checking, and so forth).
4. If the risk analysis team identified problems in requirements, design, code, or other project documents, models, or deliverables during the analysis, report those problems for resolution.

Quality risk category	Specific failure mode(s)	Priority
Functionality	Client won't boot	1
	Client mail fails	1
	User data mishandled/lost	1
	Client browse fails	1
	Client software update fails	1
	Client user interface fails	1
	Device login fails	1
	Multiuser client logins fail	1
	Mail server loses mail	1
	Update server fails/unreliable/drops updates	1
	Preferences/state server fails/unreliable/loses state information	1
	Web server fails/unreliable/drops updates	1/2
	Schedule/logging fails	1
	Sending mailer incompatibilities	1
	SPAM filtering ineffective	2
	Attachment refusal rude/silent	1
	RTF support fails/incomplete	1/2
	Basic/premiums support differentiation fails	1
	Wrong number handling invalid	1
	Area code changes mishandled	1
	Reconnect time-out fails	1
Reliability	Client crashes frequently	1
	Server crashes frequently (without failover working)	1
	Net connection fails	1
Performance	Slow e-mail uploads/downloads	2
	Slow updates	2
	Slow Web access	2
	"Jumpy" action or intermittent slowdowns	2

Figure 2 Informal quality risks analysis for an Internet appliance

5. Review, revise, and finalize the quality risk analysis document.
6. Check the quality risk analysis document into the project library under change control.
7. At regular intervals (for example, major project milestones such as the completion of the requirements, design, and implementation phases, and test readiness and exit reviews) and as new information becomes available (for example, completion of a test cycle), review and update the risk analysis, adding new items and reassessing the level of risk for the items.

The author's preference is to carry out step 3 as a single meeting, using brainstorming or similar elicitation techniques. However, he has performed this step as a series of conversations, even one-on-one, between the person charged with the risk analysis and the quality risk analysis team.

	A	B	C	D	E	F	G	H	I	J	K	L
1	Failure mode and effects analysis (quality risks analysis) form – RPN sorted											
7												
8	Initial FMEA-RPN sorted											
9	System function or feature	Potential failure mode(s) quality risk(s)	Potential effect(s) of failure	Critical?	Severity	Potential cause(s) of failure	Priority	Dejection method(s)	Detection	Risk Pri No	Recommended action	Who/ when?
10	Shreds swap files	Fails to shred	Security breach	Y	1	Program error	1	Test; debug tracing; code review	1	1	Test; debug tracing; code review	
11	Shreds swap files	Shreds excessively	Data loss	Y	1	Program error	1	Test; debug tracing; code review	1	1	Test; debug tracing; code review	
12	Compression compatibility	Damages data	Data loss	Y	1	Program error	1	Test	2	2	Test	
13	Compression compatibility	Hangs system	Data loss	Y	1	Program error	1	Test	2	2	Test	
14	Compression compatibility	Shreds improperly	Data loss	Y	1	Program error	1	Test	2	2	Test	
15	Internet files recognition	Recognizes incorrectly	Data loss	Y	1	Program error	1	Test; debug tracing; code review	2	2	Test; rules validation	
16	Network compatibility	Shreds network	Data loss	Y	1	Program error	1	Test	2	2	Test selected/ improve network; coverage	
17	Removes file name	Damages FS	Data loss	Y	1	Program error	1	Test; debug tracing; code review	2	2	Test; debug tracing; code review	

Figure 3 Failure mode and effects analysis for a PC file security utility

In addition to selecting the right technique, it is necessary to select the right participants in order to get the most out of the quality risk analysis process. One needs a cross-functional team that represents the interests of all stakeholders in testing and quality. Without representation of all interests, it is possible to miss some key risks, as well as to over- and underestimate some levels of risk.

Who are these key stakeholders? As a general rule, there are two groups. First, there are those who understand the needs and interests of the customers and/or users, or who have immediate contact with the testing process. (Customers and users themselves can be involved, too, when available.) With their insight into business considerations, they can help assess the impact of potential problems. Second, there are those who have insight into the technical details of the system. With their insight into technical considerations, they can help assess the likelihood of potential problems.

In addition to the information-gathering nature of the process, the consensus-building aspects are also critical. Both business-focused and technically focused participants can and should help prioritize the risks and select mitigation strategies.

Case Studies: Quality Risk Analysis Processes

For the Internet appliance, the author conducted the quality risk analysis as a series of interviews and discussions with the key managers and technical leaders in the organization. He had drafts of the marketing requirements and design specifications, as well as a shared high-level vision of the system among the stakeholders. The risk analysis discussion built a solid consensus around where the author and his associates would focus the test effort.

The quality risk analysis process had two interesting side effects. First, it revealed that the vision of the system was evolving and not entirely consistent, especially at the detail level. Agreeing on what was at risk, quality-wise, helped promote a detailed consensus on what it would mean for the system to have quality. Second, the risks analysis (along with later test design efforts) highlighted a number of problems in the requirements and design documents. These problems were resolved, preventing defects from entering the testing process.

For the file security application, the author's client had no written specifications. As with the Internet appliance, there was a shared vision of the system to be built. Fortunately, the author was able to get all of the stakeholders to commit to spending an afternoon in a quality risk analysis meeting. The resulting document served as a guide for testing focus and as a first step in the test design process.

In addition to creating a useful document, there were two interesting side effects. First, the development team decided to take steps to proactively prevent defects. Inspired by the quality risk analysis session, development managers and technical leads implemented quality risk mitigation strategies such as robust design and code inspections. Second, the risk analysis document became the *de facto* requirements document. Since quality risk analyses tend to focus on what not to do, they express requirements in the negative.

Focusing Testing Resources Using Aggregate Levels of Quality Risks

Quality risk analysis should identify both the risks themselves and their relative levels of risk. To determine the levels of risk, likelihood and impact are typical factors to consider. The author likes to rate both of these on a five-point scale: very high, high, medium, low, and very low. Failure mode and effect analysis uses three factors—severity, priority, and likelihood of detection—rated on a scale from 1 to 10.

To translate the two (or three) factors into a single, aggregate risk level, one can use the quality risk analysis team's collective judgment, a formula, or a table. For the Internet appliance case study, the author relied on collective judgment and decided the appropriate aggregate level of risk. For the file security case study, he followed the failure mode and effect analysis standard of multiplying the ratings for the three factors to obtain a risk priority number from 1 to 1000, which was then divided into ranges representing levels of aggregate risk. To use a table, first construct a lookup table such as the one shown in Figure 4, then use it to assign the aggregate level of risk based on the two factors for each risk item. Given the aggregate risk levels, one then uses them to determine the extent of the testing he or she wants to perform. For example, one might adopt the rules shown in Figure 5.

In Figure 5, note that one makes no commitment for testing very low and low risks areas. For medium, high, and very high risks, he or she commits increasing

IMPACT

LIKELIHOOD	Very high	High	Medium	Low	Very low
Very high	Very high	Very high	High	High	Medium
High	Very high	High	High	Medium	Medium
Medium	High	High	Medium	Low	Low
Low	High	Medium	Low	Low	Very low
Very low	Medium	Medium	Low	Very low	Very low

Figure 4 A look-up table for aggregating two risk factors

Aggregate risk	Extent of testing	Comments
Very low	None	Only report defects observed in these risk areas.
Low	Opportunistic	Leverage other tests or activities to run a test or two of an interesting condition in the related risk area, but only if it involves a very small investment of time and effort and only if the opportunity presents itself.
Medium	Cursory	Run a small number of tests that sample the most interesting conditions in the related risk areas.
High	Broad	Run a medium number of tests that exercise many different interesting conditions in the related risk areas.
Very high	Extensive	Run a large number of tests that are both broad and deep, where deep tests exercise many combinations and variations of interesting conditions.

Figure 5 Mapping relative quality risks to the extent of testing

amounts of time and effort to mitigate the related risks through testing. Where are the appropriate dividing lines between each category? This is again a question for the stakeholders. What level of testing do the stakeholders need to do to feel comfortable that each risk is adequately mitigated?

The answer to this question must be realistic. In the absence of any constraints, one might like to do extensive testing against most, if not all, risks. However, as mentioned earlier, this is not possible. So, the question each participant in the risk analysis must ask is, "What would I be willing to spend—in terms of schedule time, project budget, and possibly even foregone features—to mitigate this risk through testing?"

Case Studies: Relative Quality Risks as a Guide

For the Internet appliance project, the author followed rules like those in Figure 5. Risk served as the guide for high-level design of test suites and tools all the way down to the low-level design and implementation of test cases and data. Given that the author was working on a medium-sized project following a waterfall/V-model system development life cycle, this degree of structure was appropriate.

On the file security application project, the approach was more informal. Across the project team, everyone understood that the test team would give the highest risk areas the most attention, the medium risk areas less attention, and the lowest risk areas perhaps no attention at all. Given that the author was working on a small project following a relatively agile system development life cycle, this kind of informality was appropriate.

Risk Mitigation and Management Throughout the Life Cycle

So far, readers have seen how the quality risk analysis process and resulting document can serve as a foundation for the design of tests. However, it can also serve as a guide for the quality professional throughout the project. Let's look at seven ways one's analysis can help mitigate and manage quality risk.

First, why wait for testing to mitigate the important quality risks? As shown in the file security case study (see Figure 3), quality risk mitigation actions can include various quality assurance tasks. Requirements, design, and code reviews have proved helpful on many of the projects the author worked on. Adoption of and adherence to coding standards can help programmers avoid dangerous constructs. Defensive programming techniques such as pair programming, test-first programming, and stepping through the code with a debugger can help detect mistakes during code development. The more important the quality risk, the smarter it is to include multiple quality assurance tasks focused on it, at various stages of the life cycle, especially the early stages.

Second, as one designs and develops tests, he or she can use the quality risk analysis document to ensure completeness. Assume, for the moment, that he or she is following the approach shown in Figure 5. In this case, each test case the test team developed should map to one or more medium-, high-, or very high-risk areas. Each medium-, high-, or very high-risk risk area should map to one or more test cases. The higher the relative risk, the more tests for that risk area. If one wants to know for sure that the testers are covering all the risks appropriately, ask them to keep track of this mapping, sometimes called a *traceability matrix* (see, for example, Craig and Jaskiel 2002).

Third, as one prepares to run the tests, he or she can use this traceability from risks to test cases to pick which tests to run first. A good rule of thumb for prioritizing test case execution is: Look for the scary defects before looking for the trivial ones. So, again following the approach shown in Figure 5, the tests associated with the very high risks should precede those associated with high risks, which should precede those associated with medium risks.

Fourth, as one begins to run the tests, he or she should gather actual test results and find real—not potential—defects. The kinds and number of defects one finds in each risk area should provide feedback on the accuracy of the risk analysis. If there are a lot of defects in unexpected places, perhaps the technical risk—that is, the likelihood of defects related to some risk areas—is higher than previously thought. If there are dangerous defects where one thought there would be trivial ones, perhaps the business risk—that is, the impact of defects related to some risk areas—is higher than originally thought? If one can trace the test results and defects back to the risks from the first day of test execution, one can adjust risk analysis and testing focus based on what he or she learns (Black 2002).

Fifth, as one continues to run tests, he or she might find less time for testing than needed. Project team turnover, unanticipated specification changes, longer-than-expected testing periods, late deliverables from programmers and suppliers: All of these events can put the squeeze on testing. By tracing the relative levels of risk associated with particular test cases, one can intelligently trim the amount of testing to be done in a way that minimizes the increase in risk.

Sixth, as one reaches the end of a development project, he or she sometimes finds the need to make one more change, add one last feature, or fix one last defect. Some amount of retesting (that is, regression testing) is usually required to make sure one hasn't broken anything that worked before (that is, haven't caused regression in the system). To select a regression test set, one can—and probably should—analyze the changes being made to determine the likelihood of regression defects associated with particular changes, additions, or defect fixes. However, one can—and probably should—also use the quality risk analysis to pick the most important tests.

To cover the seventh and last benefit, notice that the author mentioned traceability many times in this section. The best way to capture and support all the benefits described here is to create a traceability database. A high-level entity-relationship diagram for such a database is shown in Figure 6. Notice

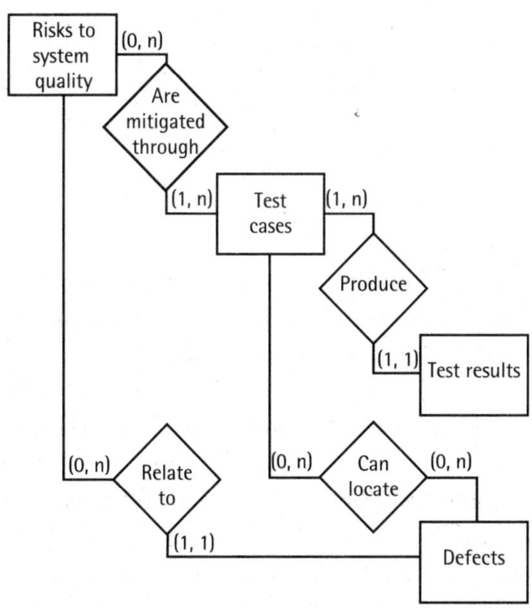

Figure 6 An entity-relationship diagram for relating risks, tests, results, and defects

how, in this diagram, one can relate quality risks to test cases, test cases to test results and defects, and test results and defects back to quality risks. This makes it possible to report test results not only in terms of the quantity of test cases (for example, run, passed, and failed) and the number of defects (for example, found, fixed, and remaining)—which after all are fairly abstract quantities—but also in terms of the risks that one has mitigated through testing and where the risks remain high.

A Cautionary Case Study

There was one engagement where the quality risk analysis process broke down. The author's client had extensive written specifications. There was also a core of about eight people who had a shared vision of where the system was to go. However, all of the stakeholders were "too busy" to spend time on risk analysis. They asked that the author and his associates perform the risk analysis.

They did so, in part by interviewing people in person, on the phone, and via e-mail, but mostly by analysis of the requirements and design specifications. They then circulated the quality risk analysis document for comments. Few stakeholders commented, because few read the document. Nevertheless, with this analysis being their only guide on where to focus, they developed tests and got ready to run them.

At that point, schedule and budget pressures caused the project managers to reduce the breadth and depth of testing. Those reductions did not follow the risk analysis at all. The project management team had no commitment to the risk analysis. They were not aware of what it could tell them. So, they arbitrarily made decisions about which tests to drop and which to keep based on their limited understanding of relative levels of quality risk. Based on this experience, the author has concluded that involving the right stakeholders and ensuring the right level of stakeholder participation is more important to the success of the quality risk analysis process than the availability of extensive documentation.

Conclusion

In this article, the author explained how and why one could use risk analysis as the foundation for testing and other quality assurance tasks. He discussed how to extend one's thinking about traditional project risk management to include the risks to system quality. He covered the factors of likelihood (technical risk) and impact (business risk) of potential problems that establish relative levels of quality risks.

Having laid out the general concepts, the author moved on to the mechanics. He examined five quality risk analysis techniques: informal; ISO 9126; cost of exposure; failure mode and effect analysis; and hazard analysis. He covered a general-purpose, adaptable process for performing a quality risk analysis.

Finally, the author looked at the many ways one can apply quality risk analysis. Quality risk analysis provides a foundation for smart test design and development. However, that's only a start. The author also showed how, throughout the project life cycle, one could continue to use the quality risks analysis to reassess, manage, and mitigate the risks to system quality.

REFERENCES

Black, R. 2003. *Critical testing processes.* Boston: Addison-Wesley.

Black, R. 2002. *Managing the testing process, second edition.* New York: John Wiley and Sons.

Craig, Rick, and Stefan Jaskiel. 2002. *Systematic software testing.* New York: Artech House.

ISO. 2000. ISO 9126-1:2000 *Information technology: Software product quality.* Geneva, Switzerland: International Organization for Standardization.

Jones, T. Capers. 1995. *Estimating software costs.* New York: McGraw-Hill.

Juran, J. M. 1988. *Juran on planning for quality.* New York: Free Press.

Stamatis, D. H. 1995. *Failure mode and effect analysis.* Milwaukee: ASQ Quality Press.

BIOGRAPHY

Rex Black, a 20-year software and systems engineering veteran, is president and principal consultant of RBCS, Inc., a leader in software, hardware, and systems testing. For more than a decade, RBCS has served its worldwide clientele with training, consulting, staffing, and on-site, off-site, and offshore project execution expertise. Black's popular first book, *Managing the Testing Process*, now in its second edition, has sold more than 17,000 copies around the world, including Japanese, Chinese, and Indian releases. His latest book, *Critical Testing Processes*, was published at the end of 2003. Black has also written numerous articles, along with presenting papers, seminars, and speeches at various U.S. and international conferences. Black can be reached by e-mail at rexblack@ix.netcom.com.

PART V

Software Metrics, Measurement, and Analytical Methods

"You can't manage what you don't measure" is a well-established rule. As we move from the management section, we next consider data collection and analysis. Clearly it is preferable to make decisions based on objective and quantitative evidence whenever possible. Yet it seems so hard to understand what to measure (and what not to measure), what appropriate statistical techniques to employ, and how best to present these results. The very act of measuring can alter and even distort a process. People get nervous and wonder: Why are you measuring that? How will the data be used? Should I do something to make the numbers "look better"? Software may be different . . . but not so different that both products and processes cannot be analyzed in ways already well understood in more mature quality measurement sectors, such as manufacturing. Measurement scales, sampling theory, quality tools such as diagrams and charts—these all offer helpful insights into the concerns of software quality.

Alex Glushkovsky begins his article by stressing that a metrics system is a business intelligence fundamental: It allows a company to analytically support the planning and controlling of activities, benchmark processes and products, and guide process improvement. "An Analytical Approach to Software Metrics Management" offers a goal-metric-data model to relate established improvement priorities to measurable feedback indications of their achievement. The author details metrics management from establishment (including business-specific customization) to determination of necessary data collection to metrics analysis and utilization. A matrix framework, built on the principles of quality function deployment, relates goals for business improvement to the selection of metrics and then to the data that are collected and analyzed.

Discussions on product quality are often based on no more than the number of reported defects and the subjective perception of stakeholders. In "Measuring

Software Product Quality," Erik van Veenendaal, Rob Hendriks, and Robert van Vonderen present a case study from the industrial development of copier/ printer controller software. They found that the usual practice of describing quality requirements in vague terms made it difficult for test engineers to verify the quality of the software product against these requirements. Instead, they developed a method to identify the most important quality characteristics by means of a risk assessment, to define completion criteria, and to subsequently measure the quality characteristics based on the ISO 9126 standard. The result: a more rigorous process for making the decision to release a given product.

"The Uses and Abuses of Software Metrics" is based on a presentation awarded "Best in Conference" at the 12th Annual International Conference on Software Quality, sponsored by the ASQ Software Division. Pat Cross admits her development of the material came out of a burst of rage. In this article she chastises the software community for what she sees as common misuses of control charts and discusses their proper application to software situations. She urges users of metrics—whether for fact-finding, prediction, comparison, or triggering a decision—to respect the data, understand their type and their precision, and not attempt to draw unwarranted deductions. Cross discusses aspects of the use of metrics beyond the goal/question/metric model presented in previous articles. The fundamental questions one should ask in metrics work are: "Why are we doing this? What is our goal?" The answers to these questions should then guide software practitioners when they choose what precision to aim for and what techniques to use.

A warning comes from Patricia McQuaid and Carol Dekkers to "Steer Clear of Hazards on the Road to Software Measurement Success." While a well designed and planned measurement program can contribute to process improvement, a poorly planned one can actually inflict damage. The authors attribute much of the waste and disillusionment from failed measurement programs to a lack of attention to the needs of analysts, management, and customers. This article outlines how to identify potential barriers to success, together with common-sense actions to avoid them. Key steps stressed include producing sustainable plans; making measurement integral to the development process; anticipating and responding to natural resistance to cultural change; and motivating to ensure the data are reported accurately, shared openly, and acted upon visibly.

An Analytical Approach to Software Metrics Management

Alex Glushkovsky

This article addresses an analytical approach that provides a practical framework for software metrics management. The matrix-based framework is applied to the following aspects of software metrics management:

1. *Metrics establishment, including conceptualization and customization according to the nature of software business*
2. *Determination of necessary data collection*
3. *Metrics analysis and utilization, including evaluation of goal achievement and guidance for business improvement*

In addition, the framework supports the following formal elements of software metrics management: documentation, review, control, maintenance, and audit.

Key words: business intelligence, matrix, metrics system, qualitative analysis, quantitative analysis

Introduction

Software metrics is an important issue in modern software development. It allows a company to analytically guide business improvement, support planning and controlling activities, benchmark processes and products, and forecast outputs of future projects. A metrics system is a business intelligence fundamental. Although the issue has been in focus for more than a decade and even supported by standards, today's software business sophistication requires an integrative software metrics management approach. This approach should provide:

1. Metrics establishment, including conceptualization and customization according to the nature of software business

2. Determination of necessary data collection
3. Implementation guidance
4. Metrics analysis and utilization, including evaluation of goal achievement and guidance for business improvement

In addition, it should support documenting, reviewing, controlling, maintenance, and auditing.

This article introduces an analytical approach that provides a practical framework for software metrics management that supports the previously mentioned elements. Once implemented, it allows one to segment business areas with respect to the achievement of established goals and optimization of decision-making, and it decreases the uncertainty of future projects.

I: G-M-D Paradigm

The improvement: goal-metric-data (I: G-M-D) paradigm (see Figure 1) is a core element of the proposed approach that was advanced from the widely used goal-question-metric paradigm (Basili and Rombach 1988; Westfall 1995; Kenett and Baker 1999). It integrates three consecutive relationships: 1) improvement: goal (I: G); 2) goal-metric (G-M); and 3) metric-data (M-D).

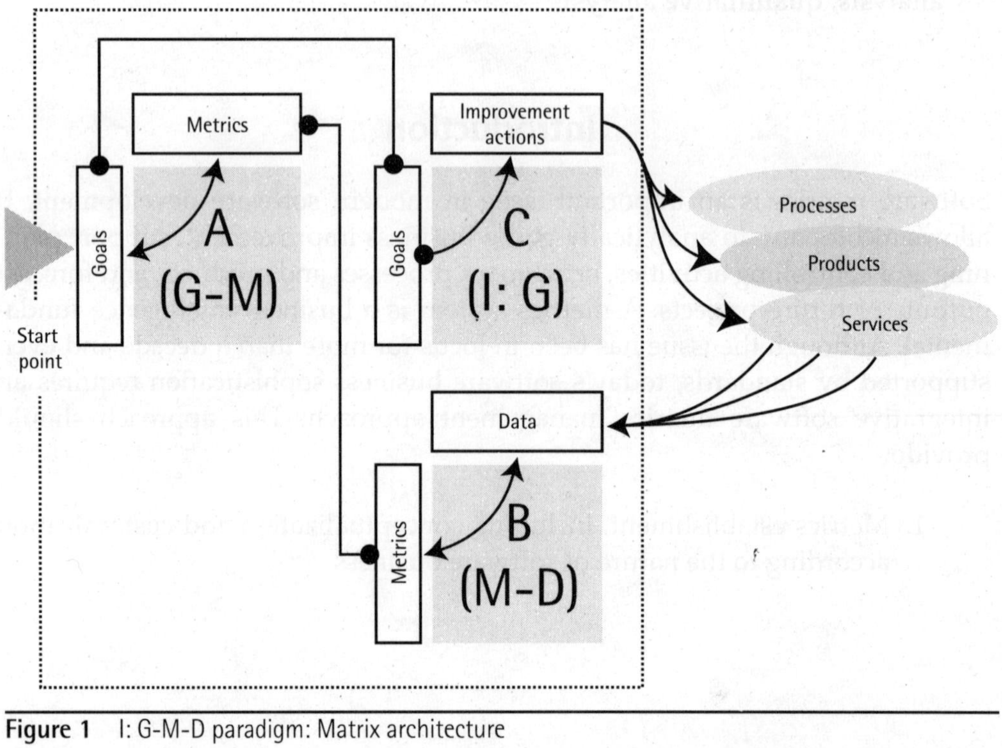

Figure 1 I: G-M-D paradigm: Matrix architecture

Improvement: Goal (I: G)

The first part of the I: G-M-D paradigm represents the principle of feedback, since the major function of metrics is to guide and control business improvement. Gap analysis of goal achievement helps to highlight and prioritize business areas to be improved, and specify corrective actions to be performed. Appropriate metrics and goal achievements indicate the results of improvement actions.

Goal-Metric (G-M)

The second part of the I: G-M-D paradigm was transformed from the goal-question-metric model. It reflects the possibility of a direct relationship between goals and metrics, assuming well-organized and multilevel structured goals. Matrices are established based on determined goals, while goal achievements are evaluated by corresponding metrics.

Metric-Data (M-D)

The third part of the I: G-M-D paradigm shows that data are essential for metrics calculation. It specifies relationships between metrics and quantitative characteristics.

Based on this approach, the success of business improvement depends on: 1) correctness of the established I: G-M-D model with respect to business nature; 2) completeness and reliability of data collections; and 3) discipline to implement determined improvement actions.

The sequence of the relationships in the I: G-M-D paradigm:

I: G, G-M, and M-D

can be visualized and formalized as a combination of three matrices (see Figure 1).

Matrices A and C can be formalized by a well-known quality function deployment (QFD) approach. The relation between matrices A and B in Figure 1 is known as the "waterfall" model, while the "linear" model presents the relationship between matrices A and C, where goals (G) guide improvement activity (I).

Quality Function Deployment

QFD is a widely used teamwork tool. Originally, it was introduced to transform customers' needs into appropriate technical requirements (Sullivan 1986; Gopalakrishnan, McIntyre, and Sprague 1992) and later was extended into different areas, including questionnaires (Glushkovsky et al. 1995) and sustainable development indicators (Glushkovsky 2001).

An ordinary QFD matrix has three major parts:

1. List of objectives (part "What?") as a row heading
2. List of technical elements (part "How?") as a column heading
3. Relationships between above-mentioned parts as a matrix entries

Matrix A in Figure 1 has a list of goals as a row heading (part "What?") and list of metrics as a column heading (part "How?"). The part "What?" relates to the question "What should be achieved?" and the part "How?" relates to the question "How will achievement be measured?" A list of goals (the part "What?") is a starting point to establish I: G-M-D model. The second step is metrics determination (part "How?" of the QFD matrix A).

Once established, the part "How?" of matrix A becomes the part "What?" in matrix B (this flip is known as the "waterfall" model). The part "How?" in matrix B relates to the question, "How are metrics calculated?"

In matrix C the part "What?" is the same as the part "What?" in matrix A, that is, a list of goals. However, the part "How?" in matrix C relates to the question, "How goals' achievement could be improved?"

In QFD, the matrix relationships between "What?" and "How?" are presented graphically as a level of intensity. Graphical models help to perform qualitative analysis of the I: G-M-D model. Usually three levels of relationship intensity are identified: strong, medium, and weak (see Figure 2). For example, there is a strong relationship between "self-controlled development" (part "What?") and "rate of defects detected in tests" (part "How?").

The formalization of relationship intensity allows quantitative analysis of the I: G-M-D model. The intensity levels strong, medium, and weak have assigned values of 9, 3, and 1, respectively. QFD practitioners usually use 9, 3, and 1 as numerical values on the strong-to-weak scale. It provides second-order stress to the strong relationship keeping the intensity range from 1 to 9. These values, as well as the number of intensity levels, can be adjusted according to specific conditions.

In addition to the three major parts described previously, the QFD matrix usually includes a column that ranks the importance of the "What?" It allows one to perform quantitative analysis based on the importance of each goal and to provide aggregation. The matrix A in Figure 2 has the column "Importance," which ranks the importance of the goals on a scale of 1 to 10, where 10 corresponds to highest level. The assigned team evaluates the rank of the goals. It should reflect the company mission and management objectives.

The formalized approach allows using QFD for the following purposes:

- Teamwork-based concept development, including determination of objectives (part "What?"), related technical elements (part "How?"), and graphical intensities of relationships between part "What?" and part "How?"

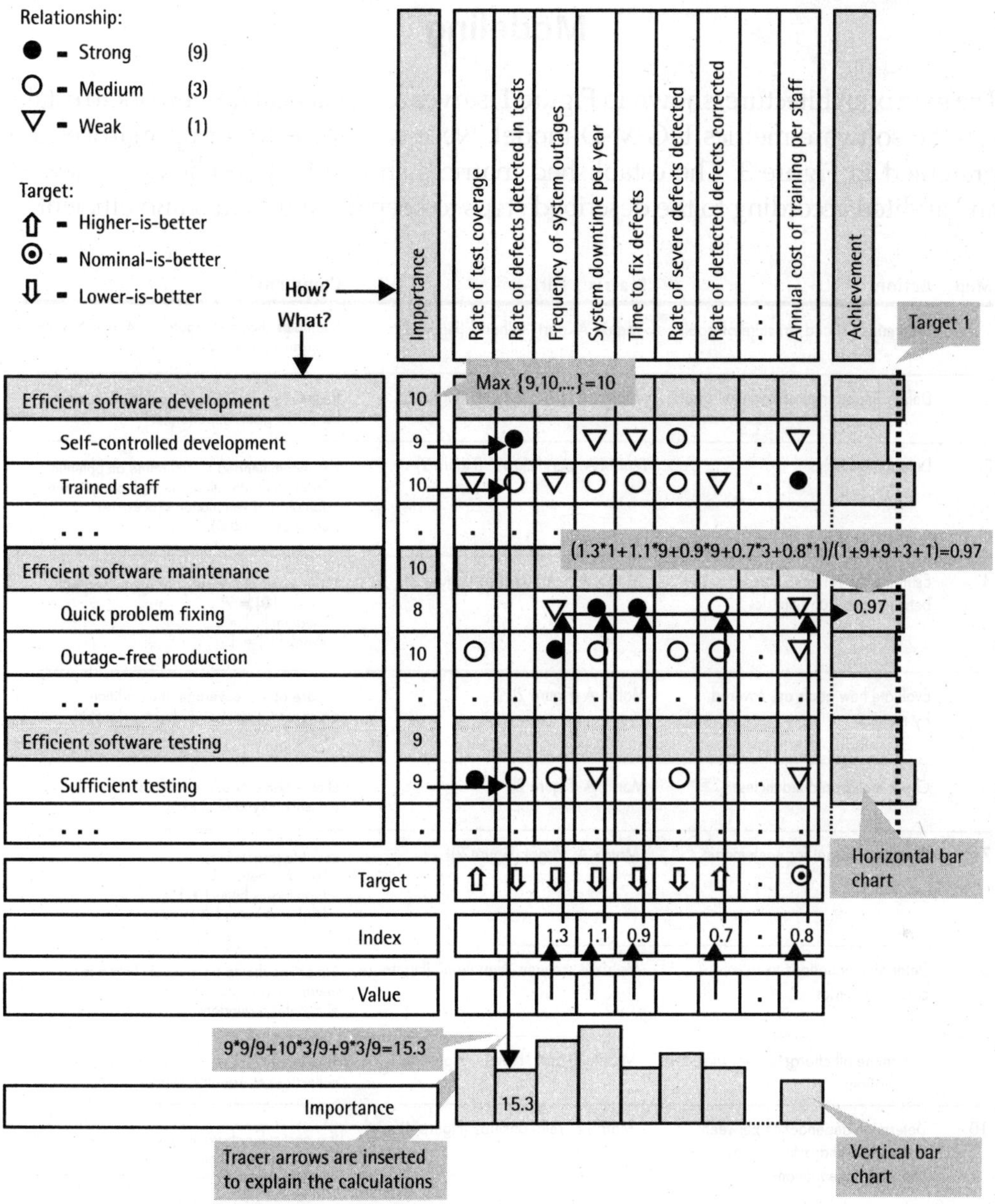

Figure 2 Matrix A (G-M): Goals vs. metrics

- Qualitative analysis, such as evaluation of coverage of part "What?" by part "How?" and detection of redundancies and conflicts
- Quantitative analysis, such as performance evaluation, prioritization of technical elements, and benchmarking

Imagination provides quick understanding, effective controlling, and memorizing of the framework objects.

Modeling

The matrix architecture, shown in Figure 1, serves as a practical framework to establish the software metrics I: G-M-D model. Necessary steps to set up matrices are presented in Figure 3. The established matrices should be periodically reviewed and audited according to the described steps to keep them updated and efficient.

Step	Action	Matrix / Part	Comment
1	Determine list and structure of goals	Matrix A, part "What?" (Figure 2)	Examples shown in Figures 2, 4, and 5 are for illustrative purposes.
2	Define importance of low-level goals	Matrix A, part "What?" (Figure 2)	It allows one to perform quantitative analysis based on goals importance.
3	Determine metrics	Matrix A, part "How?" (Figure 2)	It is recommended to determine all potential metrics, and after that proceed to implement addition and elimination procedures (see steps 5 and 6).
4	Estimate the relationships between goals and metrics	Matrix A, relationships (Figure 2)	Three levels of intensity are recommended: – Strong (●) = 9 – Medium (○) = 3 – Weak (▽) = 1
5	Evaluate how goals are covered by metrics	Matrix A (Figure 2)	In case of low coverage, the addition procedure is advised (Glushkovsky et al. 1995).
6	Check metrics redundancies	Matrix A (Figure 2)	Elimination procedure is advised (Glushkovsky et al. 1995)
7	Determine target for each metric	Matrix A, target (Figure 2)	Possible targets are: – Lower is better (⇧) – Nominal is better (◉) – Higher is better (⇩)
8	Determine equations to calculate metrics	Matrix B, column "Equation" (Figure 4)	Equations should be uniquely linked to metrics. It provides completeness and eliminates redundancies for matrix B.
9	Determine all characteristics included in equations	Matrix B, part "How?" (Figure 4)	This step is necessary to determine data collections to establish metrics system.
10	Determine dependence between metrics and characteristics by analyzing of equations	Matrix B, relationships (Figure 4)	If a particular characteristic is included in the equation, then the appropriate type of dependence should be chosed: – Negative (🠉) – Uncertain (≈) – Positive (🠋)
11	Determine possible actions for improvement	Matrix C, part "How?" (Figure 5)	It is recommended to determine a two-level structure for improvement activities: 1. Core management areas (high level) 2. Improvement actions (low level)
12	Evaluate relationships between goals and improvement actions	Matrix C, relationships (Figure 5)	Three levels of intensity are recommended: – Strong (●) = 9 – Medium (○) = 3 – Weak (▽) = 1
13	Evaluate how goals are covered by improvement actions	Matrix C (Figure 5)	In case of low coverage, the addition procedure is recommended (Glushkovsky et al. 1995).

Figure 3 Matrix B (M-D): Metrics vs. characteristics (data collections)

The start point to establish a metrics system is goals determination and structuring. Logically it should correspond to company mission and strategic goals (Juran 1986). A metrics system, as well as any other management initiative, should be oriented in accordance with the company mission. Usually the company mission and strategic goals are identified as general statements such as "to be efficient," "to be timely," "to provide noncompromised quality," and so on. These general statements should be broken down into goals and objectives. For example, the top-level goal, "efficient software development" is divided into subgoals "self-controlled development," "trained staff," "appropriate development tools," and so on (see Figure 2). A complete list of goals and correctness of their structure is very important. The recommended number of levels of goals' structure is between two and four. The example shown in Figure 2 has a two-level goals structure. A single-level structure (that is, just a list of goals) either has difficulties in association with strategic goals or provides low granularity. A metrics system that has more than four levels of goals structure becomes too complicated for management, aggregation, and control of strategic goals.

The relationships between goals and metrics are formalized for the lowest-level goals. Definitions of importance of lowest-level goals are required for formal aggregation. Aggregation to high-level goals is made based on goal structure and importance (see Figure 2).

For example, the importance of the goal "self-controlled development" is defined as 9 (that is, very-very important), while the importance of the goal "trained staff" has the maximum importance of 10 (extremely important). The importance of higher-level goals should be calculated as maximum of the included subgoals. For example, the importance of the goal "efficient software development" is 10 because it includes the extremely important subgoal "trained staff." In the case when the calculated importance of a high-level goal is not appropriate to the expected one, the review of included subgoals and their importance is required.

It should be noted that in Figure 2 three top-level goals, "efficient software development," "efficient software maintenance," and "efficient software testing," may be combined into the strategic goal "efficient operation." In this case, the structure of goals becomes a three-level one.

The aggregation of lower-level goals into strategic goals is an important issue for top management. The achievement of goals on different levels presented as a trend chart allows one to control the efficiency and tendency of business areas, and the overall system.

After the part "What?" in matrix A is set up, the next step is to determine the metrics and their relationships with the goals (see Figure 3). This step is an iterative process that requires coverage and redundancy examinations.

On the contrary, the establishment of matrix B is a straightforward process. The relationships between metrics and characteristics (data collection fields) are determined by analysis of equations. Since equations are usually simple proportions or weighted sums, this procedure is quite trivial. The part "How?" of QFD matrix B is an input to establish appropriate data collections by relating it to particular fields in databases.

The final steps are a formalization of "I: G" relationships, that is:

1. Determining the core management activities on a high level, such as project management, documentation control, risk management, configuration control, and test management
2. Determining opportunities for improvement (improvement actions)
3. Estimating relationships between improvement actions and goals

To perform determination of core management activities one can refer to the key process area (KPA) of the Capability Maturity Model (Paulk 1996) and to ISO 9000-3 clauses.

The outcome of these steps is the prioritized list of improvement actions. Improvement actions should be supported by an implementation plan that includes milestone reviews and result expectations. Review of efficiency based on the chain data-metric-goal (D-M-G) by comparing actual results to expected results triggers the advantage to the next stage of the implementation. A consistent gap between expected results and actual results requires a general review of all system elements, including coverage examination, inherent conflicts analysis, and relationships estimation.

Efficiency of improvement actions is evaluated by the achievement of related goals. A successfully implemented action closes the gap between the targeted and actual level of goal achievement, or exceeds the targeted level. In the case of an increasing gap or insufficient improvement, the review of matrix C is required with respect to goals coverage and correctness of relationships.

As was mentioned previously, step-by-step modeling (see Figure 3) is not straightforward and requires an iterative teamwork-based process. Analysis of coverage and elimination of redundancies usually are iterative processes that require relationships examination. The qualitative analysis of relationships is a major mechanism to ensure completeness and compactness of the metrics system. The ideal case is a diagonal matrix with strong relationships; however, it may be unachievable in practice.

Qualitative Analysis

The qualitative analyses of relationships for matrices are extremely important steps to ensure adequacy of software metrics and their efficiency with respect to business improvement. The addition and elimination procedures presented in (Glushkovsky et al. 1995) help to perform this analysis. These procedures improve completeness of coverage of part "What?" by part "How?" and eliminate redundancies.

An analysis of dependencies between metrics and characteristics provides the opportunity to detect inherent conflicts between metrics and, consequently, between goals with respect to determined targets. For example, there is a conflict between metrics "rate of severe defects detected" and "rate of detected defects corrected" regarding the characteristic "number of defects detected" (see Figure 4). When

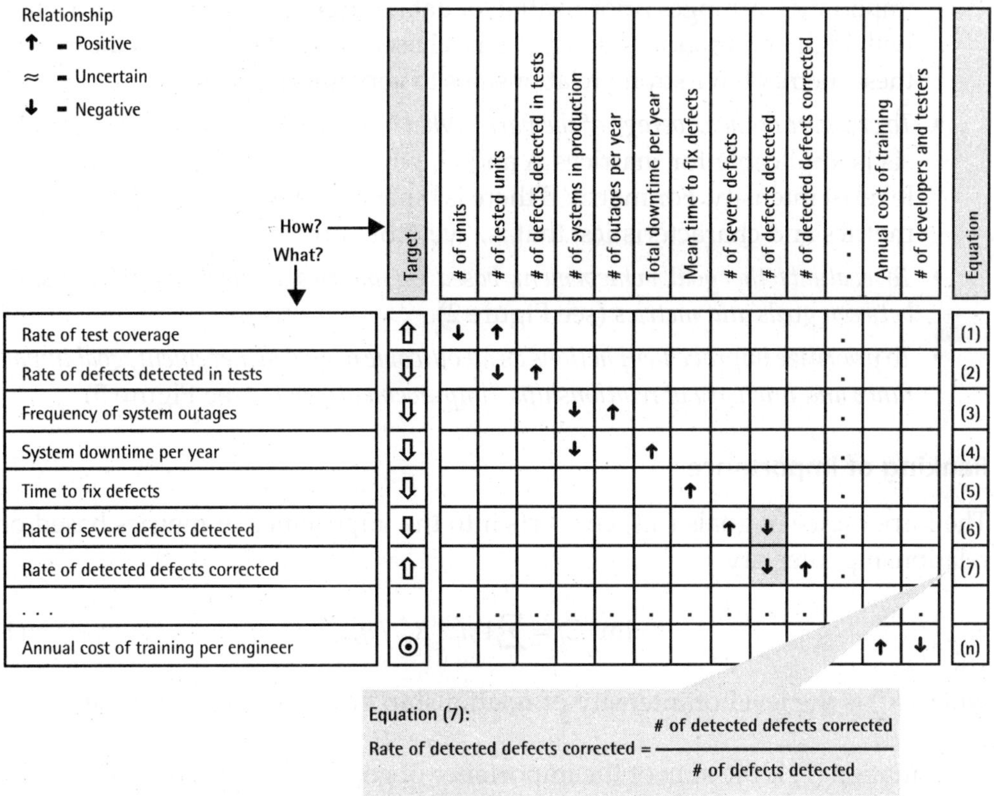

Figure 4 Matrix B (M-D): Metrics vs. characteristics (data collections)

the number of defects detected increases, then the metric "rate of severe defects detected" improves, while the metric "rate of detected defects corrected" worsens (assuming that the rest characteristics remain constant). On the contrary, there is no conflict between metrics "rate of test coverage" and "rate of defects detected in tests" regarding characteristic "number of tested units" (see Figure 4).

The conflict analysis is an analogue to the roof determination for the original QFD matrix (Gopalakrishnan, McIntyre, and Sprague 1992). When the conflict is detected, it assumes additional analysis and optimized solution, which takes into consideration the importance of the goals. This analysis provides better balancing of improvement actions.

Quantitative Analysis

The matrix-based metrics system can be used for quantitative analysis, such as:

- *To rank the of importance of metrics and related characteristics (data collections) based on defined goal importance.* The importance of high-level goals is determined according to the importance of included low-level goals. Ranking the importance of the goals, and following estimations of metrics and characteristics importance, arranges prioritization of data collections (see Figure 2). Metrics with high importance rankings can be chosen as headline ones; it means that these metrics have strong relationships to very important goals.

- *To evaluate of the coverage of the part "What?" by the part "How?"* This analysis is applicable for matrices A and C, where relationship is defined as a level of intensity. For matrix B there is binary type of relationship between metrics and characteristics, that is, "yes" or "no."
- *To evaluate the goal achievement based on metrics values and relationships between goals and metrics* (see Figure 2).
- *To prioritize improvement actions as an outcome of goal achievement, goal importance and intensity of relationships "improvement: goal"* (see Figure 5).

Ranking of Importance

The importance of goals (Im) converts into the importance of metrics based on relationship intensity:

$$\mathrm{Im}_j^{Metric} = \sum_i Im_i^{Goal} R_{ij}^A / 9, \tag{1}$$

where R_{ij}^A is the level of intensity of relationship between goal i and metric j in matrix A.

Equation (1) is the sum of the importance of goals and their normalized relationship intensities to the metric.

For example, assuming that the metric "rate of defects detected in tests" has only the following relationships:

- Strong to very-very important (9) goal "self-controlled development"
- Medium to extremely important (10) goal "trained staff"
- Medium to very-very important goal (9) "sufficient testing"

then importance of the metric is calculated as:

$$9*9/9+10*3/9+9*3/9= 15.3$$

The relative value of the importance of the metric compared to others should be taken into consideration, not the absolute value.

Accordingly, the importance of data collection (characteristic) n may be evaluated as

$$\mathrm{Im}_n^{Characteristic} = \left(\sum_i R_{jn}^B \, \mathrm{Im}_n^{Metric} \right), \tag{2}$$

where R_{jn}^B equals 1 if the characteristic n is required to calculate the metric j, or equals 0 otherwise.

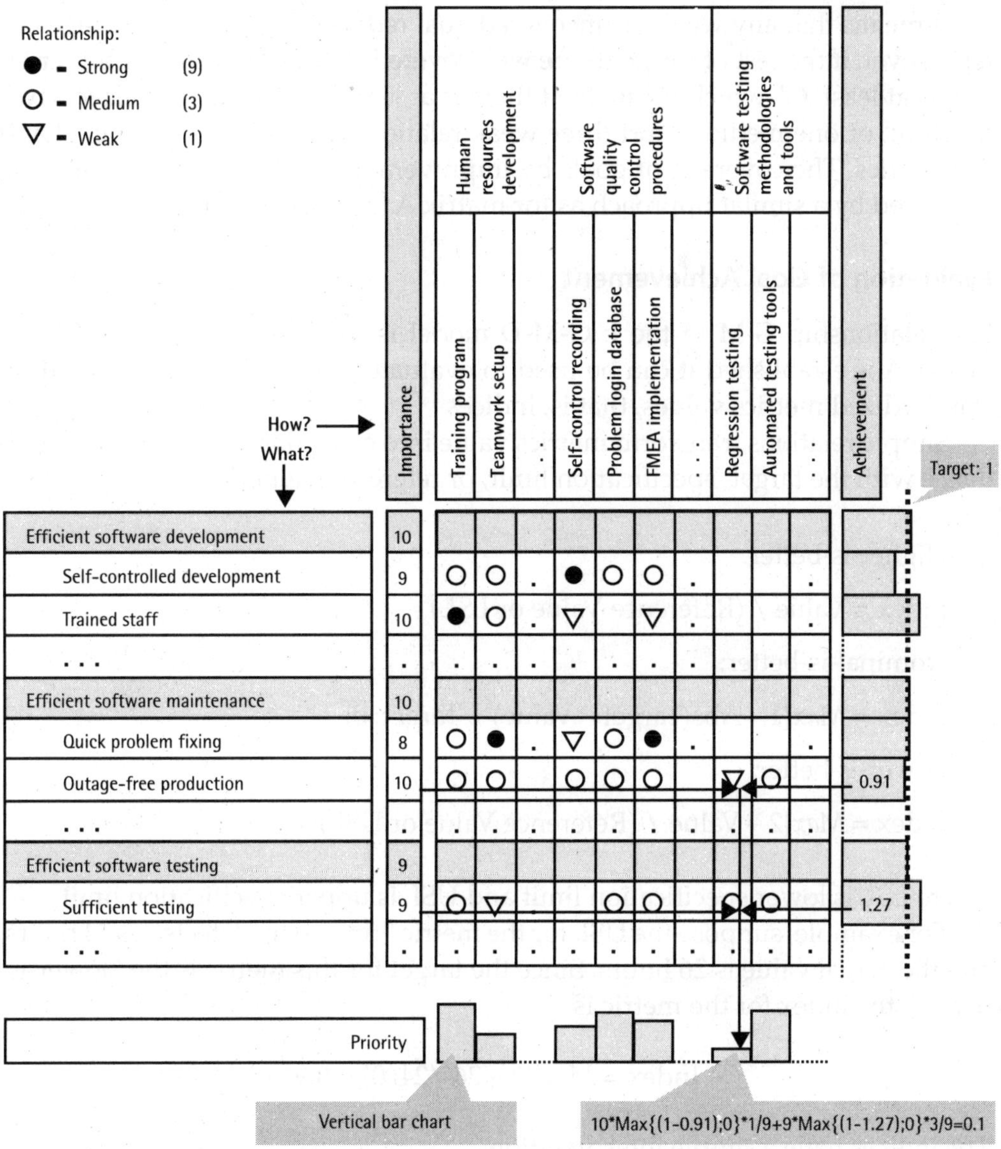

Figure 5 Matrix C (I-G): Improvement activities vs. goals

Coverage Evaluation

Coverage of goals by metrics is examined for established matrix A. The overall coverage may be presented as the following criterion:

$$Criterion^{A}_{Coverage} = \min_{i}\left(\sum_{j} R^{A}_{ij} / 9\right), \tag{3}$$

where sum indicates coverage for goal i, and goal with minimum coverage reflects overall coverage.

It means that any weak or uncovered goal reduces the overall coverage criterion even if the rest of the goals are well covered. The target level for this criterion is at least .67, which means that there is at least one strong (preferred), two medium, or one medium and three weak relationships between each goal and the metrics. The coverage of goals by improvement actions (matrix C) may be evaluated by a similar approach as for matrix A (see Equation (3)).

Evaluation of Goal Achievement

The relationship G-M in the I: G-M-D model is two-way relationship. When matrix A is established it can be used to evaluate goal achievements based on standardized metrics values, that is, indices.

Simple relations transform metrics value into a standardized index in accordance with the target, specification limit, or reference value:

Higher-is-better:

Index = Value / (Reference Value or LSL)

Nominal-is-better:

Index = *Max*{1 – Abs(Target – Value) / Target; 0}

Lower-is-better:

Index = *Max*{2 – Value / (Reference Value or USL); 0}

where LSL is lower specification limit and USL is upper specification limit.

For example, suppose the USL for the metric "time to fix defects" as 24 hours, and the actual value is 26 hours. Since the target for this metric is the "lower-is-better," the index for the metric is:

$$\text{Index} = Max\ \{2 - 26\ /24; 0\} = 0.9$$

The indices have a simple interpretation:

- Index = 1 means that the actual metric value is equal to the target, specification limit (LSL or USL), or reference value
- Index > 1 means that the actual value exceeds the desired value
- Index < 1 means that there is a gap between the actual value and desired value

Indexing provides the opportunity to evaluate, aggregate, and compare goal achievement and prioritize improvement activities.

Evaluation of goal achievement is calculated as a weighted sum of indices, taking into consideration the intensity of the relationship between metrics and goals (see Figure 2):

$$Achievement_i^{Goal} = \frac{\sum_j R_{ij}^A Index_j}{\sum_j R_{ij}^A} \tag{4}$$

For example, assuming that the goal "quick problem fixing" has only the following relationships:

- Strong to metrics "system downtime per year" and "time to fix defects"
- Medium to the metric "rate of detected defects corrected"
- Weak to metrics "frequency of system outages" and "annual cost of training per staff"

the achievement of the goal is calculated as:

$$(0.8{*}1+1.1{*}9+0.9{*}9+0.7{*}3+1.3{*}1)/(1+9+9+3+1) = 0.97$$

The calculated value of 0.97 is close to the target value of 1, and it means that at this point it does not require immediate improvement actions. However, the achievement of the goal "self-controlled development" has a significant gap from the target. Considering the very high importance (9) of the goal, the improvement of the related business area should be prioritized and controlled. Matrix C provides the necessary guidance for improving weak areas.

Achievements of strategic goals are calculated based on included lower-level goal achievements as a weighted sum:

$$Achievement^{StrategicGoal} = \frac{\sum_i Achievement_i^{Goal}\,\mathrm{Im}_i^{Goal}}{\sum_i \mathrm{Im}_i^{Goal}}, \tag{5}$$

where weights are importance of lower-level goals.

Prioritization of Improvement Actions

Priority of improvement actions are calculated as follows:

$$\mathrm{Pr}_k^{Action} = \sum_i R_{ik}^C Max\left(1 - Achievement_i^{Goal};0\right) \tag{6}$$

With respect to framework establishment, the part "How?" of matrix C (improvement actions) is more dynamic compared to "goals," "metrics," and "data." Matrix C should be reviewed systematically according to the list of improvement actions and their relationships to goals.

Calculated priorities of improvement activities provide segmentation of business areas with respect to established goals. Thus, high-priority areas require significant and immediate improvement to close the gap between targeted and actual levels of goal achievement.

Phases of Metrics System Development and Implementation

The following are common phases of metrics system development and implementation.

Phase 1: Initiation

Management initiative to establish software metrics is usually triggered by:

- Internal management's decision to improve software business efficiency based on objective analytical approach
- The customer requirement to receive metrics concerning software product quality or service efficiency (for consulting companies)
- Marketing pressure to achieve particular CMM level or to comply to consensus standards

Outputs of this stage are:

- Clarified strategic goals
- Defined management responsibilities and authorities regarding software metrics system
- Implementation team
- Initial implementation plan, including training with respect to basic knowledge on metrics and QFD methodology

Phase 2: Modeling

This critical phase corresponds to development of a matrix-based framework. The step-by-step procedure to create the I: G-M-D model is described in Figure 3. Following this approach, the metrics system is oriented on defined strategic goals. It is principally different from metrics established by an easy-to-achieve approach: "We have already had some data collections, let us extract some metrics."

Phase 3: Implementation

At this stage, the primary focus is the establishment of required data collections. Adding new or changing existing data collections are difficult tasks that require budget, resources, documented procedures, and a break of personnel inertia.

Phase 4: Utilization

At this final phase, the focus is shifted to the "improvement" part of the I: G-M-D model. The efficiency of improvement actions is evaluated by goal achievements. Systematically, regarding goal achievements problematic areas requires the review of all elements of the I: G-M-D model, particularly:

- Efficiency of improvement actions, responsibilities, and implementation discipline
- Correctness of goals structuring
- Correctness and completeness of metrics determination (goals coverage and relationships)
- Completeness and reliability of data collections

The I: G-M-D model is a dynamic one. It means that appropriate maintenance, systematic reviews, audits, and improvement efforts are required to assure its efficiency.

The proposed integrative framework (see Figure 1) can be implemented at the personnel level. It requires introductory training, technical support of personnel system creation, and integration with the general companywide metrics system. The essential element to establishing the integration is goals conformance between general system and personnel ones. On a personnel level, the system elements are subset of a general system. Implementation of the I: G-M-D metrics system on a personnel level provides employee involvement in management and increases their motivation and commitment. Furthermore, being implemented on a personnel level, the metrics system is recognized as an internal attribute of the business practice, not as a top management control initiative, which is often related to the metrics issues.

Software Metrics as a System

The model presented in Figures 1, 2, 4, and 5 serves as a system to document, control, and maintain data collections, metrics, goals, and improvement actions. In that case, the following properties should be added to the described matrix elements:

- Data collection attributes, such as:
  - —Data source
  - —Data type (that is, numeric, binary, date, or textual)
  - —Project identification
  - —Stage of development process (for example, coding, testing, validation, installation, maintenance, and so on)
  - —Period
  - —Data collection start date
  - —Updating frequency, and so on

- Metrics, goals, and improvement actions properties, such as process-oriented, project-oriented, or global
- Status (applicable for data collections, metrics, and improvement actions):
  —Formalized (documented)
  —Activated (in progress)
  —Implemented

Status analysis evaluates the readiness of the metrics system.

Data collection attributes such as project identification and stage allow focusing the software metrics on a particular area. Additionally, metrics can be presented as a dynamic chain with respect to stages, where the responses (metrics) from the previous stage are the inputs for the next stage. Furthermore, trend charts of metrics and goals achievements over time allow analyzing tendencies and forecasting.

Conclusion

The matrix-based analytical approach provides a practical framework to establish and maintain effective software metrics for systematic business control and improvement. The integrative I: G-M-D model of metrics system supports:

- Customization, modification, review, audit, and improvement of the metrics system
- Integration of the metrics system with other management programs regarding strategic goals, data collection, and improvement actions
- Minimization of the number of metrics by selecting headline ones
- Detection and resolution of inherent conflicts
- Establishment of necessary data collection
- Analysis of efficiency of improvement actions
- Communication, understandability, and results interpretability

ACKNOWLEDGMENTS

The author would like to thank David Zubrow of the Software Engineering Institute, Carnegie Mellon University, for his comments.

REFERENCES

Basili, V. R., and H. D. Rombach. 1988. The TAME Project: Towards Improvement-oriented Software Environments. In *IEEE Transactions in Software Engineering* 14 (6).

Glushkovsky, A., R. Florescu, A. Hershkovits, and D. Sipper. 1995. Avoid a flop: use QFD with questionnaires. *Quality Progress* (June): 57–62.

Glushkovsky, A. 2001. System of sustainable indicators: Object-oriented and quality control approaches. *Quality Engineering* 13, no. 3.

Gopalakrishnan, K., B. McIntyre, and J. Sprague. 1992. Implementing internal quality improvement with the house of quality. *Quality Progress* (September): 57–59.

ISO 9000-3.1997. Quality Management and Quality Assurance Standards. Guidelines for the application of ISO 9001 to the development, supply, and maintenance of software. Geneva: International Organization for Standardization.

Juran, J. M. 1986. *Juran on leadership for quality*. Wilton, Conn.: The Juran Institute, Inc.

Kenett, R. S., and E. R. Baker. 1999. *Software process quality management and control*. New York: Marcel Dekker, Inc.

Paulk, M. C. 1996. Process Improvement and Organizational Capability: Generalizing the CMM. ASQC 50th Annual Quality Congress Proceedings.

Sullivan, L. 1986. Quality function deployment. *Quality Progress* (June): 39–50.

Westfall, L. 1995. Software metrics that meet your information needs. *Software Quality* 4, no. 1: 1–7.

BIOGRAPHY

Alex Glushkovsky has 20 years of industrial, consulting, and instructing experience. He received his doctorate in mathematical simulation and optimization of technological processes from the St. Petersburg Institute of Technology. He is a fellow member of The Royal Statistical Society, a Senior member of ASQ, a CQE, and a CRE. He can be reached by e-mail at alexg@connection.com.

Measuring Software Product Quality

Erik van Veenendaal and Rob Hendriks, Improve Quality Services BV, and Robert van Vonderen, Océ Technologies

In practice, quality requirements of software products are often described in vague and general terms. As a consequence, it is difficult for test engineers to verify the quality of the software product against these requirements. This article describes a method used to identify the most important quality characteristics by means of a risk assessment, to define completion criteria, and to subsequently measure software quality characteristics using the ISO 9126 standard. The authors have applied this method, among others, during testing of copier/printer controller software at Océ Technologies, a Dutch developer and manufacturer of copying and printing equipment.

Key words: completion criteria, ISO 9126, metrics, product quality, quality profile, risk analysis, testing

Project Context

In 1997, Océ Technologies began developing a new line of copier/printer controllers to be used in a new family of monochrome high-volume hybrid copier/printers. In April 1999 this development entered the engineering phase. The engineering of the software for this controller line took place at three sites: two in The Netherlands and one in France. Approximately 60 software engineers were involved in developing this software product, hereafter referred to as the "controller software." The controller software was developed in an incremental way, with each development cycle conforming to the V-model (Myers 1979). Each increment took between three and five months.

At the start of the engineering phase a test and quality assurance team was formed with the assignment to verify correct functional behavior and to determine the quality of the controller software. One problem that the test team encountered was that the required quality level of the controller software was not specified. The only quality requirements available referred to the copier/printer product as a whole and not to its software components. However, the available requirements were easy to measure and easy to understand, for example, the mean number of copies between failures (MCBF, which pertains to all system errors) and the average copies per repair (ACPR, which is the average number of copies made between visits of a service engineer).

Quality Model: ISO 9126

The objective of the test team was to get a clear baseline of the quality requirements before beginning the testing phase. Therefore, a quality model had to be found that could help define and measure software product quality. In 1977 McCall, Richards, and Walters (1977) proposed the idea of breaking down the concept of quality into a number of quality factors. The idea has been followed by many other authors who have tried to capture software product quality in a collection of characteristics and their depending subcharacteristics, which, in turn, are connected to indicators and metrics. By doing so, every author imposes his or her own hierarchically layered model of software product quality. In these varying models some elementary characteristics keep reappearing, although their place in the hierarchy can differ. In recent years the International Organization for Standardization (ISO) and the International Electrotechnical Commission (IEC) have defined a standard set of quality characteristics. This set reflects a big step toward consensus in the software industry and thereby addresses the general notion of software quality. This ISO 9126 standard (ISO 9126-1 2001) defines six quality characteristics and the subdivision of each quality characteristic into subcharacteristics (see Figure 1). The six quality characteristics defined in ISO 9126 are: 1) functionality, 2) reliability, 3) usability, 4) efficiency, 5) maintainability, and 6) portability.

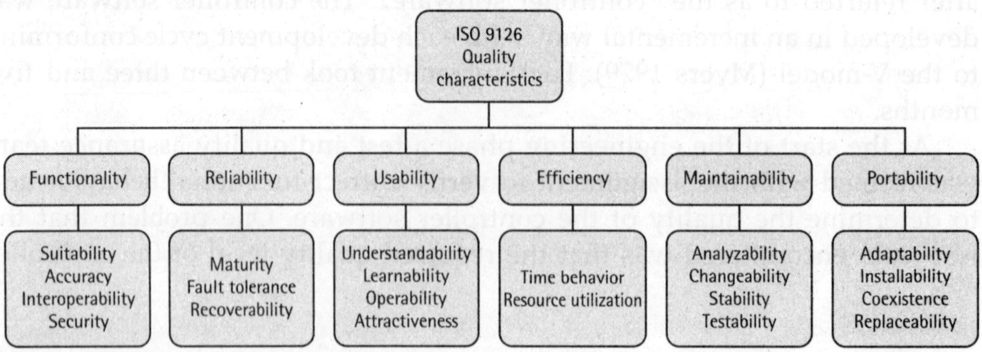

Figure 1 ISO 9126 quality characteristics overview

Selection of Product Quality Characteristics

Terminology

Not all quality characteristics are of equal importance to a software product. Portability may be unimportant when the development aims at a dedicated platform and maintainability may not be an issue when it is a product with a short life cycle. Therefore, the most important quality (sub) characteristics must be identified and selected by means of a risk assessment. This can be done by interviewing stakeholders inside the project (such as the product manager, the project manager, and the software architect) and outside the project (the various types of users are important). Copier users are not just the people operating the copier; often forgotten are stakeholders such as the service engineer and the system administrator.

The quality characteristics as defined by the ISO 9126 standard are not always easy to interpret. What does maintainability, or even worse, coexistence, mean? It is difficult to communicate regarding these quality characteristics in an unambiguous way. As it will be hard to understand for information technology (IT) professionals, it will be even harder for users of the copier, who, in general, have no or limited IT knowledge. Most of the users do not even perceive that the product contains software. The quality characteristics are usually not part of the stakeholders' terminology. It will therefore be difficult to determine those quality characteristics that are important for the software component of the product just by asking, "Do you think resource behavior is important?" The people interviewed have their own definition of the characteristics and their own view of what the system should do and what is important.

Structured Questionnaire

To overcome these problems, a questionnaire risk-based method has been developed and empirically validated in the European ESPRIT project SPACE-UFO (Van Veenendaal and McMullan 1997; Trienekens and Van Veenendaal 1997). The method relates the wishes and needs of stakeholders regarding the software product to software quality characteristics. The stakeholders' needs and requirements are explored and identified using a structured questionnaire. The questionnaire consists of a number of questions regarding so-called generic product characteristics. These product characteristics are intended to be stated in the stakeholders' language. Instead of asking whether usability is important one asks questions about the characteristics of the users that influence the usability requirements, for example, the number of users, their experience with the product (or a similar one), and their educational level. Similar questions are asked for the other quality characteristics. The answers given are used to deduct the most relevant quality (sub) characteristics by means of two-dimensional matrices. The SPACE-UFO questionnaire is a standardized questionnaire and was used without major customization for the Océ controller project.

A part of the structured questionnaire is shown in Figure 2. For each question the related quality (sub) characteristics are indicated.

Quality Profile

Within the copier/printer project four key people were selected. In addition, three representatives of the different types of users were selected. Thus, seven people were interviewed, each having his or her typical view on the copier/printer product. From the participants' answers, a list of important quality characteristics can be deducted. Furthermore, importance levels can be identified (from level D to level A). This whole process results in a so-called quality profile (ISO/IEC 14598-5 1996). A quality profile reflects the notion of quality for a certain software product and makes quality more tangible for all stakeholders

Question	Quality characteristic
What is the number of products to be sold in a certain market area? (see Trienekens and van Veenendaal 1997) 1. 1 – 1,000 2. 1,000 – 10,000 3. More than 10,000	Suitability Maturity
Does the product belong to a product family? 1. No 2. Yes	Analyzability Changeability
Can software product failures cause damage? 1. Some economic loss 2. Serious economic loss 3. Safety damage or environmental disaster	Maturity Operability
What is the average experience of the recognized user groups with regard to the product? 1. More than one-year experience 2. Less than one-year experience 3. No experience	Understandability
How many users can be identified per product? 1. 1 – 10 2. 10 – 100 3. More than 100	Maintainability Reliability Usability
Are there any alternatives to carry on with the activities when the software fails? 1. Yes 2. No	Reliability
Are certain parts of the software available on more than one platform? 1. No 2. Yes	Portability

Figure 2 Sample questions structured questionnaire

	Quality Level				
	-	D	C	B	A
Functionality				X	
Reliability				X	
Usability			X		
Efficiency		X			
Maintainability			X		
Portability	X				

Figure 3 Quality profile

(including testing). Once the initial quality profile has been defined, a consensus meeting is organized with all stakeholders to discuss the quality profile, the results of the interviews, and the observed differences. Figure 3 shows the resulting quality profile (on a quality characteristic level) for the controller software.

As can be observed in the quality profile, the quality characteristics functionality, reliability, usability, and maintainability were considered the most important for the controller software. This can be explained for the type of copier the project is developing: It is expected to run in a highly professional document production environment, where the uptime (highly related to "reliability" and "maintainability") is of utmost importance. Also, the copier/printer will be the successor product to an analog high-volume copier model, where a clear functionality demand (being compatible with existing products as well as providing an extension) is expressed. Usability scores high but was not considered further for testing the controller software. This is because usability is a property of the user interface, which was not part of the controller software development project, as it is developed in a separate project.

As a result, the test team decided to focus on three quality characteristics (functionality, reliability, and maintainability), and to develop a set of completion criteria (metrics) for these quality characteristics.

Identification of Quality Metrics

Once the quality profile has been determined, it is time to start focusing on how to evaluate and measure the relevant quality (sub) characteristics. The ISO 9126 standard defines in part two (External metrics) and part three (Internal metrics) a large number of possible metrics per characteristic, including measurement scales and application guidelines (ISO 9126-2 2002; ISO 9126-3 2002). A selection must be made of the metrics provided and, if necessary, extended with self-defined metrics. Within the project for each quality characteristic, a selection of metrics was made based on either ISO 9126 or on the product requirements (for example, MCBF). The selection of metrics to be used was mainly based on whether it was possible and easy to measure them, since this was considered to be a pilot project within Océ for measuring software product quality.

Most of the metrics were used directly from the ISO standard, but some had to be fine-tuned to the project's definitions. An example is the ISO 9126 metric mean time between failures (MTBF). This metric is often used to give an indication of the maturity of the system. For copier/printers the maturity is often indicated by means of the metric MCBF, as the number of copies made is leading instead of the up-time. Therefore a slight change for some metrics was desirable. Furthermore, the product requirements often include quality statements applicable to the product as a whole. As only the controller software was taken into account, these quality statements needed to be translated to the controller software. For example, the MCBF is higher for the controller software than for the product, because only failures caused by the controller software are considered. For example, paper jams are not important when evaluating the software maturity.

In total 16 metrics were defined, one of which was in addition to the internal and external metrics provided in the ISO 9126 standard. The availability of design documentation was considered to be a good indication of the maintainability. Therefore a metric was added to verify the amount of design documen-

Quality characteristic	Subcharacteristic	Metric	Explanation
Functionality	Suitability	*Functional implementation completeness:* Number of missing functions detected during system testing / Number of functions described in requirement specifications.	How many functions have been implemented in relation to the number of functions specified in the requirement specifications?
		Functional implementation correctness: Number of correctly implemented functions confirmed during system testing / Number of functions described in requirement specifications.	How many functions have been implemented according to the requirement specifications?
Reliability	Maturity	*Mean copies between failures:* Total number of copies during system testing / Number of defects, caused by controller software, detected during operation time.	How frequent are the defects of the controller software in operation?
		Defect detection: Absolute number of defects detected during all test phases / Number of estimated defects to be detected, measured for each release.	What is the proportion of the defects found?
		Test completeness: Number of actually executed test cases / Number of test cases to be executed.	How reliable is the test process for product quality statements?
Maintainability	Analyzability	*Availability of design documentation:* Available design documentation (that is, software architecture, top-level design, analysis views, design views, and interface specifications) / Identified design documentation.	What is the proportion of design documentation available?
		Inspected design documentation: Inspected design documentation / Available design documentation.	How reliable and correct is the content of design documentation?

Figure 4 Examples of product quality metrics

tation that was available vs. the amount of design documentation planned. An overview of some of the metrics defined can be found in Figure 4.

Defining Completion Criteria

It was decided that completion criteria, as a hypothetical baseline, had to be defined before starting actual measurement. The goal was not to measure relative improvement with each test cycle but to compare the measured quality against the completion criteria, which must be reached before the product can be released. Defining completion criteria in advance forces people to start discussion when quality targets are not met. If no baseline is defined one is tempted to accept the quality as is because no tangible reference exists. The product is easily considered to be "good enough."

These completion criteria were defined by asking some experienced engineers within the project and on comparable software projects for an estimate on each metric. These estimates were then compared and discussed in a team meeting. Each estimate needed to state the "minimum but sufficient quality level" for release. For example, the metric MCBF was defined to be 100,000. This means that only one failure, caused by the controller software, may occur every 100,000 copies. It was decided to measure all criteria (when applicable) during the system test phase of each incremental development cycle. The result of each development cycle could thus be scored against the defined baseline. In this way, both the improvements per development cycle, as well as the discrepancy with the "minimum but sufficient quality level," could be depicted and reacted upon.

Collection of the measurement data during the system test phases implied that thorough administration was necessary during test execution. In addition to defects found, it was important to record the number of copies made, the total down time of the copier/printer, the number of failures successfully restored by the system, and so on. It was important to clearly instruct the test engineers on what data should be recorded, otherwise important information necessary to calculate the metrics could be missing. The test engineers were given instructions on how to collect the metrics, and a set of supporting forms was established.

After each system test phase the measured values were evaluated to see whether the product was approaching its completion criteria. If necessary, the completion criteria can be modified, but not after a thorough discussion within the steering committee regarding the desired quality levels. Management should always formally approve a change in the completion criteria.

Real-Life Measurements

Until the first commercial release of the controller software, five development increments were evaluated and measured. For one increment, an additional system test phase was added, leading to a sixth measurement (C2 patch). Some measurement results of the increments are presented in Figure 5.

From Figure 5 one can see that the MCBF was far below the completion criteria defined. Still the completion criterion was not adjusted. The low number for MCBF for increments C1, C2, and C2 patch was mainly because the controller software was not yet robust for failures in the scanner or printer. For example, a paper jam also resulted in a failure in the controller software. From increment C3 onward the software was robust for paper jams, and the MCBF increased tremendously. Still the value was far below the initially defined quality target. It appeared that during the initial estimate it was not taken into account that the tests were aiming at finding functional defects in the software and were not defined with the objective of finding defects by producing large numbers of copies.

It is interesting to compare the measurements from increment C2 patch to those from increment C2. The software test on increment C2 was hindered by major instability and performance problems. These problems were resolved, after which measurement C2 patch took place. Although the difference between the metrics of increment C2 and increment C2 patch is relatively small (only nine major defects were solved, approximately 5 percent of the total number of defects solved), the users perceived increment C2 patch as a much "better" system. This example shows that the metrics and values indicated in Figure 5 should be interpreted with great care. For instance, when a system only shows a few critical defects in the most important part of that system, it will be of an unacceptable quality level, however the metrics may show otherwise. The severity of a defect and its location in the system are not taken into account. This means that an experience-based quantitative evaluation is needed in addition to the metrics.

Quality characteristic	Sub-characteristic	Metric	Completion criteria	Value C1	Value C2	Value C2 patch	Value C3	Value C4	Value C5
Functionality	Suitability	Functional implementation completeness	0.90	0.91	1.0	1.0	0.82	0.90	0.91
		Functional implementation correctness	0.80	0.45	0.80	0.84	0.61	0.70	0.64
Reliability	Maturity	Defect detection[1]	0.75	0.46	0.63	0.63	1.08	1.19	1.43
		Mean copies between failures	100000	not available	93	175	4880	11204	6560
		Test completeness	0.90	0.75	0.78	0.33	0.92	0.97	0.95
Maintainability	Analyzability	Available design documentation[1]	not defined	0.70	0.62	0.62	0.66	0.73	0.70
		Inspected design documentation[1]	0.75	0.71	0.67	0.67	0.59	0.49	0.49

[1]These measurement values are cumulative.

Figure 5 Measurements results

From increment C3 onward one can see that the defect detection rate is greater than 1, which shows that more defects were found than initially expected. The estimate for the defects expected to be found may be incorrect—this needs further investigation. Literature (for example, Hatton 1995 and Pfleeger, Hatton, and Howel 2001) and historical metrics from previous new products of the Océ organization were used to estimate the number of defects expected to be found. The main assumption was that on average six defects could be found per thousand lines of code (KLOC). For reused code this value was adapted to two defects per KLOC. Furthermore, automatically generated code was seen as newly developed code, and, therefore, also six defects per KLOC were expected.

The number of defects found vs. the number expected should be approximately one for each increment. Note that this is a cumulative value. In the project, however, defects were found rather late over the increments. At increment C3 the integration test process was strengthened, which may explain the rise of defect detection from that moment on.

After increment C3 a major shift of responsibilities between the test team of the controller software and the system test team of the copier/printer occurred. From that point on the functional tests were the responsibility of the copier/printer test team, while integration testing remained the responsibility of the controller software test team. Because of this shift a different test strategy was applied to system testing. The printer/copier system test team did not only focus on functionality, but also on performance and duration. Therefore, more copies were made with a minimum number of user interactions, which affected the total number of copies made during a system test phase. This affected the metric MCBF. The types of tests that have been executed are important to consider when evaluating the metrics.

Some of the measurement values show a decrease over the various increments. This can be explained by the fact that measurements for a certain increment only take into account the documentation and code that has been developed within the particular increment. For example, the metric "functional implementation completeness" is determined for the functionality developed within each increment individually. It is then possible that a measured value decreases compared to that of a previous increment. For cumulative measurements all increments are taken into account. For example, when during a particular increment many design documents are written but not inspected, this will have a negative effect on the metric "inspected design documentation."

The Release Decision Process

The software quality metrics were measured within the project for more than two years. During that period much experience was gained on the metrics themselves, how to interpret them, and how they could be used, such as for setting project priorities. The metrics were initially only applied to provide visibility on software product quality. The next step was to submit changes in the development process to improve the quality of the software and the process. For example, if the defect detection rate is lower than expected, as can be seen for releases C1 to C2 patch, but the test completeness is high (75 percent to 78 percent), it is necessary to evaluate the effectiveness of the test process. It is, of course, also possible that the engineering team makes fewer errors than expected.

Of course, if the completion criteria are not met, additional tests may be required. However, the tension between time-to-market and product quality will always remain. The metrics provided by using this method are a major input for management to support the release decision process. They allow a thorough discussion with all stakeholders on product quality and the identification of outstanding risks. As a result, the test plan may be revised to permit the relaxation (or strengthening) of the test completion criteria.

The reporting on product quality has been received well within the project, both by people involved in the quality profile definition and those only receiving the test results. The discussions on product quality are now based on more than "just" the number of defects and the subjective perception of stakeholders.

REFERENCES

Hatton, L. 1995. *Safer C: Developing software for high-integrity and safety-critical systems.* New York: McGraw-Hill.

ISO/IEC 9126-1. 2001. *Software engineering-Software product quality-Part 1: Quality model.* Geneva, Switzerland: International Organization for Standardization.

ISO/IEC DTR 9126-2. 2001. *Software engineering-Software product quality-Part 2: External metrics.* Geneva, Switzerland: International Organization for Standardization.

ISO/IEC DTR 9126-3. 2000. *Software engineering-Software product quality-Part 3: Internal metric.* Geneva, Switzerland: International Organization for Standardization.

ISO/IEC CD 14598-5. 1996. *Information technology-Software product evaluation-Part 5: Process for evaluators.* Geneva, Switzerland: International Organization for Standardization.

McCall, J. A., P. K. Richards, and G. F. Walters. 1977. *Factors in software quality* (RADC-TR-77-363). Rome, New York: Rome Air Development Center, Griffiss Air Force Base.

Myers, G. J. 1979. *The art of software testing.* New York: Wiley-Interscience.

Pfleeger S. L., L. Hatton, and Howel. 2001. *Solid software.* New York: Pearson Education Inc.

Trienekens J. J. M., and E. P. W. M. van Veenendaal. 1997. *Software quality from a business perspective.* Deventer, The Netherlands: Kluwer Bedrijfsinformatie.

Van Veenendaal, E. P. W. M., and J. McMullan, eds. 1997. *Achieving software product quality.* S-Hertogenbosch, The Netherlands: UTN Publishing.

BIOGRAPHIES

Erik van Veenendaal has been working as a practitioner and manager in the IT industry since 1987. As a test manager and quality consultant he has been involved in many projects, has implemented structured testing, and carried out test process improvements activities in a large number of organizations. He is the author of numerous papers and books on software quality and testing, including the best-seller *Testing According to TMap*. He is a regular speaker at both national and international testing conferences and a leading international (ISEB accredited) trainer in the field of software testing. At EuroStar'99 he received the best tutorial award for a tutorial on usability testing. van Veenendaal is the founder and managing director of Improve Quality Services Ltd., a company that provides consultancy and training services in the area of quality management, usability, inspection, and testing. He is also a senior lecturer at the Eindhoven University of Technology, Faculty of Technology Management. He is on the Dutch ISO standards committee for software quality. He can be reached by e-mail at eve@improveqs.nl.

Rob Hendriks has worked in the field of software quality for technical systems, with a specialization in software testing, since 1996. Currently he works as a quality and test consultant for Improve Quality Services BV. Prior to that he worked as a test coordinator and consultant within projects for consumer electronics and professional systems. He has been involved in the definition and deployment of the Software Engineering Institute's Capability Maturity Model (CMM) key process areas Software Quality Assurance within a large organization. On a regular basis Hendriks is a trainer on inspections and software testing, and he is an accredited trainer for the ISEB Foundation Certificate in Software Testing. Hendriks is a certified moderator and a member of the ISEB Software Testing Examiners Panel.

Robert van Vonderen has worked for Océ Technologies B.V. since his graduation from the Eindhoven University of Technology. He conducted a range of applied research studies in the areas of embedded software, geographical information systems, and printer controller software. In recent years he has worked as a project manager and project leader for the Océ Printing Systems division in the area of printer controllers and maintenance. He is currently responsible for the integration, testing, and quality assurance activities of the newest line of controller development.

The Uses and Abuses of Software Metrics

Pat Cross, London St. Consulting

This article discusses aspects of the use of metrics beyond the goal/question/metric paradigm. It suggests that ignoring data types and limitations, or using data analysis inappropriately, is common and leads to making incorrect decisions. Some of the major abuses of software metrics are shown through examples, some artificial and others from case studies. Given the interest of the software community in control charts, and their general misuse in software, they are explained through manufacturing examples and then their application to software situations is discussed. A simple approach, but one that tries to develop a statistical way of thinking, is advised, and a few hints are provided.

Key words: accuracy, data interpretation, data types, precision, SPC, statistics

Introduction

This article was born out of a burst of rage. One afternoon at a SPIN meeting, I saw a handout that compared the results of a questionnaire on process maturity and that had been used on a sample of 13 government organizations and 17 private-sector organizations. Averages of 62.9 percent and 57.9 percent (with standard deviations of 11.0 percent and 96.9 percent, respectively) were quoted, and the paper concluded that these government organizations were more mature than the private-sector organizations. The authors of that paper had used discrete measures as if they were continuous and had drawn conclusions of true difference between two populations using very tiny sample sizes and with results that overlapped significantly.

While still in shock over these multiple abuses of data analysis, I heard a representative from a respected high-maturity company explain that they were using control limits of one or two standard deviations (sigma) for their control charts. When I questioned why they would use these limits instead of the classic

---

This article is based on a presentation awarded "Best in Conference" at the 12th Annual International Conference on Software Quality, sponsored by the ASQ Software Division.

three sigma, my colleague told me "because we believed we could do better than that." No one in his organization knew that three sigma is deliberately chosen because it is the breakeven point between two types of errors (see Bicking and Gryna 1962).

I realized that the lessons I had absorbed through manufacturing quality on the respect one must pay to data and data analysis were not obvious in software quality, and the practitioners were often using formulas from manufacturing quality without understanding the theory behind them. The explanations and references for my positions follow.

Purpose

This article concentrates on the steps beyond understanding the importance and use of data in driving improvement and on using a goal/question/metric (GQM) approach to which data should be collected. It contains practical, not academic, approaches to avoiding poor data handling, and gives hypothetical and true case examples to clarify the ideas. It covers how to know and respect one's data and the beginnings of a statistical way of thinking, but deliberately avoids formula and detailed descriptions of techniques, preferring instead to offer simple visual ways of approaching data interpretation. This does not mean that the more detailed approach is never necessary; only that in the early stages of metrics use, the simpler methods are more likely to be applied correctly. References to more rigorous methods will be offered for further work.

Background

Gathering, analyzing, and interpreting metrics is not optional, it is essential. It is the only logical way of managing and improving any activity, including developing software. It is specifically required by both ISO 9000:2000 and the Software Engineering Institute's Capability Maturity Model for Software (SW-CMMI), which now requires a metrics program at level 2 (rather than the level 3 of SW-CMM). At maturity level 4, the model expects the performance of processes to be controlled using statistical and other quantitative techniques, and be quantitatively predictable.

However, metrics programs usually follow a boom-bust pattern. Someone realizes metrics are needed, sets up a complex program, gets results that do not "work" (reduce costs), and the metrics program gets cut. Later, the same cycle is repeated with a new batch of managers.

Historically, struggling with how to make such programs effective, the first step was to focus on clear, relatively narrow objectives, that is, to develop written goals for a metrics program specific to a company or division. The second step was to ask questions about what information would be needed to meet each goal, and the third step was to gather only those data that would supply the information. This technique was developed by Basili and Weiss (1984) and defined as the GQM method by Basili and Ronback (1988).

The metrics literature has also concentrated on the management problems of gathering and using metrics (for example, Grady 1992; Hall, Baddoo, and Wilson 2001), since the metrics usually need to be gathered by project or maintenance teams that rarely see the activity as an important priority, and the metrics group often has little power to enforce accurate gathering or changes suggested by the data analysis. An excellent review of the history is given in Fenton and Neil (1999).

More academic papers in the software area have discussed types of data and the valid transformations they can undertake (for example, Fenton 1994 and Zuse 1998). However, the papers often are written in a mathematically rigorous way, which may be hard for a person in an industrial climate to find time to assimilate. Other papers (for example, Florac, Carleton, and Barnard 2000 and Jalote 2002) have used or reported techniques based on statistical process control (SPC) borrowed from manufacturing quality to analyze their data.

What is disturbing is that many software practitioners, including very respected institutions, have either not used this knowledge, or applied it incorrectly. For example, the case studies later in this article illustrating abuses come from a very large and well-established computer company. And to clarify that the company at the SPIN meeting was not alone in its lack of understanding of the use of control charts, a recent article in *Software Quality Professional* (Jalote 2002) stated, without comment, that "Some [high maturity] organizations defined control limits as three sigma, while in others it was tighter—one sigma, two sigma, or spread in data without outliers."

I conclude that the technical basics of gathering and using software metrics are hazily understood by the average practitioner, and I hope to clarify them here without heavy mathematics. For the dangers of using techniques without care are not simply that organizations will not improve, but also that they may actually make the quality of the product or process worse than if they had not gathered metrics, interpreted them in some way, and acted on that interpretation.

Simple Examples of Use and Abuse of Metrics

Other papers (for example, Grady 1992 and McGarry et al. 2002) list the many possible ways software metrics are used in the industry. For the purposes of this article, examples will concentrate on the following four uses:

- Fact-finding
- Prediction
- Comparison
- Triggering a decision

For example, organizations will fact-find about the project before predicting the cost and schedule. As the project moves forward, they compare the actual cost and schedule to that predicted; if the actual and predicted are very different, they may decide to take action to bring them into line.

If they use the wrong data or inappropriate analysis methods or interpret the data or the analysis inappropriately, they will make wrong decisions. As a default position, practitioners should be prepared to say, "I don't know" whenever the interpretation of the data seems cloudy. It may not be what others want to hear, but it certainly will not lead the company into expensive and potentially incorrect decisions.

Here are some fictitious examples of some very simple problems that could occur. More complex problems are described later.

Fact-Finding

The customer required an efficient system. The operators take less time to do common tasks than they did before, but may take longer to do certain unusual tasks. Is this acceptable?

The problem here is that the company has not clarified the requirement. They need to understand what the customer meant by "efficient." As usual, trying to work out how they will verify the requirement (here, what metrics will be gathered) before accepting the requirement will result in a better product at the end (here, developers and customers who agree on what is meant by "efficient").

Prediction

Peer review meeting time (clock time) for component design is given in Figure 1. How will one budget (predict) reviews for 20 similar components in a new project?

If one budgets too low he or she is likely not to meet schedule when implementing the process. If one budgets too high, he or she may cause the peer reviews to be cut out from the plan. A usual way of predicting is to use the average of past results.

Time reported in minutes (to the nearest 10 min.)	Number of people reporting
60	3
120	54
150	15
300	2
750	8

Figure 1 Peer review meeting time for component design

Here the average =

$$(60 \times 3 + 120 \times 54 \ldots) / (3 + 54 \ldots) = 182.47058$$

But look at the numbers. The majority are at 120 minutes. The average is much higher because of the eight instances of 750 minutes. Why did eight meetings get reported so high? Could one even contemplate a meeting of 12 1/2 hours? Did they report the total people-hours in the meeting, or even the total preparation and meeting time? Here it is safer to use the mode (the time most people reported) rather than the average. The moral is, look at the data for odd patterns.

Comparison

Use of a checklist for ensuring compliance to company coding standards has just been introduced. Project A did not use it, but Project B (similar in most ways to Project A) did. Figure 2 shows the defects found in component testing for nine similar components in Project A and Project B. How will employees report the results to management?

If they fall into the trap of saying, "The average defects went down, you can make immediate costs savings if the coding standard is introduced for all projects," they would do the company an injustice. For if they plot the frequency of defects for each project they see (see Figure 3) the distributions overlap so much, it is not safe to say they are different, although there does seem to be a constant difference between the two sets of results. Here is a case when the correct answer is "I don't know."

Triggering an Action

The return on investment (ROI) of the last 10 projects is given below. The average is 1.1.

Project A	Project B
39	16
18	9
25	37
11	23
25	30
32	23
32	16
18	23
25	30
Average = 25	Average = 23

Figure 2 Defects found in similar code components for projects A and B

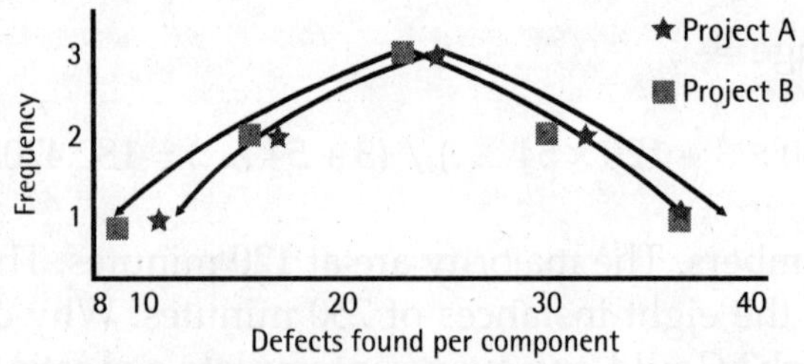

Figure 3 Frequency charts for defects before and after

$$ROI = 1.1, 1.2, 1.3, 0.8, 1.1, 1.4, 0.9, 1.2, 0.9, 1.1$$

It is suggested that the implementation of a requirements document template should be required in all projects. Before one can support this he or she needs the answers to other questions and further metrics.

- Is there evidence (metrics) that poor requirements documents are affecting the ROI?
- Are there metrics to show that the problem lies in the documentation, rather than the gathering, of requirements?
- How sensitive to the ROI of individual projects is upper management? Do they care if one-third of the ROIs are lower than 1, as long as the average is higher than 1?

Types of Measures

The Importance of Understanding Types

Programmers are familiar with using integer and floating point variables and would never dream of adding them together or manipulating an integer variable and arbitrarily treating it as a floating point. But, strangely, the same respect is not given to understanding data types and the limitations each data type places on the analyses that can be done and the inferences that can be drawn. Long before asking anyone to gather data, work out what type it will be and what actions are allowed with it.

Discrete, Continuous, and Ranking Measures

These types of measures have different names in different disciplines. A quick overview follows, so that information from one area can be lined up with information from a different background, then a simple definition is given. Finally, the strengths and weaknesses of the different types are provided.

In the more mathematical world some measurement classifications are: nominal, ordinal, ratio, and absolute (Zuse 1998). Nominal measures are those that identify without implying ranking and have no units; ordinal measures are those that rank properties, but have no units; ratio measures are those that have equal intervals (the units) along a scale whose starting point is defined and whose intervals can be (theoretically) infinitely divided. Measurements that use ratio measures can be manipulated using ordinary arithmetic. Absolute measures are defined in a complex way, but one example of them is counting.

In manufacturing quality, from which many software quality ideas are drawn, the types of data are defined in the order of easiness to handle. For probability distributions, the names "discrete" and "continuous" are used (Dudewicz 1998). These are called integer and floating point variables in programming and are loosely comparable to absolute and ratio measures mentioned previously. When using control charts, the comparable measures are attribute and variable (Dudewicz 1998). Ranking measures (ordinal as defined before) are often also called nonparametric measures (Spent 1993).

Because I think they are the most descriptive, and, therefore, easiest to understand, I have chosen to use the terms *discrete, continuous,* and *ranking* to describe these types of measures.

Discrete data are any data that are measured stepwise, the most obvious being counting—how many people, how often does this happen, how many defects, how many lines of code, what is the McCabe Complexity Metric for this module, and so on. This is usually the easiest way of measuring and the most used in young disciplines, such as software.

Continuous data are data that are measured on a well-understood, continuous scale—how much time (for example, in minutes), how much money (for example, in dollars), percentage complete, and so on. Theoretically, the divisions of these scales have no limit. Validating these scales is difficult and software practitioners usually use ones that are already in use elsewhere.

Ranking data are any data that can be ranked, but the intervals between the ranks are not equal. For example, for customer satisfaction, is the difference between how a customer feels at "somewhat satisfied" and "very satisfied" the same as the difference between how they feel at "neutral" and "somewhat satisfied"? Probably not. There is evidence that each person sets up his or her own internal scale of satisfaction when confronted by questions on this subject. Other ranking measures met in the software quality world are usability, risk, and maintainability scales.

Analysis of discrete measures is weaker than that of continuous measures (Dudewicz 1998) and often leaves one in the "I don't know" situation. Continuous data can be analyzed using ordinary arithmetic, but discrete must always "round off" results. It is very important not to forget that one cannot just change discrete to continuous by (for example) dividing by three. Respect for one's data will include remembering what was discrete and not using it as if it were continuous.

Analysis of ranking data requires more complex statistics than that used with discrete or continuous data (Spent 1993). One danger occurs when the intervals are labelled with numbers rather than words, for example, –2, –1, 0, +1, or +2 rather than very unsatisfied, somewhat unsatisfied, don't care, somewhat satisfied, or very satisfied. This is equivalent to acting as if one has discrete data, rather than ranking. One is tempted to treat the labels as if they were numbers, and, for example, average them. But a –2 and a +2 may not cancel each other out if the –2 hates the product much more than the +2 likes it (and that's the usual skew).

So as rules of thumb:

- When deciding to gather certain data, work out if it is discrete, continuous, or ranking.
- Don't try and change the type during the analysis.
- If unsure how to analyze it arithmetically, draw frequency diagrams and spend time thinking about the story they are telling.

Direct and Indirect Measures, and Indicators

A different type of classification is based on "how closely is the measure linked to the attribute you are interested in?" The closer the link, the more reliance one can have on decisions based on those data.

Direct measures allow a measurement specifically on the attribute (Fenton 1994). It may be very easy to measure, such as how much money was spent on this project or how many people were working during the requirements phase.

Indirect measures require combining two pieces of data to understand the attribute (Fenton 1994), for example, total cost per line of code, schedule variance (actual time to perform work planned/scheduled time to perform work planned).

Indicators are defined as evidence that provide clues to the measure of an attribute. Note that McGarry et al. (2002) define *indicator* to mean what Fenton called an *indirect measure* and some writers (for example, Greisdorf 2003) appear to call a similar concept to a clue or indicator a *predictive model*. In keeping with the aim of this article to use the most descriptive names so that busy managers will be able to avoid inappropriate actions, the name *indicator* will be used.

An example of when an indicator may be useful is in answering the question, "How many significant defects still exist in a set of components?" This would be useful to help predict how much more testing on each would be cost effective. But there is no way of measuring the remaining defects directly, so one might take as a clue (an indicator) the number of defects already found in each component in this phase of testing. This assumes that where a lot of defects were found, more will still be found. The action one takes depends on assumptions like this, and, of course the analysis, is much weaker than actions taken based on direct or indirect measures. Nevertheless, the indicator is often the only path open, and as long as it is used with caution, it is better than no measure at all. However, before large amounts of money are spent on the basis of an indicator, it is wise to look for back-up evidence.

Other indicators met in software quality are complexity measures used to judge the likelihood of bugs, the McCabe measure used to judge complexity itself, and size (lines of code or function points) used to predict development effort needed.

Precision and Accuracy

Precision

How close to a real value can one measure? The ultimate limitation is the scale of the measuring device, for example, a digital clock may measure in one-minute intervals (the device precision). On top of that, a person may get distracted, or it may not be obvious when an activity has ended, or the time may be recalled from memory later. The combined effect of these types of problems on the measure is known as the precision of the measure. That is why the meeting times in the prediction example of Figure 1 were quoted as measured to 10 minutes. The metric gatherer did not feel confident in getting the error lower than that.

The following is an actual case-study example. A small sample of the raw data for preparation time for peer review (in hours, as reported) is given in Figure 4.

The apparent precision here is hard to determine (see particularly, 6.75 and 40.83). The author asked what times the participants had been asked to measure to. The answer was that they had not been given a guide. So some of them had clearly measured to 15 minutes (6.75) and others to 10 minutes (40.83). There are no clues as to what the others measured to, perhaps the 20 value measured to the nearest hour. The results of analysis of these data will necessarily be suspect, or at least imprecise; one would have to round all the figures to the lowest precision used, assuming he or she could find out what it was.

The average of a set of repeated measures is expected to have a better precision (because the errors are likely to cancel one another out). For small samples (less than a hundred) as a rough approximation one can quote an average to half the interval (Topping 1957). It is not safe to quote better than half a measuring

20
12.5
6.75
12
9
16.5
10.33
40.83
5
4

Figure 4 Peer review preparation time in hours

interval unless one has statistical backing to show it is reasonable. So, for example, the calculated average of the times in the prediction example given before was 182.47058. It is clear that this is too many significant figures. Knowing that the precision of the raw data was 10 minutes, one can quote the average to a precision of five minutes, so it becomes 180 minutes.

Accuracy

A question different from "How closely do we choose to measure a characteristic?" is "How good is the measuring device?" For example, is the stopwatch sticky, since it doesn't start immediately? Does the recorder decide that deviations from the company's naming standards are not "errors," so he doesn't add them in to defect total? These errors affect the accuracy of the measurement. One cannot increase the accuracy by taking more samples, but one can sometimes pinpoint problems by plotting the data and looking at them. For a good discussion of precision and accuracy see (Juran 1962).

Using Statistics

Variability

In this world, even in software, everything varies. The same team, doing a peer review of the same code unit at different times, will find different numbers of defects. Two programmers coding the same design will produce components of differing complexities. If the environment around the code varies even slightly, the behavior of the code may vary for the same test input. If one wants to use the data to fact-find, predict, compare, or trigger a decision, which figure should he or she use?

Usually one repeats the measures and tries to analyze them to help in the task. It is easy to make incorrect assumptions about how to do this; the study of the correct way is called *statistics*.

In the 1950s W. Edwards Deming taught the people in the quality field (at that time, only manufacturing) that a strong tool for achieving quality was "a statistical way of thinking" (Kilian 1992). He did not mean that everyone needed to be a top-flight statistician, but that everyone should acknowledge variability and use the ideas to make intuitive assessments of results and choose appropriate analysis methods. He, more than anyone, brought a resurgence of the great work of Walter Shewhart (1931) 30 years earlier on control charts and other useful statistical methods. It is this approach of "does that make real-world sense?" that is aimed for in this article—a statistical way of thinking.

There are many reasons why things vary. Some of them are major. For example, a company introduces a configuration change management system, and the number of system crashes drops over six months to a third of what it was before. This is an *assignable cause* (Deming (1986) calls it a "special cause"); it is known beforehand or it is easy to see afterward.

And some of the reasons are minor. For example, in a set of meetings, one group takes a bio-break; another gets into a discussion of solutions; a third cuts off early for a company meeting; in a fourth, one of the participants has not prepared but lies that they have; in a fifth, the component being reviewed, although judged to be similar to the others in the set, is really much simpler, and so on. These are *random causes* (Deming (1986) calls them "common causes"); one cannot easily pin them down and does not think it is worth the effort.

Another way of understanding assignable vs. random causes is to think of the data just affected by random causes as one family, with the main things in common, and just small variations. But there is usually what one would call a *reason* (an assignable cause) if the data seem to be split between two families (for example, the number of system crashes before the improvement and the number of system crashes six months after the improvement).

Look at the data in Figure 5 for meeting times (in minutes to the nearest 10 minutes). By looking at the data there is little one can determine about the meetings from which the measures have been taken. One of the best ways to start interpreting the data is to make a picture of them. For example, count the frequencies of each meeting length (how many times it is reported) and plot those against the time.

Figure 6 is the frequency chart of these data and one can immediately see two different patterns emerging, which implies two different kinds of meetings are happening. The average of all the data (160) turns out to have no physical meaning. This example is a warning not to take an average unless one has confidence it has some meaning.

110	130
180	200
130	140
180	190
120	210
190	120
180	200
120	100
180	110
190	220

Average = 160

Figure 5 Meeting times in minutes to the nearest 10 minutes

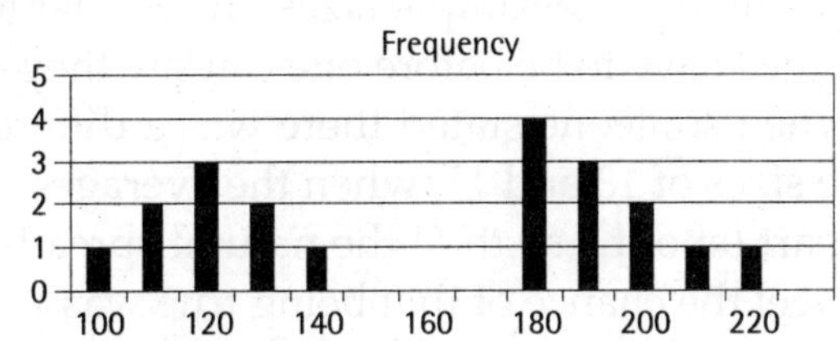

Figure 6 Frequency chart of meeting times

The reason there *are two patterns* is an assignable cause; the reasons for the *spread* of the first group from 100 to 140 are random causes and for the *spread* of the second group from 180 to 220 are (negative) growth factors.

Notice that the first pattern has a "central tendency"—it lumps up in about the middle, while the second pattern does not, but gets smaller and smaller from the initial high value. The shape of the two distributions provides a clue as to the processes happening.

In the first group, there are truly random causes that make some meetings longer and others shorter than the mode (the most usual value). This typically results in the shape shown (formally, the normal or bell curve). Times for peer reviews (or any other task-oriented meetings) typically have this distribution.

In the second group there is some restriction that does not allow meetings less than three hours; after this the curve is the "getting tired curve" (formally, negative exponential curve). In the case of meetings, this means the longer the meeting goes on, the more people there are who want it to stop. Maybe the restriction was that these were company "pep" talks and that the vice president required these meetings to be three hours, so no one felt they could stop before then. The agenda time for the peer review meeting was two hours, and the agenda time for the revival meeting was three hours.

The data gathered and the pictures or analyses that are made of them are often called the *voice of the process*, or what is actually happening. In this case, the agenda times are the *voice of the customer*, or what one hoped would happen. These two should align; however, they are different in nature.

Variability and Comparison

As the comparison abuse example of Figure 3 and the variability example of Figure 6 showed, the fundamental question in comparing two sets of data is, "Are they different frequency distributions?" Sometimes this is very easy. In the comparison example the overlap between the two sets is so great one can eyeball that there is no difference. In the variability example, the shapes are different and there is no overlap, so there is high confidence that these are two different distributions.

But in the last example, if the distributions were the same shape and were a little closer together, how could one judge whether there was a true difference? There are statistical techniques known as tests of significance. For example, a formula links the size of the sample, the spread of the data and the differences between the averages and, for a given probability, provides a yes/no on whether they are different. The smaller the sample sizes and the larger the spread, the farther apart the averages have to be before one can say they are different. That is why I was angry when someone stated there was a difference between two averages from sample sizes of 13 and 17, when the averages were less than one standard deviation apart (about a sixth of the natural spread). A statistical way of thinking made me feel the chance of that being true was very small indeed.

To read more about distributions and tests of significance see (Dudewicz 1998). However, a person who decides to use the formal method should not just look it up in a book, but learn some background statistics and get a more experienced friend to help—it is easy to misapply this. As a first step, one can plot the distributions and eyeball the results, having as a default position "I don't know."

Handling Variability in Manufacturing

Aligning the Voice of the Customer and the Voice of the Process

In manufacturing, certain product characteristics must be standardized between certain limits, usually because parts will not fit together otherwise. The limits are called the tolerances of the characteristic. For example, consider the manufacture of thousands of widgets containing a pin that fits into a hole. The engineer has decided the pin must be nominally 0.235 inches with at least a nominal overall clearance with the hole of 0.005 inches. She cannot specify the hole at 0.240 inches because that would ignore the inevitable variability that the factory will have making the pin and the hole. What she can do is specify the limits of the size of the pin and the hole. So the pin is specified at 0.235 + 0.005 inches and the hole at 0.250 + 0.005 inches; when the pin is largest (0.240 inches) and the hole is smallest (0.245 inches) there will still be a clearance of 0.005 inches. The pin is said to have a target value of 0.235 inches with tolerances of + 0.005 inches.

Now the factory must decide whether the variability caused by their equipment, material, and processes is stable; the shape is more or less symmetrical; and the natural spread is less than the interval between the tolerances. If so, the factory is satisfied that they can produce widgets with pins that will be within the tolerances.

The tolerance limits are what the engineer wants—the voice of the customer. The shape and center value of the distribution measured in the factory and the spread of the values is what one can achieve in reality—the voice of the process.

Figure 7 shows a frequency block diagram (histogram) of some factory data of pin diameter. The dotted lines are the tolerance limits required by the engineer. This looks like a symmetrical distribution (and there are statistical methods for proving this); another way of saying this is that the variability is caused by random causes.

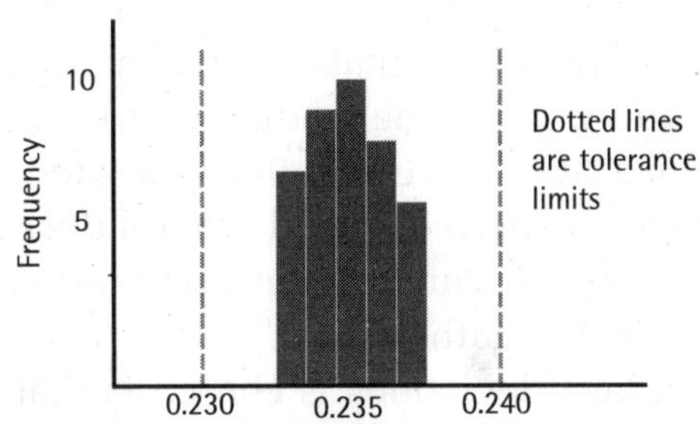

Figure 7 A symmetrical distribution inside the tolerances

In this case, the natural variability is less than the tolerances and so the voice of the customer and the voice of the process are in harmony, and all the pins produced in the future are likely to be within tolerance.

But suppose this were not so. Suppose the distribution changed over time or the shape was not symmetrical. One would have to look for obvious reasons (assignable causes) for this and try to remove them, so the distribution becomes stable and symmetrical. Suppose the spread of variability was greater than the tolerances. Then some of the parts produced would be out of tolerance and, since one does not know which parts, all must be 100 percent inspected at great cost. This is obviously a bad situation, so the factory will try to get the voice of the process in harmony with the voice of the customer. One could start by asking the engineer if the tolerances could be a bit bigger, but there may be strength and vibration reasons why they cannot be larger. So the factory will have to try to change the present distribution of the pin size (that is, change the random causes). It will have to find a major way to change the process (the combined effects of the random causes), and it will not be a trivial task.

Control Charts

Even if all is originally in harmony, the factory must keep checking to see that it stays that way. The cutting edges may wear, the material stock may have a major variation, or the operator may change the machine settings and tell no one. The factory needs a way of identifying and acting on major changes (assignable causes) before the variability is larger than the tolerances, and without being confused by the expected natural random causes. That way is SPC. The word "control" is particularly important to understand. It implies an *active feedback loop* in the system, which will force the process to remain within defined limits (Wadsworth 1998).

As long as the operator judges the distribution remains the same and only random causes are at play, the process is said to be "in control" and no adjustments are made. This is crucial. If adjustments are made when the system is actually "in control," one will introduce an assignable cause and make the variability larger (less likely to fit within the tolerances). On the other hand, if there is a clue that there has been an outside assignable cause, the system is said to be "out of control" and an adjustment should be made to bring it back to the original distribution.

So what is the clue that says an assignable cause has affected the process and made a different distribution? Even one reading that is outside the reasonable expected spread would be a clue. There are other clues, too, but they will not be covered here. The reasonable expected spread around the average is defined as +3 standard deviations where the standard deviation (also called sigma) can be calculated from the data one has gathered.

The reason three standard deviations is chosen is that it is the breakeven point between getting an early signal that the process is out of control and false alarms. Setting one's action trigger (control limits) at two standard deviations means there will be 4.5 percent of false alarms; at one standard deviation 31.7 percent of triggers will be false alarms (Bicking and Gryna 1962). This is why manufacturing does not use control limits less than three standard deviations, unless the earliness of the signal is an overriding priority. When one acts to adjust a process, but acts on what is actually a false alarm (it isn't really out of control), one forces the variability to get worse. Those "mature companies" that were quoted earlier as setting their "control limits" at one or two sigma are playing with fire.

Types of Control Charts

There are many types of control charts for different situations (see Wadsworth 1998). For the pin diameter example given previously, the manufacturing quality engineer would probably choose to take five or so samples every hour and plot both the average of the diameters and their range, with control limits on both plots (X, R). For short runs of different types of pins, normalized plots may be used, while where changes are autocorrelated and need to be caught early, a cumulative sum (Cusum) chart may be used.

The one that may be closer to the software situation occurs when the characteristic one is considering is the number of independent defects in identical units (c chart). This is particularly sensitive when the number of defects on a unit is likely to be high, but the chance of a defect occurring at any one spot is low (similar to testing software). Here the "tolerances" are zero on the lower side and "what we have been used to putting up with" on the upper side. One still has to check that the distribution is stable and more or less symmetrical. He or she can define the expected spread around the average as +3 standard deviations again, but since this is a messy calculation, it is usual to use the approximation +3 (square root of the average c). An example of a c chart is shown in the next section.

Handling Variability in Software Development or Maintenance

History and Cautions

The power of SPC in manufacturing has not been unnoticed in the software world. Claims of using it are common, but they often turn out to be analysis rather than control, that is, run charts of results are plotted and symptoms that might show the process is "out of control" (such as plots outside three sigma limits) are investigated. For example, Florac, Carleton, and Barnard (2000) reported inspection rates of space shuttle onboard software were shown to have three "invisible" subprocesses: inspection of data modules, reinspection, and inspection of design/code. Certainly, this is a useful outcome, but it is not control; it is not "an active feedback loop that will force the process to remain within defined limits."

The next sections will address possible applications of SPC to software situations, and the difficulties they pose.

Continuous Data

Since money is measured as continuous data, and is a metric of interest, one might consider using control charts for money spent per phase. To normalize the data one might plot the schedule performance index (not cumulative), that is, the value of actual work completed in each phase divided by the value of the work planned for that phase. To copy the manufacturing approach one would need the voice of the customer (the tolerances) and the voice of the process (the natural spread of the process).

One could assume the upper tolerance would be one (and the lower tolerance zero) and hope that the upper control limit, marking the natural spread of the process, would be less than one. However, the situation is presently so poor that project managers use as their trigger point for action when this ratio hits 1.05, so they are some way from using a statistical way of thinking on cost control in 2003.

And indeed, all this assumes several things, none of which may be true for one's projects:

- The distribution of the index over the time of the project is stable.
- The distributions are usually relatively symmetrical (that is, approximate normal).
- The distributions over several projects are stable enough that one can estimate the natural spread (and so the upper and lower control limits).

If one does not check that these assumptions are true, "control" charts may be drawn, but actions based on them may be misguided.

Discrete Data

Gathering the number of defects identified by testing components, one may plot a c chart such as that in Figure 8 (from a case study), the upper control limit is the upper horizontal line. In this case, a check has shown that the distribution is acceptably symmetrical, so assuming the distribution is stable, one can see that there is one point out of control—the last one. This seems like a good method to use.

However, there are many problems of assumptions and interpretation here. To use the c chart there are a series of requirements (see Bicking and Gryna 1962) shown here as a checklist.

1. Are the units (components) identical to one another? Absolutely not.
2. Are the defects independent? No, probably not.
3. Are the defect distributions likely to be relatively symmetrical (show a Poisson distribution)? No, they are not. Everyone knows that bugs cluster. There are easily understood reasons (assignable causes) for having

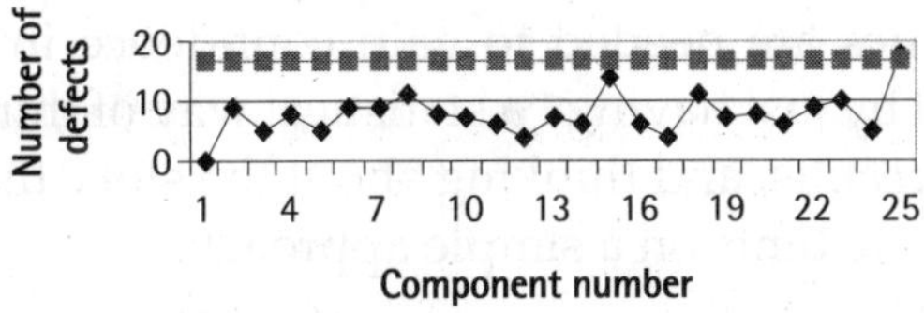

Figure 8 c chart for Test Results on Components

more defects in one component than another, such as big differences in complexity. Published defect distributions in the literature rarely show symmetrical distributions; they are significantly skewed such as Rayleigh or even Exponential.

4. Will the distributions stay stable over time? This is the most crucial point. When a company finds a defect in manufacturing, it scraps the unit or fixes it so it is identical to what it should be. When a company finds a defect in software, it changes the product. All bets are off on what the distribution of defects in the new product will be.

An even more thorny question is raised when one assumes the c chart is valid and asks what actions should be taken to bring the process back in control when the clues say it is "out of control" (for example, points beyond the control limits). Is finding more defects a good or bad situation? In manufacturing, standard inspections look for standard defects. Finding defects levels beyond the control limits means the process of production has changed. But in software it might also mean the testing process has become more efficient. It is hard to tell, so what action should one take?

Deming (1986) noted the same problem relating to the attempt to control contamination, where, as he says, the big problem is to get rid of the contamination. "One sees in practice countless control charts, most of which unfortunately are used incorrectly. It is to be feared that many of them do more harm than good. A necessary requirement for the successful use of a control chart is a smattering of the knowledge behind it."

In my opinion, for software in 2004, these charts may help one fact-find and study ways of understanding what is happening in the process, but they cannot help control the process in real time and force the standardization of the process or the product. Therefore, they should be called run charts rather than control charts so as not to mislead other readers, particularly upper management. (This opinion appears to be in disagreement with the requirements of the SW-CMM model.)

Next Steps

This article has tried to sound a warning that for metrics programs to be cost effective and help practitioners to reach their goals, not only must the GQM paradigm be used, but also the practitioner must respect the data, understand their type and their precision, and not attempt to draw unwarranted deductions. While serious statistics are needed to gain confidence in complex situations, much can be learned by just having "a statistical way of thinking"—plotting the data, looking at the results, and thinking about the story they are telling.

Following are some hints on a simple approach:

- It is usually a good idea to plot a frequency distribution and try to think about what story it is providing.
- If there is a central tendency, think about whether you are better off using the mean (the average) or the mode (the most usual value).
- Do not put numbers on ranking data; someone is sure to start adding them up.
- Do not forget that indicators do not give the whole story, just clues.
- For continuous data, decide what precision the data should be before starting, particularly if there is more than one person gathering the data. Don't expect to report better than half an interval of the precision.
- If comparing two situations, and there are not many samples available (say less than 20) *and* the spread is large, then the averages should be *far* apart before assuming there is a difference.
- For those who are really determined to use control charts, get a good manufacturing statistician to help and be prepared to do a lot of hard, basic thinking.

Last Words

The fundamental questions one asks in metrics work are "Why are we doing this? What is our goal?" The answers to these questions must guide software practitioners when they choose what precision to aim for and what techniques to use, not what new fad is out there or what does CMMI expect. The KISS principle still holds, perhaps even more so in the rather confusing and certainly expensive area of software metrics. Manufacturing has shown that the statistical way of thinking can reap rich rewards; the first steps should be simple ones, and we can hope the more complex techniques will be ours in the future.

ACKNOWLEDGMENTS

The author is grateful to the anonymous reviewers who have helped to make this a much better article.

REFERENCES

Basili, V., and Ronback. 1988. The TAME project: Towards improvement-oriented software environments. *IEEE Transactions of Software Engineering* 14, no. 6 (June): 758–773.

Basili, V., and D. Weiss. 1984. A methodology for collecting valid software engineering data. *IEEE Transactions of Software Engineering* 10, no. 6 (November): 728–738.

Bicking, C. A., and F. Gryna. 1962. Process control by statistical methods, Section 23. In *Juran's Quality Control Handbook*, Third Edition. New York: McGraw-Hill.

CMMI. 2002. *CMMI*[SM] *for Software Engineering, Version 1.1, Staged Representation (CMMI-SW, V1.1, Staged)*. Pittsburgh: Software Engineering Institute, Carnegie Mellon University.

Deming, W. E. 1986. *Out of the crisis*. Cambridge, Mass.: Massachusetts Institute of Technology, Center for Advanced Engineering Study.

Dudewicz, E. 1998. Basic statistical methods, section 44. In *Juran's Quality Handbook*, Fifth Edition. New York: McGraw-Hill.

Fenton N. E. 1994. Software measurement: A necessary scientific basis. *IEEE Transactions of Software Engineering* 20, no. 3: 199–206.

Fenton, N. E., and M. Neil. 1999. Software metrics, successes, failures and new directions. *Journal of Systems and Software* 47, no. 2: 149–157.

Florac, W. A., A. D. Carleton, and J. R. Barnard. 2000. SPC—Analyzing a space shuttle on-board software process. *IEEE Software* 17, no. 4: 97–105.

Grady, R. B. 1992. *Practical software metrics for project management and process improvement*. Englewood Cliffs, N.J.: Prentice Hall.

Greisdorf. 2003. Relevance thresholds: A multi-stage, predictive model of how users use information. *Information Processing and Management* 39, no. 3: 403–423.

Hall, T., N. Baddoo, and D. Wilson. 2001. Measurement in software process improvement. *New Approaches in Software Measurement, IWSM 2000*: 73–82.

ISO 9000:2000. Geneva, Switzerland: International Organization for Standardization.

Jalote, P. 2002. Use of metrics in high maturity companies. *Software Quality Professional* 4, no. 2: 7–13.

Juran, J. M. 1962. Measurement, section 13. In *Juran's Quality Control Handbook*, third edition. New York: McGraw-Hill.

Kilian, C. 1992. *The world of W. Edwards Deming*, second edition. Knoxville, Tenn.:. SPC Press, Inc.

McGarry, J., D. Card, S. Jones, B. Layman, E. Clark, J. Dean, and F. Hall. 2002. *Practical software measurement*. Reading, Mass.: Addison-Wesley.

Molorony, M. J. 1951. *Facts from figures*. Harmondsworth: Penguin Books.

Shewhart, W. A. 1931. *Economic control of quality of manufactured product*. New York: Vas Nostrand-Reishold. (A reprint of this classic work can be obtained from ASQ Quality Press.)

Sprent, P. 1993. *Applied non-parametric statistical methods*, second edition. CRC Press.

Topping, J. 1957. *Errors of observation and their treatment*. London: The Institute of Physics.

Wadsworth, H. M. 1998. Statistical process control, section 45. In *Juran's Quality Handbook*, Fifth Edition. New York: McGraw-Hill.

Zuse, H. 1998. *A framework for software measurement*. Berlin: Walter de Gruyer.

BIOGRAPHY

Pat Cross has an extremely varied background. She has a bachelor of science degree in physics, a master's degree in textile technology, and a doctorate in consumer studies. Her working life has been in teaching, technical management, and consulting, mainly in the area of quality achievement. While her introduction to quality achievement was through manufacturing, she has been supporting the achievement of quality in control and IT software for the past 17 years. She was with Spar Aerospace for 12 years, introducing and managing the discipline of software quality assurance specifically for the Robot Arm for the International Space Station (Canadarm 2) and other projects. She presently runs London St. Consulting, supporting companies (mainly in IT) making a step-change in achieving software quality. Cross can be reached by e-mail at patcross@londonst.com.

Appendix

Some Useful and Simple Books

- The classic quality book is *Juran's Quality Handbook*. More a bible than a focused textbook, dipping into this regularly will educate readers in many aspects of quality achievement that were mostly started in manufacturing quality, but have now spread into software development and several types of services. The newest edition is the fifth (1998) and it covers a wider range than older editions; however, it has sacrificed detail to do this. That is why sometimes I have referenced the fifth edition and sometimes the third (1962).
- There is a very old book (Moroney 1951) that explains how to safely interpret repeated data in a straightforward and simple way. It uses old-fashioned and specifically English examples, but it is direct and doesn't assume one knows complex mathematics. In his last chapter, Moroney makes the following comments, which I believe are particularly relevant to software quality at this point in time:

  "There is something very sad in the disparity of our passion for figures and our ability to make use of them once they are in our hands.

  "Learn something about statistics as soon as you can. Don't dismiss it through ignorance or because it calls for thought. . . . Whoever you are, if your work calls for the interpretation of data, you may be able to do so without statistics, but you won't do so well."

  Amazon.com says that this book is now out of print (while giving it five stars), but offers a few used paperbacks.

- For those who use ranking measures in a serious way, consider a relatively simple book directly on their statistics (Spent 1993). "Relatively simple" in this case means one knows some basic statistics and is comfortable in a statistical way of thinking.

Steer Clear of Hazards on the Road to Software Measurement Success

Patricia A. McQuaid, California Polytechnic State University, and Carol A. Dekkers, Quality Plus Technologies, Inc.

While a well-designed and planned measurement program can definitively illustrate the results of process improvement, a poorly planned measurement program can actually inflict damage—leaving an organization and its members with volumes of data and unanticipated dysfunction.

This article outlines how to identify potential barriers to success, together with common-sense actions to avoid them. The goal is to increase the return on investment for companies contemplating fact-based management through measurement.

Key words: measurement program, practical software and systems measurement, systems engineering, unintended measurement side-effects

Introduction

Examine any engineering- and scientific-based discipline and one will find that measurement is a core component. Imagine running a manufacturing line or implementing a just-in-time warehouse inventory control system without measurement. Measurement has become second nature in these engineering disciplines, and with the emergence of "software and systems engineering," measurement is becoming more common in information technology (IT).

While it is good news to observe this more "engineering-like" approach to information technology, it is disheartening that the Standish organization's reports still cite software project failures and over-budget and behind-schedule projects as the norm. They state, "Project success rates have increased to just over a third or 34 percent of all projects. This is a 100 percent plus improvement over the 16 percent rate in 1994. Project failures have declined to 15 percent of all projects, which is more than half the 31 percent in 1994. Challenged projects account for the remaining 51 percent" (Standish Report 2003). While these statistics are better than before, the numbers are still depressing.

Measurement is often cited as the silver bullet for correcting these software ailments; however, care must be taken to ensure that the measurement outcomes match the goals and expectations. To do so requires careful planning of not only the technical aspects of measurement (measures, accuracy, variances, interpretation of data, collection mechanisms, and so on), but also of the nontechnical aspects of measurement (people and cultural issues).

The authors' observations and research indicate caution should be used when engaging in measurement practices if one is to realize the tremendous gains that are possible. With statistics showing that a mere 20 percent of software measurement programs survive past their second birthday (Dekkers and Bradley 1999), it is clear that there is more to measurement than technical implementation. Coupled with stories of dysfunction and actual damage caused by unplanned measurement activities, this article explores the rationale behind measurement failure and recommends preventive action to achieve measurement success.

Background

Since the mid-1990s, Harvard Business School professor Robert Austin (Austin 1996) has warned organizations about unintended measurement side effects. Austin's research demonstrates how an organization's poorly planned measurement program can result in dysfunctional behavior, and, in fact, can actually degrade performance—instead of facilitating improvement.

"It is imperative for any organization interested in quality to be alert and careful about metrics," writes independent consultant Doug Hoffman. "Even organizations that have well-established programs, *especially* organizations with long-established metrics programs, ought to consider whether the metrics have the desired meanings and identify what side effects are caused. Where efforts are diverted without improving the product or its quality, some questioning should be made as to the appropriateness of the measures and metrics. The unintended side effects may be slowing rather than streamlining the organization" (Hoffman 2000).

Successful Measurement Programs Overcome Common Hazards

Independent consultant Esther Derby describes a useful measurement as: "one that helps you understand and make decisions. The cost of gathering the information can't exceed the benefit it provides, and the measurement shouldn't have lots of unintended side effects" (Derby 2000). While this may appear to be intuitively obvious, in practice, these guidelines are often cast aside in pursuit of "technically perfect" measurement programs.

The 80 percent failure rate cited earlier (Dekkers 2000) has been consistent since the 1980s, and occurs in spite of increased industry expertise and the release of models and frameworks outlining how to set up *technically sound* measurement. Current software measurement literature overwhelmingly focuses on the *technical* aspects of measurement, and virtually ignores the cultural or human side of its implementation. While important, the technical design and implementation (technical correctness of the measures themselves and the collection processes) are only equal in importance to these nontechnical people-issues. British author and measurement practitioner Paul Goodman acknowledged this importance in the close of his 1993 book *Practical Implementation of Software Metrics* by stating: "Perhaps you have been surprised by the relatively small part that 'metrics' have to play in this work, and how much the involvement of people can affect the success or failure of such a program" (Goodman 1993).

The factors that follow, presented as hazards of measurement initiatives, are based on more than a decade of firsthand software measurement consultation and the observation of measurement successes.

Hazard No. 1: Lack of Sustainable Measurement Plans

The adage "No one plans to fail, yet many fail to plan" holds special meaning in the context of measurement programs. While few software projects would be financed without at least sketchy requirements, there are many measurement programs funded without goals and objectives.

Robert Grady, noted metrics expert from Hewlett-Packard, identified both tactical and strategic reasons for measurement. He states that project managers must "define the right product, execute the project effectively, (and) release the product at the right time. . . . Software metrics help to clarify those details," and later, "As more people and organizations have adopted metrics, metric usage has evolved to become a strategic advantage" (through software process improvement) (Grady 1992). Overall, a properly planned and implemented measurement program allows a company to identify, standardize, improve, and leverage its software development best practices—and clearly observe where process improvements can be made.

Recommendation

One of the best ways to ensure measurement program success is to implement it as a development project, complete with requirements, design, and build phases, and including formal project management. In so doing, the software measurement program must justify itself in the same way as any other initiative seeking funding, and obtains the necessary framework to succeed. Companies with successful programs take metrics seriously from the start. Goals are set and measures are aligned to support key decision making. Whatever one's goals for measurement, ensure they are aligned with those that are important to the company. Measurement programs that lack this rigor and simply start collecting measures soon find themselves scrambling to assemble the collected data into something meaningful to the business. The goal/question/metric approach, first introduced by Victor Basili at the University of Maryland in the mid-1980s and updated in the goal/question/metric method (van Solingen, Rini, and Egon Berghout 1999), outlines a systematic, technical approach to ensuring that measurement will meet the desired goals. This approach to sustainable measurement was also embraced by the Practical Software & Systems Measurement (PSM) initiative by the U.S. Department of Defense in cooperation with the Software Engineering Institute (SEI), and is published in their recent book of the same name (McGarry et al. 2002).

Example from Industry

A federal government department decided to measure the size of their software application portfolio three years ago. The result was that they found out how large their portfolio was (in function points) and that was all. Having spent more than $100,000, they discovered that a single measurement alone (size) did not provide any insights for decision making. What could they have done differently? The organization should have set out their goals (perhaps to improve the quality of their software), asked determined questions (such as what is the current level of quality, the incremental improvement in quality due to corrective action, and so on), then set out to select metrics to meet that need. As such, the resultant metric may have been defects (defined) per 1000 function point (FP) of application delivery. In this case, the FP application sizes would have contributed to the required metric. Instead, today the department simply knows how big their application portfolio was three years ago.

Hazard No. 2: Measurement Is the Goal

Successful measurement supports and works *with* software development processes—it should not become an overhead process. It is important to understand what measurement can and cannot do, and to recognize how critical it is to plan (as in Hazard no. 1). Properly chosen measures and analysis can become a powerful tool that enables management to make key, fact-based decisions and streamline processes. If done haphazardly, measurement can easily create obstacles to process improvement (by injecting inappropriate stop points to collect useless measures) and (de)motivate workers to lower productivity. Organizations need to maximize the return on investment in measurement by targeting their goals, questions, and metrics to support key decision-making processes, and maximize the use of current data collection procedures to meet their needs. To be successful, measurement must be the means to an end—the end being the organization's goals of improved quality, productivity, or software estimation, not an end in itself.

Recommendation

Most organizations embarking on a software measurement program engage in software development as a core competence. When this core process is superceded by measurement work, the resulting output is measurement data and reports—not software. This almost guarantees failure and usually results in metrics program "abandonment." Companies with failed measurement programs voice a common complaint about their measurement initiatives: "Measurement was perceived as overhead, similar to training, and was cut when management needed to trim nonessential services."

Example from Industry

An outsourcing company was contracted for application development services to a client. Measurement criteria were put into place to assess the relative increases in productivity of the enterprise across all projects on an annual basis. Because bonus or penalty mechanisms were based on the achievement of the productivity increases, the development teams began to fixate and focus on trying to tweak the productivity numbers rather than delivering good software faster. Eventually, the teams became so entrenched in the measurement process in itself that the software delivery process actually got slower instead of more productive.

Hazard No. 3: Cast Aside Cultural Issues as Common Resistance to Change

When people and their concerns about software measurement are ignored as a viable force, damage and insurgency arise. Measurement changes how people view their work, their interactions with peers and superiors, and how they perform their work. Measurement involves cultural change, one of the hardest types of change to implement. As DeMarco and Lister write in their latest version of *Peopleware*, "Most managers are willing to concede the idea that they've got more people worries than technical worries. But they seldom manage that way. . . . The most strongly people-oriented aspects of their responsibility are often given the lowest priority. . . . The major problems of our work are not so much technological as sociological in nature" (DeMarco and Lister 1987). Measurement programs are successful because people *allow* them to succeed. When staff members are involved in the overall development of the measurement program, they more readily can embrace the changes associated with measurement itself.

For many of people, measurement is a part of everyday life, illustrated by sports averages, finance, and medical history (blood pressure, weight, age), all of which are predominantly related to "personal" attributes or behaviors. When it comes to software measurement and the use of the word "productivity" people naturally assume that the metrics will be used to measure them and their work. To overcome this tendency, companies have started to educate their developers about measurement and what it can or cannot do—*prior* to implementing the measures. Metrics coordinators understand the importance of why frequent, short exposures to new concepts are critical to people's understanding. In addition, metrics often carry personal connotations (for example, productivity implies how productive *people* are). Replacing "productivity" by the more accurate term "delivery rate" depersonalizes the meaning of the metric and gives rise to less defensiveness.

Recommendation

While measurement transforms an organization's business from "managing by feeling" to "managing by fact," its people are forced to change their business "culture." It is critical for management to accept that resistance to change is human nature and should be expected and tolerated if one wants to succeed with measurement.

Additional information describing the effects of people on a measurement program can be found in (Dekkers and Bradley 1999). The article identifies and tackles common myths held by management and professionals about software measurement. To cite a few examples:

Myth: There always will be people who resist change. Just give them time and they will come around.

Myth: People can manage the startup of the measurement program in addition to their current job.

Myth: Measurement data bring their own rewards.

It is critical to consider the impact of cultural change when planning to introduce software measurement in an organization.

Example from industry: A financial institution implemented software measurement but did not tell their IT department why they were doing so. After a short period of time, rumors started to fly that the organization was measuring so that they could figure out which staff to furlough, when the reality was that the organization wanted to assess the potential advantages of one technology over another based on measured productivity rates.

Hazard No. 4: Data Are the Responsibility of Those Being Measured

Many companies mistakenly assume that measurement data reflect the people rather than the processes they use. Measurement data are passive—the data simply report the "status quo" of where the current processes are performing. "Shooting the messenger" (that is, penalizing the people who bring or report truthful measurement data) creates an unhealthy atmosphere of fear and facilitates the propagation of false reported data. Accurate data are the cornerstone to any measurement program—without them measurement might as well be built on sand because there is no foundation from which to base improvement.

It is critical to measurement success to collect and report *true data*. With accurate data, managers can develop corrective-action plans that result in true process improvement. This does not happen naturally, especially if the reward or incentive systems are at odds with the reporting of true data. Data are passive, and unless people can report data without being punished for how bad or good they may appear to be, measurement will succeed. Success comes from being able to accept the current situation (whether it is good news or bad), and then acting to improve on it. When fear dominates, accurate data will be withheld and measurement ends up masking problems. The measurement initiative will ultimately fail because it will be based on false data. In simple terms, what gets rewarded improves, and support for measurement will only emerge when people are not punished with the data they report.

An important corollary to this is to provide contributors of data with access to the analysis and results, and collect the data using consistent measurement definitions. The introduction of measurement implies that there is room for improvement, and professionals resent any such implications about *their* work. Providing appropriate and ready access to the collected measurement data helps to alleviate fears of its misuse and minimizes the degree of speculation about management motives (outsourcing, downsizing, personal measurement).

Recommendation

Accept the data reported (especially prior to process improvement or measurement activities) as the status quo, without assigning goodness or badness to it. In addition, auditing and validating the correctness of the collected data are critical steps to gaining measurement acceptance. Once again, in the words of Robert Grady (1992), "You have to convince people of the importance of measurement, *and* you have to follow through by building an environment of trust with consistent, correct use of data."

Example from Industry

A utility company implemented defect collection measures and was assessing the data by comparing raw defect numbers across projects, and drilling down to potential root causes. When the analysis came back with minimal useful information, the IT professionals whose projects were being measured asked why there were no defect density equations being used. The IT professionals knew that the project sizes varied widely and therefore the only sensible comparison of defects was using defect density (defects/FP). Management tried to make sense of defects reported per project (which were "all over the map" because each project was a different size)—and their root-cause conclusions ended up to be nonsensical. As a result, the project teams soon learned that by doing smaller projects, they could truthfully report lower numbers of defects per project and would escape the eye of management determined to reduce defect levels. This was a dysfunctional outcome of measurement as the project teams began to create (and justify) miniproject releases that were high in overhead (as a percentage of the project), delivered minimal functionality, and resulted in lower raw numbers of defects. Fortunately, management realized the error of their ways and implemented software size measurement as a denominator value and examined defect density to correctly align the measures.

Hazard No. 5: Measurement Results Are Kept "Secret"

Even when organizations state that their measurement purpose is process improvement, skeptics abound. The perceptions of measurement misuse and secrecy become reality if measurement results are hidden, and the results stockpiled in reports on management shelves. Organizations with successful measurement programs *actively* respond to what the measurement data tell them. If the quality decreases for a product or process being measured, an investigation into the root cause is launched and appropriate remedial actions are taken. If the quality does not increase as a result of this subsequent action, further investigation is done and other changes are made until the processes are brought under control.

Recommendation

Why measure unless one intends to act on the resultant analysis? A measurement program whose motto is "measurement for measurement sake" will not deliver value, and will become a target for early funding withdrawal. Measurement must provide a return on investment if it is to become an integrated part of doing business. Many measurement programs fail because they produce merely charts and reports and are not tied to process improvement or decision making.

Example from Industry

An insurance company implemented a solid measurement program complete with data collection, analysis, and wall charts. After analyzing the data, the measurement team recommended that management arrange for training of junior staff in newer technologies that they were lacking. Management responded by saying that the timing was wrong and because their budgets were cut, they were unwilling to make any changes or spend any money on process improvement initiatives. No corrective measures were acted upon or implemented as a result, and the metrics team became ineffective and was viewed as overhead. It was no surprise that the metrics team was the first of many cost-cutting activities when budget cuts were made. If the timing is wrong and management is not committed to making decisions or acting on the results of measurement, then doing measurement for measurement sake will result in failure. Einstein is often quoted for his statement about insanity: Insanity is doing the same thing over and over and expecting different results. In this example, the metrics team may have had chances of success by implementing small pilot measures and corrective actions on projects that were in trouble, and then reporting positive small-scaled results. This would have reduced the investment and risks of measurement and provided management with insight into the potential benefits of well-planned measurement. Instead, the initiative was untargeted and delivered what management considered were "nonresults."

Summary

While software measurement success is not guaranteed, there are benefits to implementing a technically and nontechnically correct measurement program. Without measurement, it is virtually impossible to objectively demonstrate the results of software process improvement, yet many programs will commence with purely technical plans. Software process measurement can be *the* catalyst in process improvement, yet without considering the nontechnical (people) aspects of measurement, there can be a high cost of implementation. Why not plan to increase one's company's chances of measurement success by taking the nontechnical people issues into the planning process? We hope that by doing so, one can avoid the hazards along the pathway to software measurement success and enjoy positive ROI with measurement.

REFERENCES

Austin, Robert. 1996. *Measuring and managing performance in organizations*. New York: Dorset House Publishing.

Dekkers, Carol A. 2000. Unleash the POWER to improve. *Software Quality Professional* (December): 48–51.

Dekkers, Carol, and Mary Bradley. 1999. It is the people who count in measurement: The truth about measurement myths. *Crosstalk, The Journal of Defense Engineering* (June): 12–14.

DeMarco, Tom, and Timothy Lister. 1987. *Peopleware, productive project and teams*. New York: Dorset House Publishing.

Derby, Esther. 2000. Designing useful metrics. *Software Testing & Quality Engineering Journal* (May/June): 50–53.

Goodman, Paul. 1993. *Practical implementation of software metrics*. New York: McGraw-Hill International, Ltd.

Grady, Robert. 1992. *Practical software metrics for project management and process improvement*. Englewood Cliffs, N.J.: Prentice-Hall, Inc.

Hoffman, Doug. 2000. The darker side of metrics. In *Proceedings of the Pacific Northwest Software Quality Conference*, Portland, Oregon.

McGarry, John, et al. 2002. *Practical software measurement—Objective information for decision makers*. New York: Addison-Wesley.

Standish Report. 2003. Press release. (March) See URL: http://www.standishgroup.com/press/article.php?id=2.

van Solingen, Rini, and Egon Berghout. 1999. *The goal/question/metric method—A practical guide for quality improvement of software development*. United Kingdom: McGraw Hill International Ltd.

BIOGRAPHIES

Patricia A. McQuaid is a professor of information systems at California Polytechnic State University. She has taught in both the Colleges of Business and Engineering throughout her career and has worked in the banking and manufacturing industries. Her research interests include software project management, software quality management, software process improvement, software testing, and complexity metrics. She has a doctorate in computer science and engineering from Auburn University, an MBA from Eastern Michigan University, and an undergraduate degree in accounting from Case-Western Reserve University. She is a Certified Information Systems Auditor (CISA).

McQuaid served as the program chair for the Americas for the Third World Congress for Software Quality, held in Munich, Germany, in 2005. She held the same position for the Second World Congress for Software Quality that was held in Japan in 2000.

McQuaid is a Senior member of ASQ, a member of the editorial board for the *Software Quality Professional*, and a member of ASQ's Software Division Council. She was a contributing author to the recently published *Fundamental Concepts for the Software Quality Engineer* (ASQ Quality Press) and is one of the authors of the forthcoming *ASQ Software Quality Engineering Handbook* (ASQ Quality Press). She is also a member of IEEE and the IEEE Computer Society. She can be reached by e-mail at pmcquaid@calpoly.edu.

Carol A. Dekkers is the principal consultant and president of Quality Plus Technologies, Inc., specializing in consulting and training in software quality, fact-based management (using measurement), process improvement, ISO and CMMI standards, and functional size measurement (based on IFPUG Function Points and other methods). She is known internationally as a presenter and authority on quality and measurement with clients including Nielsen Media Research, Citicorp, Anheuser-Busch, the Department of Defense, insurance companies, and others.

Dekkers is a Certified Management Consultant (CMC), a Certified Function Point Specialist (CFPS), a professional engineer (Canada), an Information Systems Professional (ISP), and an ISO project editor (software engineering standards), and involved in leadership positions for ASQ, PMI, IFPUG, and ISO. She is a member of the editorial board for the *Software Quality Professional*, and is the track chair for ASQ's Software Division at the Annual Quality Congress. In 2000, ASQ's *Quality Progress* magazine named Dekkers as one of its 21 New Voices of Quality for the 21st Century, and in 2003 Dekkers was accepted to the PMI Leadership Institute Class of 2004. Dekkers is one of the authors of the forthcoming *ASQ Software Quality Engineering Handbook* (ASQ Quality Press). Dekkers can be contacted by phone at 727-393-6048, or by e-mail at Dekkers@qualityplustech.com.

PART VI

Software Verification and Validation (V&V)

Controlling quality—meeting requirements—involves both prevention and appraisal. Preventing defects is the role of the software engineering processes already discussed. Appraising how well the prevention has been completed is the role of techniques addressed in this section. These techniques of appraisal include inspections, walkthroughs, audits, technical analyses, and testing. Each of these techniques needs to be fit into the processes and culture of a given organization if it is to contribute to its full potential. Some, such as testing, are essentially projects unto themselves, with their own life cycles and complex management issues.

Wayne Woodruff's "Introduction of Test Process Improvement and the Impact on the Organization" describes a four-year-long sequence of process analysis and improvement activities. His software testing organization, as is typical, was under pressure to test products, with little time to spend on process improvement. By developing and following a process improvement plan, they have dramatically increased productivity, as well as the accuracy of scheduling and resource planning. Not least, the organization has a great sense of pride and accomplishment. The sequence described begins with configuration management (see Part VII) and then progresses through formal inspections, requirements management, and finally "Planning to Track, Tracking to Plan."

"Optimizing Software Inspections with Statistical Quality Techniques" describes a self-optimizing closed-loop process. The authors, Ellen George and Stephen Janiszewski, share performance data from both large and small inspection teams, as well as from single-person bench checks. Measuring effort, product size, and defects allows for management of the quality of the inspection process and the quality of the product being inspected. Further, it is possible to forecast the number of defects found in downstream test processes and to compare the predictions with actual values using statistical techniques. Defect data from tests are then fed back into the inspection checklist. This article provides data on the correlation between inspection rate and inspection yield, the number of defects identified per code volume inspected, and relative costs of inspection and test.

Test cases are important in the arsenal of practices used to assure software quality. Techniques for evaluating software using test cases inspired by an algorithm's design technique are presented by Thomas Griffin, Thomas Lucy-Bouler, Nancy Davidson, and Robert Gehling. Their "Design-Appropriate Test Cases" discusses how knowledge of the design technique used to create an algorithm can be used to develop better test cases for evaluating that algorithm. The authors illustrate with test cases for specific design techniques: brute force algorithms, recursive algorithms, divide and conquer, greedy design, and iterative methods. Consideration of algorithm design in the development of test cases is shown to be another tool supporting the intelligent and efficient selection of test cases that can be used at any point in the development process.

Finally, we hear from Ugo Piazzalunga and Paolo Salvaneschi on "How to Test Usability of Security Sensitive Systems." While security testing of software is becoming an important topic, little attention has been paid to the critical aspect of usability. Security testing has focused on finding vulnerabilities in the software regardless of whether additional security problems result from designs with poor usability. The authors argue for a systemic approach in designing security software and systems. In this article they propose a framework for testing the usability of security-sensitive systems. Applying this framework to test the usability of alternative realizations of a widespread system reveals how usability issues lead to security problems. Interpretation of these test results offers recommendations for software practitioners to properly address usability of security devices.

Introduction of Test Process Improvement and the Impact on the Organization

Wayne D. Woodruff, Motorola Broadband Communication Sector

Testing organizations are often under the gun to test products, and they have little time to spend on process improvement. By developing and following a process improvement plan, an organization can make substantive improvement and improve productivity.

Often the mere mention of a process improvement project will instill fear into the team and kill the project. One effective way to avoid this common pitfall is to avoid making a commotion about the project and steer the team in small steps along the path to improvement.

Key words: inspections, process improvement, requirement management, traceability

Introduction

This article describes the process analysis and process improvement activities that took place over a four-year period in a software testing organization. The process improvement plan was based upon the Software Capability Maturity Model (SW-CMM) (Paulk et al. 1993). This was found to be an excellent foundation on which to build our processes. As one will see, our improvement plan closely follows the Level 2 key process areas (KPAs) and at least one Level 3 KPA.

This test process improvement project was implemented by a test group that is part of a product development group (hardware and software). This product development group produces products used in the Cable-TV industry. My involvement in this project was as the manager of the test department that underwent these process improvement activities.

Initial Assessment

Using existing knowledge of the SW-CMM, an informal assessment was performed. The assessment comprised comparisons between group activities and behaviors and the Level 2 KPA. No questionnaires were filled out and no formal results were presented. The assessment results were not shared with the group, nor were the improvement plans. While this flies in the face of accepted practices, reality is that when a person is confronted with change, there is usually a negative reaction to that change. Rather than emphasize the plan and raise the fear level, it was decided to implement changes in small steps, almost covertly. Why announce a large process improvement project when the same thing can be accomplished by introducing subtle, but meaningful changes in a way that reduces or eliminates the fear and subsequent stress?

In a paper by Oliver Recklies (2001), a seven-stage model was described that depicts the changes a person goes through when confronted by change. By minimizing the fear factor, we skipped the first few steps in the model and put the staff through fewer emotional swings.

The main reason for this approach was that in a prior process improvement project the improvement plan was well publicized and became the center of attention. Many of the people involved in the project were reluctant to embrace the change concepts and felt the process was "being shoved down their throats" by a corporate mandate.

Rather than let history repeat itself, I decided to take a totally opposite approach in this project. This approach was to make subtle, incremental changes and celebrate the intermediate successes rather than make a big announcement, and present the details up front.

Configuration Management and Requirement Management KPAs

Examining the test development side of the group, test specifications were written and informally reviewed by the test group. Little, if any, influence outside the test organization was brought in. Once complete, the specifications were placed under formal version control. From the test specification, tests were developed and integrated. Errors found in the test specifications during test development and integration were not routinely captured in a document revision. Essentially, once the document was under configuration management (CM) control, it was rarely revised. The impetus for updating the spec was usually the addition of a significant new feature. Major revisions rarely contained updates for previously identified problems, because the problems were not tracked. Test requirements were not clearly identified and tagged; consequently, there was no management of enumerated requirements.

For the test execution side of things, a proprietary tool was used for creating and executing test scripts. These test scripts were poorly managed as well. All machines that ran scripts were attached to LAN, and the scripts were run from a server. Because of network problems, the server was frequently unavailable. Since the testers needed to continue to make progress, they simply copied the scripts from the server to their local hard drives. Files were not systematically managed and the scripts on the machines often did not match the scripts on the server, nor was there any correlation between identically named scripts on the various machines.

Project Planning/Project Tracking and Oversight KPAs

Estimates were never generated for new test development; therefore, progress against plans was never tracked.

Regression test planning was instituted as soon as the project started. These plans identified the following:

- Code objects under test
- The testers responsible for execution of a particular subset of the regression suite
- The areas of functionality that were not being tested
- An estimate for the calendar time for test execution
- A list of risks
- Identification of where the test results could be found

The planning was a start, but it needed to be more accurate and contain more information for it to have any credibility.

Regression tracking was performed by keeping pass/fail status for all the tests in a spreadsheet. The tests were prioritized, and time estimates were kept for each test. Unfortunately, no process existed to capture and analyze actual test execution times, so the estimates were never revised and had no credibility. Likewise, there was no link between the plan and the actual test run. We had a nice plan that stated what we intended to do, but there was no way of verifying the plan was actually followed.

Software Quality Assurance KPA and Subcontract Management KPA

The organization did not have a separate SQA function, and we did not outsource any activities.

Assessment Summary

The results of the assessment were not pretty. Numerous problems were identified. Following are the most serious:

- It was impossible to understand how much effort a test cycle actually took.
- It was difficult to assess the status of the test cycle in real time.
- We had no empirical data from which to draw estimates for test development or test execution.

- When a test failed, the results could not necessarily be duplicated because the test script or environment had likely changed.
- The test status sheet was hard to read and understand.
- Certain tests had to be run by certain people. Little cross training was done. If a key person was out, that test had to wait until he or she returned.
- The only person who understood a particular suite of tests was the person who developed those tests.
- There was little control over the test configuration. There was no standard test station. The test environment was not controlled.
- Test requirements were not enumerated and managed.
- Errors found after the test specification was complete were not systematically corrected.
- The test organization had little credibility, and morale was poor.

From the management perspective, there were several key objectives of the process improvement project:

- To obtain up-to-date status of any test object under test at any time
- To accurately understand the effort to run components of the test cycles, so test effort could be predicted
- To be able to reliably reproduce test failures
- To improve group morale, and give the test team a sense of accomplishment

The Plan

Once the assessment was completed, a four-phase plan was devised. The idea was to fix the major problems and come back later for fine details. The four phases in the improvement project are:

1. Configuration management
2. Formal inspections
3. Requirements management
4. Planning to track/tracking to plan

One might ask, "Why these phases and this order?" It is my opinion that CM is the basis for all development. Without it, chaos will rule. Likewise, it is my opinion that inspections have a well-documented return on investment and provide numerous additional benefits. Requirements management requires a bit more discipline and maturity in the organization, so that was saved for later. Planning to track/tracking to plan was last because I believe that this particular phase requires the most maturity in an organization.

As the manager, I thought there were several critical success factors that were required for the team to succeed:

1. At the start of any phase, explain to the team the reason for a change. Explain the problem that the team is attempting to solve and the desired results. Be sure the desired results are obtainable.
2. Give the team training on any new tools for the current phase and allow the team adequate time to become familiar with the tools and processes as the project evolved. Training does not need to be formal; mentoring or on-the-job training is actually more desirable.
3. Do not mandate a solution. Provide guidelines. Allow the team to develop the solution.
4. Do not abandon the process when a crisis arises.
5. Make small but substantive changes.

By committing to the process, I tried to show the team that I believed in the process and the subsequent outcome. This seemed to inspire them to exceed the goal, rather than to think of it as a passing fad.

Phase 1: Configuration Management

In the CM phase, all configuration items were identified. Configuration items included the test specifications, test scripts, test application source code, and the test environment. The team had felt the pain of the lack of CM, so they were ready to embrace change.

As discussed before, the test scripts were a mess and were addressed first. These were fairly simple to fix, but time consuming. The network infrastructure problems were quickly solved. The next task was to get the scripts under control of a commercially available CM tool. To perform that task, all the scripts had to be reviewed to determine the appropriate scripts to use as the configuration managed version. This was done as the scripts were used during test cycles, and it consumed the better part of four months as well as several regression cycles. Once this was completed, the testers were mentored on CM concepts and the tool. Scripts were checked into the CM tool, and the most current revisions of the scripts were sent to a well-known location on the network. The test environment was modified so that the test stations all used the same location for test scripts. The CM tool was used to handle ongoing maintenance of the scripts.

Another step in this process was to define a standard test station. Each section of the test suite was examined to determine if it had any special equipment requirements. All stations were identical, except for one station that had additional equipment for running one set of tests. Over time, the special dependency was removed and all test stations now have identical configurations.

Finally, the test environment was located in a laboratory that was also shared by development and test personnel. Often, the development personnel made changes to the lab that would affect testing. A cross-functional team of development and test people was formed and asked to define a shared environment so that development personnel had the ability to make lab changes that would no longer impact testing. Any subsequent changes made to the lab were now scrutinized for cross-functional impact.

These simple changes made a world of difference. Other aspects of CM, namely the management of test specifications and test requirements, were deferred to the requirement management phase, since they are so closely related.

Phase 2: Formal Inspections

Just five months after this project started, the leaders of the test team were trained as inspection moderators. They were trained to use a Fagan-like process (Fagan 1986) and have used this process for more than four years. My unstated goal was to inspect 90 percent of our test specifications. It took discipline on the team's part, but the process became a part of our culture within a year, and to date, we have achieved 100 percent inspection of the test requirement specifications. The team members were reluctant at first to participate in an inspection, especially if they were the producer. I helped by being a participant in every inspection for the first two years and reassuring them that this was not a witch hunt. I also had the team inspect some documentation that I produced to show them how they could help me.

The inspection team usually consisted of five people and included the author of the document, also known as the producer, a software developer (preferable the one who designed the code), and at least one of the people responsible for running the test (testers). The other two team members were the moderator and recorder. The moderator runs the defect-logging meeting and the recorder records the results of both the defect-logging meeting and the individual inspections. Inspectors had at least a week to review the document and generate a list of defects using standard forms and checklists. The results were captured in a master defect list during a defect-logging meeting. The producer was given the master list and fixed the issues. Depending upon the nature of the defects, a reinspection may have been warranted; the inspection team was empowered to decide whether to reinspect the test requirements document.

Measurements were taken as part of the process and from those measurements the following metrics were computed:

- Inspection efficiency—minutes of inspection per defect found. This includes both inspection and logging time. For comparison sake, this is also computed in dollars.
- Defects per inspected page
- Cost to find a defect (historical)

Based on three major product developments and 98 inspections over the last four years, it takes only 17 minutes to find a defect in an inspection, and assuming a labor rate of $100/hour, it costs us $28 to find a defect. Another notable benefit of the inspection process is that it offered the opportunity for the testers and developers to interact during the inspection, so that developers helped identify tests that may have been missed. The testers, the people who actually run the tests, also received advance notice of upcoming new tests. It allowed the test team the opportunity to identify diagnostic requirements so the software requirements could be validated. It was a great opportunity to train test staff, to share ideas, and to reinforce excellent working relationships between developers and testers.

Phase 3: Requirements Management

This phase introduced formal requirements management, but had strong ties to the inspection process and the CM process. This was a big change, since it involved the introduction of a new tool. This phase took the longest to institutionalize.

About a year after the process improvement project began, the company began to develop a major new product. Having had many years of experience with a commercially available requirements management tool, I convinced the software team to let the test team capture the software requirements in the tool. The software developers and testers needed some training on the tool for the management of requirements, but since the tool used the same word processor, it was fairly simple. Once the document was brought in to the tool, we allowed the tool to scan the document for a keyword and create a database of software requirements. For software requirements, we chose "shall" as the keyword and "shall verify" for test requirements.

For each software requirements specification (SRS), a test lead was assigned. That lead person analyzed the SRS and developed a test requirement specification. After a draft document was completed, the test lead would meet with the software engineer and try to clarify any software requirements we did not think were testable. Note that the software team does not use inspections, so their document was official after one or more reviews of the document. It was entirely possible that the SRS could be released with untestable requirements!

Once that effort was completed, a formal inspection of the test specification was conducted. After the test requirements specification was revised, it was captured in the requirements management tool and the database was augmented with the test requirements.

The next step was to trace the test requirements back to the software requirements. Again, the requirements management tool fully supported traceability, so it was a matter of allowing the team time to perform the traceability and subsequent analysis. This is one area that we must focus on for future improvement. The traceability should be included as part of the inspection process, not conducted after the inspection is complete.

Once traceability was completed, some key metrics were generated and reviewed. These include number of traced software requirements, number of untraced requirements, and ratio of test requirements to software requirements. Software requirements that did not have test requirements that were traced to them were investigated. Root-cause analysis of those untraced requirements showed that approximately 90 percent of them were attributed to being design requirements, which were not testable. As mentioned previously, the software requirements are reviewed but not inspected. The test group often found defects in the software requirements during the inspection of the test specification, as they were always used as a reference document for the test specification inspection.

One advantage of the requirements management tool was that it had a built-in CM that was better than the company's existing CM tool. It kept revision information on every requirement as well as on each document and the project as a whole. Our CM tool would only maintain revision history on the project, so we chose to use the abilities of the requirements management tool.

Some test specifications were not based on software or hardware requirements. One example was our product that employed a proprietary communications interface. The protocol definition was external to the requirements repository. We had developed numerous test specifications for the protocol and updated our specifications when the protocol definition was expanded. While it would be nice to trace back to the protocol requirements, we manage without. The protocol specification is not frequently updated, so updates are very well documented, so we can easily establish the impact to the tests.

Likewise, there are numerous implicit requirements, based on a historical perspective, both product and industry. We handled them in the same manner. We developed test specifications and captured test requirements; they were not just traced back to originating hardware or software requirements. The policy was that every test we ran must be documented in a specification.

Phase 4: Planning to Track, Tracking to Plan

The approach of this phase was to put together a simple and effective way of capturing test execution status. Later in the phase, the planning aspect fell out of that status reporting mechanism.

Our existing tracking spreadsheet was poor (see Figure 1). It had several worksheets: one for each major test area, and one for the summarized pass/fail status. The summary sheet was particularly confusing. Ran was defined as pass plus fail, so %ran was ran divided by number of tests. Total coverage was the sum of ran, can't test, and not tested. The "definition" of total coverage was vague and was ignored.

Looking at the detailed status sheet (see Figure 2), each major test area worksheet had a different format, which contributed to the confusion, but most worksheets had a core set of columns: test number, functional requirement, test case, test script, and pass/fail.

The *test number* was just a sequentially numbered value that was not traceable to any software requirement. The *functional requirement* was a description of the test. Unfortunately, its origin was thought to be a generic description entered by the test developer and was very subjective. The *test case* was a cryptic string of letters and numbers whose origin was unknown. The *test script* defined the script that the tester was to use. The *pass/fail* was the result the testers arrived at by running the test and had one of four possible test outcomes: pass, fail, can't test, and not tested.

Basically, the spreadsheet tracked the status of running the scripts. If a test had a status of other than "pass," there were not any notations of why it failed, could not be tested, or was not tested. If the test failed, there was no link to a defect report. Each time a test cycle was run, the same bug occurred. After a while, the tester who ran it knew which tests would not pass and stopped running tests. If the bug was fixed, the fix was never verified!

The requirements for improvement were that the status had to be easy for the testers to use to track detailed progress against, but provide planning and summary status for management. In the past, a document was generated with the plan for the regression cycle. There was no mechanism for verifying that the plan was actually executed, so the ideal tracking method would also include the planning information.

	Test A	Test B	Test C	Test D	Test E	Not Supported		Totals
Number of tests	52	179	119	15	26	10		401
Ran	51	168	94	12	0	0		325
Pass	48	163	94	12	0	0		317
Fail	3	5	0	0	0	0		8
Can't Test	1	11	25	3	0	0		40
Not Tested	0	0	0	0	0	0		0
Total	52	179	119	15	0	0		365
% RAN	98.1%	93.9%	79.0%	80.0%	0.0%	0.0%		81.0%
Total Coverage % (Run+CT+NT)	100.0%	100.0%	100.0%	100.0%	0.0%	0.0%		91.0%

Figure 1 Old summary status

Test #	Functional requirement	Test case	Test script	Pass/Fail
23	The product will illuminate the front panel...	DCTACC-FW-04	Xyx.txt	P

Figure 2 Old detailed status sheet

The fix was rather drastic. The first step was to create a consistent look and feel to the detailed status sheet. One of the test managers mulled this over for a few weeks and suggested that test requirements be exported from the repository and brought into individual status worksheets. By doing so, we captured the test requirement number and test requirement text from the database, along with the name of the application or script that was used to test this requirement. These are represented in the spreadsheet as TR# and test requirement, respectively. This solved a multitude of problems and the worksheets had a consistent look and feel.

A second effort was to create clear and consistent definitions for the status-reporting column. This required a few iterations as we realized that the existing test status definitions did not clearly state the result. Over time, the four grew to seven with the following definitions:

P—Pass

Testing completed and expected results achieved.

F—Fail

Testing completed and expected results were not achieved. A new defect must be written. To facilitate testing of future code releases, the tester enters the bug number from the defect tracking system and the code version into the Code CR (change request) column.

CT—Can't test (external problem)

Lack of verification mechanism

External equipment missing/broken

Test developed, software functionality not supported

NT—Not tested (test group internal problem)

Test script/app under development

Test script/app needs maintenance

KI—Known issue

An existing defect within another area of code, does not allow further testing to be completed.

Test verification mechanism (that is, diagnostic output) requested but not implemented.

KF—Known failures

Test fails because of an existing defect, which was not fixed in this release.

PV—Pass verified

When retesting a known defect, and expected test results are achieved.

The following columns were added to the spreadsheet:

- Code CR—Identifies a defect report and is used when a test fails and there is a defect in the product.
- App/Script CR—Identifies a defect report and is used when a test fails and there is a defect in the test.
- Comments

The result is shown in Figure 3. Likewise, we added information to the summary table.

First, we added in the name of the tester who ran the major section and how many hours were spent on that test. Over the course of many test cycles, all testers had the opportunity to run each test suite several times. This served several purposes. All the testers became familiar with all of the test suites and the average execution time could be computed from the empirical data. Since the average execution time for each suite was well known, a very accurate schedule could be produced. This also allowed for accurate schedule generation in cases where resource levels fluctuated.

We added a column for "Testing Planned." Normally, we run the complete regression cycles on each software release, so each entry would be "yes." In the case where we decide to run a reduced regression cycle, we assess the changes to the software and what test will exercise those changes. Any tests that do not need to be run get marked with a "no." Based on the "yes" entries in the testing planned column, the total number of test requirements is computed. Once the planning was completed, the testers printed the detailed worksheet (see Figure 3) for the areas they were going to test. The detailed spreadsheet contained all the information the tester needed to do his/her job. Each tester kept a paper copy and

TR#	Test requirement	App/Script	P/F/CT/NT/KI/KF/PV	Code CR	App/Script CR	Comment
TR1063	Verify the xyz shall ...	Abc.txt	F	1234-5678 1.21		
TR1064	Verify the sun rises...	Qec.txt	KF	1234-5660 1.19		Bug not yet fixed
...						

Figure 3 New detailed status worksheet

noted updates on this copy as he or she ran tests. Once a day, each tester used the data on the paper copy to update the electronic spreadsheet.

A worksheet was added to list any new defects found in a release. This allowed testers to easily share any new defects without the need to query the bug database. All testers knew to check the defect worksheet prior to submitting a bug so duplicates were not entered. The total number of bugs found were computed and added on the summary page.

Since we had new defects found and hours testing used, we computed how many hours of testing it takes to find a new defect. Empirical data tell us it takes between 14 and 30 hours of test time to find a defect during a regression cycle. Based on the $100/hour rate, this translates to $1400 to $3000 to find a defect during regression testing. The dollar figure is not that notable, but the hours are. If we plan to spend 150 hours testing a new release, on average, the software team can expect at least five bugs from that effort. We call this metric "the cost to find a defect" metric. The resulting summary status page is shown in Figure 4.

We used this process for a short period of time, but it still wasn't quite right. To create a status sheet for a new test cycle, we copied the results from the last cycle and deleted the pass/fail status. This allowed us to carry over the defects and comments from the prior cycle. The problem with this was if we added or modified any test requirements, our status sheet would not contain those new or modified test requirements. The only way to accomplish this was to update the spreadsheet by entering/modifying test requirements in both the database and the spreadsheet. We needed to resolve these issues to make the process better.

We actually introduced two new improvements as a next step. Whenever a new defect was found, the tester enters the code defect number as well as a code version in which the defect was found in the requirements repository against the test requirement. This kept the requirement database current with new failures. Likewise, if a test that previously failed now passed, the tester removed the defect number from the requirements repository. In order to keep this from being a burden to the testers, they waited until the current test cycle was completed and made all the updates at one time.

Test area	Testing planned	# Test requirements	Ran	Pass	Fail	Can't test	Not tested	Known issues	Known failures	Tester	Time
Area 1	Yes	35	35	32	2	1	0	0	0	Jim	3.5
...											
Area n	No	45	0	0	0	0	0	0	0		
Total tests planned		437	429	412	15	1	0	1	0		80.5
New CRs found	12										
Hours/ new CR	6.7										

Figure 4 New summary status information from spreadsheet

Secondly, at the start of any test cycle, we exported the test requirements from the database and used them to create a new status tracking spreadsheet. By doing so, we corrected all the problems. The status sheet would contain the latest test requirements and the results from the prior test cycle.

This really closed the loop and guaranteed that each test cycle had the most current test requirements and defect history. A series of spreadsheet macros was developed that automated the building of the status sheet and made the process more user friendly. Now, we had the most current test requirements and the issues found in the last cycle were automatically carried over to the next cycle.

A separate spreadsheet was maintained for each software version tested. This was beneficial in that there was a snapshot of the exact tests run and the status of those tests for each version of code. As the test suite was enhanced over time, the history of the test evolution was saved.

The Results

After four years of hard work, benefits of the process are being enjoyed (see Figure 5).

More impressive is that we increased our productivity dramatically, without adding a single resource! As a matter of fact, at the end of year three, we *lost* a resource!

Our test cycle schedule accuracy is excellent. We know how long it will take to run the cycle and how many resources it will take. We rarely miss the deadline! We can pull the schedule in by adding resources (to a point). Overtime is the exception rather than the rule.

Next Steps

There are two areas for us to focus on in the short term. First, we should start inspecting our test scripts and the source code for test applications. In the original concept of the plan, source code and script inspection was thought to be too expensive and we should focus on the upstream documentation first. After

Year of improvement project	Number of test cycles run	Percent increase from year two	Number of test requirements covered by a test cycle	Percent increase from year two
2	48	N/A	1600	N/A
3	48	0	1800	11
4	79	65	2640	65

Figure 5 Improvement results

several years of inspection documents, the belief that code/script inspections are too expensive has passed.

Second, I would like to expand the planning to track/tracking to plan to include test development. We routinely develop schedules for test development, but we do not track it like we do a regression cycle. Granted, this is a considerably different process, but estimating and measuring our development will only help to improve those as well.

Conclusions

The project is a resounding success. I write "is" because the project is not over and it never will be. Improvement is a journey, not a destination. Continuous improvement provides valuable insight to the organization and has fundamentally changed how we do our job. We have and will continue to make substantive improvements to how we do our job. Our team is very agile and has very predictable schedules.

- We now have great understanding of how much effort a test cycle actually requires.
- We have real-time test status.
- We have empirical data from which to draw estimates for test execution.
- We can readily duplicate test results.
- The test status sheet is much easier to read and understand.
- Cross training is a way of life. We are rarely bound to a single person owning a test.
- There is a standard test station. The test environment is tightly controlled.
- Test requirements are enumerated and managed.
- Errors found after the test specification was complete are systematically corrected.
- The test organization has a great sense of pride and accomplishment.

I'd like to reveal an interesting endnote. After developing this process for three years, I was commenting to one of my managers about how our process had improved. The manager gave me a puzzled look and asked me what I meant. I showed the manager a flowchart of the process and described the process. After looking at it for about 30 seconds, the manager's eyes opened wider and the manager smiled and said, "I had no idea that we were following such a process." Likewise, a few months ago, I was asked to present our process improvement project to corporate management. Afterward, I decided to present it to my staff. I got a similar comment from one of my senior developers after the presentation. While there are several ways to interpret this, my understanding of the response was that I had created an environment of continuous improvement, without people feeling burdened by the process.

REFERENCES

Fagan, M. E. 1986. Advances in software inspections. *IEEE Transactions on Software Engineering* 12, no. 7 (July).

Paulk, M., B. Curtis, M. B. Chrissis, and C. Weber. 1993. Capability Maturity Model for Software, version 1.1 (CMU/SEI-93-TR-024). Pittsburgh: Software Engineering Institute, Carnegie Mellon University.

Recklies, O. 2001. *Managing change: Definition and phases in change processes.* See URL www.themanager.org/Strategy/Change_Phases.htm.

BIOGRAPHY

Wayne Woodruff is a senior manager for Motorola Broadband Communication Sector, where he is responsibie for software development for Advanced Interactive Digital Cable Settop boxes. This article was written while he managed testing of Advanced Interactive Digital Cable Settop boxes. He has been working in embedded systems design, development, and testing for more than 23 years. Woodruff has a master of electrical engineering degree from Villanova University and a bachelor of electrical engineering technology degree from Spring Garden College. He has published numerous articles ranging from Embedded Systems Design to Integrated Development environments to Requirements Management, which can be viewed at http://www.jtan.com/~wayne/publications.html.

Woodruff is a member of ASQ, and he can be reached at wwoodruff@motorola.com

Optimizing Software Inspections with Statistical Quality Techniques

Ellen George and Stephen Janiszewski, Software Six Sigma

Software inspections can be an extremely effective method for removing defects early in the software life cycle while the removal cost is still relatively low, but an open-loop inspection process that is not measured and proactively managed could actually cost more than it saves.

By measuring effort, product size, and defects, it becomes possible to manage the quality of the inspection process and the quality of the product being inspected. It is possible to forecast the number of defects found in downstream test processes and to compare the predictions to actuals using statistical techniques. Defect data from test can be fed back into the inspection checklist resulting in a self-optimizing closed-loop process. Use of a structured defect prevention process in tandem with the inspection process engages the developers in process improvement and greatly improves the quality of defect data and ultimately of process yield.

Key words: appraisals, defect prevention, inspections, Fagan inspections, Gilb inspections, quality management, Six Sigma, software process improvement, statistical process control

Introduction

Software inspections can be a good method for removing defects early in the software life cycle while the removal cost is still relatively low. Many organizations don't understand how to measure the effectiveness of their inspection process and therefore don't manage their inspection process effectively. An open-loop inspection process that is not measured and proactively managed is unlikely to perform as well as it could. In fact, it could actually cost more than it saves.

This article summarizes the authors' experience implementing, managing, and optimizing an inspection process at a large aerospace organization. It presents performance data from large and small inspection teams as well as from single-person bench checks, including the correlation between inspection rate and inspection yield, number of defects identified per thousand lines of code (KLOC) inspected, and relative cost of inspection and test.

Inspection Goals and Measurements

Prior to beginning any software process improvement effort, members of an organization should have a clear understanding of the problems they are trying to solve and the goals they are trying to achieve. Without explicit linkage to business objectives, it becomes very difficult to maintain active senior management support of the initiative.

The organization's employees were given an explicit objective to improve productivity. Their goal was to get a 7 percent productivity improvement on all new development activities. They wanted to select a process improvement initiative that would provide a quick, visible return on investment, in order to solidify management sponsorship. The company chose to use inspections to remove defects early at a lower overall cost, with the expectation that they would reduce integration and test time.

Since integration and system test accounted for approximately 30 percent of the company's life-cycle costs, a 7 percent productivity improvement could be achieved by reducing the number of defects that escaped into integration and system test by approximately 25 percent. Employees had an additional constraint to recover the process improvement cost within one year.

The company decided to measure the improvement in productivity by measuring the overall decrease in cost of quality for the software development process. Cost of quality is the sum of three terms: failure cost of quality, appraisal cost of quality, and prevention cost of quality. *Failure cost of quality* is the percentage of total project effort expended correcting defects found in test. *Appraisal cost of quality* is the percentage of total project effort expended performing bench checks and inspections. *Prevention cost of quality* is the percentage of total project effort expended in training and defect prevention activities. A net decrease in cost of quality corresponds to more effort expended generating product and less effort wasted correcting defects. A comparison of the changes in the appraisal and failure cost of quality allowed the company to measure its progress against its goal.

Measurements

There are only three types of measurements required to manage the inspection process: effort, size, and defects. *Effort* is the individual effort expended by each inspection participant to prepare for, hold, and fix the defects found in the inspection. *Size* is the size of the work product inspected, which is often measured in lines of code (LOC). *Defects* is the quantity, type, effort required to fix and verify, point of injection, point of removal, and description of the defect.

Derived metric	Definition
Inspection rate	LOC/hr
Defect density	Defects/KLOC
Defect removal rate	Defects/hr
Yield	Defects removed/(defects removed + defects not removed)
Defect removal leverage	Inspection removal rate/test removal rate
Appraisal cost of quality	Cost of all inspection activities expressed as a % of project cost
Failure cost of quality	Cost of all rework related activities required to complete compilation and test expressed as a % of project cost

Figure 1 Derived metrics

Although a defect measurement consists of several pieces of data, it is collected as a single measurement at a discrete point in time.

These three measurements are simple and economical to record in process with an automated tool. A typical effort or size measurement requires about 15 seconds to perform. A defect measurement requires about 30 seconds. All other metrics are derived from these three measurements. Figure 1 provides a list of the derived metrics used to fully characterize the inspection process.

The Inspection Process

Types of Reviews

The organization used two types of reviews to optimize its inspection process: bench checks and team inspections.

Bench Checks

Bench checks are used to clear the majority of the simpler defects prior to team inspection.

Bench checks are personal inspections conducted by the author immediately after completing a work product or a portion of a work product. They are checklist based. The checklist is generated from a list of defects found by the author in downstream activities such as code and unit test. Once the author has completed a product development phase such as design or code, he or she inspects the product against his or her personal checklist, systematically proving that each application question is not a problem. Bench checks are based on PSP personal reviews (Humphrey 1995).

Team Inspections

The company's team inspections were based on the standard Fagan process (Fagan 1976). A small team conducts the inspection. The team includes the author, reviewers, a moderator, and a recorder.

Open-Loop Inspection Process

The team introduced the organization to inspections by training the developers in standard Fagan inspections. One cannot emphasize enough the importance of providing the staff with formal training in order to rapidly move the organization to a repeatable, stable process. Honeywell's initial inspection process is depicted in Figure 2.

The author submits material for inspection. When there are approximately 1000 LOC to be inspected, the moderator calls for an inspection.

The moderator gathers the material and invites the inspection team members to a preliminary meeting. The reviewers are given the source and product material; told how it fits into the overall project; provided the checklist, standards, and procedures; and told when the inspection meeting will be held. Each reviewer is expected to review the material at his or her desk against the checklist and come into the meeting with defects identified. The product size, time spent in the preliminary meeting, and time spent reviewing the material are recorded.

Initially the team used the same standard checklists across all projects. The checklist questions were based on typical "industry data."

The moderator facilitates the inspection meeting. Beginning with the first question on the checklist, the moderator asks each reviewer, starting with the author, to identify any issues they logged. Issues are identified and discussed objectively. All issues are recorded. The moderator moves the group through the remaining checklist questions, always starting with the author. Time spent in the inspection meeting and issues identified in each product are recorded.

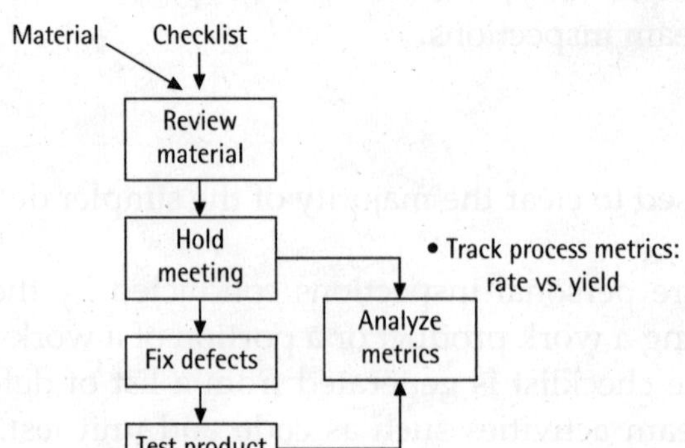

Figure 2 Open-loop inspection process

It is left to each author and his or her supervisor to determine how each issue is to be resolved. They could decide that an issue is a defect that needs to be fixed immediately, a defect that will be scheduled for fix in the future, or that the issue is not a defect at all. Discussion time between the author and the supervisor is recorded.

The author fixes the agreed-upon defects and creates problem reports for those that were deferred. For each defect, the author records the defect fix time, defect type, life-cycle phase in which it was introduced, life-cycle phase in which it was removed, and a description of the defect. When the repair work is completed, the author moves on to the next life-cycle phase.

In unit test, and again in each subsequent test step, the author records time spent in phase and defects identified and fixed. For the most part, test phase time is composed of the time spent finding and fixing defects.

The organization was clearly saving money by finding and fixing defects earlier in the life cycle when they were less expensive, but as yet they had not started quantifying their savings as part of normal activities. It was apparent that there was ample opportunity to improve the process.

The Software Engineering Process Group (SEPG) reviewed and analyzed the metric data. The data analysis report was being provided to the development organization on a monthly basis, but the developers never had the time to look at it.

The developers' objective was to hurry up and get their code tested and delivered. Since they rarely took time to look at the data, they were typically unaware of how much time the inspection process was saving for them in test. They thought inspections were good in a vague way because they provided a learning opportunity and "improved quality." They could not quantify either the cost or benefits of the inspection process. As such, they continued to do what they were comfortable with, rushing through their inspections so that they could get their product into test.

Closed-Loop Inspection Process

The solution to this problem was to involve the developers in the analysis of the inspection data. They were trained in basic Six Sigma tools such as run charts, Pareto analysis, root-cause analysis diagrams, and in how to calculate return on investment (ROI).

The inspection process was modified to give the developers responsibility for performing the data analysis step and for implementing the continuous process improvement resulting from the data analysis (see Figure 3). Successful completion of data analysis was treated as a "phase gate," that is, it became an inspection process exit criteria. The development team members learned to calculate their own ROI, and were able to convince themselves that the time in inspections was worth spending.

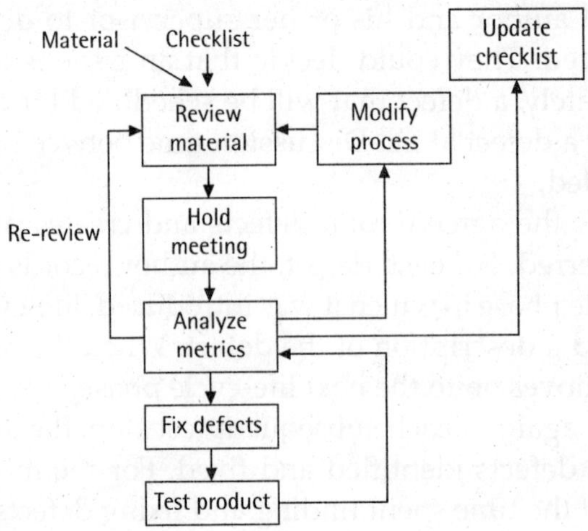

Figure 3 Closed-loop inspection process

The development teams on each project took over responsibility for creating and managing their own checklists. Checklists were now based on local defect data from test and were designed to prevent repeated escapes of the same defect type. Each development team set quantitative improvement goals to improve the defect containment rate of their inspections. It was the team's responsibility to suggest and pilot improvements to the process and to take actions that would result in higher product quality and higher inspection process effectiveness.

The SEPG served as a consultant to the inspection teams, mentoring them on data analysis techniques and helping them implement improvement recommendations. The SEPG fostered communication between teams by sponsoring a bimonthly meeting at which the development teams shared the results of their inspection improvement activities.

Data Analysis

Measuring Process Performance with Run Charts

After some preliminary analysis, the inspection team chose to characterize the inspection process by two measurements: inspection rate (LOCs/person-hour) and density of defects identified during the inspection (defects/KLOC). For products of similar quality, density of defects identified at inspection should be related to yield. The advantage of using density of defects identified at inspection is that it is not a lagging variable, that is, one doesn't have to wait until the project is over to measure it. Defect density identified was selected to characterize the effectiveness of the inspection process; inspection rate was selected to characterize the actual execution of the process.

Process measurements always include some random variation. In order to recognize trends or shift in process performance, one must put measurements in a temporal context by plotting them as a time series. This will also allow one to see the range of normal process variation, so that he or she can test apparent changes in process performance for statistical significance before using measurements as inputs to a decision-making process. Otherwise one runs the risks of taking management action in response to normal statistical variation in the data. At best this can waste a lot of effort, at worst it is likely to be counterproductive.

For inspections, the team characterized process performance with individual XmR charts, as depicted in Figure 4. The X chart is a run chart plotting the history of the values of a variable over time. An average of the data values is calculated and plotted on the chart. Upper control limits (UCL) and lower control limits (LCL) are calculated and plotted as well. The UCL and the LCL are typically drawn three standard deviations (3s) above and below the mean. When the LCL is less than zero, it is generally not drawn. The value of sigma is estimated from the average of the moving range.

The X chart is used to identify data points that fall outside the natural limits of process variation. These points can then be analyzed for assignable causes. The difference between upper and lower control limits defines the normal variation of the process. The mean defines average process performance. The moving range (mR) chart, is used to monitor process stability. This chart shows a moving range of the data values, or the absolute difference between each pair of values plotted on the X chart. When the range chart is out of control, it is generally not possible to draw conclusions about the X chart.

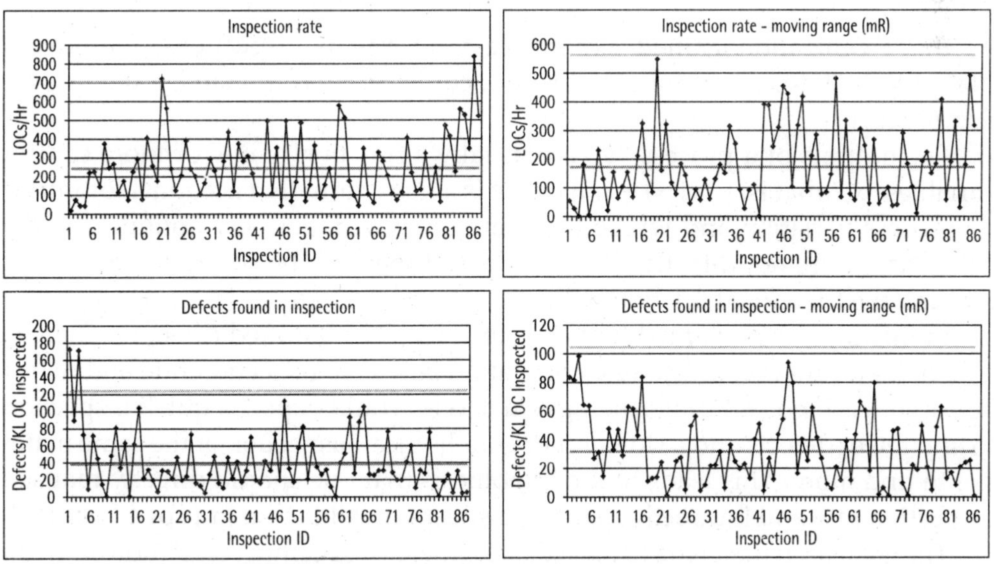

Figure 4 XmR charts for inspection rate and defect density found in inspection

Once a process is stable, shifts in process performance can be detected using the following tests:

- At least two out of three successive values fall on the same side of, and more than two sigma units away from, the centerline.
- At least four out of five successive values fall on the same side of, and more than one sigma unit away from, the centerline.
- At least eight successive values fall on the same side of the centerline.

The team used run charts of the defect density identified and inspection rate to monitor process performance.

The open-loop process was basically stable throughout most of this project, although it had considerable variability. The last 10 or so inspections show a trend toward increasing inspection rate and a corresponding trend to decreasing defect density identified. One didn't need to look far for an assignable cause to realize that the inspection teams were rushing against a looming project deadline. In fact, the previous peak in the inspection rate data that broke through the three-sigma limit represented an inspection done just before a holiday shutdown

The defect density identified chart also shows a few out-of-control points early on. These represent the first products through inspection when the inspection process was deployed in the organization. Once the developers realized that inspections were finding a lot of defects, they began to clean up the code before submitting it to inspection, and the defect density identified rapidly fell off to a lower range.

Control Variables

As the organization gained experience with Fagan inspections, employees started to look for a control variable that could be used to manage the inspection process.

The outputs of a process "y" are usually a function of one or more control variables "x," that is, $y = f(x) + \varepsilon$, where ε is a noise term that accounts for intrinsic process variation and where f is some unknown, possibly nonlinear, function. The y's are not directly controllable, but they can be controlled indirectly through the functional relation with x.

In this case, they wanted higher defect density identified (their y). There is a lot of literature that indicates a correlation between inspection rate and defect density identified. All things being equal, one would expect a quick inspection to find fewer defects and a slower more methodical inspection of the same material to find more. This leads to the hypothesis that one should directly manage inspection rate and indirectly manage inspection yield to an improved value.

The team used their data to investigate if there was really a correlation between inspection rate and the number of defects per KLOC found during inspection. Figure 5 shows a scatter plot of defect density identified vs. inspection rate and a curve fit by a nonlinear function. The fit has a correlation coefficient $r^2 = 0.67$. While not a particularly high value, it is good enough to be useful. These data suggested a target inspection rate in the range of 100 to 200 LOC/hour. This is far slower than normal reading speed, and it takes some training, practice, and reinforcement for reviewers to be able to consistently operate at this rate.

In the closed-loop inspection process the team set a target inspection rate of 100 to 200 LOC/hour and took corrective action when they missed the target. The average inspection rate was used as an entry criterion to the inspection meeting. If the rate was too high, the meeting was called off and the material given back to the reviewers.

The target inspection rate should be set based on actual data for a given application and project team. The team has seen some applications, typically safety critical code implemented in assembly language, where the target inspection rate was in the range of 50 LOC/hour.

Figure 6 shows the effect that proactively managing inspection rate has on the inspection run charts. When compared with the open-loop charts in Figure 4, it is obvious that the average inspection rate is lower and the variation in inspection rate is much lower. This is to be expected owing to the closed-loop nature of the control on rate. The improvement in average defect density identified is larger than expected based on Figure 5, and the improvement in defect removal rate shown in Figure 7 (6 defects/hour to 15 defects/hour) is even more dramatic. The shift in the process mean is obvious in the run chart. A t-test yields t = 2.93 allowing one to reject the null hypothesis that there is no significant difference in the process means at a significance level of 0.01. The reason that the improvement in defect rate is so dramatic is that the team introduced a number of other changes as they shifted to the closed-loop process.

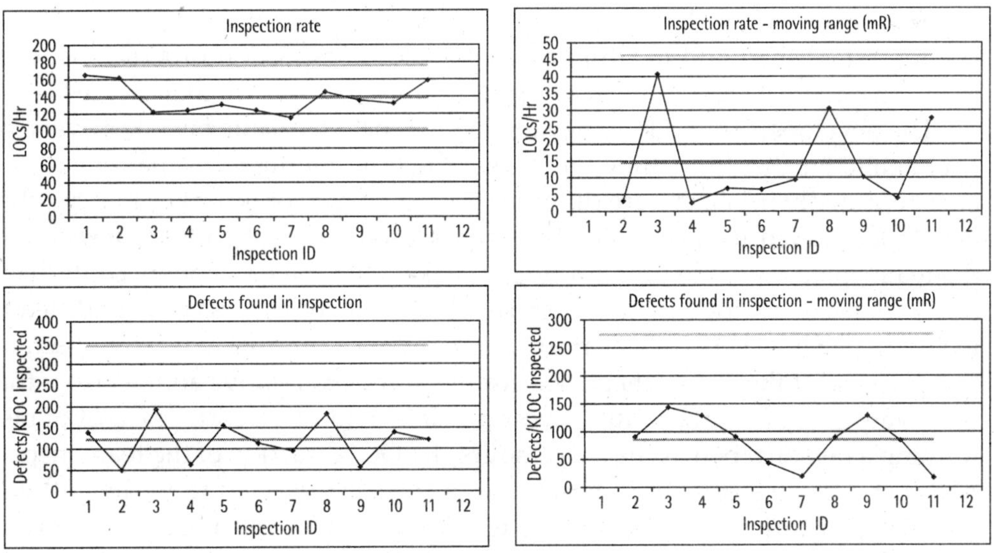

Figure 5 Correlation plot

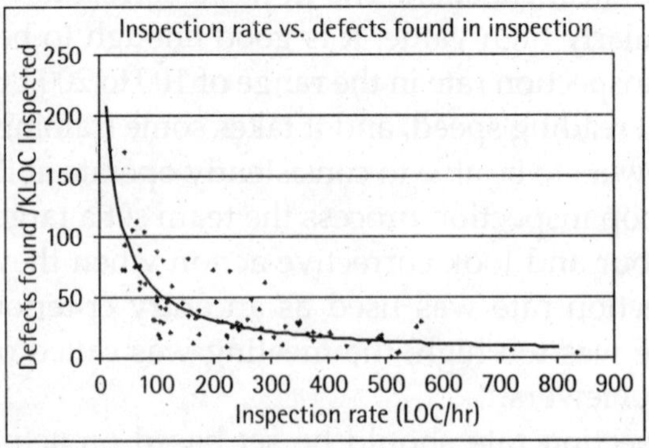

Figure 6 Managed inspections

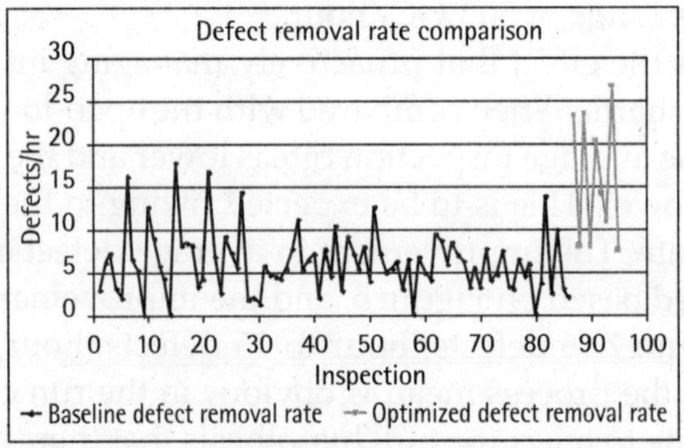

Figure 7 Comparison of defect removal rate before and after optimization

Optimization Strategies

Having established and institutionalized a stable inspection process, the team found that there were a number of opportunities to optimize their process.

The developers found that they tended to repeat the same mistakes over and over again. Furthermore, they found that the types of mistakes that one developer repeatedly injected were different from the types of mistakes that another developer tended to inject. Finally, when a product went to team inspection, the team spent valuable time finding mistakes that the developers could have easily found or avoided themselves. The development process was modified to include a personal bench check prior to submitting a product to team inspection. The purpose of the bench check was for the author to remove all the errors that they were likely to make at the lowest possible inspection cost. The cost of performing a personal bench check is 5 hours/KLOC, a fraction of the team inspection cost. The personal bench check uses a checklist derived from the author's own list of historical compilation and test defects. These checklist questions flag areas of high risk where the author has a history of making mistakes. By removing these defects prior to team inspection, they are removed at a lower cost, and the team inspection can focus on finding defects that the author would have been less likely to find.

Each inspection in the development process had a different objective. The checklists for personal bench checks were focused around the types of design and code defects that the author had a history of making. The team inspection checklists focused on interface- and requirements-related issues that cannot easily be found in the personal bench checks.

The team also found that their inspection process was creating a lag between the completion of the design or code phase and the subsequent phases. They had been holding off scheduling inspections until there was approximately 1000 LOC to be reviewed. It took up to a week after a product was submitted before the inspection was completed and the product returned to the author. The team implemented shorter, more frequent team inspections. Reviewers were assigned a day that they were "on duty." As developers submitted their product for inspection, it went to the team on duty for the day. Size of the inspections was limited to a few hundred lines at a time, reducing preparation time to one to two hours. The inspection team reviewed the material in the morning, the inspection meeting was held after lunch, and the reviewed product was back in the hands of the author within two to three hours of submitting it. This eliminated the lags in the system, removing the temptation for the author to move forward into test before the inspection had taken place.

Reducing the size of the product inspected also made it easier to control the inspection rate. Inspection teams tend to rush with larger products. In fact, the correlation between product size and defects per KLOC found in inspection is as strong as that with inspection rate as shown in Figure 8. The plot has $r^2 = 0.68$ and clearly shows a nonlinear relationship between product size and number of defects per KLOC found in inspection. Investigation of these data show a correlation between product size and inspection rate, larger products having a tendency to be rushed through inspection.

Inspection teams typically had an author and four reviewers. The size of the inspection teams was reduced to the author plus two reviewers. This reduced the cost of the inspection by 40 percent without significantly diminishing the

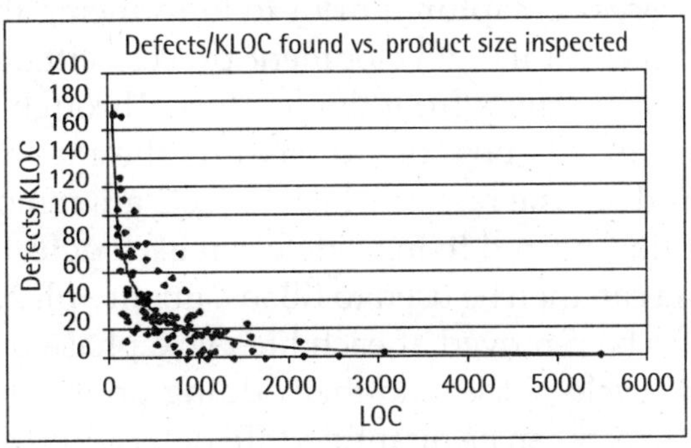

Figure 8 Effect of product size on number of defects found in inspection

inspection yield. Whenever possible, the internal "customer" for the product was included on the inspection team, helping to eliminate product handoffs between groups (that is, requirements to development).

Periodic defect prevention meetings provided the development team with an opportunity to review their data and define approaches to detect defects earlier or prevent them entirely. They found that defect prevention could be implemented in a CMM level 2 organization that is performing inspections and collecting defect data. Each development team became a defect prevention team, setting and managing to their own goal. The goals were aligned with the overall business objectives. The developers use their own defect data, captured during inspections and testing, as the basis for their defect prevention activities. The defects were analyzed using Pareto charts to identify most expensive, most frequent, and so on. The team determined what actions to take to prevent a chosen defect type from recurring in the future. Typical actions included modifying checklists, or changing coding and design standards. The team members convinced themselves of the value of the inspection and defect prevention activities by calculating their own ROI. The role of the SEPG became one of mentoring the defect prevention teams. Lessons learned were shared periodically with other defect prevention teams.

A key lesson learned through the introduction of defect prevention into the organization was that the people collecting the data must regularly use them; otherwise, they will stop collecting them! During defect prevention training, the team asked each developer to bring a dozen of their recently logged defects to the class. In one of the exercises, the developers were asked to read their defect descriptions and group the defects. The defect descriptions were so poorly written that the developers were unable to read their own defects! They had been collecting the data for someone else to use. They thought their job was to get to code and test. Now that their job included analyzing their own defect data, the quality of the defect reporting improved dramatically.

Measuring Return on Investment

The ROI of the inspection process can be directly measured. A cost analysis of the development process is captured prior to introducing the process improvement activity. Each step in the development process either injects defects into the product or removes defects from the product. Through measurement and/or anecdotal evidence, it is possible to baseline the rate at which defects are injected into the product, the rate at which defects are removed from the product, and the cost of finding and fixing a defect at each defect removal step in the life cycle. These data can then be used to fill in a quality plan. By multiplying the number of defects to be removed at each life-cycle phase by the cost of removing them in that life-cycle phase, and then adding up the costs, the total cost of finding and fixing defects can be quantified. To determine the savings relative to implementing inspections, the baseline cost of defect removal is first calculated without inspections (see Figure 9).

	Defects leaked from prev phase	New defects injected	Phase yield	Defects contained	Defects leaked	Defect removal cost	Total removal cost (hrs)
Design	0.0	40	0%	0.0	40.0	n/a	0.00
Design bench check	40.0	0	0%	0.0	40.0	10 mins	0.00
Design inspection	40.0	0	0%	0.0	40.0	30 mins	0.00
Code	40.0	60	0%	0.0	100.0	n/a	0.00
Code bench check	100.0	0	0%	0.0	100.0	5 mins	0.00
Compile	100.0	0	50%	50.0	50.0	1 min	0.83
Code inspection	50.0	0	0%	0.0	50.0	15 mins	0.00
Unit test	50.0	0	50%	25.0	25.0	15 mins	6.25
Integration test	25.0	0	35%	8.8	16.3	18 hrs	157
System test	16.3	0	35%	5.7	10.6	18 hrs	102
Customer	10.6						267

Figure 9 Quality plan—baseline

On average, developers injected 40 defects/KLOC in design and 60 defects/KLOC in code. None of the defects were removed in inspection, and between 35 percent and 50 percent of the defects were removed during each testing activity. When multiplied out, company employees found that they were spending about 267 hours/KLOC to remove defects. They also found that with this scenario, they still expected to have 10 defects/KLOC in the product post system test.

The cost of removing defects with inspections is calculated next, as captured in Figure 10.

	Defects leaked from prev phase	New defects injected	Phase yield	Defects contained	Defects leaked	Defect removal cost	Total removal cost (hrs)
Design	0.0	40	0%	0.0	40.0	n/a	0.00
Design bench check	40.0	0	50%	20.0	20.0	10 mins	3.33
Design inspection	20.0	0	50%	10.0	10.0	30 mins	5.00
Code	10.0	60	0%	0.0	70.0	n/a	0.00
Code bench check	70.0	0	70%	49.0	21.0	5 mins	4.08
Compile	21.0	0	50%	10.5	10.5	1 min	0.18
Code inspection	10.5	0	60%	6.3	4.2	15 mins	1.58
Unit test	4.2	0	50%	2.1	2.1	15 mins	0.53
Integration test	2.1	0	35%	0.7	1.4	18 hrs	13.23
System test	1.4	0	35%	0.5	0.9	18 hrs	8.60
Customer	0.9						37

Figure 10 Quality plan—baseline

New defect injection rates during design and code remained unchanged at 40 defects/KLOC in design and 60 defects/KLOC in code. Defect removal costs and yields were measured and inserted into the plan for bench check and inspection activities. Yields for testing activities remained unchanged. The total cost of defect removal was added up. With inspections, the company expected to spend a total of 37 hours fixing defects per KLOC of developed code. Additionally, they now expected to find less than one defect per KLOC post system test.

The baseline cost to find and fix defects per KLOC without inspections was 267 hours. The cost to fix those same defects when using bench checks and inspections was 37 hours. The difference between the two costs represents the savings realized per KLOC developed as a result of implementing inspections.

Before completing the ROI calculations, one must also consider the cost of performing the inspections. The predominant cost is the inspection preparation time and the meeting time. For a 1000 LOC inspection, a team of four developers each spent approximately half an hour in the kickoff meeting, 10 hours reviewing the material at 100 LOC/hour, and one hour in the inspection meeting. In addition, there was time spent by the author to categorize and fix the defects plus time spent by the inspection moderator to verify the defects had been fixed and to close the inspection meeting. In all, the cost of holding an inspection of 1000 LOC was about 50 hours. Since there is a design inspection and a code inspection, one must double this figure to get a total cost of about 100 hours. The design and code bench checks will add another 20 hours, for a total appraisal cost of about 120 hours.

The total cost of defect removal for 1000 LOC without inspections was 267 hours. With inspections, this cost drops to 37 hours, a savings of 230 hours. The cost of holding all of the inspections is about 120 hours. This indicates that the net savings, or ROI, for inspections was 267 – (37 + 120) = 110 hours/KLOC. In addition, one could expect a 10x improvement in delivered quality to the customer.

So the ongoing savings are about 110 hours/KLOC. The company still needs to consider the startup costs. They used one and a half days of inspection training and two days of defect prevention training per person. Assume a class size of 10, the total cost of labor for the instructor and the students will be about 310 hours. Since the savings per KLOC are about 110 hours, it will require the development of at least 3 KLOC to recover the training cost. This number is almost certainly too optimistic. The first inspections will be relatively ineffective because the team will be inexperienced. As the team gains experience, the quality of the inspections will improve dramatically. So a more realistic assumption is that training costs for 10 people can be recovered after the development of 6 to 10 KLOC.

The cost of defect removal in integration and system test drives the economics of the inspection process. In this case, the cost of defect removal in integration and system test was 18 hours/defect. The company was developing mission-critical embedded software, a situation where this number is fairly high. For other applications, with lower defect removal costs, the savings per KLOC would be smaller and the time to recover training costs would be longer.

Inspections by their very nature are more predictable and controllable than testing. One can budget 120 hours with a high level of confidence for every 1000 LOC to be inspected. The time required to test, however, remains highly unpredictable. While one can use average defect fix times in test for his or her calculations, the range of time required to fix any given defect can be very large. The more defects that have to be fixed in test, the less accurate the estimate for completion will be. Since appraisal cost is more predictable than testing cost, estimating accuracy will improve as a result of implementing inspections.

Finally, the number of defects removed in unit test is an indicator of the number of defects remaining in the software. Unit tests removed approximately 50 percent of the existing defects in the product. This means that the number of defects remaining in the product as it enters integration is about the same as the number of defects found in unit test. By introducing inspections, the number of defects leaked from unit test to integration test dropped from 25 per KLOC to around 2 per KLOC. Fewer defects in integration and system test results in the largest component of the cost savings from implementing inspections.

Quality Is Free

Earlier on in our careers, when we first introduced inspections, we frequently met managers who said something like this: "I know inspections are a good thing to do and that they will get our quality up but we don't have the time (or budget) to do them right now." Once one understands the dynamics of an effective inspection process, it becomes obvious that this argument is a fallacy. It assumes that inspections add cost without realizing a corresponding savings in test. If the savings in test is larger than the cost of the inspections, then one can cut costs and improve project cycle time by doing more inspections not fewer.

Actually there is some truth in both points of view. Ineffective inspections are likely to add more costs than they save. Well-managed closed-loop inspections produce a net savings. In order to understand how quickly one could recover the inspection cost, the team did some analysis on personal bench check data.

They looked at productivity from design through unit test before implementing bench checks and after implementing bench checks. They found that there was no significant difference in the productivity, even though they were taking time to perform the inspections. As appraisal costs increased and defects were found earlier, unit test costs decreased. In fact, the total cost of quality (appraisal plus testing) remained unchanged between design and unit test. This showed that there is no net cost to performing appraisals. Furthermore, the cost is recovered before the product exits unit test. Reductions in defects in integration and system level test go directly to the project bottom line.

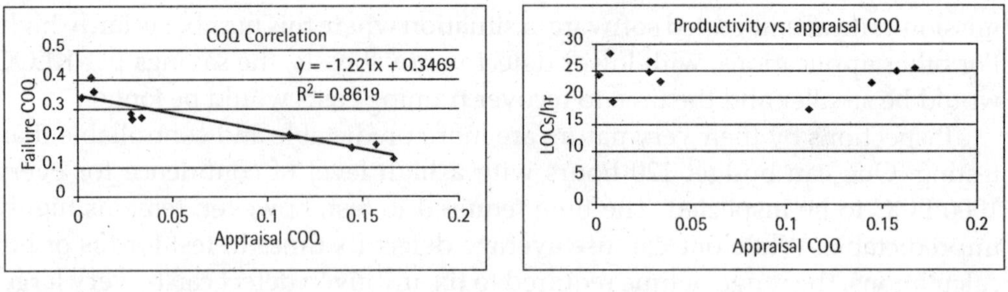

Figure 11 COQ relationships

Figure 11 summarizes the results. There is no correlation between appraisal COQ and productivity, that is, spending a longer time in inspection does not degrade productivity. There is a linear relationship between appraisal COQ and failure COQ, that is, increasing appraisal COQ tends to decrease failure COQ. As long as the slope is larger in absolute magnitude than –1 (in this case it is –1.22), the inspections result in a net cost decrease. But be warned, without active management, it is possible for the slope to go the wrong way!

Results

Over a five-year period the organization gradually implemented the optimization strategies described previously. Through this time, inspection yields increased from 60 percent to 80 percent and defects into integration reduced from 10 per KLOC to 3 per KLOC. At the same time, cost of performing inspections decreased by 40 percent, as they reduced the size of the inspection teams. The results are shown in Figure 12.

Summary

The organization's experience has shown that inspections can be characterized by a relatively small number of measurements: effort, product size, and defects.

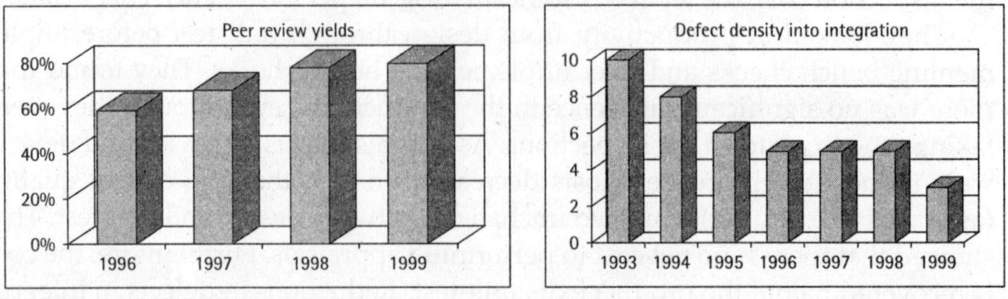

Figure 12 Inspection benefits

When these characteristics are measured consistently, it becomes possible to manage the quality of the inspection process and the quality of the product under inspection. This entails tracking product quality costs across the software life cycle and understanding and quantitatively managing the correlation between inspection rate and inspection yield.

The organization has seen that it is possible to forecast the number of defects found in downstream test processes and to compare the predictions to actuals using statistical techniques. If a product shows an unexpectedly high number of defects in test, it can be returned to inspection.

Defect data from test can be fed back into the inspection checklist resulting in a self-optimizing closed-loop process. Use of a structured defect prevention process in tandem with the inspection process engages the developers in process improvement and greatly improved the quality of defect data and ultimately of process yield.

Several optimization strategies were identified, including the use of bench checks prior to team inspections, optimizing the size of the inspection team, inspection meeting duration, and inspection frequency. Frequent short inspections covering a relatively small number of products can have a significant performance advantage over less frequent inspections that attempt to cover larger work products.

The key to managing inspections is gathering and using data. Well-managed inspections can produce outstanding results, but when inspections are not managed the results can range from mediocre to poor.

REFERENCES

Fagan, Michael. 1976. Design and code inspections to reduce errors in program development. *IBM Systems Journal* 15, no. 3.

Gilb, Tom, and Dorothy Graham. 1993. *Software inspections*. Reading Mass.: Addison-Wesley.

Humphrey, Watts. 1995. *A discipline for software engineering*. Reading, Mass.: Addison-Wesley.

BIOGRAPHIES

Ellen George has 20 years of experience in software development, software process improvement, and project management. She has held positions ranging from software developer to software manager of large-scale embedded development programs to manager of the Software Engineering Process Group (SEPG). George headed the SEPG at AlliedSignal's Teterboro, N.J., site, helping the site to become the first CMM Level 4 site within the corporation. She later became the software project manager of AlliedSignal's first PSP/TSP project. George has since become an SEI authorized PSP instructor and TSP launch coach. More recently, she was a member of Honeywell's corporate Software Six Sigma organization, helping to lead the deployment of software process improvement initiatives in more than 100 sites worldwide. She has been active in training and management consulting on the application of software process. George holds a bachelor's degree in math from Fordham University, and master's degrees in computer science and technology management from the Stevens Institute of Technology.

Steve Janiszewski has 30 years of experience in all phases of software development, management, and process improvement. As manager of AlliedSignal's Software Engineering Department in Teterboro, N.J., he led the organization to become the first CMM Level 4 site within AlliedSignal Corporation. Beginning 1997, Janiszewski championed the introduction of PSP and TSP at AlliedSignal. He chaired the AlliedSignal Software Process Improvement Council and he was also active in consulting on the application of software process to diverse domains including aerospace, medical instrumentation, industrial automation, automotive system, and financial systems. Prior to joining PS&J, Janiszewski was the director of the Honeywell corporate system and Software Six Sigma organization. At Honeywell, Janiszewski's responsibilities included providing process assessments, training, management consulting, and improvement planning assistance throughout the corporation, providing service to more than 6000 software engineers in more than 100 locations worldwide. Janiszewski is an SEI authorized PSP instructor and TSP Launch Coach. He holds a master's degree and doctorate in theoretical physics from NYU. He can be reached at stevejaniszewski@softwaresixsigma.com.

Six Sigma Fundamentals

Overview

Six Sigma (6σ) is a multifaceted approach to business improvement. It includes a philosophy, set of metrics, set of improvement frameworks, and toolkit.

Philosophy

The Six Sigma philosophy is to improve customer satisfaction through defect elimination and prevention and, as a result, increase business profitability. *Defects* are defined in terms of the customer's (not engineer's) viewpoint. The business profitability motive is crucial; improvement for improvement's sake, without positive impact on the bottom line, does not align with the Six Sigma philosophy.

Metrics

Among the most commonly cited metrics in Six Sigma are defect rate (parts per million, ppm) and sigma level. Conceptually, the *sigma level* of a process or product is where its customer-driven specifications intersect its distribution. A centered six-sigma process has a normal distribution with mean equal to target and specifications placed six standard deviations to either side of the mean. At this point, the portions of the distribution that are beyond the specifications contain 0.002 ppm of the data (0.001 on each side). Practice has shown that most manufacturing processes experience a shift of 1.5 standard deviations (due to drift over time) where the mean no longer equals target. When this occurs in a six-sigma process, a larger portion of the distribution extends beyond the specification limits: 3.4 ppm.

Figure A depicts a 1.5-sigma-shifted distribution with six-sigma annotations. In manufacturing, this shift results from issues such as mechanical wear over time and causes the six-sigma defect rate to become 3.4 ppm. The magnitude of the shift may vary, but empirical evidence indicates that 1.5 is about average. Does this shift exist in the software process? While it will take time to build sufficient data repositories to verify this assumption within the software and systems sector, it is reasonable to presume that there are factors that would contribute to such a shift. Possible examples are declining procedural adherence, technology learning curve, and constantly changing tools and technologies (hardware and software).

Other metrics that are used to report performance levels include defects per unit, defects per million opportunities, and yield or productivity. Within specific improvement projects, cycle time, defects, cost, product

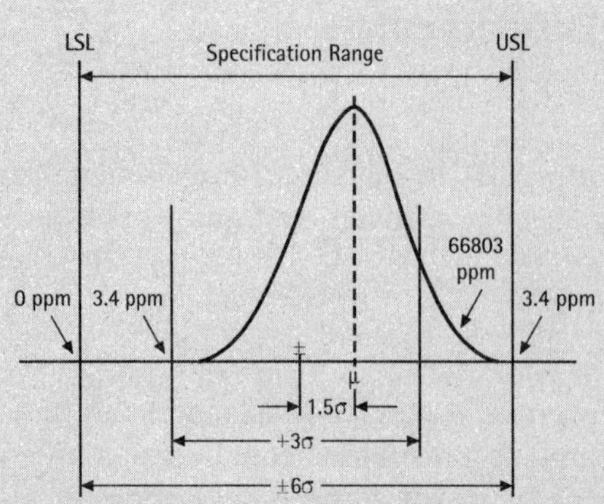

Assumptions:

- Normal distribution
- Process mean shift of 1.5s from nominal is likely
- Process mean and standard
- Deviations are known
- Defects are randomly distributed throughout units
- Parts and process steps are independent
- For this discussion, original nominal value equals the target

Figure A 1.5-sigma-shifted distribution with 6-sigma annotations

performance (or their variability), as well as bottom-line savings, may become paramount.

Some things to remember: Six Sigma measures should be expressed in customer terms. Target sigma-level performances should be driven by customer and business needs. Project-specific technical measures (in process defects, for example) may be needed to understand the processes and implement improvements, but they should always be linked to customer measures.

Frameworks

There are currently two main Six Sigma frameworks:

1. *DMAIC* (define-measure-analyze-improve-control) is used to improve and optimize existing processes and products.
2. *DFSS* (Design for Six Sigma) is used to design new products and processes. It is also used to redesign existing processes and products that have been optimized but still do not meet performance goals (that is, the desired sigma level). The latter case is believed to frequently occur when moving from a five-sigma level of performance to a six-sigma level. While DMAIC enjoys a relatively high degree of consistency across industry, DFSS is much more varied in its implementation. An example of the key DFSS steps is define-measure-analyze-design-verify.

LeanSigma, another approach to Six Sigma, may emerge as a third framework. However, lean techniques vary significantly across industry, and many organizations are implementing them within their existing DMAIC or DFSS frameworks.

Toolkit

The Six Sigma toolkit includes proven statistical and nonstatistical methods from previous evolutions of quality and business improvement initiatives. Figure B is an example of a toolkit showing the DMAIC phases where tools are commonly (but not exclusively) used.

It is important to remember that the Six Sigma toolkit is dynamic and organization-specific. The decision to adapt, add, or focus on specific methods should be based on the improved ability to deliver on customer needs and business benefit.

Define	Measure	Analyze	Improve	Control
Benchmark baseline Contract/charter Kano model Voice of the customer Voice of the business Quality function deployment Process flow map Project management "Management by fact"	Defect metrics Data collection methods Sampling techniques Measurement system evaluation	Seven basic tools Cause & effect diagrams, matrix Failure mode & effects analysis Statistical inference Reliability analysis Root cause analysis Five whys Hypothesis test ANOVA	Design of experiments Modeling Tolerancing Robust design Systems thinking Decision & risk analysis	Statistical controls: • Control charts • Time series methods Nonstatistical controls: • Procedural adherence • Performance management • Preventive activities

LeanSigma is a registered trademark of Maytag Corp.

Figure B A Six Sigma Toolkit

Six Sigma Fundamentals sidebar provided by Jeannine M. Siviy, Software Engineering Institute, e-mail jmsiviy@sei.cmu.edu.

Design-Appropriate Test Cases

Thomas F. Griffin, Thomas Lucy-Bouler, Nancy W. Davidson, and Robert Gehling, Auburn University Montgomery

Test cases are important in the arsenal of practices used to assure software quality. This article describes techniques for evaluating software using design-appropriate test cases. Design-appropriate test cases are test cases inspired by algorithm's design technique. Algorithm design is a part of most traditional books on algorithms. Design-appropriate test cases are discussed for brute force, recursive, divide and conquer, greedy design, and iterative design techniques.

Key words: algorithm design, software testing, test cases

Introduction

The classification of algorithm design techniques is included in many books on algorithms. Algorithm design is a useful guide to the selection of an approach to solving complex problems more efficiently than using a brute force alternative. This article illustrates how knowledge of the design technique used to create an algorithm can be used to develop better test cases for evaluating the algorithm.

Levitin (2000) provides an informative discussion of traditional design techniques such as divide and conquer, greedy approach, dynamic programming, backtracking, and branch-and-bound. He cites a number of recent books (Brassard and Bradley 1996; Horowitz, Sahni, and Rajasekaran 1996; Neapolitan and Naimipour 1997) that are organized around this familiar list of design techniques. The classes of design techniques have appeared in the computer science literature for decades (for example, Aho, Hopcroft, and Ullman 1974).

Because of its underlying design technique an algorithm may be deterministic or non-deterministic. Software to balance one's checking account at a point in time is deterministic. It should give exactly the same answer every time one uses it. Test cases are well suited to this category of software. Deterministic algorithms based on different design techniques would be expected to benefit from, if not require, testing and evaluation approaches tailored to the algorithm's design approach.

Pressman (2001) identifies several common computational errors including misunderstood or incorrect arithmetic precedence, mixed mode operations, incorrect initialization, precision accuracy, and incorrect symbolic representation of an expression. Many of these errors may affect comparison operations. Since change in program flow may happen after a comparison operation, Pressman asserts that test cases should be designed to uncover these errors. The algorithm design technique used to create a program is the roadmap for designing test cases that can detect many common computational errors.

Design-Appropriate Test Cases

This article seeks to explore software evaluation for brute force, recursive, divide and conquer, greedy, and iterative algorithms. It describes how common computational errors can be discovered by using test cases tailored to the algorithm's design. Jarvis and Crandall (1997) identify several kinds of test cases. Computation test cases verify mathematical calculations with normal data containing no purposely created error conditions. Boundary analysis test cases extend the data to the minimum and maximum allowable values plus or minus one. Boundary tests should not only demonstrate that the algorithm works properly within designed boundaries, but that it gives the expected behavior when outside the designed boundary. Cause and effect and logic cases extend the test cases to both valid and invalid data and test for the correct reaction of the system to both.

Brute Force Algorithms

The baseline algorithm to which all others are compared is the brute force algorithm. Brute force algorithms are typically simplistic in design, slow in execution, and tedious to test. For example, suppose an algorithm was required to compute the correct change to be given with the smallest number of coins possible. A brute force algorithm could be written to try every possible combination of coins that equaled the correct change, and then select the combination with the fewest coins. Unfortunately, testing a program based on this design would require testing every possible solution. As will be shown later, this "correct change" problem has more efficient solutions from both the standpoint of execution and testing.

Finding the largest of a set of unsorted numbers is a common programming task for which a brute force algorithm may be the most appropriate solution. A simple brute force algorithm would compare each number to the "largest number yet found" and, if necessary, update the "largest number yet found" with the value of the number currently being evaluated. Similar problems involve identifying whether a data set contains unique values, and the multiplication of matrices. Many algorithms of this type are implemented with iteration structures and may involve the processing data stored in arrays.

Boundary analysis test cases would typically explore the minimum and maximum values plus or minus one to be processed by the algorithm. To find the largest of a set of unsorted numbers, the "black box" approach to boundary analysis test case development would lead to test cases based on data sets based the largest number and the smallest number the algorithm should process. The largest and smallest numbers could be dependent on the application requirements (for example, zero might be the smallest number the data set is allowed to contain) or machine capability (for example, the largest value an integer may store). Additional test cases would contain the largest number allowed plus and minus one and the smallest number allowed plus and minus one.

For algorithms that process data in arrays, extending the "boundary test" concept to include correct processing at the boundaries of the array can create design-appropriate test cases. Just as basis path analysis can be used to assure that all of the code in an algorithm is executed, care must be taken to assure that all elements of an array are examined. Just as important, care must be taken to assure that only the elements of the array that should be examined are examined. In the case of the maximum value problem, this can be accomplished by testing the algorithm with different data sets, each with the maximum value element at a different location in the array. Possible locations for the maximum value element should include: a location in the body of the table (that is, not on an edge), locations at the corners of the table, and locations outside the edge of the table. The idea of searching locations outside the valid portion of an array may seem strange at first. However, if the table to be searched has columns 1 through n and rows 1 through m, common mistakes would include processing rows 1 through n and columns 1 through m, processing columns 1 through $n+1$ and rows 1 through $m+1$, or processing columns 0 through n and rows 0 through m.

If the simple brute force algorithm compares each number to the "largest number yet found" and, if necessary, updates the "largest number yet found" with the value of the number currently being evaluated, one must test for correct initialization of the "largest number yet found." If the largest number yet found is not initialized, or null, then comparisons to this value may always fail. If the initialization value is incorrectly set to zero, the algorithm will not find the largest of a set of negative numbers. It is appropriate to initialize the "largest number yet found" with the value of an element of the array. Cause and effect and logic test cases should ensure an algorithm responds properly with both valid and invalid data contained in the initialization element. As noted previously, null values in the initialization element can cause incorrect conclusions from comparisons. Null values in the data set may or may not be valid data and appropriate program behavior should be observed.

Obviously, it would not be possible to test an algorithm with every set of numbers from which the largest value would need to be found. In addition, "sampling" would not necessarily assure the accuracy of the program. However, a number of appropriate test cases can be deduced from knowledge of the design technique used to create the program. In combination, these design-appropriate test cases can assure the quality of the program.

Recursive Algorithms

A familiar recursive algorithm solves the problem of n factorial ($n!$). In this case the integer n is the input size of the algorithm. $n!$ is defined as the product of n, n-1, n-2 . . . 1. A "black box" approach to boundary testing at the upper limit might involve using n equal to the largest allowable integer value plus or minus one and at the lower limit the value one plus or minus one.

The recursive algorithm, F, solves $n!$, F(n), by returning (n)·F(n-1) unless $n = 0$, in which case it F(0) returns 1 and the algorithm ceases. In this example, $n = 0$ is defined as the initial condition or "base case" of the algorithm. Testing recursive algorithms should include boundary analysis. In the case of recursive algorithms, the base case represents the design-appropriate lower boundary to be tested regardless of the smallest value of n for which $n!$ will be calculated. A common error is to assume the base case for this algorithm is $n = 1$ since $n!$ is the product of all numbers from n to 1. Many statistical problems require the calculation of the special case of $n!$, where $n = 0$. Other recursive algorithms may have different base case values representing the lower boundary test case. Lower boundary tests should be conducted with the input size (n) equal to the base case and base case plus or minus one.

The upper boundary would represent the largest value the algorithm can process. Setting n equal to the largest possible integer value may not be the appropriate upper boundary for a recursive algorithm. In this case, $n!$ is always larger than n except when $n = 1$. If both n and $n!$ are integers, the limiting factor is the largest number that can be stored in the integer data type used to store $n!$. The upper boundary test case is the value of n that results in the largest value of $n!$ that can be stored in the data type used for $n!$. Boundary analysis at the upper boundary should produce an appropriate error code when the largest value that can be processed is exceeded.

The benefit of design-appropriate is readily apparent when considering an algorithm that calculates $n!/m!$ for n greater than or equal to m. Based on the preceding example, this problem could be solved by using a recursive algorithm to solve for $n!$ and, then, $m!$ (that is, F(n)/F(m) and the algorithm, F, could be tested using the procedure described above. Depending on the values of n and m, it could be much more efficient to solve $n!/m!$ as F(n) where the base case of F is m. The lower boundary test cases would include n equal to m, m plus one and m minus one.

Divide and Conquer

In the divide and conquer algorithm, a problem is divided, perhaps recursively, into two or more smaller problems, hopefully of equal size, which are independently solved by a simple solution and their solutions combined. A mergesort algorithm might take eight elements and divide them into two sets of four. Each set of four might be further divided into sets of two. The items in each set of two are ordered with a simple comparison. The sets of two forming each original set of four are merged in sorted order. The sets of four are merged in sorted order to produce the original eight items in sorted order.

Quicksort algorithms operate in a similar manner. Quicksort algorithms operate by picking any element, a pivot value, and placing all elements less than the pivot ahead of the pivot and all elements greater than the pivot after the pivot. Recursively perform the quicksort on elements less than the pivot and on elements greater than the pivot and concatenate them. The base case is a list of size zero or one.

Testing algorithms of this type should include tests that assure the problem is divided correctly into mutually exclusive, complementary sub-problems. If the divisions are not mutually exclusive and complementary, the resulting merged set may be larger, smaller, or different from the original set. Test cases using even and odd numbers of elements to be sorted and, in the case of quicksort, multiple values of the pivot element should be used.

Because the mergesort involves many comparisons as the data are merged, the boundary conditions for the comparison include more than just the highest and lowest values. Ultimately, every value in the data set becomes one of two values being compared. Test cases involving values that ultimately become members of sets to be merged should be tested as if one were the boundary value of the other (that is, setting one value equal to the other, then larger, and finally smaller). Thus, at the lowest level of the mergesort, a sub-problem may contain two unequal values, two equal values, one value, or zero values. For each value in the first sub-problem a second sub-problem should be constructed with values that are equal to, larger, and smaller than the values in the first sub-problem. Table 1 contains the possible value combinations for boundary analysis test cases.

Once the possible values are enumerated and duplications are removed it is possible to specify test cases. Table 2 contains an enumeration of boundary test cases for a mergesort.

Greedy Techniques

Greedy methods build solutions a piece at a time. Each added piece represents the locally optimum piece to add to the partial solution. The choice selected is

First sub-problem		Second sub-problem	
	Values	Possible boundary values	Possible value pairs for each value in first sub-problem
Two unequal values	10	11, 10, 9	(11,11) (11,10) (11,9) (10,10) (10,9) (9,9) (11) (10) (9)
	9	10, 9, 8	(10,10) (10,9) (10,8) (9,8) (9,9) (8,8) (10) (9) (8)
Two equal values	10	11, 10, 9	(11,11) (11,10) (11,9) (10,10) (10,9) (9,9) (11) (10) (9)
	10	11, 10, 9	(11,11) (11,10) (11,9) (10,10) (10,9) (9,9) (11) (10) (9)
One value	10	11, 10, 9	(11,11) (11,10) (11,9) (10,10) (10,9) (9,9) (11) (10) (9)
Zero values		11, 10, 9	(11) (10) (9)

Table 1 Possible boundary analysis values

	First sub-problem Values	Second sub-problem Values by test case													
Test no.		1	2	3	4	5	6	7	8	9	10	11	12	13	14
Two unequal values	10	11	11	11	11	10	10	10	9	9	8	11	10	9	8
	9	11	10	9	8	10	9	8	9	8	8				
Two equal values	10	11	11	11	10		9	11	10	9					
	10	11	10	9	10		9								
One value	10	11	11	11			9	11	10	9					
		11	10	9			9								
Zero values		11													

Table 2 Boundary analysis test cases for mergesort

that which produces the largest immediate gain. On the first step a solution to part of a problem is selected from the best alternative available. At each step the choice is the best of the remaining choices. "Choices" in greedy methods are irrevocable, meaning they are not revised. For example, in the "Traveling Salesman Problem" one must find the cheapest roundtrip route given a number of cities and the cost to travel between each city. The greedy method would select the next city by choosing the unvisited city with the lowest cost to reach from the current city. Choosing the lowest cost city is locally optimum, but it may not lead to a globally optimum solution.

An example, given by Levitin (2003), involves selecting the minimum number of coins required to give 48¢ in change. The choices are from an unlimited supply of U. S. coins in denominations of 25¢, 10¢, 5¢, and 1¢. The first step would be to select a quarter (25¢) since this provides the greatest gain toward 48¢. This step could be done recursively until less than 25¢ remains to be given in change. The second step cannot be a quarter since it would exceed the maximum change to be given. In the second step a dime (10¢) is selected as the optimum choice. In the third step another dime is selected. In the final three steps, pennies (1¢) are selected to reach 48¢. In this case the solution is globally optimum, but greedy techniques do not guarantee a globally optimum solution. Consider a second case of giving 10¢ in change where the denominations are 7¢, 5¢, and 1¢. A greedy approach would give a solution of one 7¢ coin, the locally optimum choice for the first step. After that choice, three pennies on succeeding steps would be chosen. This solution is not globally optimum since it requires four coins. The globally optimum solution requires only two coins—two 5¢ coins.

Greedy techniques are applicable to optimization problems and should be designed to assure that the problem to which the greedy algorithm will be applied is such that only globally optimum solutions will result, if possible, or that locally optimum solutions can at least be identified. Test cases should verify that the locally optimum solution for each step is correctly calculated and selected. Further, when a locally optimum step is selected the problem remaining to be solved must be accurately calculated.

In Levitin's example (with pennies, nickels, dimes, and quarters) the problem is a special case of giving between 1¢ and 99¢ in change with the fewest possible coins. However, basing boundary test cases on only the extreme values of 1¢ and 99¢ would miss many opportunities for testing. Logically, the boundary conditions to be tested can be derived from upper and lower limits of the problem and the denominations of the coins involved. Table 3 gives the candidate "change given" boundary values for test cases resulting from having either the minimum or the maximum number of each type of coin in a solution. The minimum number of coins of a particular type in a solution is zero. The "boundary" of exactly one of each coin in the solution should be tested. In addition, there is a "boundary" determined by the maximum number of coins of a type that can be included in a solution. The maximum number of pennies is four, nickels is one, dimes is two, and quarters is three. The values plus or minus one will ensure that coins of the correct type are selected.

The boundary analysis test cases reduce to giving the following amounts in change: 0, 1, 3, 4, 5, 6, 10, 19, 20, 21, 25, 74, 75, 76, 99, and 100¢. It can be argued that some of the candidate test cases in the table are redundant. For example, to calculate the correct solution for giving 99¢ in change, the algorithm must correctly solve the problem of giving 75¢, 20¢, and 4¢ in change. After elimination of duplication the remaining values for design-appropriate boundary test cases would be: 0, 6, 19, 21, 76, 99, and 100¢.

Iterative Methods

Moret and Shapiro (1990) mention that iterative methods, a particularly difficult class of algorithms to evaluate, are used as an approach to optimization problems.

> "Iterative methods start with any feasible solution and proceed to improve upon the solution by repeated applications of a simple step.

	Candidate change values in cents				
Denominations	Min Coins	Min Coins+1	Max Value-1	Max Value	Max Value+1
Penny (1¢)	0	1	3	4	5
Nickel (5¢)	0	5	4	5	6
Dime (10¢)	0	10	19	20	21
Quarter (25¢)	0	25	74	75	76

Min is the change of value based on the minimum number of each type of coin possible in a solution.
Max is the change of value based on the largest number of each type of coin possible in a change solution.

Table 3 Table of candidate "change given" values for test cases

> The step typically involves a small, localized change, which improves the value of the objective function."

Unlike greedy methods, iterative methods can easily allow a portion of the solution to be revisited and possibly changed. In addition, at each step in the process, iterative algorithms may or may not maximize the gain toward the final solution. Indeed, they may simply move in the direction of the maximum gain by a predetermined amount, the step amount. Iterative algorithms may start with any feasible solution, including a randomly generated solution, and step toward what appears to be the best direction for a solution. During each iteration the algorithm recalculates the best direction for a solution and takes a step toward it.

Some type of halting principle is necessary to prevent iteration from continuing indefinitely. Halting is usually based on examining the gain or improvement in the quality of the solution. First, when the algorithm determines that improvement on the next step is less than some predetermined amount, the algorithm halts with a solution that is "close enough." It is as if someone were walking across a field by going one-half of the remaining distance each day. The first day half the field is crossed, the second day three-fourths is crossed, the third day seven-eighths is crossed, and so on. The only way to get to the other side is to declare victory when the next step is negligibly small. Second, halting can occur if the best possible next step produces a solution that is not as good as the present solution, for example, if someone were walking across a distance of 10 feet by taking three-foot steps. After moving nine feet, the next step would take the person farther from the goal than he or she was before taking the step. As in the case of greedy methods, it is possible to find a locally optimum solution before a globally optimum solution is encountered. Indeed, any number of locally optimum solutions may be possible.

Algorithms based on this method may be capable of producing many different solutions from the same data. This is because the starting solution may be random; therefore, a different starting solution may be used each time the data are analyzed. As these algorithms approach a final solution from a different starting point they may halt the process prior to finding a global solution. This is because the algorithm cannot move to a solution even if it can calculate it. It can only move by the "step amount" toward the solution and must halt because of the halting rules whether it has reached the solution or not.

A second problem is that the data to be processed may be expected to contain errors and internal inconsistencies. These errors may be due to measurement or other sources. In fact, the ability of these algorithms to tolerate problems with the data is one of their most attractive features. Even if errors in the data have a mean of zero they may cause the global solution to be quite different from the solution that would have been obtained with error-free data. For example, if the input data contain the lengths of three sides of a triangle, it is quite possible for the data with errors to be consistent with a different triangle, which the algorithm might easily identify. This example illustrates that it is possible for the algorithm to find a globally optimum solution (a triangle that perfectly matches the data), but find a solution that is wrong (not the triangle that was measured). It is also possible that no solution may be perfectly consistent with the data supplied to the algorithm.

Performance testing involves testing the ability of the finished product to meet requirements. Typically, the requirements are measurable characteristics such as transactions per second, response time under a given level of user load, or time to complete a given task. These measures may be sufficient for algorithms that produce a unique solution and whose ability to do so has been verified prior to performance testing. For algorithms based on iterative methods it may be necessary to include "solution accuracy" in the plan for performance testing. Monte Carlo methods in conjunction with experimental design concepts are effective approaches to measuring accuracy (Griffin 2001). Generating test cases via Monte Carlo methods could be classified as functional or black boxes testing, since test cases do not rely on a knowledge of the internal design of the software (Rakitin 1997). However, the authors take the view that Monte Carlo simulation is the design-appropriate method for generating test cases for non-deterministic software.

Simulation has long been recognized as an effective means for testing and debugging software. In many industries process simulation is viewed as the best method for verification and logic validation of control software (Purcell 1999). In this circumstance, offline testing is faster and safer than online testing of control systems.

Summary

This article has discussed algorithm design as a factor in planning software evaluations. Design-appropriate tests based on the algorithm's design technique have been shown to be a useful addition to the development of standard test cases. If one knows the design technique of the algorithm used in a software solution, he or she has a better chance of selecting the test cases necessary to assure the quality of the software. If one does not have, or use, this valuable information, it is entirely possible that he or she would fail to include tests that should be run. The alternative is simply to design and run large numbers of tests, many of which would be either redundant or useless, with the hope that the correct tests will by chance be included in the set.

Test case generation based on algorithm design is a technique that could be used by developers doing unit testing of simple algorithms. In some cases this technique may require more time for planning and testing than developers would, or should, spend. Testing by a professional tester assigned to the developer may be a more realistic approach for using this technique. For large complex systems such as refinery control systems, Monte Carlo simulation is a design-appropriate method for testing. The technique is not limited to unit testing by developers. Consideration of algorithm design in the development of test cases is simply another tool supporting the intelligent and efficient selection of test cases that can be used at any point in the development process.

REFERENCES

Aho, A. V., J. E. Hopcroft, and J. D. Ullman. 1974. *The design and analysis of computer algorithms.* Reading, Mass.: Addison-Wesley.

Brassard, G., and P. Bradley. 1996. *Fundamentals of algorithmics.* Englewood Cliffs, N. J.: Prentice Hall.

Griffin, T. F. 2001. Measuring software accuracy. In *Proceedings of the 6th International Conference of the Decision Science Institute,* Chihuahua, Mexico.

Horowitz, E., S. Sahni, and B. Rajasekaran. 1996. *Computer algorithms.* Rockville, Md.: Computer Science Press.

Jarvis, A., and V. Crandall. 1997. *Inroads to software quality.* Englewood Cliffs, N. J.: Prentice Hall.

Levitin, A. 2003. *Introduction to the design and analysis of algorithms.* Reading, Mass.: Addison-Wesley.

Levitin, A. 2000. A new road map of algorithm design techniques: Picking up where traditional classification leaves off. *Dr. Dobbs Journal* (April): 23–28.

Moret, B., and H. Shapiro. 1990. *Algorithms from P to NP, volume I: Design and efficiency.* Reading, Mass.: Addison-Wesley.

Neapolitan, R., and K. Naimipour. 1997. *Foundations of algorithms.* Boston: Jones and Bartlett.

Pressman, R. S. 2001. *Software engineering: A practitioner's approach,* fifth edition. New York: McGraw-Hill.

Purcell, J. 1999. Simulation software cuts time and expense. *Control Magazine* (October).

Rakitin, S. R. 1997. *Software verification and validation: A practitioner's guide.* Boston: Artech House.

BIOGRAPHIES

Thomas F. Griffin is professor and acting head of the Department of Information Systems and Decision Science at Auburn University Montgomery. He is a Senior member of ASQ and a member of its Software Division, having served as a member of the Division Council, publications chair, newsletter editor, and as a past speaker at the International Conference on Software Quality and ASQ's Annual Quality Congress. He holds a doctorate from the University of Alabama. His primary research interests are in the fields of software project management and software quality. He can be reached by e-mail at tgriffin@mail.aum.edu.

Thomas Lucy-Bouler is an associate professor at Auburn University Montgomery (AUM). He has been at AUM for 15 years. His research interests include small business information systems, neural networks, and healthcare information systems. He currently is working on several articles in the healthcare information system field. He holds a doctorate in management science with an emphasis in artificial intelligence from the University of Alabama.

Nancy W. Davidson is an assistant professor in the Information Systems/Decision Sciences Department at Auburn University Montgomery. She teaches systems analysis and design, database management, and information management at the undergraduate level. At the graduate level, her primary areas of teaching are in information resource management, database management, and systems analysis and design.

Her research interests include information technology performance and infrastructure issues, information technology policy and strategy, and business policy and strategy as they relate to information technology. Her publications have appeared in *The Academy of Management Executive*, *Information & Management*, **and** *Journal of Information Technology Management*.

Robert (Bob) Gehling is an assistant professor in the Department of Information Systems and Decision Sciences in the School of Business at Auburn University Montgomery (AUM). Gehling has degrees from Auburn University, the University of North Florida, and Austin Peay State University. He has more than 20 years of experience in the management of information technology. Prior to joining AUM, he served as chief technology officer and director of information technology services at the State University of West Georgia, and as the director of information systems support at Auburn University. He also served as an assistant controller at the University of Florida. Gehling's research interests include network and data security, technology outsourcing, and end-user computing support. His primary areas of teaching include data communications, network security, and information technology disaster preparedness.

How to Test Usability of Security Sensitive Systems

Ugo Piazzalunga, Eutron Infosecurity Srl, and Paolo Salvaneschi, University of Bergamo

While security testing for software is becoming an important topic among software testers, little attention has been paid to a critical aspect of security: its usability. Security testing is focused on finding vulnerabilities of the software, regardless of whether additional security problems occur from bad usability designs. This article proposes a framework for testing the usability of security sensitive systems. Based on the systemic approach to usability, it defines general usability attributes and calls for their experimental evaluation. The authors apply this framework to test the usability of alternative realizations of a widespread PKI-based system. These alternatives differ for the personal security devices used, that is, traditional cryptographic smart cards or USB tokens. The tests clearly show that usability issues lead to security problems. The interpretation and explanation of the test results bring up recommendations for software practitioners to properly address usability in security software based on security devices.

Key words: security, testing, usability

Introduction

Software quality professionals can no longer consider security superficially. Their reputation and business is in jeopardy without proper security in place. According to E. Dash's article "Visa to bar transactions by processor," published in the *New York Times*, July 19, 2005, companies have lost their business because of security breaches, and even Microsoft struggles to recover from the bad security reputation it has gained over the past few years (Schneier 2005). Companies must therefore test against security issues. But while much literature exists on testing against security vulnerabilities (see, for example, Whittaker and Thompson 2003), there is little on testing security *and* usability. If a company has a system that is highly secure but unusable, it won't sell. On the other hand, if a company has a system that is usable but not secure, it will put its reputation and business at risk. What should the company do then? This article presents a test methodology that can be used to assess that a proper balance between usability and security is in place.

It would be better, of course, if one could rely on software engineers to design software that is both usable and secure (this is possible—see Cranor and Garfinkel 2005). (It would be better, too, if one could rely on software engineers to design correct reliable bug-free software!) It is beyond the scope of this article to thoroughly discuss why this rarely happens, yet the following two observations appear to be relevant.

First, software architects and developers tend to accuse users of being foolish, doing their best to avoid and circumvent the smart, strongly secure—but unusable—technologies and policies they designed and implemented (Adams and Sasse 1999). This stand is wrong. If one wants to achieve real security he or she must take into consideration the usability of the software, accepting the responsibility to deliver software that is both usable and secure.

Second, while security vulnerabilities get plenty of attention on the Web and in the news, as well as broad coverage on the economics of their impacts, appropriate awareness of the security versus usability issue is missing. For example, what is the cost of user accounts that were violated because of a badly chosen password? Or how many information technology (IT) organizations establish policies that allow users to set secure and usable passwords? Password usability represents just one of the many examples of usability issues that affect security. It is far from being alone. Wool (2004) studied how often firewall configurations violate well-established security guidelines, while this article presents the impacts on security of the usability of different form factors of security devices.

The authors argue that the main reason behind usability versus security problems is a missing systemic view and approach while designing security software and systems. Addressing usability without taking into account: 1) the social and physical contexts (including the security software and users' security devices); 2) the users; and 3) the tasks that these users have to achieve are prone to failure (Sasseff, Brostoff, and Weirich 1999). The systemic view of usability is required while defining usability attributes. The definition of these attributes represents the first step of the approach the authors propose for testing usability and security. A second step is the objective measurement of these attributes; it is common to find even contrasting usability claims that are not supported by any research or experimental evidence. The primary purpose of the authors' approach is for testing; experimental tests, however, are interesting not only for evaluation and comparison purposes, but also for explanations and suggestions for better system design.

There is not a rich set of published works related to the experimental evaluation of usability and usability-security interaction for security systems. Wu, Garfinkel, and Miller (2004) propose an authentication system based on mobile phones and describe a user study done to confront its usability and security with respect to other authentication systems. Usability was evaluated apparently only through scores collected from user questionnaires, while security was measured by simulating attacks during the user tests. The authors' work presents usability attributes and associated metrics, most of them measured without relying only on subjective user ratings. It is unclear whether the security metric they measured is affected by usability issues or, rather, is just a direct measure of security per se. The authors explicitly introduce the usability attribute "security interaction" to focus on the impact that usability might have on security. Usability studies related to specific identification and authentication mechanisms may be found for user-names and password usability (Adams and Sasse 1999) and biometric usability (Coventry, De Angeli, and Johnson 2003). The paper by A. Whitten and J. D. Tygar (1999) focuses on Public-Key Infrastructure (PKI) usability, in particular, of PGP; their conclusions are similar to the authors' conclusions—"We need to know the usability limits of security software"—but the authors' work differs for the focus on the systemic approach and the generality of the experimental testing method proposed.

Testing the Usability of Security Systems

The experimental evaluation the authors propose for testing the usability of security systems requires a careful test design, implementation, processing, and interpretation of results. Their usability test takes advantage of the methods used in the current best practices of Human Computer Interfaces evaluation (Dix et al. 2004). Moreover, it integrates the usability test method with the approach of the quality models for software products evaluation (ISO 9126 1991). This is done through the definition of a set of metrics and how they combine to give quality attribute scores. The methodology includes the following steps:

1. Purpose, context, and roles definition: Define the aims of the test (for example, the comparison of the usability of two different security GUIs of a system) and set the limits of the test. The context for the experimental scenario is designed, including the real environment one wants to simulate, the roles of the users, the type of tasks, and so on.
2. User selection and task definition: The selection criteria of users are defined according to the selected context and aims. The number of users must provide a wide enough sample to support the statistical analysis of data. The tasks to be executed by each user (sequence of steps, input data, output data) are defined.
3. Measurement apparatus design: Choose the usability attributes, the metrics, and specify their relationships. For each metric, define the name, description, scale, and procedures to collect the data and compute the measurement.
4. Execution and data collection.
5. Processing for statistical significance.
6. Computation of the quality attributes scores: The ISO 9126 quality model is a tree where the usability is linked to a set of attributes, and

each attribute is evaluated through a set of metrics. To draw the quality profile of a product, it is required to compute, through a suitable procedure, the score for each quality attribute by considering the contribution of a number of metrics.

7. Results interpretation and explanation: Interpret the whole set of results and suggest possible causal explanations to support design recommendations.

The authors explain their approach in more detail through the discussion of a specific experimental study related to the usability of a class of PKI-based systems.

An Experimental Study of PKI-Based Systems Usability

Purpose, Context, and Roles Definition

The scenario set up for this study compares the usability (and the usability-security interaction) of three alternative realizations of a simple but widespread PKI-based system. These alternatives differ for the personal security devices used: the traditional plastic smart card with a USB smart card reader and two types of USB tokens (labelled as "base" and "advanced" token). The base type of USB tokens integrates, in one object, both the smart card reader and the cryptographic smart card IC. The advanced USB token adds a mass storage to the base type; when connected to the host system, this token will make available as separate resources both the smart card (and its reader) and a removable hard drive for general purpose storage. The e-mail client was Microsoft Outlook Express running on Windows XP and Windows 2000. Except for low-level drivers, all three systems shared the same middleware (for example, Microsoft CAPI). The role assigned to the participants was to be responsible for the preparation and launch of an advertising campaign to promote a new product. Tasks for this job included frequent travel among company sites. The material had to be sent to colleagues through e-mails with a strong level of security protection. The test involved a number of participants (the users) and a supervisor. The supervisor had the following roles: drive the initial phase of the test; give the user all the required inputs; collect the measures and act as customer support service during the test; and drive the final phase to collect the questionnaire.

User Selection and Tasks Definition

The authors selected 10 participants for the user test (a wide enough sample: 10 samples for each system type to support the statistical analysis of data). All of the participants were in their second or third year of undergraduate studies in an engineering college, skilled with the use of computers, but without any previous experience securing e-mail or with cryptographic devices. Before executing the user test, the supervisor introduced each participant to the test scenario and the required task. Installation and user manuals were made available, together with the hardware of the first system. Participants had to move across three company sites. Three workstations in three different university labs simulated this setup. At each site the user had to execute the following tasks and then proceed to the next site:

- Install drivers and software for the device.
- Send an encrypted and signed e-mail message to a colleague through the standard Outlook encryption and signing procedure, which requires him or her to provide the password to authorize the signature operations on the device. The text and the recipient of the e-mail were contained in the documents handed out; the e-mail client was configured to include the digital certificate of the recipient. The user's digital certificate was automatically available after the device was inserted.

At the end of the three sites, the supervisor gave the user the hardware for the second system, and the user repeated the steps. The same was repeated for the third one. The systems presentation sequence was designed to balance the frequencies of the presentation order. During the execution phase the supervisor measured the values of the defined metrics using a standard sheet to write the results. When there was failure to correctly complete a task, the supervisor requested that the task be repeated. At the end of the test, the user was asked to answer a few questions in the form of a questionnaire.

Usability Attributes and Measurement Apparatus

The authors tried to capture many of the important and general usability attributes that most people will likely find applicable. Their attributes definition is based on the ISO 9126 standard. The ISO 9126 software quality model defines six independent software quality characteristics, and each of them is decomposed into a set of subcharacteristics. Usability studies of security systems deal not only with software aspects but also with systemic aspects. Moreover, they require the evaluation of interactions between different quality attributes like usability and security (an ISO subcharacteristic of functionality). The following security interaction attribute the authors are proposing evaluates how poor usability may lead to security problems. Therefore, while the ISO standard is an important reference point, it has to be extended and adapted to accommodate the specific aspects of interest. The usability attributes the authors adopted are an extension of the following three ISO 9126 usability subcharacteristics:

- *Learnability*. The effort required to learn the use of the security system.
- *Operability*. The effort required to properly carry out the assigned tasks.
- *Attractiveness*. The extent that a security system is attractive to the user.

Operability is a very broad attribute and can be broken down into the following attributes:

- *Mobility*. The ease of operation of the security system from different computers, since organizations are increasingly requiring nomadic workers and professionals.
- *Installability*. The ability to easily install the required software.
- *User friendliness*. The ease with which users are able to operate the system.
- *Low costs to operate*. The workload of customer support calls that the security system demands, and the time spent by users to carry out their tasks.
- *Security interaction*. The system must provide enhanced security without inducing dangerous errors. Do usability problems lead to security failures? Do security constraints lead to usability issues?

The adaptation of the ISO model of software quality to the specific type of systems requires some additional comments. The first concerns the hierarchical relationship among the attributes. In the authors' approach, each subattribute of operability has the same relevance level of learnability and attractiveness. The subattributes are simply classified under the common name of operability. A further comment is related to the security interaction. With a somewhat arbitrary choice, the authors placed it under the heading "operability." The ISO standard does not model this type of attribute, because it describes an interaction between properties (usability and security).

The proposed experimental approach is driven by the usability attributes defined previously. Each attribute will be evaluated through a set of defined metrics. Figure 1 lists the metrics and defines their relationships with the usability attributes.

Hesitations are conditions in which the user has doubts on how to proceed and do not necessarily imply an error.

The following errors are classified as security errors:

- Failure to encrypt an e-mail. The secret supposed to be protected was sent in clear.
- Failure to sign an e-mail. It prevents the recipient from verifying the author and the integrity of the e-mail.
- Failure to bring the cryptographic device in the new location. The device is left on the desk or plugged in the workstation; this situation may allow attackers to get access to the user's private key.

The focus here is mainly on how usability impacts security. In general, however, the interaction between security and usability goes in both directions: usability can affect security and security can affect usability (such as the usability problems due to constraints set on user passwords (see, for example, Adams and Sasse 1999)).

Metrics	Learnability	Attractiveness	Installability	User friendliness	Low cost to operate	Security interaction	Mobility
No. of references to the manual	X						
No. of requests to the customer service	X				X		
Time for installation			X				
No. of errors during installation			X				
No. of hesitations during installation			X				
Time for sending e-mail				X	X		
No. of errors in sending e-mail				X			
No. of hesitations in sending e-mail				X			
No. of security errors						X	
No. of mobility errors							X
Evaluation of mobility (questionnaire)		X					X
Evaluation of usability (questionnaire)		X					
Discretional use (questionnaire)		X					

Figure 1 Metrics and their relationships with the usability attributes

A mobility error may occur moving from site to site, for example, if the user fails to bring the CD-ROM containing the installation software, the smart card, the reader, or the token. A mobility error is also a security error only if the object forgotten is either the smart card or the token. The last three metrics are based on the questionnaire answers; participants were asked to express a score from 1 (bad) to 5 (excellent) on the overall system usability and mobility. A preference of purchase was also included.

Statistical Processing and Computation of the Quality Attributes Scores

The data were examined to find possible outlying values that might skew the test results, then the collected data were processed to test their statistical significance. Where applicable, the measured results were processed to compute the mean value and the standard deviation. Given a set of three mean values (and the associated standard deviations) coming from a metric applied to the three systems, the authors computed the t-test to each pair of values to evaluate the statistical significance of the differences. Figures 2, 3, and 4 show some examples of these measured values, their standard deviations, and the related probability levels.

The data were then processed to compute the quality attributes scores. For each quality attribute, the computation takes as input the set of values coming from a number of metrics (both quantitative and qualitative values; see Figure 1). The computation is done through interpretation functions, which map

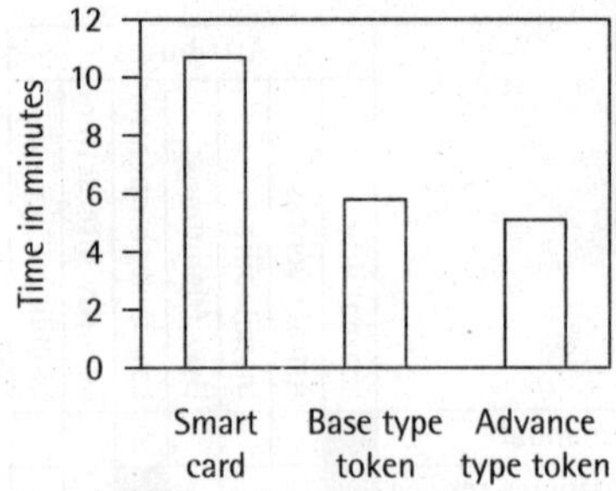

	mean	std. dev.
SC	10.7	4.0
BT	5.8	2.5
AT	5.1	1.7

	p
SC-BT	0.01
SC-AT	0.01
BT-AT	0.50

Figure 2 Mean time required to a user to complete the e-mail sending tasks on the three sites

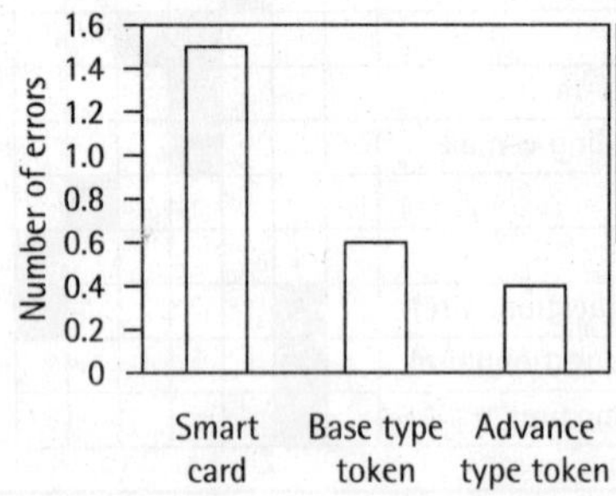

	mean	std. dev.
SC	1.5	1.4
BT	0.6	0.8
AT	0.4	0.7

	p
SC-BT	0.10
SC-AT	0.05
BT-AT	0.60

Figure 3 Mean number of errors that occurred while sending the e-mails on the three sites

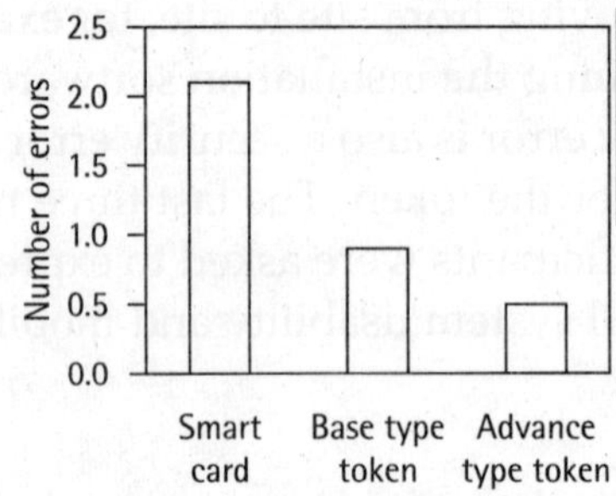

	mean	std. dev.
SC	2.1	1.4
BT	0.9	0.9
AT	0.5	0.7

	p
SC-BT	0.05
SC-AT	0.01
BT-AT	0.30

Figure 4 Mean number of security errors to complete the tasks on the three sites

the measured values (for example, the mean time is three minutes) onto merit values (for example, the mean time is high) and integrates a set of merit values into a unique score. The computation steps are:

- A mapping function translates the value of each metric into a qualitative space "very good, good, medium, bad" (for example, the values from zero to the maximum time required to send three protected e-mails are divided into four intervals of equal amplitude, each pointing to a qualitative value).
- A decision table maps each set of qualitative values into a unique attribute score from 1 (bad) to 7 (excellent). For example, a two-entry decision table (an

attribute is influenced by two measures) maps the values "very good, very good" into the score 7 and the values "very good, good" into the score 6.

Figure 6 shows the outcome of this procedure. To explain the reasons for the approach, consider as an example the evaluation of the maintainability of a software product. One can get a number of measures from design and code documents that are related to the maintainability of the product (for example, the modularity of the code, or the ratio comments/lines of code or an expert evaluation of the design document). To evaluate the global maintainability, the following steps are needed. The first one is the interpretation of each measured value. A given value of comments/lines of code ratio is bad or good?

The second step is related to the following type of questions: If the architectural design is very good, the modularity is medium, and the number of comments is sufficient, how do you rate the maintainability? This rating may be done through a form of evidential reasoning where each interpreted value provides evidence for a global quality value. The reasoning may be codified through a set of rules (or decision tables). This approach can manage both quantitative and qualitative evaluations and host different types of rules with a higher flexibility than, for exampie, averaging the metrics. The procedure is somewhat arbitrary, but useful to provide a global quality profile. This profile may be also combined with the detailed discussion of specific quantitative measures.

Results, Interpretation, and Explanation

Figure 2 shows the mean time needed to perform the e-mail protection tasks, which required each participant to send three protected e-mails, one for each site.

("Mean" is the mean of the collected data. "Std.dev." is the standard deviation of the collected data (10 users). "P" is the significance level of the difference between the means values for two devices. "SC," "BT," and "AT" denote, respectively, the smart card, the base type token and the advanced type token.)

The time needed while using the smart cards ended up being about twice the time needed while using the tokens. The existence of more hardware pieces and the need to properly connect them was the main reason for this result (note that in a nonnomadic context this difference would likely decrease). Figure 3 shows the mean number of errors that occurred while sending the e-mails on the three sites.

While the figure shows a remarkable difference between the tokens and the smart card (with smart cards, users made more than three times the mistakes made with the advanced token) it does not convey what the actual frequency of these errors is. The following numbers complement Figure 3 by reporting on the overall error impact: The frequency of errors is 43 percent for smart cards, 20 percent for the base tokens, and 9 percent for the advanced ones. Figure 4 shows the mean number of security errors to complete the tasks on the three sites, while Figure 5 supports a causal explanation of the nature of the security errors.

A node of the graph represents a type of events, while an oriented arc defines an influence relation between a node and its parents. The numbers n/t means that, out of a total of "t" events, "n" influenced the linked event. The data were coming

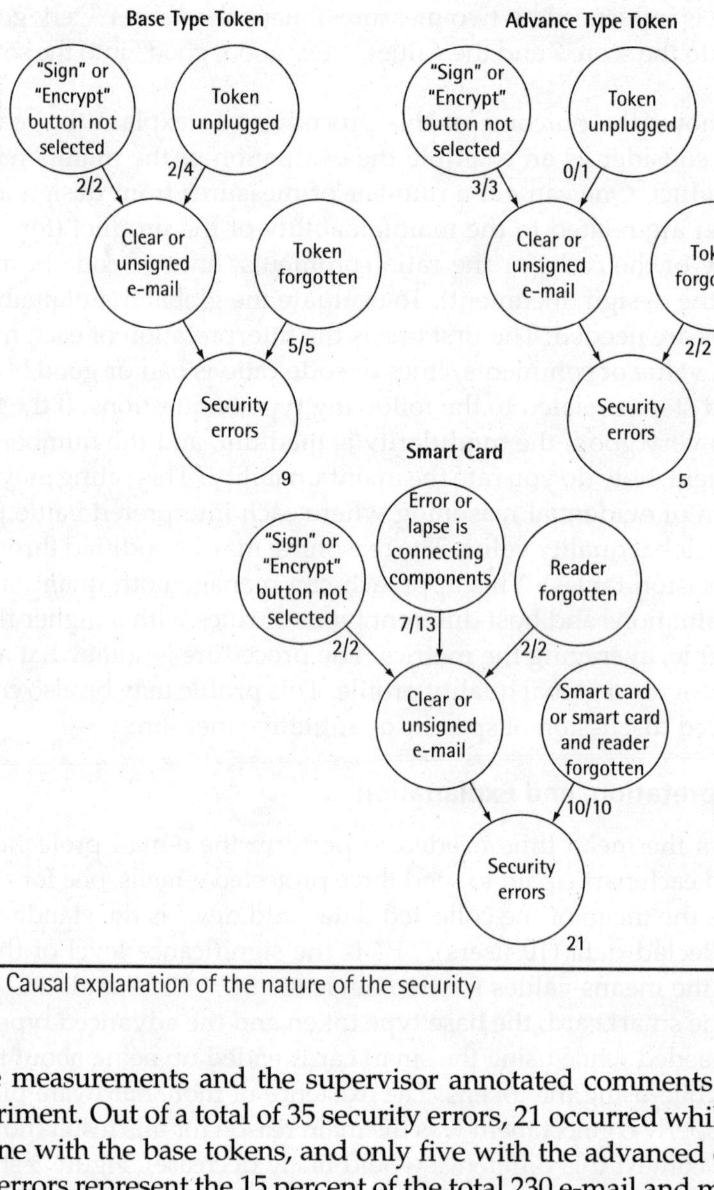

Figure 5 Causal explanation of the nature of the security

from the measurements and the supervisor annotated comments taken during the experiment. Out of a total of 35 security errors, 21 occurred while using smart cards, nine with the base tokens, and only five with the advanced ones (these 35 security errors represent the 15 percent of the total 230 e-mail and mobility tasks). Most of the errors were due to: 1) improper connections of the devices; or 2) the failure to bring along the hardware when moving to a different location.

This result indicates that the number of hardware components users have to deal with increases the complexity and negatively affects the security. The few errors occurred when the advanced token appeared to be linked to trivial but effective causes. First, the need for a single hardware piece makes the user less prone to forget it. Second, users praised the mass storage functionality: it was presumably a natural tendency of participants to care more about this object since it had a greater value to them. Finally, since the advanced token carries the installation software, it was plugged in for the e-mail protection task when users reached a new location. Figure 6 provides a graphical summary of all the

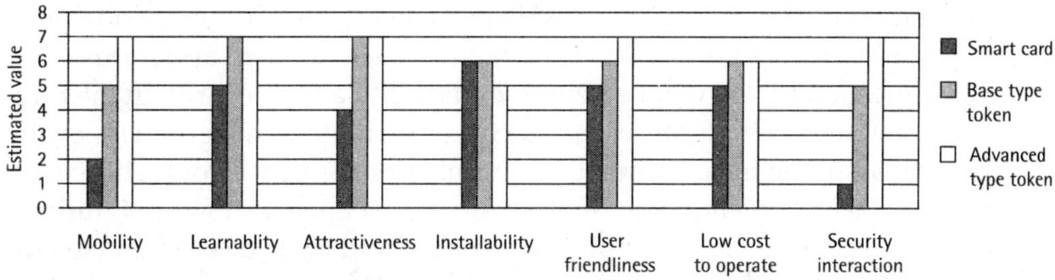

Figure 6 Comparison among the usability attributes of the three systems

usability attributes scores. (See Piazzalunga, Salvaneschi, and Coffetti 2005 for a detailed report of all the metrics.)

The reason for a better usability of the USB tokens is rooted in the minor number of components involved and the well-designed usability of the USB connector (users can plug a USB device in one way only). The advanced tokens' best results are further linked to a side effect of the e-mail client usability; the token was already plugged in because of its use in installation. Therefore, it bypassed the failure of the software to remind users to insert the device for signing e-mails. The usability is a systemic property and is affected by the interaction of the hardware and software components. E-mail client software should give specific feedback that the device is plugged in and, therefore, the certificate and associated private key is available for e-mail signature. Advising users to unplug the device when they finish a session could also help them remember to carry along their cryptographic credentials.

Limits of the Experiment

In the experiment the authors took some measurements, they interpreted them as values of more abstract properties, and they compared them providing some conclusions. Are the conclusions well founded? A reasonable answer requires answering different detailed questions.

The first one is: "Are the measured values significantly different in the three realizations of the PKI-based systems?" The t-test shows that, if one considers each measurement (Figure 2, 3, and 4), there is a significant difference between the cryptographic smart card and each USB token. It is more questionable if there is a difference between the two USB tokens, but this was not the primary goal of the experiment. More robust experiments and a more rigorous statistical analysis (for example, ANOVA) could provide more reliable evaluations.

The second question is: "Is the usability of the three systems significantly different?" Figure 6 shows the differences between the three usability profiles. While the comparison between the single measurements is well-founded in the design of the experiment and the statistical analysis, the answer to this second question includes a subjective component. It depends on the definition of the measurement tree (one can choose different variables to be measured) and on the interpretation rules. A well-founded experiment (from an engineering point of view) should include the consensus about the measurement apparatus.

A final question is: "To what extent does usability affect security in the three PKI-based systems?" The "security interaction" attribute (see Figure 1) is evaluated through a unique measurement, the number of security errors. This choice reduces the subjective component of the evaluation. Figure 4 shows a significant difference between the cryptographic smart card and each USB token (see the first question). One can ask if the security errors really capture the effects of usability problems. In the experiment the question is not answered using a statistical approach (for example, ANOVA). The answer is found on the causal network of Figure 5 (derived from the evidence collected during the experiment). This causal network supports the interpretation that indeed the security errors were caused by usability problems.

Applicability of the Methodological Approach

The authors' definition of the measurement apparatus is based on the ISO 9126 standard. This does not mean that their method is constrained to the ISO 9126 software quality model. The same approach can easily be applied to other frameworks because they are based on variations of a quality attributes tree linking measurements to more abstract properties. See, for example, the original work of McCall (McCall, Richards, and Walters 1977) and the overview in (Fenton and Neil 2000).

The authors explained their approach in more detail through the discussion of a specific experimental study related to the usability of a class of PKI-based systems. Yet the methodological approach they are proposing can be applied to any (end-user) security system. Take the example of "personal firewalls." Not only is the methodology described previously still applicable, but also the usability attributes and measurement apparatus can be translated easily to personal firewalls. All proposed attributes are applicable—it is significant to ask what is the effort required by the end user to learn it (learnability), the extent to which the specific personal firewall used is attractive to the user (attractiveness), or potential negative influences that usability issues might have on security (security interaction). Mobility might appear at odds with personal firewalls, yet it is meaningful to ask what the effort is for porting a specific configuration to a different machine (for example, from the user notebook to her desktop). An interesting application to this domain would be the usability test assessment of personal fire-walls implemented by different vendors.

Conclusions

In this article, the authors presented an approach for testing the usability of security systems and the interaction between usability and security. The approach introduces a measurement apparatus, a set of usability attributes, and a method to drive the experimental evaluation of them. They applied this approach to measure the usability of alternative types of a subclass of security systems, the cryptographic smart cards. The results of the application of their approach to the specific experiment show that different realizations of the same PKI based system do have different levels of usability and that usability affects security. From the experiment results and the final interpretation and explanations of data, one can draw general recommendations for the design of security systems. The first one is that the quality of usability arises from the interaction of social, human, and technical components. Every evaluation or design activity must take into account the whole system. As the results presented previously demonstrate, software designers often ignore this key point. A second aspect is that users prefer simple systems to those that are more complex or those that have more parts. With simpler systems, the user makes fewer security errors.

REFERENCES

Adams, A., and M. A. Sasse. 1999. Users are not the enemy. *Communications of the ACM* 42, no. 12.

Coventry, L., A. De Angeli, and G. Johnson. 2003. Usability of large scale public systems: Usability and biometric verification at the ATM interface. In *Proceedings of the Conference on Human Factors in Computing Systems*. ACM Press: 153–160.

Cranor, F., and S. Garfinkel, eds. 2005. *Security and usability*. Sebastopol, Calif.: O'Reilly.

Dix, A., J. Finlay, G. D. Abowd, and R. Beale. 2004. *Human-computer interaction*. Boston: Pearson.

Fenton N. E., and M. Neil. 2000. Software metrics: Roadmap. In *The Future of Software Engineering*, ed. A. Finkelstein. New York: ACM Press.

ISO. 1991. *International Standard ISO/IEC 9126. Information technology—Software product evaluation—Quality characteristics and guidelines for their use.* Geneva, Switzerland: International Organization for Standardization.

McCall, J. A., P. K. Richards, and G. F. Walters. 1977. Factors in software quality. RADC TR-77-363. Rome, N.Y.: Rome Air Development Center, Griffits Air Force Base.

Piazzalunga, U., P. Salvaneschi, and P. Coffetti. 2005. The usability of security devices. In *Security and Usability*, eds. L. Cranor and S. Garfinkel. Sebastopol, Calif.: O'Reilly.

Sasse, M. A., S. Brostoff, and D. Weirich. 1999. Transforming the "weakest link": A human-computer interaction approach to usable and effective security. *BT Technology Journal* 19-3: 122–131.

Schneier, B. 2005. Internet Explorer Sucks. Available at: http://www.schneier.com/blog/archives/2005/12/internet_explor.html

Whittaker, J. A., and H. Thompson. 2003. *How to break software security*. Boston: Pearson.

Whitten, A., and J. D. Tygar. 1999. Why Johnny can't encrypt: A usability case study of PGP 5.0. In *Proceedings of the 8th USENIX Security Symposium*.

Wool, A. 2004. A quantitative study of firewall configuration errors. *Computer* (June): 62–67.

Wu, M., S. Garfinkel, and R. Miller. 2004. Secure Web Authentication with Mobile Phones. Available at: http://www.mit.edu/~minwu/

BIOGRAPHIES

Ugo Piazzalunga is technical director at Eutron Infosecurity Srl. His technical interests include software security and the design of secure usable USB devices. He is a member of the ACM and of the IEEE Computer Society. He can be reached by e-mail at upiazzalunga@acm.org.

Paolo Salvaneschi is associate professor of software engineering at the University of Bergamo. He joined the university after spending 20 years as software architect and head of software development groups in industry and research labs. His interests include quality evaluation of software products, software design methods, and A.I. based data interpretation. He can be reached by e-mail at pasalvan@tin.it.

PART VII

Software Configuration Management

Software configuration management (SCM) remains a part of the CSQE Body of Knowledge—and who would argue with the need for configuration management for all deliverables of the software development process? A software project must be managed, and SCM is the set of processes you put into place to do that managing. Software has gotten so big that there needs to be a good process for keeping track of all specifications, reviews, code, test plans, test results, and so forth. Who can keep track of all the pieces of even a small project? And what about fixes? If they aren't tracked to a particular part of the code, how can they be reviewed or tested? It all needs to fit together, and that is the role of SCM. It isn't the exciting part of the process—and it is hard to find good materials to support the principles. We've picked two articles to explain some of the basic parts of this least understood area of software engineering, SCM.

What is the purpose of a "Defect Tracking and Management Process"? David Fern offers his experiences in a practitioner-oriented article. He tracks the process from defect detection and reporting through defect evaluation and finally to defect repair, retest, and closure. His organization's use of the tools and procedures described provided status accounting and allowed defects to be triaged and properly addressed in a systematic fashion.

In "Software Measurement Using SCM," by Jeffrey Holmes, we learn how to put some additional value into configuration management. SCM systems allow a multiperson team to work on the same software while reducing the chance that individuals will overwrite each other's work. SCM also provides a mechanism for identifying the files that make up a release. This article proposes a way to use project history that is stored in the SCM system to identify problematic areas of the code. In addition, the article illustrates how the SCM system can be used to monitor a project's progress.

Defect Tracking and Management Process

David Fern, Micros Systems, Inc.

Software development matures by moving from an ad-hoc process to one in which quality assessment activities are directed by procedural means. Management of defect processing is one key component of such maturing. This personal narrative elaborates on a sequence of defect identification and reporting, followed by evaluation and finally repair and closure. The author provides templates and definitions of various documentation elements throughout the process. His focus on defect management during testing activities can be generalized to other portions of the software development life cycle.

Key words: evaluation, problem resolution, progress reporting, repair, testing process, triage

Introduction

The purpose of a defect tracking and management process is to accurately and efficiently determine the state of the software and status of every known defect in the software at any given time. While this process is not the only tool for determining the software's state, this article will focus on defect tracking and management during testing activities.

The defect tracking and management process records and tracks defects from their discovery through their repair and finally closure. Keeping track of thousands of defects is a difficult task and requires a process and tools to be managed correctly.

Tools such as the defect repository and periodic reports are mainly used to determine the state of the software, but they are also used as an archive on future projects. The team can better plan and react to situations by having metrics available from past projects. Metrics may include defect counts and percentages by module, defect turnaround times, and number of builds required to complete a project.

A defect tracking and management process can promote the resolution of issues in a systematic fashion, build teamwork, and create a record of the project that can be used in future projects.

Why Use a Defect Tracking and Management Process?

Our software development group as a rule was an ad hoc-testing group, which had a rudimentary defect-tracking database but no defined process. Every project was "fly by the seat of your pants." Testing was considered only a final step and many times an impediment to release. The developers would fix the defects they wanted to fix, and, in many cases, they would fix only those defects that were easy to fix and ignore the defects crucial to the project's advancement and completion. The lack of a clear process was causing the group to have unsuccessful releases and multiple patches on a single version as defects were reported from the field. As our group was planning to embark on a one-year project to convert our product to the Microsoft Windows operating system we found it prudent to overhaul the test group and establish a process to ensure the project's success.

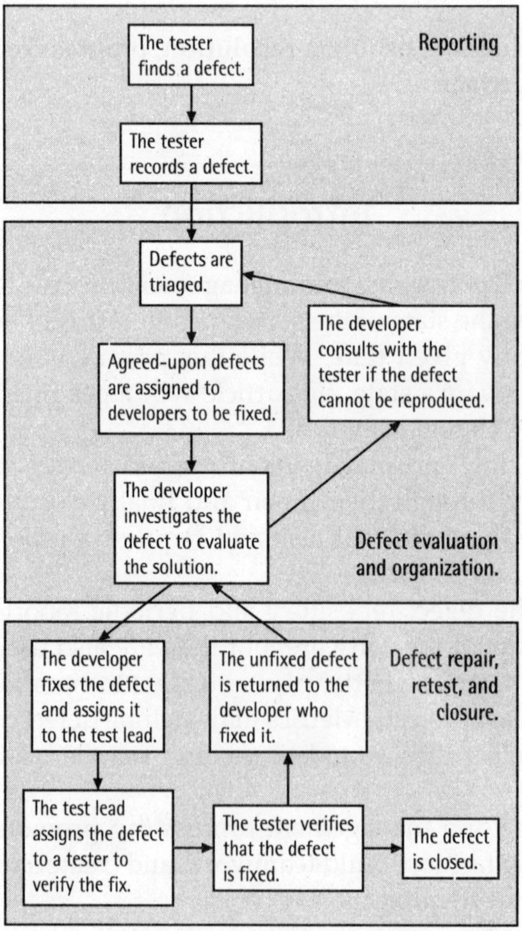

Figure 1

The process ensures that there will be procedures to follow, a way for everyone to easily see the current condition of the project at any time, defect metrics, and an archived record of the decisions made during the project.

The procedures ensure that during the development of each project there are carefully created steps to ensure that all details are addressed. The next major goal was to make the process easily accessible to everyone so that at anytime anyone can easily see the current condition of the project. Third, we created defect metrics that help in decision-making by giving quantitative information as to the condition of the software. One should be cautious, however, when measuring the progress of the project in terms of defect counts. Defect counts do help to determine that a project is far from release, but they cannot tell that a project is ready for release (Kaner, Bach, and Pettichord 2002). Finally, we created an archived record of the project decisions. This archive is a trail of why we treated a defect in a certain way or why we followed a certain procedure as issues arose. It helps allocate time when planning future projects as well as identify areas with higher concentrations of defects. One should also keep in mind the Pesticide Paradox, which states that if testing does a good job exposing defects and quality assurance reports its findings to the programmers, they are unlikely to repeat their mistakes in the future (Beizer 1995). Finally, the archive can become invaluable in a legal dispute.

By setting up and following a process for defect tracking and management the project can be more organized and will have a better chance of success. Since our software development group has put the process into place we have been able to release higher quality software and in faster time frames, giving us more confidence in our software. In our organization the normal defect tracking process looks like Figure 1.

These steps are easily divided into three major sections: reporting, defect evaluation, and defect repair.

The *reporting* section deals with the processes and tools that the tester follows as he or she finds and reports a defect. The *defect evaluation* section deals with the tools and processes used to evaluate, triage, organize, and assign the defects to the engineers for repair. Finally, the *defect repair* section deals with the tools and processes the developer, test lead, and tester use as the defect is fixed, verified, and closed or resubmitted to development to be repaired again.

Reporting

The reporting section of the process is composed of two steps: 1) the tester finding a defect, and 2) recording it in the defect database. Finding the defect can be difficult and time consuming and is dependent on the test planning and test-case design. Recording the defect sounds simple but can be very difficult, as the entire process depends on how accurately and completely this task is performed. We have a tool and a process for the tester to follow for properly recording a defect.

What is a defect? According to Koomen (1999) a defect is "the difference between the expectation and the actual results." The expectation can come from a request made by the customer or the requirements specification. The testers in our organization are at a disadvantage in that most of our work is on legacy products that we do not have proper requirements specification on, and there is no usability testing in place for customer requests and proper requirements documentation. For these reasons some issues that appear to be defects are not. This often creates defect reports that are not true product defects but rather issues with requirements that are to be sorted out in triage.

The tool our group uses to record defects is a defect tracking database. There are many different kinds on the market, but there are a few key features that must be incorporated. It must be able to create reports, create custom queries, and integrate with the other tools.

The ability to create reports becomes extremely important as the test team, project manager, and development team need to quickly and easily run and view preprogrammed reports related to different aspects of the defect database for database maintenance and determining project status.

All team members need the ability to create custom queries. Being able to query the database helps in its maintenance and it allows the data to be viewed in different ways. Data from the queries will be used to create reports later.

It is important to have the ability to interface with other tools such as the test case repository, requirements software, or project planning software. Product integration can save time and has the ability to more efficiently control the entire development process as each product can draw pertinent data from its counterparts.

Even if one has the best defect tracking database fully integrated with the other software development tools one needs a process for its maintenance and, more important, for the consistency and integrity of the information that is being inputted.

The maintenance process requires the test lead to maintain the database for his or her project. The maintenance entails the daily review of all new defects that are entered into the project to ensure that they are complete and according to the standard templates. It also requires running reports and queries to ensure that all entries are updated and moving through the process correctly. The test lead will normally spend 15 to 30 minutes a day on this task depending on where we are in the project. Sometimes we may not find a defect for days and other times we may find 10 or 20 in a day. Our process for recording a defect involves the tester recording the defect using the following template, assigning it to the development owner, and classifying it as "defect verified." Part of the process involves having consistent standards for classifying and reporting the defects.

Defect Reporting Template

All defects must include the following information:

- Title
- Description
- Problem
- Steps to reproduce
- Actual result
- Expected result
- Reproducibility—How often does this defect occur?
- Test case that detected the defect
- Attachments—Any files that pertain to the defect, such as screen captures or log files
- Item type—The item type for the defect can be selected from the list of item types in the next section.
- Severity—The severity of the defect is determined here. A list of all severity ratings is in the next section.
- Module
- Submitter—The name of the tester entering the defect
- Owner—Who is the owner of the defect?
- Status—What is going on with this defect. The status ratings are in the section after severity.
- Origin—Classify the origin as tester, beta site, site, or automated testing. This helps us to see where and how the defects are being discovered.
- State—This is opened or closed when the defect has been fix verified.
- Defect repository definitions for item type
- Defect verified—Assigned by the tester when the defect is a defect at the creation of the defect report
- Design issue—Assigned to a defect that has some type of design flaw and can be assigned this status by anyone at any time
- Feature request—Assigned to the product manager by anyone when they see that an added feature would be advantageous
- Question—Assigned to development by someone on the test team
- Update doc spec—Assigned by anyone to update some documentation
- Usability—Assigned to the development team by someone in quality assurance concerning an issue that is not a defect but should be redesigned for the user

Defect Repository Definitions for Item Type

Item type identifies what type of issue is being reported.

- **Bug verified**—Assigned by the tester when the defect is a bug at the creation of the defect report
- **Design issue**—Assigned to a defect that has some type of design flaw and can be assigned this status by anyone at any time
- **Feature request**—Assigned to the product manager by anyone when they see that an added feature would be advantageous
- **Question**—Assigned to development by someone on the test team
- **Update doc spec**—Assigned by anyone to update some documentation
- **Usability**—Assigned to the development team by someone in quality assurance concerning an issue that is not a defect but should be redesigned for the user

Defect Repository Definitions for Severity

Severity identifies how crucial the defect is to get it fixed.

- **Zero**—A severity of zero means that the defect has no impact on the software.
- **Low**—A severity of low means that the defect involves enhancements and design issues, or minor irregularities that do not affect the software's functionality.
- **Medium**—A severity of medium means that the defect creates disruption in a module or the system but does not prevent main functionality.
- **High**—A severity of high means that a module does not function. These are serious errors that prevent testing for a particular module.
- **Showstopper**—A severity of showstopper shuts down the system, or the module is nonfunctional, flagrant errors that prevent further testing. The defect fix team should turn around showstopper errors in 24 hours.

Defect Repository Definitions for Status

Status defines what is going on with the defect.

- **Answered**—The defect originated as a question posed to development or product management. This type of defect is resolved by answering the question.
- **Defect verified (assigned)**—The defect has been completely recorded and has been assigned from test to the development owner.

- **By design**—The feature is working to specifications, but may need a change in the design.
- **Configuration error**—The reported defect is not a defect but a configuration or programming error.
- **Doc open**—Used when defect has been assigned to the documentation group
- **Doc resolved**—Used when the documentation group has included the issue in documentation and closed the defect
- **Doc verify**—Used when the documentation group assigns the defect test for technical edits
- **Duplicate**—Used when the defect reported already exists and is then closed
- **Fix verified**—Used when test has verified that the defect has been fixed
- **Fixed**—Used by development when they have fixed the defect and assigned it to test (quality assurance owner) for verification
- **Need more information**—When the development team requires that the test team supply further information
- **Not reproduced**—Used by development telling test that it cannot reproduce the defect and assigns it back to the tester for reevaluation. Nonreproducible defects are reproducible. If you know the conditions you can re-create the failure (Kaner, Bach, and Pettichord 2002).
- **Not fixed**—When test reassigns the defect back to development with a note as to why the defect is not fixed or still exists
- **Postponed**—Used by product management when the defect is deferred until further action is taken by product management
- **Will not fix**—Used by product management if they have decided that the defect will not be fixed

The setup requires the configuration of a defect-tracking database. This step must be done with care and consideration because it is the main tool and it must be set up correctly to get the maximum benefit.

Defect Evaluation

The defect evaluation and organization section of the defect tracking management process includes triaging and developments beginning the correction of the defect. The tools used in this section are weekly module and build reports, the hot list, and task list, with the process tying all of the tools together.

The first step in this section is triage. The defect triage process is a weekly meeting where the lead developer and lead tester agree on the defects that will be fixed in the upcoming week's build cycle. The time of the meeting can vary depending on the number of defects and where the group is in the cycle. For example, about three weeks from beta we will have a long triage ensuring that all defects that should be included are included, but the week before beta we may meet for 10 minutes and agree that there is only one final defect to correct.

Triage is the chance for the lead tester and lead developer to reach a consensus and address the most severe defects. Triage is also the place to discuss overlapping problems or issues such as development flow and related problem reports. Triage is also the place to discuss why a defect should not be fixed. In most cases, addressing the most severe defects enables testing to continue. This also increases test's ability to improve the depth of its reporting on the state of the software each week. Triage also provides a time for discussion and risk analysis between the test and engineering teams.

The test lead will generally start the meeting with comments or questions about the weekly build, the testing effort, or technical questions that the engineer is best suited to answer. Test produces a "hot list," which includes the top defects as designated by the test team. Development and test then decide which defects will be fixed during the week. It is also verified that the past week's commitments have been met. An important item to note is that development should not be using its time fixing defects that are not on the list without the approval of test.

The expected outcome of the meeting is that test and development have addressed the highest priority defects and decided which ones will be in the next build. This is executed by assigning a specific developer the responsibility to fix the defect. Putting the developer's name beside a defect on the hot list places necessary pressure to fix it in the allotted time. It is imperative that the list be maintained since many decisions are based on it. Once the meeting has adjourned, the test lead will update the defect database and begin to build the test suite. The test lead maintains the list, which is always kept on a shared drive so everyone has access to the information at all times.

The idea here is to prioritize the defects into a weekly hot list and have "fix commitments" that everyone agrees to. The test lead can continually update the hot list so we can always see the current state of the software. At the weekly triage the defects are distributed among the engineers so they get about one week's worth of work to complete. If a showstopper is discovered, it is immediately put on the hot list and an engineer is assigned.

At triage the test lead presents the grades from the last week's build in a tool called the weekly cycle build report. This report is a way to look at software as a whole and how it has changed over the past week.

In establishing grading criteria it becomes important to consider key elements and divide the entire project into modules. The key element that our group uses is the ability of the software to be successfully installed. We divide the project into modules. These modules are then grouped into infrastructure, core, and noncore. The infrastructure is composed of those modules that directly relate to the overall functioning of the software. The core modules are those that are important in the functionality of the software, and, finally, the noncore modules are those that are nice to have but are not essential. By categorizing the modules the build grading becomes easier. The criteria used in the weekly build grading are based on the information in Figure 2.

The criteria that our group uses for a beta is an overall grade of "B." An "A" is awarded after a beta installation and no further defects are uncovered. The criteria that we use for general release is an overall grade of "A."

The test lead is again responsible for maintaining the build grades, which are also kept on a shared drive. A sample of the weekly cycle build grade report can be seen in Figure 3.

The test lead also grades each module of the software on a weekly basis. Some module's grades will remain static while test recommends that development focus on more severe modules. The ultimate goal is to have all modules at a letter grade that is agreed upon in the test plan. The module grades are calculated using the same counts and scale as the weekly builds.

The module grades are a way to look at software by module and to lend additional insight into the weekly build grade. Everyone focuses on how individual modules have fluctuated over the past week. An important item to note is that it is

E =
- The install was unsuccessful.
- The application would not start.
- The infrastructure modules contain showstopper defects.
- The core modules contain showstopper defects.
- The noncore modules contain showstoppers.

D =
- The install has moderate to serious usability issues.
- The infrastructure modules contain excessive severity high defect counts.
- The core modules contain excessive severity high defect counts.
- The aggregate of noncore modules contain excessive severity high defect counts.

C =
- The infrastructure modules contain moderate severity high and excessive severity medium defect counts.
- The core modules contain moderate severity high and excessive severity medium defect counts.
- The aggregate of noncore modules contain moderate severity high and excessive severity medium defect counts.

B =
- The infrastructure modules contain moderate severity medium defect counts.
- The core modules contain moderate severity medium defect counts.
- The aggregate of noncore modules contain moderate severity medium defect counts.

A =
- The aggregate of defect counts for the entire system is low and the severity is low.

Figure 2 Sample grading scheme

Cycle	Date	Grade	Submitted SCR's					Current Defects				Total Open Defects	Total SCR's	Closure Rate
			SS	High	Med	Low	Total	SS	High	Med	Low			
D03 – Dev Cycles	#####	F												
D02	#####	F		6	10	15	31		65	89	57	211		
D01	#####	D		0	0	0	0		65	89	57	211		
A01 – Alpha Cycles	#####	D		12	10	3	25		54	92	75	221		
A02	#####	D		3	18	9	20		39	108	60	222	347	39
A03	#####	D		12	22	8	46		51	123	67	258	393	10
A04	#####	F		6	1	3	10		57	115	69	257	396	9
A05	#####	F		6	11	10	31		54	114	72	257	429	33
A06	#####	F		18	13	10	43		54	98	52	216	471	58
A07	#####	F		9	10	9	29		55	95	56	216	500	26
A08	#####	F		13	7	8	30		69	109	74	225	530	18
A09	#####	F		16	4	5	25		72	96	90	258	555	35
A10	#####	F		14	9	5	29		62	83	59	218	582	23
A11	#####	F		17	8	3	28		65	87	56	220	610	27
A12	#####	F		10	3	4	18		73	88	59	234	630	5
A13	#####	F		8	11	5	26		77	95	61	248	656	17
A14	#####	F		11	2	0	13		75	90	55	232	670	32
A15	#####	F		5	9	12	28		70	72	54	209	696	52

Figure 3 Sample weekly cycle build grade

imperative to have modules set up in the defect repository correctly. Too few or too many modules will skew the module reporting. The size of the module and quantity of defects are considered when evaluating the modules and assigning grades.

This report is created in a spreadsheet and compiled by the test lead using the defect repository database. We multiply the number of defects in each module by their respective weight and then add each to get the weighted total. This can be easily set up as a formula in the spreadsheet. The total software score is calculated by an average of each module.

The test lead is also responsible for maintaining the module grades, which are also kept on a shared drive. A sample weekly module grade report is shown in Figure 4.

Many times in the triage meeting various tasks or questions arise that cannot be resolved immediately. These concerns are recorded in a tool called the "task list."

The purpose of the task list is to ensure that no concern goes unaddressed. We do not believe that every item or concern should be submitted as a defect because the database can easily become clogged with questions.

Module	Number of open SCR's					Weighted total	Test Dept Score	Grade	Comments
	Stop=5	High=4	Med=3	Low=2	Total				
Module 1	0	0	0	0	0	0	0	0	
Module 2	0	0	0	0	0	0	0	0	
Module 3	0	0	0	0	0	0	0	0	
Module 4	0	0	0	0	0	0	0	0	
Module 5	0	0	0	0	0	0	0	0	
Total	0	0	0	0	0	0	0		
Average						0.00			
Percent of total	0.00%	0.0%	100.0%	0.0%					

0	E	Fail (defect count contains showstopper defects, not in stable condition.) 0 - 30
31	D	Below Average (defect count for module contains excessive severity high, needs work) 31 - 50
51	C	Average (defect count for module contains moderate severity high, needs improvement) 51 - 70
71	B	Good (defect count for module is low and severity is medium, may be released) 71 - 90
91	A	Excellent (defect count for module is low and severity is low, "zero defect") 91 - 100
		The size of the module and content of the system change requests (SCR) are considered when evaluating the modules.

Figure 4 A sample weekly module grade report

The next step in this section is for the developer to investigate the defect to determine the solution. This is where the developer digs into the code and reproduces the defect to decide how it will be corrected. If the developer cannot reproduce the defect, it is sent back to the original tester. Normally about 1 percent of defects are sent back to the tester for more information. The status at this point is "needs more information" and the owner is the original tester. If the developer can correct the defect he or she does so and reassigns the defect to the test lead and marks it as fixed.

After seeing how we handle the reporting phase of the process one may ask what effort and manpower are required to set up and maintain this process. The setup requires establishing the core defect tracking process and triage. The core defect tracking process is referring to the mindset that there need to be changes in the organization, which dictate that once we are code complete quality assurance determines the path to release. In some organizations this may be difficult to implement. Once one has the buy-in from engineering, however, the entire team will understand and see the benefits. Managing the triage is also key to the success of this process. This is where the defects are discussed, prioritized, and assigned to be fixed. Specifics on setting up these processes were discussed previously.

The setup requires the setup of the metrics for the hot list, task list, module grades, and build grades. The specifics on these metrics were described previously, but one will want to adapt it to his or her specific needs.

The maintenance of this section is imperative to the success of the project. All data must be up to date and accurate because many people are silently looking at the data and making decisions based on its timeliness and accuracy.

Defect Repair

The final section follows the defect from the developer repairing the defect to the tester verifying that the defect has been fixed and then closing or resubmitting it for repair. The tools used in this section are the defect repository hot list and task list. In this section the developer fixes the defect and assigns it to the test lead with a release note in the defect tracking database and release notes that accompany the build. The release notes in the database let the tester know what has happened to the defect, and the build release notes allow the test team to see exactly what defects have been fixed in this build.

The test lead assigns the defect to a tester for retest to ensure that the defect has been corrected. According to Kaner, Bach, and Pettichord (2002), defect reports should be closed by testers. We agree with this lesson because the tester opened the issue and it should not be closed until he or she is satisfied with the resolution. If everyone can close defects the submitter may lose track of the issue and not know why it has been closed.

The tester will now either close the defect in the defect repository with a closing note indicating that the problem is resolved or change the status to "not fixed" and return it to the engineer who fixed it. From this point the developer starts the defect in the cycle again.

In this section the test lead is continually updating the other tools, the hot list, task list, module, and build grades in anticipation for the next triage. By following the process of updating the tools with consistent complete documentation and assigning the defect to the next person, it is assured that all defects flow consistently from engineer to test lead to tester to closure.

Why Our Defect Tracking and Management Process Works

Why should a company consider using our defect tracking and management process? First, our plan now has a proven track record. Since the process has been implemented, all projects have been on time and in an organized manner. Previously about 20 percent of our group's projects were late, and the last-minute discovery of important defects in the database prolonged the agony. The only cost to this process is the manpower used to maintain the system, which is far less resource intensive than the rework in emergency situations in the past. We have determined that when software is in beta or released it becomes 10 times more expensive to repair than when it can be repaired in development. Finally, this process is easily adaptable between projects and even other sections of the development cycle, as discussed previously. With a few minor changes this entire process can be duplicated when it comes time to move on to the next project. Our process can also be used in other phases of the company and in development where defects can be encountered with minor modifications. Some other areas where it can be used are:

- Escalations
- Engineering code walkthroughs

- Beta testing
- Automation test group
- Design
- Requirements

We designed this process by taking pieces from other processes and putting them together in a plan that works for us, so it is not specifically documented anywhere. As we looked around and gathered information to set up our process, we did not find another complete plan that fit our organization. The only drawback to this process is that every part must be up to date and accurate because people are always looking at the data and making decisions based on what they see. We do not need to ask around for the project status because it is always available.

Conclusion

After spending hours constructing and executing test cases we want every defect to be properly addressed. Our defect tracking and management process is divided into three sections: reporting, defect evaluation, and defect repair.

The reporting section involves setting up a defect database correctly and following established processes. The defect evaluation and organization section uses tools such as the task list, weekly build grade report, weekly module report, and a triage process to properly manage the defect tracking process. Finally the defect repair, retest, and defect closure section uses the defect tracking database, hot list, module, and weekly build grades and a process for closing the defect.

By using tools and following the processes in place we are able to know the status of the software at anytime and properly address every defect in an effort to produce software of the highest quality.

REFERENCES

Beizer, B. 1995. *Black box testing: Techniques for functional testing of software and systems.* New York: John Wiley and Sons.

Kaner, Bach, Pettichord, eds. 2002. *Lessons learned in software testing*. New York: John Wiley and Sons.

Koomen, P., ed. 1999. *Test process improvement: A practical step-by-step guide to structured testing*. Reading, Mass.: Addison-Wesley.

BIOGRAPHY

David Fern is an automation test engineer in research and development at Micros Systems in Columbia, Md. During the past four years he has been involved in all aspects of food service point-of-sale application and devices, specializing in the development of large restaurant and hotel computer systems. Fern recently had an article entitled "Testing Point of Sale Software" published in the November 2000 *Quality Techniques* newsletter and "When is Software Really Ready to Ship" in the 2001 *Quality Techniques* newsletter. Fern has a master's degree in industrial technology from the University of Maryland, College Park, and a bachelor's degree in business management. He can be reached by e-mail at dfern@micros.com.

Software Measurement Using SCM

Jeffrey S. Holmes, Motorola, Inc.

Software development teams have used software configuration management (SCM) systems for years. SCM systems allow a multiperson team to work on the same software while reducing the chance that individuals will overwrite each other's work. SCM also provides a mechanism for identifying the files that make up a release. This article proposes a way to utilize the project history that is stored in the SCM system to identify problematic areas of the code. In addition, the article will illustrate how the SCM system can be used to monitor a project's progress.

Key words: comparative methods, nonparametric statistics, Six Sigma, software configuration management, statistical process control

Introduction

The Base Transceiver System Center of Excellence team in Fort Worth, Texas, maintains all software files using the Rational ClearCase configuration management tool. The tool allows the developers to monitor the versions of the files, share files during development, and identify or label a set of files for a release. The tool also contains a history of the changes that have been made to the files. This article will strive to demonstrate how the SCM history can be tapped to gain a better understanding of the software team's activities and the software product itself.

In addition to monitoring team performance, there are efforts under way within Motorola to identify problematic files (files that have caused the development team the most trouble). This study proposes that the problematic files can be determined by querying the SCM system to see which files are changing the most. Using the SCM data, a set of problematic files was identified. These files were then compared to a list of the files that were changed as a result of post-release testing, which confirmed that using the SCM data was valid in identifying problematic files. This information could then be used to ensure rigid peer reviews, and testing is conducted when these problematic files are changed in the future.

The technique used for monitoring the software team's activities involved extracting the changes being made to the files in the SCM system and analyzing the data using Six Sigma techniques to determine the team's capability and then monitor the team versus this capability. Using SCM to monitor the team's progress can provide a nonintrusive, real-time view of the team when it is in the coding phase.

The use of the SCM system for software measurement has many advantages, including no manual data entry for the engineers, real-time status capability, and a low cost, since most groups already have their software under configuration management.

The project employed the Six Sigma technique of define, measure, analyze, improve, and control (DMAIC). DMAIC is a methodology that is used when one wants to minimize the variation that causes defects in an existing product or process. This article covers the first four steps of the DMAIC methodology, which were used on this project. At the time the article was written, the project was entering the control step.

Define Opportunities

The first question to consider when searching for ways to measure the software development life cycle is "What's important?" Some of the more desirable goals of software measurement would be:

- Accuracy (Are the data accurate?)
- Timeliness (Can the data be retrieved on demand?)
- Impact to developers
- Cost

Taking these goals into consideration, SCM offers an attractive opportunity to the software community. Data pulled from the SCM system will be very accurate. The developer, date, time, file, and what was changed are all captured when the developer "checks in" a change into configuration management. On some systems, the developer even enters an explanation of the change and the defect tracking number associated with the change.

SCM-based measurements can be retrieved daily to show what types of changes have been placed into configuration management up until the time of the retrieval. The SCM measurements are truly a measure of the work that is being performed and require no manual entry. The fact that developers are not required to do anything to generate the data is a huge benefit of this approach. The development team can conduct "business as usual" and focus on generating product. Removing the manual entry also eliminates the possibility of data entry errors.

The cost of SCM-based measurements should be minimal since most organizations already pay for the SCM software. The big hurdle is being able to pull the data from SCM. A skilled SCM person who is familiar with the system can build the scripts to pull this information. After the initial cost of developing the scripts, the SCM measurements would be a byproduct of the work being done in the SCM system. Additional costs should be minimal.

The aforementioned goals are desirable to the project, but the project should also be able to correlate these goals to the goals of the customer and the company. The bottom line that could be affected by this opportunity for both the customer and the company is in terms of revenue. Accurate project tracking and estimating can allow projects to be delivered on time with confidence. In addition, insights gained from the SCM data could provide optimizations that result in reduced cycle time and/or improved quality. This optimization could then result in improved revenues for the both the customer and the company.

Measure Performance

The plan for gathering the data consisted of pulling the file change history from the configuration management system, converting the data into a usable format, analyzing the data, and displaying the data in the desired chart/report format. This article will use the following data types.

- Updates—An update is the act of placing a new file version into the configuration management system. Depending on the SCM system, some updates may not be relevant to the analysis. For example, if a developer habitually checks his or her work at the end of each day, that information may not be as useful as updates that are checked in to make an official release.
- Updates/month—The number of updates that are made in a month.
- Added—The lines of code that are added during an update.
- Modified—The lines of code modified during an update.
- Deleted—The lines of code deleted during an update.
- Total changed—The total lines of code added, modified, and deleted in a month.
- Problem report—An issue logged into the defect tracking system that caused an update to the software. A query for problems reported by the subsystem test team over a two-month period prior to this article provided the problem report data set.

An examination of the updates for files that have been changed because of a problem report was conducted to determine if there were a statistically significant number of the changed files that had been changed multiple times. Confirmation that a majority of the files corrected because of problem reports have been updated more often than files updated without problem reports provided evidence that there is a subset of the source code files that contain the majority of the defects.

These measures were also used to measure the team performance by examining both the updates per month and the total changed per month. The SCM data monitored over time revealed the team's development capability in terms of how many updates and lines of code the team can produce in a month. A comparison was then made to ensure the team was not performing at a level beyond its capability.

All of these data, except for problem report information, are available through the SCM system. Problem report information is retrieved from the team's defect tracking system. The granularity of the data that are available on problem reports is limited to the structure/process of the defect tracking system. For example, some teams may not capture in the problem report what files were changed. If this is the case, it provides further need for the SCM measures that can identify the problematic code.

Analyze Opportunity

Two different types of analyses were performed on the SCM data. The first was a comparative method analysis to determine if the most updated files were in fact the most problematic. The second analysis examined the number of updates over time to identify the team's capability and demonstrate how the team performance can be measured using the SCM system.

Comparative Method—Are the Most Problematic the Most Updated Files?

Using comparative methods techniques, a null hypothesis is developed for the problematic code. The following two statements are the null hypothesis (H_0) and the alternative hypothesis (H_A).

- H_0: The number of updates to files updated because of problem reports is greater than (>) the updates to files not updated because of the problem reports.
- H_A: The number of updates to files updated because of problem reports is equal to or less than (<=) the updates to files not updated because of the problem reports.

A 5 percent risk of incorrectly concluding that the files that were changed because of problem reports are problematic is acceptable.

The analysis attempted a one-to-one comparison with two means. The distribution of number of updates was examined for files that were changed because of problem reports. The data set consisted of a list of all the files. The files that were changed as the result of a problem report were identified. Using this identification, the comparative method could be performed using a "fit y by x" check.

The initial step in the statistical analysis is to determine whether the data set is normal. A distribution was created for the number of updates. The normality checks failed indicating the data set was nonnormal. Figure 1 illustrates the failed normality checks. The normal quantile plot illustrates a nonnormal data set and the "goodness of fit" value Prob<W being less than 0.05 confirms the data set is nonnormal. Transformation of the data was unsuccessful, thus

Distributions

Number of Updates

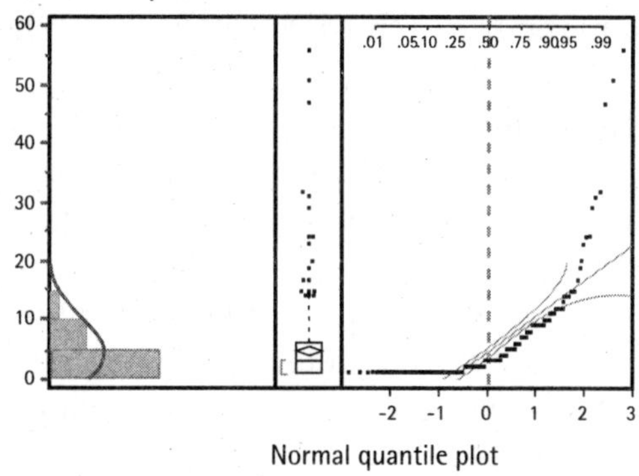

—Normal (4.71259,6.08985)

Quantiles

100%	maximum	56.000
99.5%		50.560
97.5%		19.450
90.0%		10.000
75.0%	quartile	6.000
50.0%	median	3.000
25.0%	quartile	1.000
10.0%		1.000
2.5%		1.000
0.5%		1.000
0.0%	minimum	1.000

Moments

Mean	4.7125891
Std Dev	6.0898478
Std Err Mean	0.296801
upper 95% Mean	5.2959896
lower 95% Mean	4.1291886
N	421
Sum Wgts	50

Fitted normal

Parameter estimates

Type	Parameter	Estimate	Lower 95%	Upper 95%
Location	Mu	4.712589	4.129189	5.295990
Disperson	Sigma	6.089848	5.704409	6.531575

Goodness-of-fit test

Shapiro-Wilk W Test

W	Prob<W
0.607463	0.0000

Figure 1 Normality check for updates to files

the nonparametric approach of Wilcoxon/Kruskal-Wallis tests was used in the comparative method.

A "fit y by x" check was performed using the update counts as the "y" and the flag indicating a file change due to a problem report. This produces the one-way analysis of variance (ANOVA). Examining the Wilcoxon/Kruskal-Wallis tests, the one-way test ChiSquare approximation provides a "Prob>ChiSq," which is less than 0.05. This information fails to reject the null hypothesis. In other words, the statistical analysis did not disprove that files updated because of a problem report have been updated more than files that were not updated from one of the problem reports in the data set. Figure 2 shows the results of the "fit y by x" analysis.

The software engineering findings from this analysis indicate that examining the number of times a file has been updated may provide insight into whether the file is problematic. Examining the most changed files revealed that eight of the 10 most changed files were changed as a result of a problem report. The software project manager can now use this information to either proactively investigate the most changed files to determine what the issues are or to monitor future changes to these file to ensure senior developers are involved with inspections and testing of these files.

Process Capability

The ability to determine the development team's capability from the SCM data will use control charts to identify the "voice of the process." The control limits that are calculated based on the data are the "voice of the process." Using the control limits from historical data, specification limits that represent the "voice of the customer" can be established for future projects. Monitoring the team's status against the control limits allows management to see if the team is performing within the boundaries that it is capable of performing. Comparing team performance against the specification limits gives an indication of whether the team is on track to complete the project on time.

The number of updates is one way to measure the team's capability, as this measures the number of changes a team is implementing. Consideration should also be given to the amount of change being performed. In other words, how many lines are being added, modified, and/or deleted for the updates? The project management should be aware that 10 updates were made, but these updates only affected 50 lines of code.

In order to develop control charts for the data, they must first be examined for normality to ensure the proper type of control chart is performed. The analysis of the number of updates per month and the amount of change per month for normality is shown in Figures 3 and 4.

One-way analysis of number of updates by problem report mod

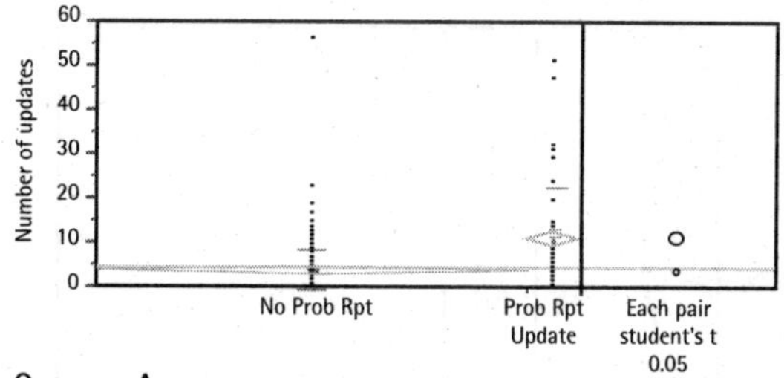

One-way Anova

Summary of fit

RSquare	0.145969
RSquare Adj	0.14393
Root Mean Square Error	5.634573
Mean of Response	4.712589
Observations (or Sum Wgts)	421

t-test

	Difference	t-test	DF	Prob > |t|
Estimate	-7.4492	-8.463	419	<.0001
Std Error	0.8803			
Lower 95%	-9.1794			
Upper 95%	-5.7189			

Assuming equal variances

Analysis of variance

Source	DF	Sum of Square	Mean Square	F Ratio	Prob > F
Prob Rpt Mod	1	2273.639	2273.64	71.6143	<.0001
Error	419	13302.584	31.75		
C. Total	420	15576.223			

Means for one-way Anova

Level	Number	Mean	Std Error	Lower 95%	Upper 95%
No Prob Rpt	375	3.8987	0.29097	3.3267	4.471
Prob Rpt Update	46	11.3478	0.83077	9.7148	12.981

Std Error uses a pooled estimate of error variance

Means and standard deviations

Level	Number	Mean	Std Dev	Std Err Mean	Lower 95%	Upper 95%
No Prob Rpt	375	3.8987	4.5203	0.2334	3.4397	4.358
Prob Rpt Update	46	11.3478	11.2155	1.6536	8.0172	14.678

Means comparisons

Dif=Mean[i]-Mean[j]

	Prob Rpt Update	No Prob Rpt
Prob Rpt Update	0.0000	7.4492
No Prob Rpt	-7.4492	0.0000

Alpha= 0.05

Comparisons for each pair using Student's t

t
1.96564

Abs(Dif) - LSD

	Prob Rpt Update	No Prob Rpt
Prob Rpt Update	-2.3094	5.7189
No Prob Rpt	-5.7189	-0.8088

Positive values show pairs of means that are significantly different.

Wilcoxon/Kruskal-Wallis tests (rank sums)

Level	Count	Score sum	Score mean	(Mean-Mean0)/Std0
No Prob Rpt	375	74096	197.589	-6.593
Prob Rpt Update	46	14735	320.326	6.593

Two-sample test, normal approximation

S	Z	Prob>|Z|
14735	6.59335	0.0000

One-sample test, ChiSquare approximation

ChiSquare	DF	Prob>ChiSq
43.4809	1	<.0001

Figure 2 Fit y by x one-way ANOVA results

Distributions

Number of updates

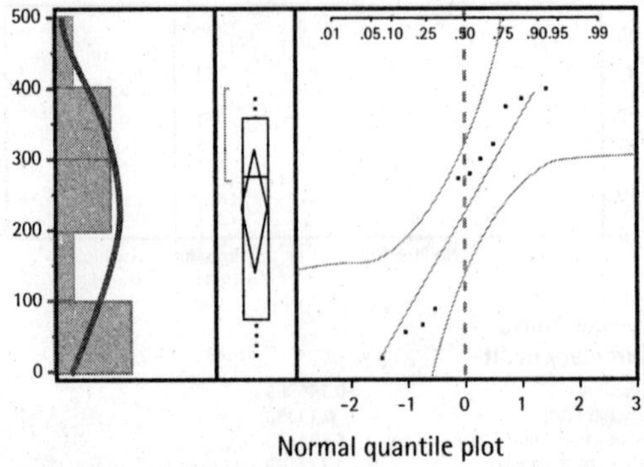

—Normal (4.71259,6.08985)

Quantiles

100% maximum	401.00
99.5%	401.00
97.5%	401.00
90.0%	395.90
75.0% quartile	358.75
50.0% median	274.50
25.0% quartile	72.75
10.0%	32.20
2.5%	22.00
0.5%	22.00
0.0% minimum	22.00

Moments

Mean	228.66667
Std Dev	138.58856
Std Err Mean	40.00707
upper 95% Mean	316.72163
lower 95% Mean	140.6117
N	12

Fitted normal

Parameter estimates

Type	Parameter	Estimate	Lower 95%	Upper 95%
Location	Mu	228.6667	140.6117	316.7216
Disperson	Sigma	138.5886	98.1755	235.3065

Goodness-of-fit test

Shapiro-Wilk W Test

W	Prob<W
0.900728	0.1549

Figure 3 Normality check for file updates

The "goodness of fit" confirms that both of these data sets are normally distributed. The "goodness of fit" determines if the sample under analysis was drawn from a population that follows some specified distribution. The normal distribution allows the generation of control charts to examine the team activity over time and establish the "voice of the process."

Distributions

Total changed

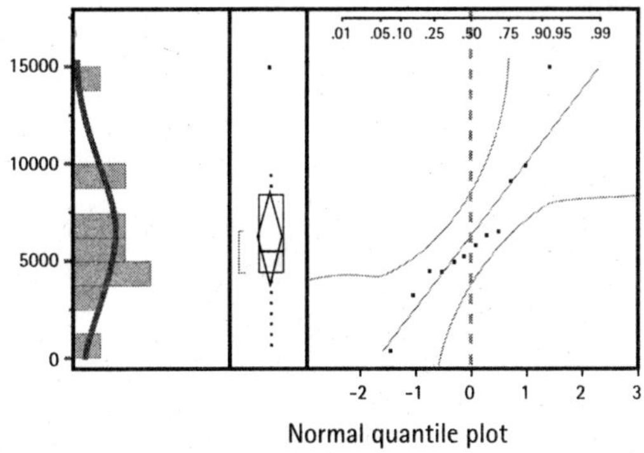

Normal (6261.08,3698.6)

Quantiles

100%	maximum	14981
99.5%		14981
97.5%		14981
90.0%		13443
75.0%	quartile	8402
50.0%	median	5504
25.0%	quartile	4439
10.0%		1213
2.5%		352
0.5%		352
0.0%	minimum	352

Moments

Mean	6261.0833
Std Dev	3698.597
Std Err Mean	1067.693
upper 95% Mean	8611.0598
lower 95% Mean	3911.1069
N	12

Fitted normal

Parameter estimates

Type	Parameter	Estimate	Lower 95%	Upper 95%
Location	Mu	6261.083	3911.107	8611.060
Disperson	Sigma	3698.597	2620.068	6279.767

Goodness-of-fit test

Shapiro-Wilk W Test

W	Prob<W
0.916606	0.2456

Figure 4 Normality check for total changed

Figures 5 and 6 are the control charts that were generated for the updates and total changed. Figure 5 graphs the number of updates performed for the project. This graph demonstrates three stages the project went through in 2002. The project team is working "out of control" for the months of July, August, and September. This project completed its coding phase in September 2002,

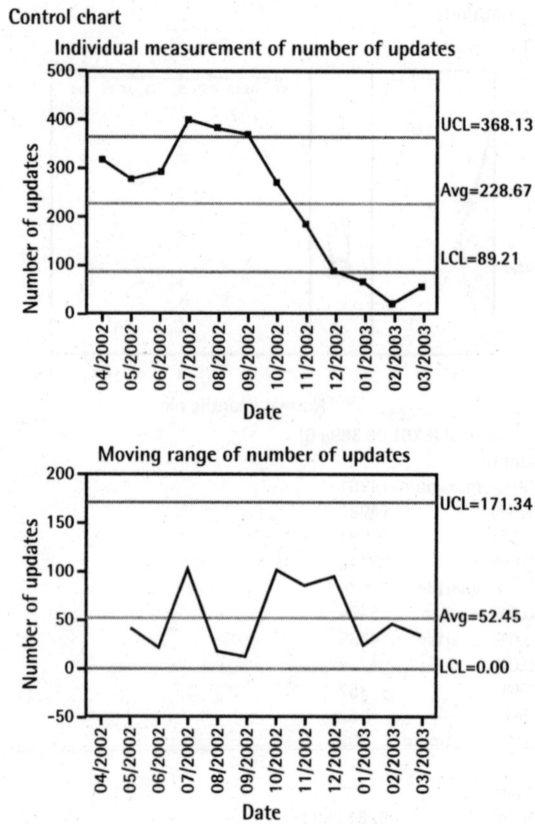

Figure 5 Control chart for updates

which correlates to the drop in activity after September. October and November indicate the team is working within its capability. After December, the team is below its lower control limit indicating that the team has completed the bulk of the development on this project and is responding to issues found after the software was released. In Figure 6, the team is operating "under control" but there is a definite downward trend. The downward trend in both number of updates and the amount of change confirm that the team has entered the test phase where changes are made to correct issues found in test.

Software project management can use these charts to monitor the team progress to ensure that the activity in the configuration management system is matching the project schedule. For example, if the project shown in Figure 5 was scheduled to complete the coding phase in July 2002 and the chart was provided in August 2002, the project lead could easily see that the coding phase had extended past the deadline.

As a demonstration of another scenario that can be revealed by monitoring the SCM system, Figure 7 illustrates a project that is struggling. Months five and

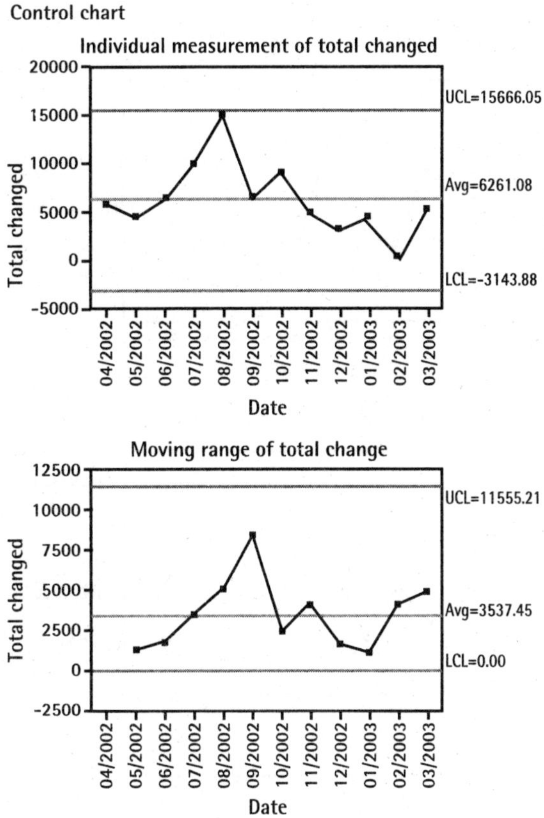

Figure 6 Control chart for total changed

nine of the project exceeded the upper control limit. A project leader with this information can quantitatively see that the project team may be working too hard. The team is exceeding its capability, which could result in the development of a low quality product.

Using the information from these control limits the project management has the ability to characterize the team's capability to develop code. The next step is to use this information to find ways to optimize the productivity. The productivity numbers from SCM should always be considered against the team's quality capability to prevent increasing productivity at the cost of reducing quality.

The information can also be used to respond to the "voice of the customer." Project management can use the data in planning to make accurate estimations on completion dates to the customer. The project management can set specification limits that will allow the team to meet the customer dates. Monitoring the SCM data against the specification limits can provide warning of possible schedule deviations.

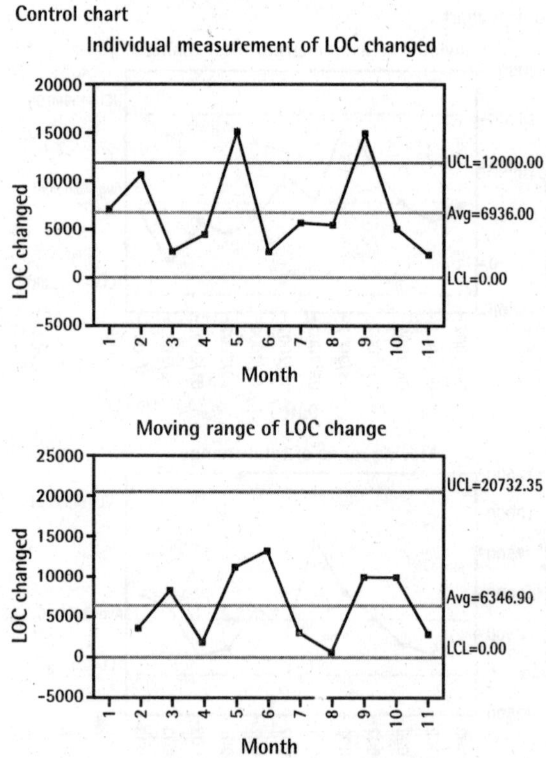

Figure 7 Control of project that is "out of control"

Improve Performance

The initial step for any performance improvement is to establish the current working capability. The use of SCM measurements is an accurate way to determine a team's capability by examining the historical evidence stored in the SCM system. The analysis requires no inputs from the developers and is a method for measuring the developers' work activities.

The next step in performance improvement is to identify areas to improve. Using SCM data, the project can identify problematic files to provide lessons-learned information to the development team. The team should examine the files most changed because of problems or issues. As stated previously, some files are expected to be updated frequently. For example, an include file containing the software version may be updated for each release. These files should be excluded from the analysis since they obviously are not problematic. The team's performance history can also be correlated to problem data and inspection data to further identify improvements to the process.

The SCM system can then be monitored to determine the impact of the process improvements on the team's performance. Once again, this information should be examined with the quality data to ensure the "improvements" did not cause a degradation in quality.

Conclusion

The need for accurate and timely data is paramount to successfully estimating and monitoring a software team's development activities. Accurate and timely data allow project management to know what a team's development capabilities truly are and to monitor the team's activities to ensure the team is performing within the boundaries of its capabilities. Another key factor in managing software development is identifying and isolating problematic code areas. A team that can identify where the majority of its defects originate can proactively restructure the problem area or at least ensure senior developers are involved in any changes to those areas.

Use of the SCM system can satisfy both of these needs. This article demonstrated how examining SCM data can identify problem areas within the code. The article compared the number of updates made to files that were the result of a problem against files that were changed for other reasons. The statistical evidence indicated a linkage between files that had problems and files that had been updated multiple times.

A team's development capability can be determined by using historical SCM data. Project leadership can use the team's history to determine the optimal level at which the team can be expected to operate. This information can be used to estimate future projects as well as to identify areas for optimizing the team's performance.

SCM also provides a nonintrusive, real-time method for examining a project's status. The SCM data can be extracted without interfering with the software developer's work. It is a measurement of the team member's work as the work is being performed. This allows management to identify the current team status on a daily basis without interrupting the work of the developers. The data should also be accurate, as it requires no manual data entry. It is truly a measurement of the work that is being performed.

This article attempted to demonstrate the powerful capabilities of using SCM measurements for estimating and monitoring software projects. The SCM system also contains update history that can provide insights to improving product quality. These facts should make SCM data an integral part of every software development metric program.

A second, less obvious, goal of this article was to demonstrate the use of Six Sigma techniques on software development data. The techniques used in this analysis included comparative methods, nonparametric statistics, problem solving, and statistical process control. This analysis demonstrated how these techniques can be applied to software data to provide insights to the software development team.

As software development teams search for ways to optimize the development processes while improving quality, the use of Six Sigma statistical techniques and SCM data could prove to be invaluable resources.

BIOGRAPHY

Jeffrey Holmes has 16 years of experience in software engineering. The majority of this time has been spent developing real-time software for avionic and telecommunications systems. Holmes joined Motorola in April 1994. He is currently working as a principal staff software engineer on the Motorola Base Transceiver System Center of Excellence team in Fort Worth, Texas.

Holmes has a bachelor's degree in computer science from Texas A&M University and a master's of software engineering degree from Texas Christian University. He is a recognized Motorola Six Sigma Black Belt and has used the Personal Software Process for the past eight years. He can be reached by e-mail at J.Holmes@motorola.com.

Closing Thoughts

Phil Crosby identified what he saw as the five stages of quality management maturity: uncertainty, awakening, enlightenment, wisdom, and certainty. Applied to software, this model has been translated into organizational maturity levels called initial, repeatable, defined, managed, and optimized. Whether for an organization or an individual, the useful image is one of a journey, a progression to higher stages and deeper insights.

Professional development is exactly that kind of journey. Each of us has had that anxiety and uncertainty the first day on the job. Perhaps it extended over the first weeks and months. Perhaps it repeated itself as an experience of novelty at multiple new assignments, multiple new jobs, or multiple new organizations. The old joke is, "Do you have 20 years of experience, or 1 year of experience repeated 20 times?" Well, it might feel like that every time we start over with a new staff or a new company. But we should be progressing. We should be finding that we can see patterns and make connections so that novelty is not complete uncertainty.

The software quality profession is relatively new, as evidenced by the few years we have had the CSQE certification and the *SQP* journal. Yet it draws from a depth of historical experience within the larger quality profession. Many of the articles collected in this volume were informed by well established quality principles and techniques—in data gathering, analysis, and display; in quantitatively driven management; in standards-based practices; in feedback mechanisms; and in process improvement.

You see, none of us is on this journey alone. We have mentors and colleagues old and new, near and far. If we are attentive, we can learn from their experiences, avoid their mistakes, and model their positive attributes. Where do we find these fellow travelers? They are in the pages of our professional literature. In training sessions and seminars. At society meetings and conferences, whether in our hometowns or halfway around the world.

We can and should help each other move higher and deeper in our journeys of professional development. The authors who have contributed material, first for the journal and now for this book, have shown their willingness to share. And they will be enriched if you, in turn, respond—with questions, with objections, or with reports of how you have tried to put what they described into practice in your own setting.

We all need that feedback and mutual support. Won't you renew your commitment to the journey? Won't you join those colleagues who are also striving for greater maturity? Won't you reach back to those who are less experienced and more uncertain, with a hand of encouragement and companionship?

Let's continue the journey. I look forward to seeing you along the way.

—Taz Daughtrey

APPENDIX

Certified Software Quality Engineer (CSQE) Body of Knowledge

The topics in this Body of Knowledge include additional detail in the form of subtext explanations and the cognitive level at which the questions will be written. This information will provide useful guidance for both the Examination Development Committee and the candidates preparing to take the exam. The subtext is not intended to limit the subject matter or be all-inclusive of what might be covered in an exam. It is intended to clarify the type of content to be included in the exam. The descriptor in parentheses at the end of each entry refers to the highest cognitive level at which the topic will be tested. A more complete description of cognitive levels is provided at the end of this appendix.

I. General Knowledge, Conduct, and Ethics (16 Questions)

A. Quality philosophy and principles

1. Benefits of software quality

   Describe how software quality engineering can benefit an organization. (Comprehension)

2. Prevention vs. detection

   Describe how quality engineering methodologies can reduce the length of time for testing and can influence other defect detection methods. (Comprehension)

3. Organizational and process benchmarking

   Identify, analyze, and model best practices at the macro (organizational) and micro (process and project) levels. Identify and develop business objectives, use metrics to monitor their achievement, and provide feedback to close the process improvement loop. (Analysis)

The CSQE Body of Knowledge is updated periodically based on practitioner input to reflect changes in the software quality field. See http://www.asq.org/certification/software-quality-engineer/bok.html for the most current Body of Knowledge.

B. Standards, specifications, and models

Identify and use software process and assessment models, including ISO 9001, ISO 15504, IEEE software standards, IEEE/EIA 12207, SEI Capability Maturity Model Integrated (CMMI), etc., in a variety of situations. (Application)

C. Leadership tools and skills

1. Organizational leadership

   Define, describe, and apply leadership tools and techniques, including analyzing current situations, proposing, justifying, implementing, and managing change (using change-agent tools), developing and implementing quality initiatives, obtaining cross-functional commitment and collaboration, ensuring knowledge transfer, motivating personnel, etc. (Application)

2. Team management

   Define and use various team management techniques, including identifying and assigning roles and responsibilities (e.g., champion, sponsor, facilitator, leader, coach), identifying and assessing team member skills, interpreting team dynamics and stages of team development, handling dominant or disruptive team members, recognizing how diversity in teams strengthens the creative process, etc. (Application)

3. Team tools

   Define, describe, and use tools such as brainstorming, nominal group technique (NGT), joint application development (JAD), rapid application development (RAD), etc. (Application)

4. Facilitation Skills

   Use various tools to manage and resolve conflict. Use negotiation techniques to produce win-win outcomes. Identify and use time and meeting management tools to maximize performance. (Application)

5. Communication skills

   Define, describe, and apply various communication elements used in verbal, written, and presentation formats, including interviewing and listening skills. Apply communication elements to create effective process and procedural documents, including identifying roles and responsibilities. (Application)

D. Ethical conduct and professional development

1. ASQ Code of Ethics

   Determine appropriate behavior in situations requiring ethical decisions, including identifying conflicts of interest and recognizing/resolving ethical issues related to software licensing and use. (Evaluation)

2. Software liability and safety issues

   Identify legal issues related to software product liability and safety, including negligence, customer notification requirements, and other legal or regulatory issues. (Application) [NOTE: Other aspects of product safety and hazard analysis are covered in IV.C.4.]

3. Professional training and development

   Define, describe, and apply training needs analysis methods for software quality professionals, and manage training resources and materials. (Application)

II. Software Quality Management (30 Questions)

A. Goals and objectives

1. Quality goals and objectives

   Describe, analyze, and evaluate quality goals and objectives for programs, projects, and products. (Evaluation)

2. Outsourced services

   Define, analyze, and evaluate the impact of acquisitions, subcontractor services, and other external resources on the organization's goals and objectives. (Evaluation)

3. Planning

   Identify, apply, and evaluate scheduling and resource requirements necessary to achieve quality goals and objectives. (Evaluation)

4. Software quality management (SQM) systems documentation

   Identify and describe various elements related to SQM system documentation. (Comprehension)

5. Customer requirements

   Analyze and evaluate customer requirements and their effect on programs, projects, and products. (Evaluation) [NOTE: *Changes* in requirements are covered in III.B.3. The focus in this section is to ensure that customer requirements are evaluated properly.]

B. Methodologies

1. Review, inspection, and testing

   Define, describe, evaluate, and differentiate between these defect detection methods. (Evaluation)

2. Change management methods

   Identify and apply various methods appropriate for responding to changes in technology, organizations, environment, human performance, etc. (Evaluation) [NOTE: Change-agent tools are covered in I.C.1.]

3. Cost of quality (COQ)

   Define, differentiate, and analyze COQ categories (prevention, appraisal, internal failure, external failure) and their impact on products and processes. (Analysis) [NOTE: Interpreting and reporting COQ data are covered in IV.B.2.]

4. Quality data tracking

   Define, describe, select, and implement information systems and models used to track quality data in various situations. (Evaluation)

5. Problem reporting and corrective action procedures

   Define, describe, analyze, and distinguish between these procedures for software defects, process nonconformances, and other quality system deficiencies. (Evaluation)

6. Quality improvement processes

   Define, describe, analyze and distinguish between various defect prevention, detection, and removal processes, and evaluate process improvement opportunities in relation to these tools. (Evaluation)

C. Audits

1. Program development and administration

   Identify roles and responsibilities for various audit participants, including team leader, team members, auditee, auditor, etc. (Comprehension)

2. Audit preparation and execution

   Define and distinguish between various audit types, including process, compliance, supplier, system, etc. Define and describe various steps in the audit process, from scheduling the audit through the closing meeting and subsequent follow-up activities. Define and identify various tools and procedures used in conducting audits. (Comprehension)

3. Audit reporting and follow up

   Identify, describe, and apply the steps of audit reporting and follow up, including the need for and verification of corrective action. (Application)

III. Software Engineering Processes (26 Questions)

A. Environmental conditions

1. Life cycles

   Compare and evaluate the characteristics of spiral, waterfall, incremental, rapid prototyping, Vmodel, etc. Differentiate these life cycles, describe what they are designed to do, what their benefits are, and in what situations they should be used. (Evaluation)

2. Systems architecture

   Identify, describe, evaluate, and distinguish between system architectures, including client server, n tier, B to B, B to C, and B to E, web (internet/intranet/extranet) and wireless development, messaging and collaboration software, etc. (Analysis)

B. Requirements management

1. Requirements prioritization and evaluation

   Describe, assess, prioritize, and evaluate the requirements for verifying software correctness, consistency, completeness, and testability. Determine what should be covered in a requirements statement, how to specify a requirement, etc. (Evaluation)

2. Requirements change management

   Define, describe, and evaluate various elements of managing requirements change, including what processes should be followed, when requirements need to change, what review processes to use, etc. Define the effect of changing requirements at various stages of the project life cycle. (Evaluation)

3. Bi-directional requirements traceability

   Describe, select, and evaluate various traceability elements, including requirements to design, design to code, and requirements to test. Describe and apply traceability tools and mechanisms, such as system verification diagrams, traceability matrices, etc. (Evaluation) [NOTE: Traceability of configuration items is covered in VII.C.5.]

C. Requirements engineering

1. Requirement types

   Define, describe, and analyze various requirement types such as security, regulatory, quality, feature and product functionality, etc., and the significant elements of each. (Analysis)

2. Requirements elicitation

   Define and describe various elicitation methods, including using tools such as quality function deployment (QFD), joint application development (JAD), customer needs analysis, etc. Describe the key steps necessary for gathering product requirement details, and identify common causes of failure to comply with requirements. (Comprehension)

3. Requirements analysis and modeling

   Describe, select, and use tools such as data flow diagrams (DFDs), entity relationship diagrams (ERDs), use cases, etc. Describe how they are used at different phases of development and requirements specifications. (Analysis)

4. System and software requirements specifications

   Define and distinguish between these two types of specifications and their purpose, and describe their relationship to each other. (Analysis)

D. Analysis, design, and development methods and tools

1. Software design methods

   Define and use various design methods, including object-oriented analysis and design (OOAD), structured analysis and design (SAD), unified modeling language (UML), etc. Identify the steps used in program design and explain their uses. (Application)

2. Types of software reuse

   Define, describe, and differentiate the use of various reuse methods including reengineering, reverse engineering, plug-and-play, etc., and describe the design paradigms that address these concepts. (Application)

3. Cleanroom and other formal methods

   Define and describe these methods and their benefits. (Comprehension)

4. Software development tools

   Identify, describe, use, and distinguish between various tools used for modeling, code analysis, documentation, relational databases, etc. (Application)

E. Maintenance management

1. Maintenance types

   Describe the characteristics of corrective, adaptive, and perfective maintenance types and their benefits and risks. (Comprehension)

2. Operational maintenance

   Describe the various categories of and activities involved in providing operational services to the customer, managing application portfolios, and providing basic software maintenance. (Comprehension)

IV. Program and Project Management (24 Questions)

A. Planning

1. Project planning elements

   Describe and use factors such as forecasts, resources, schedules, etc., to develop, initiate, and accomplish project goals. (Application)

2. Goal-setting and deployment

   Identify and use milestones, objectives achieved, task duration, and other goal-setting and deployment methods. (Application)

3. Project planning tools

   Define, apply, and analyze various methods of managing risk, estimating costs, scheduling resources, etc. using tools such as PERT charts, critical path method (CPM), work breakdown structure (WBS), etc. (Analysis) [NOTE: Gantt charts are covered in IV.B.1.]

4. Cost and value data

   Identify and use various methods for calculating project-related data such as earned value, development investment costs, etc. (Application)

B. Tracking and controlling

1. Phase transition control techniques

   Develop and use various control techniques for tracking projects, including entry/exit criteria, phase gate reviews, Gantt charts, etc. (Analysis)

2. Interpreting and reporting cost of quality (COQ) data

   Review, interpret, and report COQ data and evaluate how each category is affected by continuous improvement strategies. (Evaluation) [NOTE: The definitions and distinctions between these categories are covered in II.B.3.]

3. Tracking elements and methods

   Describe, assess, and apply different tracking methods, including establishing metrics for costs, deliverables, productivity, etc., creating and evaluating status reports and life-cycle phase reports, measuring changes in earned value, evaluating changes in business conditions, etc. (Evaluation) [NOTE: Calculating earned value is covered in IV. A. 4.]

4. Project reviews

   Define, use, and differentiate various types of reviews, including post-project, senior management, team, etc., and use closed-loop methodologies to improve projects as a result of lessons learned. (Analysis)

C. Risk management

1. Risk management planning methods

   Define, integrate, and analyze various risk management methods, including assessing, preventing, and mitigating risk with respect to critical aspects of a project and its supporting strategies. (Synthesis)

2. Risk probability

   Describe and evaluate various risk warning signs, assess risk probability and impact, and develop contingency plans. (Evaluation)

3. Product release decisions

   Identify situations and factors that require trade-offs on product release decisions. Develop and analyze various ways of bringing a project back on track when problems occur that affect quality, scheduling, customer requirements, product functionality, etc. (Evaluation)

4. Software security, safety, and hazard analysis issues

   Identify, review, and evaluate various factors related to software security, safety-critical software, and hazard analyses. Identify and describe rationales for developing safety plans and for implementing hazard analyses. (Analysis) [NOTE: The legal aspects of product safety are covered in I.D.2.]

V. Software Metrics, Measurement, and Analytical Methods (24 Questions)

A. Metrics and measurement theory

1. Definitions

   Define, describe, and explain various terms related to metrics and measurement, including error, reliability, internal vs. external validity, explicit vs. derived measures, etc. (Comprehension)

2. Basic measurement theory and techniques

   Define, describe, and use basic measurement scales (nominal, ordinal, ratio, interval), the central limit theorem and related terms, including mean, median, mode, standard deviation, variance, etc. (Application)

3. Psychology of metrics

   Define and describe various uses of metrics. Compare and contrast how metrics affect people and how people affect metrics. (Comprehension)

B. Process and product measurement

1. Process, product, and resource metrics

   Describe and use various metrics to assess processes, products, and resources. (Application)

2. Commonly used metrics

   Define and use metrics to measure various aspects of software, including software complexity, lines of code (LOC), non-commented lines of code (NCLOC), design defects, requirements volatility, system performance, etc. (Application) [NOTE: Code coverage metrics are covered in VI.D.4.]

3. Software quality attributes

   Identify and describe various criteria for measuring attributes such as maintainability, verifiability, reliability, usability, reusability, testability, expandability, etc. (Comprehension)

4. Defect detection effectiveness measures

   Define, describe, and use defect detection measures such as cost, yield, customer impact, etc., and track their effectiveness. (Application)

5. Program performance and process effectiveness

   Identify and use various methods of examining performance and effectiveness. (Analysis)

C. Analytical techniques

1. Data integrity

   Define, use, and interpret various techniques to ensure the quality of metrics data, its accuracy, completeness, timeliness, etc. (Synthesis)

2. Sampling theory and techniques

   Describe, differentiate, and analyze various sampling techniques for use in auditing, testing, product acceptance, etc. (Analysis)

3. Quality tools: Charts

   Define, select, and use tools such as flowcharts, Pareto charts, scatter diagrams, control/run charts, histograms, process decision program charts (PDPCs), etc. (Analysis)

4. Quality tools: Diagrams

   Define, select, and use tools such as cause and effect diagrams, scatter diagrams, affinity diagrams, tree diagrams, activity network diagrams, etc. (Analysis)

5. Miscellaneous quality tools

   Define, select, and use various problem-solving tools such as root cause analysis, interrelationship digraphs, prioritization matrices, etc. (Analysis)

VI. Software Verification and Validation (V&V) (24 Questions)

A. Theory

1. V&V planning procedures and tasks

   Identify and select various methods for verification and validation, including static analysis, structural analysis, mathematical proof, simulation, etc. Identify and analyze which tasks should be iterated as a result of proposed or completed modifications. (Synthesis)

2. V&V program

   Describe and analyze methods for managing and reviewing a V&V program, including technical accomplishments, resource utilization, program status, etc. (Analysis)

3. Evaluating software products and processes

   Analyze and select various ways of evaluating documentation, source code, test and audit results, etc., to determine whether user needs and project objectives have been satisfied. (Synthesis)

4. Interfaces

   Identify various interfaces used with hardware, user, operator, and software applications. (Comprehension)

B. Reviews and inspections

1. Types

   Define, describe, and use various types of reviews and inspections, including desk-checking, walkthroughs, Fagan and Gilb inspections, technical accomplishments, resource utilization, future planning, etc. (Application)

2. Items

   Identify, describe, and use various review and inspection items, including proposals, project charters, specifications, code, tests, etc. (Application)

3. Processes

   Define, describe, and use various review and inspection processes to examine objectives, criteria, techniques, methods, etc. (Application)

4. Data collection, reports, and summaries

   Define, describe, and use terms related to data collection, including preparation rates, defect density yield, phase containment, etc. (Application)

C. Test planning and design

1. Types of tests

   Select, apply, and develop various types of test, including functional, performance, regression, certification, environmental load, stress, worst case, perfective, exploratory, etc. (Synthesis)

2. Test tools

   Define and describe the application and capabilities of commonly used test tools such as acceptance test suites, utilities (for memory, screen capture, string-finding, file viewer, file comparison, etc.), and diagnostics (for hardware, software, configuration, etc.). (Comprehension)

3. Test strategies

   Identify, analyze, and apply various test strategies, including top-down, bottom-up, black-box, white-box, simulation, automation, etc. (Synthesis)

4. Test design

   Identify, describe, and apply various types of test design including fault insertion, fault-error handling, equivalence class partitioning, boundary value, etc. (Application)

5. Test coverage of specifications

   Identify, apply, and develop various test coverage specifications, including functions, states, data and time domains, etc. (Synthesis)

6. Test environments

   Identify various environments and use tools such as test libraries, drivers, stubs, harnesses, etc., in those environments, and describe how simulations can be used in test environments. (Synthesis)

7. Supplier components and products

   Identify the common risks and benefits of incorporating purchased software into other software products. Use various methods to test supplier components and products in the larger system. (Application)

8. Test plans

   Identify, describe, and apply methods for creating and evaluating test plans including system, acceptance, validation, etc., to determine whether project objectives are being met. (Application)

D. Test execution and evaluation

1. Test implementation

   Define, describe, and use various implementation elements, including scheduling, freezing, dependencies, V-model, error repair models, acceptance testing, etc. (Application)

2. Test documentation

   Define, describe, and use various documentation procedures, including defect recording and tracking, test report completion metrics, trouble reports, input/output specifications, etc. (Application)

3. Test Reviews

   Describe, develop, and analyze various methods of reviewing test efforts, including technical accomplishments, future planning, risk management, etc. (Synthesis)

4. Code coverage metrics

   Define and apply various metrics including branch-to-branch, condition, domain, McCabe's cyclomatic complexity, boundary, etc. (Application) [NOTE: Other types of metrics are covered in V.B.2.]

5. Customer deliverables

   Identify and select various methods for testing the accuracy of customer deliverables, including packaged or downloaded products, license keys, user documentation, marketing and training materials, etc. (Synthesis)

6. Severity of anomalies

   Identify and select various methods for evaluating severity of anomalies in software operations. (Evaluation)

VII. Software Configuration Management (16 Questions)

A. Configuration infrastructure

1. Configuration management

   Describe the roles and responsibilities of the configuration management group. (Comprehension)

2. Library/repository processes

   Define and identify processes used in a library system including dynamic, static, controlled, etc., and their related procedures. (Comprehension)

3. Defect tracking and library tools

   Define and describe configuration management tools used for defect tracking, library management tools, etc. (Comprehension)

B. Configuration identification

1. Configuration items

   Define, select, and use various items, including documentation, code interfaces, training materials, customer-supplied equipment, etc. (Application)

2. Baselines

   Define and identify when configuration baselines are created and used. (Comprehension)

3. Configuration identification methods

   Define and describe how these methods relate to schemes, naming conventions, versions, serializations, etc. (Comprehension)

4. Software builds

   Define and describe the primary purpose of software builds and their relation to configuration management functions. Describe and use various methods for controlling builds, including automation, new-version builds, etc. (Synthesis)

C. Configuration control

1. Item and baseline control

   Define, describe, and apply various control processes, including version control, traceability requirements, specifications, concurrent development, verifying milestones, etc. (Application)

2. Proposed modifications

   Describe how to assess proposed modifications, enhancements, or additions in terms of their impact on an existing or planned system. (Comprehension)

3. Review and configuration control boards (CCBs)

   Define, describe, and differentiate the roles and responsibilities of and procedures used by these boards. (Application)

4. Concurrent development

   Describe how configuration management control principles can be used in concurrent development processes. (Application)

5. Traceability

   Identify and apply various tools and methods for establishing and maintaining traceability design, including backward and forward traceability, naming conventions, etc., and explain how they are related to configuration management objectives. (Application) [NOTE: Traceability through product development is covered in III.B.3. The focus for this area is on traceability and evolution of configuration items in code archives and other configuration management elements.]

6. Version control

   Define, describe, and use version control methods such as source code version management and others, and how such methods can be used effectively by both small and large development teams. (Application)

7. Configuration item interfaces

   Define, describe, and apply management control processes for configuration item interfaces. (Application)

D. Configuration status accounting

1. Status reporting

   Describe various processes for establishing, maintaining, and reporting the status of configuration items. (Comprehension)

2. Changes to configuration items and baselines

   Describe the processes that should be used when changes are proposed to configuration items and baselines. (Comprehension)

3. Documentation control

   Define and describe related procedures for document distribution, approval, storage, retrieval, revision, etc. (Comprehension)

E. Configuration audits

1. Functional configuration audit

   Describe the primary purpose of these types of audits in relation to product specifications and in contrast to physical configuration audits. (Comprehension)

2. Physical configuration audit

   Describe the primary purpose of these types of audits in relation to product specifications and in contrast to functional configuration audits. (Comprehension)

F. Release and distribution issues

1. Product release process issues

   Identify and describe product release issues such as planning, scheduling, hardware and software dependencies, etc. (Comprehension)

2. Packaging, production, and distribution

   Define and describe these components in relation to product release requirements and related issues. (Knowledge)

Six Levels of Cognition based on Bloom's Taxonomy (1956)

In addition to *content* specifics, the subtext detail also indicates the intended *complexity level* of the test questions for that topic. These levels are based on "Levels of Cognition" (from *Bloom's Taxonomy*, 1956) and are presented below in rank order, from least complex to most complex.

Knowledge Level

(Also commonly referred to as recognition, recall, or rote knowledge) Being able to remember or recognize terminology, definitions, facts, ideas, materials, patterns, sequences, methodologies, principles, etc.

Comprehension Level

Be able to read and understand descriptions, communications, reports, tables, diagrams, directions, regulations, etc.

Application Level

Be able to apply ideas, procedures, methods, formulas, principles, theories, etc., in job-related situations.

Analysis

Be able to break down information into its constituent parts and recognize the parts' relationship to one another and how they are organized; identify sublevel factors or salient data from a complex scenario.

Synthesis

Be able to put parts or elements together in such a way as to show a pattern or structure not clearly there before; identify which data or information from a complex set is appropriate to examine further or from which supported conclusions can be drawn.

Evaluation

Be able to make judgments regarding the value of proposed ideas, solutions, methodologies, etc., by using appropriate criteria or standards to estimate accuracy, effectiveness, economic benefits, etc.

Index

O

P

Q

R

S

T

U

V

W

Y

Also Available from ASQ Quality Press Exclusively Published by New Age International Pvt.Ltd.

Analysis of Customer Satisfaction Data
Derek R. Allen, Tanniru R. Rao
ISBN: 978-81-224-2800-1, Original Edition Price: $ 66.00, Indian Edition Price: Rs. 395.00

An Introduction to Design of Experiments: A Simplified Approach
Larry B. Barrentine
ISBN: 978-81-224-3112-4, Original Edition Price: $ 40.00, Indian Edition Price: Rs. 150.00

Computer-Based Robust Engineering Essentials for DFSS
Genichi Taguchi, Rajesh Jugulum, Shin Taguchi
ISBN:978-81-224-2791-2, Original Edition Price: $ 57.75, Indian Edition Price: Rs. 395.00

Common Sense Project Management
Wayne Turk
ISBN:978-81-224-3102-5, Original Edition Price: $ 46.00, Indian Edition Price: Rs. 250.00

Customer Satisfaction Research Management
Derek R. Allen
ISBN: 978-81-224-2797-4, Original Edition Price: $ 66.00, Indian Edition Price: Rs. 395.00

Design of Experiments with Minitab
Paul Mathews
ISBN: 978-81-224-3111-7, Original Edition Price: $ 116.00, Indian Edition Price: Rs. 595.00

Effective Implementation of ISO 14001
Marilyn R. Block
ISBN: 978-81-224-3114-8, Original Edition Price: $ 110.00, Indian Edition Price: Rs. 495.00

Environmental Management Quick and Easy: Creating an Effective ISO 14001 EMS in Half the Time
Joe Kausek
ISBN: 978-81-224-3113-1, Original Edition Price: $ 87.00, Indian Edition Price: Rs. 395.00

Enabling Excellence: The Seven Elements Essential to Achieving Competitive Advantage
Timothy A. Pine
ISBN: 978-81-224-3105-6, Original Edition Price: $ 41.00, Indian Edition Price: Rs. 150.00

Fundamental Concepts for the Software Quality Engineer, Volume-2
Sue Carroll and Taz Daughtrey, *Editors*
ISBN: 978-81-224-3107-0, Original Edition Price: $ 72.00, Indian Edition Price: Rs. 399.00

Integrating Reengineering with Total Quality
Joseph N. Kelada
ISBN: 978-81-224-3110-0, Original Edition Price: $ 88.00, Indian Edition Price: Rs. 495.00

Improving Performance Through Statistical Thinking
Galen C. Britz, Donald W. Emerling, Lynne B. Hare, Roger W. Hoerl
Sturat J. Janis, Janice E. Shade
ISBN: 978-81-224-2796-7, Original Edition Price: $ 39.00, Indian Edition Price: Rs. 200.00

ISO 9001:2008 Explained Third Edition
John E. "Jack" West, Charles A. Cianfrani, Joseph J. Tsiakals
ISBN:978-81-224-3101-8, Original Edition Price: $ 105.00, Indian Edition Price: Rs. 395.00

Integrating ISO 14001 into a Quality Management System, Second Edition
Marilyn R. Block and I. Robert Marash
ISBN: 978-81-224-3115-5, Original Edition Price: $ 39.00, Indian Edition Price: Rs. 395.00

Measuring Customer Satisfaction and Loyalty
(Survey Design, Use, and Statistical Analysis Methods)
Bob E. Hayes
ISBN: 978-81-224-2799-8, Original Edition Price: $ 53.00, Indian Edition Price: Rs. 395.00

Principles and Practices of Organizational Performance Excellence
Thomas J. Cartin
ISBN: 978-81-224-2793-6, Original Edition Price: $ 44.00, Indian Edition Price: Rs. 495.00

Quality Engineering Statistics
Robert A. Dovich
ISBN: 978-81-224-3108-7, Original Edition Price: $ 43.00, Indian Edition Price: Rs. 150.00

SPC Essentials and Productivity Improvements: A Manufacturing Approach
William A. Levinson, Frank Tumbelty
ISBN: 978-81-224-3116-2, Original Edition Price: $ 40.00, Indian Edition Price: Rs. 399.00

Statistical Engineering An Algorithm for Reducing Variation in Manufacturing Processes
Stefan H. Steiner and R. Jock Mackay
ISBN: 978-81-224-3109-4, Original Edition Price: $ 99.00, Indian Edition Price: Rs. 395.00

Six Sigma Project Management (A Pocket Guide)
Jeffrey N. Lowenthal
ISBN: 978-81-224-2802-5, Original Edition Price: $ 24.00, Indian Edition Price: Rs. 50.00

Six Sigma for the New Millennium: A CSSBB Guidebook, Second Edition
Kim H. Pries
ISBN: 978-81-224-3103-2, Original Edition Price: $ 97.00, Indian Edition Price: Rs. 399.00

The ASQ Auditing Handbook, Third Edition
J.P. Russell, Editor
ISBN: 978-81-224-3104-9, Original Edition Price: $ 139.00, Indian Edition Price: Rs. 495.00

The Certified Software Quality Engineer Handbook
Linda Westfall
ISBN: 978-81-224-3117-9, Original Edition Price: $ 133.00, Indian Edition Price: Rs. 699.00

The Certified Reliability Engineer Handbook
Donald W. Benbow and Hugh W. Broome
ISBN: 978-81-224-2792-9, Original Edition Price: $ 121.00, Indian Edition Price: Rs. 495.00

The Certified Quality Engineer Handbook
Connie M. Borror, Editor
ISBN: 978-81-224-2794-3, Original Edition Price: $ 139.00, Indian Edition Price: Rs. 795.00

The Certified Quality Process Analyst Handbook
Eldon H. Christensen, Kathleen M. Coombes-Betz, Marilyn S. Stein
ISBN: 978-81-224-3106-3, Original Edition Price: $ 76.00, Indian Edition Price: Rs. 495.00

The Certified Quality Technician Handbook
Donald W. Benbow, Ahmad K. Elshennawy, H. Fred Walker
ISBN: 978-81-224-2790-5, Original Edition Price: $ 121.00, Indian Edition Price: Rs. 495.00

The Desk Reference of Statistical Quality Methods: Second Edition
Mark L. Crossley
ISBN: 978-81-224-3118-6, Original Edition Price: $ 104.00, Indian Edition Price: Rs. 499.00

The Metrology Handbook
Jay L. Bucher, Editor
ISBN:978-81-224-2789-9, Original Edition Price: $ 121.00, Indian Edition Price: Rs. 695.00

The Making of a World-Class Organization
E. David Spong and Debbie J. Collard
ISBN: 978-81-224-2798-1, Original Edition Price: $ 42.00, Indian Edition Price: Rs. 150.00

The Supplier Management Handbook
James L. Bossert, Editor
ISBN: 978-81-224-2801-8, Original Edition Price: $ 81.00, Indian Edition Price: Rs. 395.00